C0-DUQ-335

The
World's Worst
Bet

Also by David J. Lynch

When the Luck of the Irish Ran Out:
The World's Most Resilient Country and Its Struggle to Rise Again

The
World's Worst
Bet

HOW THE GLOBALIZATION GAMBLE

WENT WRONG

(AND WHAT WOULD MAKE IT RIGHT)

David J. Lynch

PUBLICAFFAIRS

New York

Copyright © 2025 by David J. Lynch

Cover design by Ann Kirchner
Cover image © Lauren Nicole via Getty Images; © Titus JP / Shutterstock.com;
© Elfangor / Shutterstock.com
Cover copyright © 2025 by Hachette Book Group, Inc.

Hachette Book Group supports the right to free expression and the value of
copyright. The purpose of copyright is to encourage writers and artists to produce
the creative works that enrich our culture.

The scanning, uploading, and distribution of this book without permission is a theft
of the author's intellectual property. If you would like permission to use material from
the book (other than for review purposes), please contact permissions@hbgusa.com.
Thank you for your support of the author's rights.

PublicAffairs
Hachette Book Group
1290 Avenue of the Americas, New York, NY 10104
www.publicaffairsbooks.com
@Public_Affairs

Printed in the United States of America

First Edition: September 2025

Published by PublicAffairs, an imprint of Hachette Book Group, Inc. The
PublicAffairs name and logo is a registered trademark of the Hachette Book Group.

The Hachette Speakers Bureau provides a wide range of authors for speaking
events. To find out more, go to hachettespeakersbureau.com or email
HachetteSpeakers@hbgusa.com.

PublicAffairs books may be purchased in bulk for business, educational, or
promotional use. For more information, please contact your local bookseller or the
Hachette Book Group Special Markets Department at special.markets@hbgusa.com.

The publisher is not responsible for websites (or their content) that are not owned by
the publisher.

Print book interior design by Six Red Marbles.

Library of Congress Control Number: 2025000912

ISBNs: 9781541704060 (hardcover), 9781541704084 (ebook)

LSC-C

Printing 1, 2025

For my wife Kathy
and our three wonderful sons,
Jack, Patrick, and Declan

Contents

Prologue

An Attractive Theory

The swollen, blackened bodies on the tile floor were barely recognizable as human. Just an occasional belt buckle or fragment of clothing revealed that these charred forms, shrouded in plastic sheeting, had once been someone's husband, friend, mother, or child. The dead lying at my feet were casualties of powerful forces reshaping the global economy, forces that eventually would contribute to historic changes in my own country. But on that sweltering May afternoon in 1998, I couldn't know that.

I was in Jakarta to cover the uprising that within days would end the thirty-two-year reign of the Indonesian dictator Suharto. Massive street protests had begun after he imposed sharp price increases on food, fuel, transport, and electricity, meeting conditions set by the International Monetary Fund in return for $43 billion that Indonesia needed to stay afloat.

What started a few days earlier as a peaceful demonstration had degenerated into mob violence against ethnic Chinese shopkeepers, who were resented for their relative affluence. The bodies lying in the airless morgue were Indonesians who had been caught in fires set by rioters at the Glodok shopping center. In the morgue that day, I spoke with a man named Tamin, who was searching for his twenty-year-old daughter. "I don't know whether she is here or not," the anguished father told me.

I had flown in from London the day before to fill in for a colleague. When I arrived, the airport was crowded with expatriates and wealthy

Indonesians fleeing the chaos. In a taxi heading downtown, I could see fires burning in the fields along the highway. Jakarta's streets were lined by armored personnel carriers full of soldiers awaiting orders. With tens of thousands of students, activists, and union representatives demanding a new government, there were fears of a Tiananmen Square–style ending. I stuck around long enough to cover Suharto's surprisingly peaceful fall and then moved on to my next assignment.

Indonesia's turmoil came nearly a year into an Asian financial crisis that began in Thailand, when the foreign investors who had flocked to the country during its boom years suddenly took flight. The upheaval spread to other emerging markets, including Russia, where the era's hopes of democracy were already souring. Before the summer's end, I found myself in Moscow, reporting on the aftermath of a ruble devaluation that impoverished ordinary Russians. Long queues formed outside banks as people withdrew whatever money they could get their hands on. I spent some time one afternoon with Mikhail Gorbachev, long out of power, listening to him blame everyone but himself for Russia's plight.

I grew up during the Cold War and spent years studying and writing about the nuclear standoff between the United States and the Soviet Union. To be reporting in a free Russia, whatever its economic circumstances, seemed a marvel. But I failed to understand the implications of what I was seeing in places like Indonesia and Russia. I thought, wrongly, that they were temporary difficulties amid the steady march of markets and democracy. Instead, they were alarm bells that continue to reverberate more than a quarter century later.

Trouble abroad posed a stark contrast to the triumphalism back home, where Americans were enjoying a tech-fueled boom marked by low unemployment and high stock prices. A broad political consensus favored market dictates and trade liberalization. It seemed obvious that removing arbitrary restrictions on the flow of goods and capital was the right thing to do; no one nation could produce everything it needed any more than any one state or city could.

In those exhilarating days, globalization promised a double-barreled win: prosperity at home and peace abroad. True, integrating three billion or so people from China, India, and former Soviet-bloc countries into the global economy would be disruptive. And the adjustment costs would fall most heavily on the least-skilled and least-educated workers in the United States. But free trade advocates—and who in those days wasn't one of those?—insisted that globalization's "losers" would be compensated with the retraining and financial support needed to ease their transition to the new world. Meanwhile, authoritarian nations such as China and Russia would inevitably become freer as globalization encouraged the development of a property-owning middle class that would demand a greater voice in governing.

It was an attractive theory, and for a while it looked like it might even be true. I moved to Beijing in the summer of 2002, just a few months after China joined the World Trade Organization. The capital was a disorienting mix of medieval and modern. The occasional donkey-drawn wagon competed for pavement with fleets of navy-blue Buick minivans. In many ways, what was happening in China reminded me of the transformation that swept the United States after World War II. People were growing richer, buying apartments, and enjoying middle-class comforts like televisions, DVD players, air conditioners, and automobiles that would have been unknown to their parents' generation. The country itself was being remade, with a network of highways and dozens of new airports, subways, ports, and rail lines.

The changes in China appeared to validate the forecasts of globalization enthusiasts. As the Chinese became more affluent, the political system faced pressure for reform. On the campus of Beijing University, one of the country's finest educational institutions, students told me Communist Party membership held little appeal. Later that year, General Secretary Jiang Zemin for the first time officially invited capitalists to become members of the Communist Party, the proletariat's revolutionary vanguard. Mao Zedong had vilified businessmen and landlords as enemies of the people. Now Jiang welcomed them as allies. This extraordinary ideological relaxation—even if largely symbolic—reflected a political system that seemed, however slowly, to be remaking itself alongside a changing economy. Some Chinese villages had even experimented with elections that included a handful of non-Communist candidates.

In factories, offices, and mines all over the country, I saw China emerge as a manufacturing power, for better and worse. Appliance maker Haier supplied American college students with affordable compact refrigerators for their dorm rooms while textile factories full of low-wage laborers siphoned business from mills in North Carolina. Meanwhile, hundreds of thousands of Chinese people each year traveled to the United States to study, engage in business, or just see the sights.

At the time, it was hard to see China's rise as an imminent threat. The US economy then was almost eight times larger than China's. Once you left the major cities, the evident prosperity vanished. I once took my oldest son, then just six or seven years old, on a Cub Scout camping trip, near the Great Wall. Hiking through the countryside, our group met a farmer, bent at the waist with a thick bundle of firewood on his back. When he told us how much money he earned in a year, I realized I was carrying more than that in my pocket.

I had other experiences that, with the benefit of hindsight, should have raised more questions. In the spring of 2003, an outbreak of an unfamiliar respiratory virus began shutting down the economy. Severe acute respiratory syndrome (SARS) was like a dress rehearsal for the economic impacts of covid-19. As people suddenly sickened, downtown restaurants emptied and farmers stopped slaughtering their pigs. In Seattle, a ship full of Chinese cargo sat at the dock while longshoremen refused to touch what they thought were possibly contaminated containers. Back in Beijing, one of our expat neighbors fled for the airport, panicked over rumors that the government was about to declare martial law and close the border. I'd like to say that I saw the danger to the global economy of a more serious pandemic. But to me, SARS was just something that thinned the traffic on my daily commute.

While China was clearly a freer place than it had been in the past, both for Chinese citizens and visiting journalists, the government still was repressive. We took for granted that the security services could listen in on our telephone conversations or follow us whenever they wanted. I was briefly detained by local officials when I went to nearby Hebei Province to report on SARS. But on the drive back to the capital, I and a colleague were able to sneak into a small village, past a policeman who was slumbering in his patrol car. On another trip to a coal town in the northeast, where miners had recently died in a bad accident, officials showed up while I was interviewing a mine supervisor, threw me out of town, and demoted him. When I wrote a story about the Communist Party's historic persecution of capitalists, illustrated by an old black-and-white photograph of businessmen being paraded through the streets during the Cultural Revolution, government censors physically removed the page from the newspapers on sale in Beijing.

We moved back to the US in 2005, in time for the last few years of semi-normalcy before our country went off the rails. By 2008, the pro-trade consensus was starting to crumble. In the Democratic presidential primaries that year, both Barack Obama and Hillary Clinton called for the North American Free Trade Agreement to be renegotiated. I interviewed Clinton during the Pennsylvania primary. Seated in a school gym teacher's cramped office, she accused China of manipulating its currency, violating American copyrights, and rigging its domestic market to benefit government-backed firms. She also endorsed the kind of industrial policies that a Democratic president would eventually implement almost fifteen years later. "We have to adjust our views of this," she told me. Her remarks would have been welcome to the factory workers I had met in Ohio one month earlier—if they still believed anything politicians said. The men had lost their jobs when their plant relocated to an industrial park in Mexico. They'd spent their final workdays training their Mexican replacements.

Economists like to say the plural of *anecdote* isn't *data*, meaning that these sorts of stories don't prove anything. But like the dead in Jakarta, and the bank-running Russians in Moscow, these Midwestern factory workers were economic casualties, too. I still appreciated the financial logic behind moving basic manufacturing to a lower-wage country. But I wondered why more couldn't be done to help the workers left behind. By this point, I'd been seeing the human costs of these economic transitions for decades.

I was born in Holyoke, Massachusetts, one of the places where the Industrial Revolution began in nineteenth-century America. My Irish immigrant ancestors had worked in paper mills along the Connecticut River until those jobs went south where wages were lower. In the first years after the Cold War's end, I'd reported on the so-called peace dividend as it played out in Southern California, where almost one-third of the state's five-hundred-thousand-plus aerospace workers lost their jobs in five years. Whether the cause was trade, technology, or geopolitics, the available remedies for sudden unemployment did not seem adequate.

A few years after I returned to the United States, my own industry suffered a similar winnowing. Employment at the nation's newspapers was cut in half over little more than a decade, as advertising disappeared and audiences resisted paying for news on the internet. In late 2015, after more than three decades as a reporter, the trend finally caught up with me when Bloomberg News laid me off. The experience was unsettling, but I was luckier than most. I quickly found a new job in the business and in a couple of years worked my way to a better position than the one I'd lost. But my brief spell of unemployment gave me more empathy for other men and women who found themselves jobless. I'd been fortunate enough to have received severance pay. What would it feel like to watch your savings drain away while you searched for a new job you might never find?

In Jakarta and Moscow, I saw the raw power of global capital flows. Living in Beijing, I witnessed the rise of the globe's new manufacturing leader. But it took moving home for me to really experience the backlash against globalization—and to recognize that a new economic model was emerging.

I have mixed feelings about all this. My life, after all, illustrates globalization's promise. I have lived abroad with my wife and our three children, two of whom were born outside the United States. We travel frequently and enjoy other cultures. Both of the cars in my garage carry Japanese nameplates, though they were manufactured in Mexico and Mississippi. The political opposition to globalization often struck me as hidebound and even nutty. Every time someone complained about the allegedly sinister influence of the World Economic Forum, I had to laugh. I had attended the organization's annual meeting in Davos several times. For all the self-regarding hoopla, it was just a fancy business conference, hardly an all-powerful globalist conspiracy.

Like most people, I didn't think Donald Trump had much chance to be elected president in 2016. But it was obvious on the campaign trail that he was tapping into a reservoir of popular resentment over the ways the country and its relationship with the world were changing. On Maryland's conservative eastern shore, one Republican told me flatly: "There's too much globalization going on."

Trump's upset win was evidence that unfettered globalization had run into a dead end. The Manhattan businessman had long been a protectionist; trade and immigration were the rare public policy issues on which he held strong beliefs. For most of his four years in office, Trump imposed or threatened tariffs on products from China, Germany, Mexico, Canada, and any other country that caught his eye.

The erratic nature of Trump's multifront trade wars probably delayed my recognition that something fundamental was changing. It was easy to dismiss his scattershot rants and sometimes hard to take him seriously. In December 2019, for example, the president said on Twitter that he was imposing tariffs on Brazil and Argentina over their alleged currency manipulation—"effective immediately"—and then, after an uproar, never actually got around to doing so.

Events conspired to change my mind. The first sign that the coronavirus was going to be a major problem for the United States emerged in global supply chains. As a rolling wave of shutdowns hit factories—first in China, then in Europe and the United States—production of a range of goods stuttered and stalled. Suddenly, consumers couldn't obtain what they wanted, when they wanted it.

The first products in short supply were the masks, gloves, and wipes people needed to protect themselves from the pandemic. Then, a shortage of semiconductors made it almost impossible to find a new car. On a reporting trip in the summer of 2021, I found myself in a sailboat off the coast of Southern California, threading my way through a cargo-ship flotilla idling outside the Port of Los Angeles. The offshore backlog topped one hundred vessels at one point, an unprecedented traffic jam that illustrated the risks American companies had run by concentrating their supply chains in distant Asia. Six months later, the war in Ukraine sent commodity prices rocketing and exposed Europe's folly in betting its economy on Russian energy supplies. When prominent figures in Washington began calling for a decoupling from China, it just confirmed that the old approach to globalization was fading fast.

I don't know precisely what will replace it. I don't think anyone does. But it feels as if we're drifting toward trouble. A quarter century ago, there was a broad consensus in Washington that the market had all the answers and that bringing China, and Russia, into the global trading system would cement a peaceful future. Now there is almost as much certainty that the government should be shaping economic outcomes—through subsidies, high tariffs, or both—and that China is a hostile power bent on leading an alternative international order.

What's required now is the sort of policy nuance that was lacking in the 1990s, which began a period that economists describe pejoratively as "hyper-globalization." It should be possible to stiffen our approach to China without acting as if military conflict were inevitable, as some in Congress and the commentariat often insist. Likewise, there is a logic to having the government take a more active role in critical markets in order to safeguard national security, given the lessons of the pandemic, China's inward turn, and the wars in Ukraine and the Middle East. But uncommon political discipline will be required to prevent such efforts from descending into boondoggles, waste, and cronyism.

We have embarked on a new era of à la carte globalization. It will be at least as difficult to manage as the original. But if we ignore the lessons of the past, it may not be manageable at all.

Introduction

We Might Have Done Things Differently, If We Had Known What Was Coming

It was easy to be an optimist in the United States at the dawn of the twenty-first century. The economy was strong. The nation was un-challenged on the world stage. The American model of free markets and free elections was sweeping the globe. So when Congress on September 19, 2000, took up legislation normalizing trade relations with China, a step toward admitting it to the World Trade Organization, it did so from a position of strength.

Among the optimists was Joe Biden, the senator from Delaware, who was an enthusiastic proponent of the China bill. As the senior Democrat on the Senate Foreign Relations Committee, his views reflected a bipartisan consensus that expanded trade would encourage greater freedom in authoritarian regimes. Enlisting Communist China and post-Soviet Russia in a US-led economic order would lead to shared prosperity, peace, and political liberalization—or so many policymakers said at the time.

The labor unions that were among Biden's chief political supporters, however, were vehemently opposed to greater trade with China, fearing it would place Americans in competition with low-wage Chinese workers who lacked the right to strike or bargain collectively. But speaking on the Senate floor, Biden minimized the likely consequences of China's rise. After all, the US economy was almost ten times the size of China's, making any risks seem manageable. Advocates on both sides of the debate had "oversold" the bill's economic impact, he said. "I do not anticipate a dramatic explosion in American jobs, suddenly created to fuel a flood of exports to China. Nor do I see the collapse of the American manufacturing economy, as China, a nation with the impact on the world economy about the size of the Netherlands', suddenly becomes our major economic competitor," Biden said.

China was changing, Biden said, and could be encouraged to change more quickly through trade. "They have been forced to acknowledge the failure of communism, and have conceded the irrefutable superiority of an open market economy. The result has been a marked improvement in living standards for hundreds of millions of Chinese citizens," Biden said in September 2000. "This growing prosperity for the Chinese people, in turn, has put China on a path toward ever greater political and economic freedom. The Chinese people, taking responsibility for their own economic livelihood, are demanding a greater voice in the governance of China."[1]

Frank Jannuzi, a longtime Biden foreign policy adviser, said the senator viewed trade relations with China—and the country's proposed WTO membership—as a strategic issue more than an economic one. It was all about bringing leverage to bear on Chinese leaders to continue steering the country toward a market-based approach, and promoting stability by enmeshing China in a global system whose rules had largely been written in the United States.[2]

That said, China's human rights practices remained a concern. The United States objected to Beijing's harsh treatment of pro-democracy dissidents, the restive province of Tibet, and the self-governing island of Taiwan, which it claimed as sovereign Chinese territory. When the Senate held its final debate on the China trade bill, lawmakers from both parties drew explicit links between incorporating the Chinese into the global economy and political change. Flooding China with American information technology products would inevitably undermine government control of society, said Sen. Dick Durbin, a Democrat from Illinois. "It's time to bring democracy to China via the Internet, via US-Chinese commerce relationships, via other US products," said Durbin. "Expanding trade...will lead China into democracy, into freedom, closer to what we value as principles in this country."

In the early days of China's economic opening, Deng Xiaoping had used a metaphor to describe the costs and benefits of reform. Opening a window would inevitably allow some flies into the room, Deng said, but the fresh air would be worth it. Now, hardliners in China's Communist establishment—with clear memories of the bloody events in Tiananmen Square little more than a decade earlier—were less sanguine about what might fly in China's open windows. Their opposition to WTO membership was taken in Washington as proof that trade liberalization would undermine Chinese authoritarianism. "The changes are a direct threat to the communist establishment in China. As the Chinese people become more aware of the opportunities that exist for improving one's life that are inherent in a free society, they will demand more rights from their government and will demand that the government become more responsive to the will of the people," said Sen. Christopher "Kit" Bond of Missouri.

China faced a choice between "irreconcilable interests": economic liberalization or political repression, according to Sen. Bob Kerrey, the Nebraska Democrat. It could open itself to the world through greater trade, and accept the destabilizing effects of Western values that would arrive via the internet, cable television, and Western periodicals, or it could maintain its apparatus of authoritarian control. But it could not do both.

"What better way to promote democracy in China?" Kerrey said. "China does in fact represent a case for economic engagement as a mechanism for effecting political change."

Habits of liberty

There were precedents for the political transformation that many American lawmakers anticipated. Prosperity and freedom had risen in tandem across East Asia over the previous two decades; China seemed likely to follow the same path as its smaller neighbors. "I believe in trade as a liberalizing force. A country cannot accept our goods and services and not be exposed to our ideas and values," said Sen. Herb Kohl, a Democrat from Wisconsin. "One has only to look around the Pacific to see countries that have made the move from dictatorship to democracy and see their focus on trade to see the connection. South Korea, Taiwan and Indonesia have all made steps toward greater democracy and all three have been engines for economic growth in the region. As capitalism penetrates Chinese society, the push for greater democracy will inexorably follow."

American politicians were equally confident about the outlook for Chinese behavior outside its borders. Greater US trade with China, they said, would reduce the chances of the two countries engaging in armed conflict. "History teaches us that conflicts among trading partners are less likely than conflicts between countries that do not have strong economic ties," said Sen. Kent Conrad, a North Dakota Democrat, overlooking World War I, when the United Kingdom and Germany waged a ruinous war despite their extensive commercial links.

Still, Conrad wasn't alone. His Republican colleague, South Carolina's Sen. Strom Thurmond, insisted that trade would protect Taiwan from forced reunification with the mainland. "The more China trades, the more it has to lose from war," Thurmond said.

For some, the link between economic development and political freedom was a matter of ideological faith. Sen. Orrin Hatch of Utah, a conservative Republican, quoted Austrian economist Friedrich Hayek and Milton Friedman, an American monetarist, to demonstrate that time was running out for Chinese communism. "Capitalism cannot exist without expanding individual freedoms," Hatch said. "And the growth of individual freedom is antithetical to authoritarian control. . . . Capitalism corrodes communism."

What explained this certitude? Experience and hubris. The China debate occurred at a moment when the United States enjoyed unquestioned global dominance as a singular "hyperpower" and was growing ever wealthier thanks to an internet-fueled boom.[3] The men and women on the Senate floor that early fall day had witnessed the collapse of the Berlin Wall, the demise of the Soviet Union, and the extension of democracy to perhaps seven hundred million people. They were living, many believed, through what the political scientist Francis Fukuyama called "the End of History," the permanent triumph of Western liberal democracy and free market capitalism. From this vantage point, some degree of eventual Chinese democratization hardly seemed any more unlikely than the global events that already had occurred.

After all, when Richard Nixon journeyed to Beijing in February 1972, China was still mired in the isolation and insanity of Mao's Cultural Revolution. Private markets were illegal. Labor camps were crowded with political prisoners. Now, China was visibly changing. Deng's economic reforms, which began as experiments in limited coastal zones, had spread nationwide. Even before the WTO deal was finalized, American businesses were stepping up their investment in the country, drawn by a market of more than one billion people. Two-way trade between the United States and China had doubled since 1994.

Supporters of granting China "permanent normal trade relations" dominated both political parties, and included prominent business, religious, and civil figures. Former Presidents Gerald Ford and Jimmy Carter; Federal Reserve Chair Alan Greenspan; Christian broadcaster Pat Robertson; and Leonard Woodcock, former president of the United Auto Workers labor union, were among those who backed the Senate legislation. "This may be one of those rare occasions on an important issue where there's virtually no downside to taking affirmative action," said Brent Scowcroft, who had helped bring the Cold War to a graceful conclusion as national security advisor to President George H. W. Bush.[4]

Indeed, Biden's rosy assessment of China's prospects was widely shared. Economist Henry S. Rowen, a former RAND Corporation president who had served at the Pentagon under Dick Cheney, predicted in 1996 that China would become a full-blown democracy once per-person annual income hit $7,000, which Rowen predicted would occur around 2015.[5] Countries like Spain, South Korea, Chile, Argentina, and Taiwan all had embraced popular rule when they hit that mark. There seemed no reason to believe China would be any different.

Granting China normal US trade relations—and thus doing away with the annual pro forma review of its access to the American market—was pushed through Congress by Bill Clinton, a Democratic president. But his eventual Republican successor was equally enthusiastic.

"The case for trade is not just monetary, but moral. Economic freedom creates habits of liberty. And habits of liberty create expectations of democracy," said Texas Governor George W. Bush as he campaigned for the presidency.[6] After eleven days of debate, the China trade bill cleared the Senate with eighty-three yes votes.

Quick and painless

Democratic hopes still flickered in Russia, which at the end of its first post-Soviet decade had stumbled into a currency crisis that saw the ruble lose roughly two-thirds of its value, leaving Russians poor and resentful. By the time Bush spoke, an aging Boris Yeltsin had resigned the presidency, giving power to his designated successor, a former KGB officer named Vladimir Putin.

At the Cold War's end, the Russian and Chinese economies in dollar terms had been of similar size. But Russia was an economic wreck by the year 2000. It was China's emergence that would define the twenty-first century. Yet, as time passed, it became clear that globalization had not delivered the political liberalization that had been anticipated. China reached the $7,000 income level in 2013, two years earlier than Rowen had forecast. But far from introducing democratic reforms, China's new leader, Xi Jinping, doubled down on authoritarianism. Using sophisticated technologies—many imported from the United States—Xi created a surveillance state that kept tabs on Chinese citizens, imprisoned more than one million residents of Muslim-majority Xinjiang Province, and engaged in practices the US government labeled "genocide."

China's U-turn toward renewed repression was not the only unexpected development. A few years after Xi came to power, Americans embraced a populist leader who saw trade as only a negative, leaving the world for a time without traditional US leadership on international economics. Global supply chains that once seemed a marvel of efficiency proved brittle when stressed. And the post–Cold War peace among major powers that had facilitated widespread prosperity crumbled as Russia invaded its European neighbor and China's president insisted that Taiwan would soon return to Beijing's rule one way or the other.

To be sure, globalization—meaning the easier movement across borders of goods, services, money, people, and ideas—delivered impressive economic gains. In 2023, the $93 trillion world economy was more than three times bigger than it had been in 1985 when Mikhail Gorbachev came to power.[7] Knitting together low-wage workers in the developing world with consumers in the United States and Europe helped lift nearly 1.5 billion people out of crushing poverty, according to the International Monetary Fund. Countless individual lives were enriched by the lowering of trade barriers and the rise of a more integrated world.

Most of those people were in China and other developing nations. But globalization also paid economic dividends in the United States. Thanks to growing trade, American consumers enjoyed a greater array of products at more affordable prices. Low-cost production from abroad helped keep a lid on inflation for two decades, enabling families to stretch their budgets.[8] The typical American household in 2007 had gained an extra $1,500 in annual purchasing power since 2000, according to a detailed study of hundreds of thousands of individual product prices.[9]

The gains associated with globalization, however, were not evenly distributed. Highly educated Americans living in coastal cities flourished while those whose schooling had ended with a high school diploma, or who lived in rural areas or factory towns, often lagged. The benefits of freer trade were spread throughout the economy in ways that made them hard for average consumers to detect and easy to take for granted. How much more would a shirt from Walmart cost if trade barriers were higher? Who could say? Did many Americans know that Apple's iPhone, in one frequently cited example, might cost twice as much if produced in the United States rather than China? Probably not.

So with costs concentrated and obvious, and benefits dispersed and often imperceptible, a backlash began building. After China joined the WTO at the end of 2001, its factories moved to the center of global supply chains for consumer electronics, industrial equipment, auto parts, and clothing. By 2005, the United States each year was importing almost one-quarter of a trillion dollars' worth of Chinese goods, three times as much as in 1999. That was good news for American consumers—and the many American factories that relied upon Chinese parts. But China's rise accelerated the long-term decline of US manufacturing employment, dealing a crippling blow to many working-class communities.

In factory towns like Union City, Tennessee; Martinsville, Virginia; Dalton, Georgia; and Hickory, North Carolina, employment plummeted as low-cost Chinese products flooded US markets. The economy overall gained better jobs and greater wealth thanks to trade. But in just three years starting in the summer of 2000, three million American factory workers lost their jobs. (During the previous three years, the level of manufacturing employment had remained essentially flat.) Trade was not solely, or even chiefly, responsible for the decline. Most economists blamed automation, which enabled factories to produce the same output with fewer workers, as the culprit behind most of the job losses. The recession that followed the terrorist attacks on September 11 also did not help.

Manufacturing payrolls had been dropping since 1979. If trade liberalization received disproportionate blame for that decline, one reason was that it represented a visible national policy choice. Trade deals were debated at length in public and then voted up or down in Congress. No one got to vote on whether Boeing or Caterpillar or General Electric would automate an assembly line. The benefits of trade agreements also were exaggerated by politicians, who promised they would create plenty of new jobs—even though standard economic teaching held that trade affected the mix of jobs in an economy, not their number.

The factory job losses, unlike the gains, also were not spread evenly across the country. Instead, the pain was concentrated in manufacturing-dependent communities, especially in the Midwest and the South. When the housing bubble burst a few years later, igniting a global financial crisis, many of these towns were dealt a second blow. It wasn't obvious at first, but globalization was implicated in this crisis, too. Huge sums of money had flowed into the US bond market from investors in China and Europe, which fueled the bubble and ultimately aggravated its implosion.[10]

In the aftermath, the nation suffered through the weakest recovery since World War II. The human consequences of the China shock, financial crisis, and subsequent government austerity extended beyond dollars and cents as powerful global forces collided with an American system that largely left the victims of labor market adjustments to their own devices. A profound malaise stalked middle-aged whites, in particular, with "deaths of despair" from suicide, drug overdoses, and alcoholic liver disease spiking, according to research by economists Anne Case and Angus Deaton. Hardest hit were white men without a college education, whose incomes had stagnated for decades.[11]

"The mistake in the conventional account of gains from trade was to imagine that the transition from the old jobs to the new jobs would be quick and painless, and to suppose, without proposing policies to make it happen, that the gains to consumers would somehow compensate for the losses to (erstwhile) producers," Case and Deaton wrote.[12]

We all should have thought about this much earlier

The political consequences were also striking. In the years after the financial crisis, countries adopted more than three times as many protectionist measures each year as they had previously.[13] The United Kingdom quit the European Union following its 2016 Brexit referendum. Later that same year, Donald Trump won the US presidency after campaigning on a platform of full-throated economic nationalism. Of the voters who believed international trade cost American jobs, 64 percent voted for Trump, well above his 46 percent overall share of the vote. Trump's strongest support came from white men without a college degree; they chose him over Hillary Clinton by a margin of 71 percent to 23 percent.[14]

It is impossible, of course, to attribute Trump's victory to any single factor. The complacency that kept Hillary Clinton from campaigning in Wisconsin; generalized anti-elite discontent; and racism all played a part. But among a critical segment of the electorate— Trump voters who had cast a ballot for Barack Obama in 2012—anti-globalization sentiments exerted a disproportionate influence. Such voters were the most anti-trade and anti-immigration of Obama's supporters. And they were the most economically insecure of Trump's. "Switchers appear to be against all aspects of globalization—trade, immigration, and finance," one review of the academic literature concluded.[15] These voters propelled Trump to victory in normally Democratic states such as manufacturing-heavy Michigan, Wisconsin, and Pennsylvania.

President Bill Clinton, hosting a 1997 gathering of world leaders in Denver, had proclaimed globalization "irreversible." But there was nothing permanent about the rapid growth in global trade and investment that characterized the first decades after the Cold War. While the amount of goods and cash moving across national borders increased for another decade following Clinton's confident assertion, globalization plateaued following the 2008 financial crisis. In 2023, merchandise trade equaled 59 percent of the global economy, down slightly from a decade and a half earlier.[16] Global banking also retrenched. Bankers loaned customers in other countries almost four times as much in early 2008 as they had at the turn of the century. In the fifteen years following the crisis, even as the global economy grew by more than 50 percent, those flows stagnated.[17]

Years of deteriorating US-China relations and failed global trade talks stalled the tighter integration that Clinton had anticipated. Russia's invasion of Ukraine and the financial sanctions imposed by the United States and its allies in response showed that the triumphant globalization that began more than thirty years ago had reached a dead end. Biden's presidency, which some had expected to revive the flagging enthusiasm for expanded trade, instead marked an emphatic turn toward industrial policy and domestic manufacturing.

During his five decades in Washington, the Democrat had backed controversial trade deals with Mexico and China in the face of opposition from his labor union allies. As a presidential candidate in 2020, Biden criticized Trump's tariffs on Chinese goods as "erratic" and "self-defeating." But once in the White House, he retained them and erected new barriers, cutting off China's access to the most sophisticated American semiconductors and the machines and experts who produced them. As his four-year term limped to a close, Biden on trade more closely resembled his "America First" predecessor than the Democrat he had served as vice president.

Globalization's fraying was more than just a US-China story. Biden choreographed Russia's economic exile following the invasion of Ukraine and criticized the WTO for infringing on American prerogatives in terms that Trump might have applauded. His administration disparaged the traditional trade agreements negotiated by his Democratic predecessors Clinton and Obama, saying they had failed to convert China or Russia into satisfied members of a US-led order and had left too many working Americans empty-handed. Reducing trade barriers no longer was a US priority. Instead, Biden concentrated on fortifying supply chains against threats such as a new pandemic or geopolitical coercion by China.

Of greatest significance, Biden did more to encourage domestic production at the expense of imports than any president in decades. He put new teeth in "Buy America" requirements, even if they slowed progress on other administration priorities, and pushed through Congress three major pieces of legislation, on infrastructure, climate change, and semiconductor production. Analysts estimated the initiatives would pump a combined $4 trillion into the US economy over a decade, marking the most consequential shift in American economic thinking since the Reagan era. After four decades of habitual government deference to the market, Washington was back in charge. Biden's industrial policy measures, including generous subsidies for clean energy development, were aimed at China. But they also hit US allies: French President Emmanuel Macron warned that Biden's protectionism could "fragment the West."[18]

A quarter century earlier, former enemies were becoming commercial and political partners. Companies were gaining vast new markets where they could serve billions of customers and locate low-cost production facilities. Consumers were enjoying the start of years of almost-nonexistent inflation.

Today, former enemies are, once again, enemies. Economic walls are going up, not coming down. Geopolitics, disease, and extreme weather events have exposed the risks of supply chains designed purely to minimize cost. Europe has learned the hard way that depending upon

Russian energy supplies was a bad idea, and the United States feels the same about its reliance on China for pharmaceutical ingredients and the critical minerals needed for the transition to a low-carbon economy. As governments prioritize more secure supply lines, and companies modify just-in-time production strategies, consumers will pay the price.

"We all should have thought about this much earlier," said Jamie Dimon, CEO of JPMorgan Chase, the nation's largest bank. "Like about ten or fifteen years ago, we should have said, you know, globalization is great. But we can't rely on China for all of the ingredients that go into pharmaceuticals. 100 percent of penicillin. Rare earths that go into the F-35. You know, seventeen fabs in Taiwan, which produce 80 percent of all the complex chips in the world. That was a mistake."[19]

Freedom and democracy

These are among the most dramatic shifts in global economics in a generation. How and why did they come about?

The seeds of globalization's rethinking were planted years before Donald Trump first entered the White House, but were ignored by a complacent pro-trade establishment. "We were too busy admiring the upside of openness" to notice what was happening to the public mood, wrote Glenn Hubbard, chairman of the White House Council of Economic Advisers under President George W. Bush.[20]

Despite ample warning of the dangers, policymakers and business executives failed to equitably spread globalization's gains and were remarkably blasé about its costs for manufacturing workers in advanced economies like the United States. Mainstream economists based their forecasts on the modest domestic impact of trade when it occurred largely between high-wage economies, such as the United States and Germany or the United Kingdom. As a result, they underestimated the effects on US factory employment of soaring imports from low-wage developing countries like China, which were responsible for "more than half" of the jobs lost between 1997 and 2005.[21] Paul Krugman, who earned a Nobel Prize for his academic work on international trade, would later concede: "Globalization produced far more disruption and cost for some workers than the consensus had envisaged....We might have done things differently if we had known what was coming."[22]

Conventional wisdom held that trade created winners and losers and that the losers should be compensated—both as a matter of morality and to maintain political support for further global integration. And yet somehow, that never seemed to happen. Proposals that would have insured Americans against a sudden loss of wages or created a comprehensive social safety net went nowhere. An existing workforce-retraining program, known as Trade Adjustment Assistance, was chronically underfunded. It finally lapsed under the Biden administration, which billed its trade policy as "worker centered." Even though trade's negative effects were known to fall most heavily on specific communities, the government tried few geographically targeted or "place-based" responses.

This failure to address obvious needs began under the Clinton administration when the federal budget, for the first time in decades, was in or near balance.[23] The United States—the wealthiest country on Earth—could have afforded greater aid to cushion the blow of globalization. Policymakers, constrained by a political climate that fetishized a balanced federal budget, chose not to spend the money. The failure to adequately provide for those who would be hurt by globalization had the entirely predictable consequence of fueling political forces that were opposed to its continuation.

"Globalization not only failed to spread liberal values, because freedom and democracy do not necessarily travel with goods and services, but also weakened them in the countries that were its strongest proponents and fed instead the rise of inward-looking forces," Mario Draghi, the former president of the European Central Bank, said in early 2024.[24]

With the benefit of hindsight, prominent Democrats and Republicans alike lamented the failure to better equip Americans for the transition to a new economy. Hubbard was a prominent conservative economist, not normally given to promoting new government programs. But he became convinced that the failure to help workers upended by globalization drove Americans toward protectionism. The government, he argued in a 2022 book, should spend more on enhanced social insurance, retraining, and other aid.

"We felt that markets, whether they're markets for labor or markets for goods and services, would adjust more frictionlessly than they did," Hubbard said in an interview. "There was a feeling somehow that it would quote 'work out.' Indeed if you think of political elites instead of economists, whether they're center left or center right, there wasn't a lot of attention to this problem."[25]

At the other end of the political spectrum, Michael Froman, Barack Obama's chief trade negotiator, said working-class Americans had legitimate gripes about the way their leaders had managed global integration. "Where I think both Republican and Democratic administrations failed is that we never put together the domestic set of policies that would make globalization work for everybody.... There's a whole agenda. But it was never pursued with as much gusto as it could have been or should have been."[26]

Those who favored globalization also were excessively optimistic that expanded trade would promote the liberalization of autocratic regimes. *New York Times* columnist Thomas Friedman wrote in 1997 that China's capitalist development would inevitably require the societal institutions that accompanied free markets everywhere else. "China's going to have a free press," he wrote. ". . . China's rapid growth actually fuels internal pressures for change, by creating new constituencies— like shareholders—who demand reform for their own self-interest."[27] Instead, Chinese leaders recognized the potential danger and proved adept at maintaining undemocratic rule.[28] Though trade grew rapidly, hopes for political change in China and Russia withered; eventually, there seemed little obvious relationship between commercial engagement and political liberalization. For a time, the Chinese people enjoyed both more material wealth and personal freedom than their ancestors ever could have anticipated. Yet after taking power in 2012, Xi cracked down on the country's most successful entrepreneurs, reemphasized the Communist Party's supremacy over the economy and the state, and obliterated norms limiting Chinese presidents to ten years in office.

"I thought putting China in the WTO was going to open them up and make them get closer to democracy and capitalism. That's a vote I might take back," former House Speaker Paul Ryan, an avowed free trader, said in 2023.[29]

With no end to his rule in sight, Xi is the most powerful Chinese leader since Mao. But he was not single-handedly responsible for China's turn toward renewed autocracy. Under his colorless predecessor, Hu Jintao, the ruling Communist Party in 2006 launched well-funded industrial policies aimed at reducing China's dependence upon foreigners for key technologies. State security officials in preparation for the 2008 Beijing Olympics tightened controls over the media and the internet that they never relaxed. And in the wake of a global financial crisis that originated on Wall Street, China's rulers shed any remaining deference to American leaders.[30]

Oversold, under-resourced, and poorly administered

Globalization advocates behaved as if the geopolitical calm that followed the Cold War would endure, permitting trade and finance to grow undisturbed. In fact, American political and corporate leaders were wrong in their claims about how trade would spread freedom and about how reliable global supply chains centered in China would prove in the face of multiple foreseeable threats. The alarms that were missed or ignored included the outbreak in 2003 of an unfamiliar respiratory virus in China known as SARS; the lessons of the 2008 financial crisis; the 2011 nuclear accident in Fukushima, Japan; Russia's annexation of Crimea in 2014; and evidence of chronic US port and rail inadequacies. Now, after getting it wrong with its initial sanguine consensus, the United States risks compounding the error by overindulging in protectionist industrial policies and tariffs or decoupling from China.

American policymakers in the 1990s did something that was both the most natural thing in the world and the most audacious. In trying to cobble together a world of free markets and free peoples under their leadership, US officials proceeded along a path their predecessors had blazed following World War II. By adding China to the global trading system, however, they embarked on an unprecedented experiment. China's sheer size argued for caution. But its rise came at a time when American officials were not in a cautious mood. In this new age of globalization, they already had weathered crises in Mexico, Thailand, South Korea, Russia, and Brazil, leading *Time* magazine to hail the crisis-fighting trio of Federal Reserve Chair Alan Greenspan, Treasury Secretary Robert Rubin, and Deputy Treasury Secretary Lawrence Summers as the "Committee to Save the World." [31]

Clearly, the arrival on the global economic scene of China's several hundred million factory workers, all willing to toil longer hours for less pay than their advanced economy counterparts, would have far-reaching consequences, both good and bad. Americans welcomed the good but made little provision for the bad. "There was a general recognition that China with its large population would become a large and important economy. But it didn't matter much at that time because we had a lot of other things to worry about," Rubin said. "In hindsight, we could have been more focused on matters related to trade." [32]

The United States effectively gambled that embarking upon unrestrained globalization would generate widespread prosperity at home while encouraging political liberalization abroad. Instead, the increasing global flows of goods and finance produced lopsided economic benefits in the United States while leaving little mark on the political systems of Communist China and post-Communist Russia. Compounding the error, many multinational corporations—fixated on efficiency above all else—concentrated their supply chains in a single country, one that grew increasingly hostile to US national interests. American leaders launched their unprecedented project of global integration for all the best reasons. But they did so without investing in the guardrails that were needed to make it safe for all segments of society—and that were required to maintain political support for its continuation. Little effort was made to offer affected workers adequate retraining or financial support as they weathered the transition. And as problems arose that threatened the project, such as import surges that overwhelmed individual US industries, policymakers chose not to use the protections they had negotiated into the terms of China's WTO membership.

Globalization went awry, in this sense, because of policy choices, inaction, and error.

Decades later, the American bet on globalization—oversold, underresourced, and poorly administered—has not paid off in the ways that had been expected. Seen from the vantage point of the 1990s, the current situation would have seemed almost unimaginable. China, rather than advancing however slowly toward greater pluralism, has doubled down on Maoist repression and state capitalism. Russia has been virtually excommunicated from the global economy, left to wither under the weight of financial sanctions. Perhaps most surprising, the United States, whose leaders created the rules-based global trading system, has all but abandoned it under three consecutive presidencies. The WTO has been relegated to near-irrelevancy as American officials increasingly choose unilateral action over cooperative engagement. The political support that once existed for trade liberalization has evaporated, supplanted first by populist rage, then by industrial policy, and finally by a national turn inward with Donald Trump's triumphant return to the White House. Worse, an era that began with Washington confidently promoting to other nations its greatest export—democracy—concludes with the American democratic system under threat at home from an unorthodox president determined to centralize power in the White House. US leaders once felt sure that the technological miracles invented in Silicon Valley would undermine the world's autocrats. Now they recognize that technology can cement undemocratic rule more readily than threaten it. At home and abroad, the situation that confronts Americans today is not at all what an earlier generation anticipated amid "the End of History."

Now the US is placing another big bet, this time on the most sweeping tariffs in nearly a century and wary engagement abroad. Supply chains are being redesigned to reduce US dependence on Chinese factories, even if it means higher costs. More than a decade after the "China shock" largely ended, new labor market upheavals loom in the rise of artificial intelligence and the shift to a low-carbon economy. Yet America's social safety net remains as thin as ever, meaning that workers who will be displaced in these transitions could well become fresh recruits for the populist ranks.

How in the world did the United States arrive at this juncture? The answers can be found in the experiences of two presidents and a representative handful of their constituents: a factory worker, an activist, a journalist, a corporate executive, and an investor. Seeing the past few decades through their eyes will illuminate what went right with globalization, what went wrong, and what needs to change for Americans to navigate its shifting currents.

1

The Strongest in the World

On a warm Saturday in June 1997, Bill Clinton awaited his guests. Every few minutes, accompanied by a fanfare of trumpets, a foreign dignitary would arrive outside Denver's striking public library, where the American president was hosting a global summit. Seven times, he and another leader gave a quick wave to onlookers before pivoting for the obligatory photo. When German Chancellor Helmut Kohl stepped out of a massive white bus to join him, an ebullient Clinton joked with photographers: "You like his limo? I do." [1]

The American president had reason to be in a good mood. The US economy was expanding at an annual rate of nearly 7 percent while unemployment was at its lowest level in twenty-four years. On Wall Street, stocks were on their way to their third consecutive year of 20-percent-plus returns. The president had opened the summit weekend by proclaiming: "America's economy is the healthiest in a generation and the strongest in the world." [2]

The self-satisfaction irked American allies, as did US officials' repeated suggestions that Europe and Japan should mimic the American economic formula of low taxes and light regulation. The French, in particular, took offense at their hosts' swagger. "We have our own model and we plan to stick to it," said French President Jacques Chirac. The Parisian daily *Libération* summarized Clinton's message with the sarcastic headline "Why Can't You Be American?" The president finally told his more voluble aides to "cool it."[3]

Clinton and the other leaders confronted a sprawling agenda for their weekend gathering in the Mile High City: the fragile peace in Bosnia, globalization, terrorism, the imminent reversion of Hong Kong to Chinese control, NATO enlargement, and global warming. In a June 16 memo to the president, senior Clinton aides identified nine separate objectives for him to pursue during the thirty-six-hour conclave.[4]

What distinguished this summit from previous such events was the presence of the eighth participant, Russian President Boris Yeltsin. For the first time, the leader of a free Russia was joining the annual meeting of the world's seven industrial democracies. The leaders gathering in the shadow of the Rocky Mountains sensed the best opportunity in half a century to spread peace and prosperity.

Some members of the G7—which included Canada, France, Great Britain, Germany, Italy, and Japan—had resisted inviting Yeltsin to the "Summit of the Eight." Less than six years after the Soviet Union's collapse, Russia remained dependent upon Western financial aid.[5] But throughout the weekend, Clinton made sure Yeltsin was seated right next to him at the leaders' round cherry-and-aspen wood-veneer table. When Clinton gave a brief public statement to conclude the summit, Yeltsin stood so close the two men were practically touching. It was the Russian's hand that Clinton shook first when he finished speaking.

Despite Russia's weakness, Yeltsin's presence in Denver symbolized a new era for the global economy. For more than four decades after the end of the Second World War, the world had been divided into rival blocs, one free, the other unfree. But that had changed.

The Berlin Wall, the physical embodiment of the East-West divide, had come down, and the Soviet Union had dissolved. India had abandoned socialism. Ten times as much money flowed into emerging markets such as Brazil, Mexico, and South Africa as had just one decade earlier.[6] A few weeks after the summit, the general secretary of China's Communist Party, Jiang Zemin, would ring the opening bell on the New York Stock Exchange before dining with two hundred American business leaders at the Waldorf Astoria, where he sought US support for Beijing's bid to join the World Trade Organization.[7]

Russia, long America's enemy, was now its political and commercial partner. One day earlier, Yeltsin and Clinton had met for an hour in a downtown hotel. Clinton greeted Yeltsin, who had lost sixty-five pounds since their last meeting four months earlier, with a compliment.

"You look in good shape," Clinton said.

Patting his stomach, Yeltsin replied, "Something is lacking here."

When Clinton repeated, "You look good," Yeltsin replied: "I prefer that women would tell me that!"[8] The men laughed, then sped through talks on arms control, NATO, and the latest crisis with Iraq. The Russian leader informed Clinton that he had settled several disputes with Ukraine, the former Soviet republic that had declared independence, including the division of the Soviet-era Black Sea Fleet, based in the Crimean port of Sevastopol.

The two leaders talked mostly about integrating Russia into global capitalism. Yeltsin thanked Clinton for resolving the last hurdles to Russia rejoining the Paris Club of creditors, which symbolized Moscow's new standing and gave it hopes of collecting some of the $140 billion that the former Soviet Union had lent its allies.[9] Despite doubts about Russia's political stability, its bid for full membership in the global community enjoyed unmistakable momentum. The next step would be entry into the WTO, perhaps as soon as the following year. "We need to intensify our efforts and need to keep these things going," Clinton told Yeltsin.

It had been less than a decade since the Cold War shuddered to an end. All of the former Warsaw Pact countries were virgin economic terrain, just waiting for the right dose of modern American entrepreneurial brio. A comprehensive reshaping of global economic patterns was just beginning. But it was one that would confound the assumptions and expectations of nearly everyone.

A climate for democratic change

Clinton's White House predecessor at first had been skeptical when Mikhail Gorbachev began overhauling the Soviet Union. President George H. W. Bush suspected a Communist trap. But he soon warmed to the new Soviet leader. In May 1989, Bush agreed to cut US forces in Europe to match Soviet reductions. Seven months later at a summit in

Malta, the two sides agreed to extend Western trade and investment to Moscow and complete two arms treaties. By the spring of 1991, when he traveled to New Haven to give the commencement address at Yale University, Bush had accepted "the end of a long era of cold war and conflict."

Russia now was a democracy, and Bush hoped he could someday say the same about China. Two years earlier, Chinese authorities had brutally repressed pro-democracy protests in the center of the capital Beijing. To American officials, the Tiananmen Square massacre marked an interruption in Chinese democratization, not its end. While critics called for Bush to withdraw China's trade privileges, known as "most favored nation" status, he saw commerce as a way to shape Beijing's behavior. Raising tariffs against Chinese products would in particular hurt the merchants of southern Guangdong Province, which Bush described as a hotbed of resistance to Communist rule. "We can help create a climate for democratic change," Bush told the Yale audience. "No nation on Earth has discovered a way to import the world's goods and services while stopping foreign ideas at the border. Just as the democratic idea has transformed nations on every continent, so, too, change will inevitably come to China."[10]

The world economy certainly was changing. In 1992, the total value of imports and exports for the first time reached 40 percent of the global economy, up from just one-quarter in 1970. As merchandise trade swelled, the amount of money racing across borders—to buy stocks and bonds or to build new factories—likewise soared.

During the 1992 presidential campaign, two countries dominated the debate over how the United States should engage with this new era: Mexico and China. In August of that year, negotiators wrapped up a proposed North American Free Trade Agreement that would link the United States, Mexico, and Canada in a single trading bloc. With many Democrats and organized labor opposed to the pact, Clinton delayed taking a stand until thirty days before the election.

After an agonizing debate with his political advisers, Clinton opted to support the deal with reservations. Pressed to choose between his image as a pro-business "New Democrat" and the support of Democrats' traditional labor allies, he sought to have both. Only if new "side agreements" on labor and environmental issues were added to the pact would he submit it to Congress, he said in a speech at North Carolina State University.[11]

Clinton had previewed this nuanced approach in a closed-door address to the AFL-CIO in California a few months earlier, as the primary campaign wound down. Companies already were moving low-skilled factory jobs to Mexican maquiladoras, tariff-free facilities that had existed just across the border for decades, he said. And that would continue with or without the new treaty. At the same time, working Americans were hurting because their government was slow to adapt to globalization. Countries like Germany did a better job of training and educating their workers. If we do NAFTA right, Clinton said, his administration would secure federal funds for new training and investments in infrastructure and technology that would provide jobs for the unemployed.

"Essentially he had a lot of the assumptions of the anti-NAFTA people and the conclusions of the pro-NAFTA people and you really couldn't find any human being on earth except him who saw it that way," David Kusnet, Clinton's chief speechwriter, later recalled.[12]

When Clinton moved from candidate to president, even some of his top White House aides were ambivalent about the deal. Before joining the campaign, speechwriter Michael Waldman, working for consumer activist Ralph Nader, had lobbied Congress against the proposal. Drafted to handle communications for Clinton's NAFTA war room, Waldman and other in-house skeptics made "NAFTA cuz we hafta" their unofficial slogan.[13]

As negotiations over the side letters proceeded with Canada and Mexico, Lawrence Katz, the chief economist at the Labor Department, bargained with US labor and business groups over a major expansion of the social safety net. The idea was to replace the limited Trade Adjustment Assistance program with a sweeping package of aid for all dislocated workers—not just those who lost their jobs because of trade deals.

In talks that consumed the first half of 1993, Katz, who was on leave from teaching at Harvard University, proposed a roughly $4 billion program that included training, job search help, more generous unemployment benefits, and wage insurance. He saw a rare opportunity to expand the safety net with bipartisan support: Republican lawmakers would back the proposal to boost NAFTA's chances of getting through

Congress while Democrats would be attracted to the idea of helping more workers.

But the effort collapsed amid opposition from the AFL-CIO leadership, President Lane Kirkland, Secretary-Treasurer Thomas Donahue, and Chief Economist Rudolph Oswald, according to Katz. The union leaders were afraid that Congress would starve a broader social program of needed funds. And they detected political and institutional advantages in the existing arrangement.

"They liked the fact that trade was separated out because they believed that pointed out how terrible trade was, to see lots of people called 'dislocated' by trade. And they also liked the fact that because [TAA] was a complicated process, you had an advantage if you were a union member," he said. "And so that moment sort of disappeared."[14]

Instead of Katz's $4 billion plan to permanently expand the social safety net, American workers were left with a paltry $30 million transitional training program, which Congress established when it approved the trade deal and which would last for just five years.

Clinton began his NAFTA lobbying push in a mid-September ceremony in the White House East Room. Joined by former Presidents Bush, Carter, and Ford, Clinton framed the debate as a choice between adapting to a changing world or clinging to the past. The treaty—improved by labor and environmental codicils that he had persuaded Mexico and Canada to accept—would create two hundred thousand American jobs in its first two years and reduce illegal immigration, he promised. To assuage workers' fears of competition with Mexicans willing to work for far less, Clinton vowed to create "a reemployment system" to replace the nation's outdated unemployment program.[15]

The president had rejected a speech draft that emphasized the treaty's importance to American global leadership, preferring to focus on what an integrated North American market meant for working Americans. "I got to sit with him as he was lobbying Democratic Congress members in groups of like ten or fifteen, you know, day in and day out. And I sat in the corner and took notes so I could use them in the speeches. And over and over again, he was saying, 'Look, I agree with you on this; I agree with you on that. That's going to happen anyway. This plant is going to Mexico with or without NAFTA. The question is, what can we do to make it work for us, and our people, and our economy?'" Waldman said. "He was always very focused on that."[16]

The lobbying effort crested with a televised debate between Vice President Al Gore and Texas businessman Ross Perot, who had run for president as an independent in 1992 famously warning that the treaty would create a "giant sucking sound" as American jobs fled south. "Our people are really angry about this. Working people all across the United States are extremely angry. There is no way to stop 'em. They are not going to tolerate having their jobs continued to be shipped all over the world," Perot said on CNN.[17]

Perot's blunt talk and unvarnished personality once had captivated Americans tired of polished politicians. But his appeal waned during his on-again, off-again 1992 presidential campaign, and seated alongside Gore, his anti-NAFTA passion came off as querulous. Gore, meanwhile, argued that the treaty would encourage Mexico's democratic reforms while the side agreements that the administration had negotiated would enable the US to use sanctions to protect the environment. Less than ten days later, the House approved the deal 234–200 with 102 Democrats in assent; the Senate soon followed suit by a 61–38 margin.[18]

At the national level, Perot's "giant sucking sound" was never heard: Factory employment stayed above pre-NAFTA levels for seven years after the treaty took effect.[19] But in the cities and towns most exposed to competition from Mexican imports—particularly in textiles, apparel, shoes, and leather—"NAFTA had a significant, negative effect on employment," a quartet of economists later concluded.[20] The trade deal's localized downsides also fueled an exodus from the Democratic Party of affected workers, especially white men. It was an early indication that even as trade benefited the economy as a whole, its distributional consequences could be troubling and profound.

A substantial degree of ignorance

With China, Clinton faced a daunting learning curve. He had promised during the 1992 campaign not to "coddle tyrants" as Bush had by sending "emissaries to raise a toast" with the Chinese leaders who crushed the pro-democracy protests in Tiananmen Square.

In practice, Clinton's stance meant conditioning China's trade privileges on its human rights record. Given the size of the US market, Clinton believed he could dangle commercial benefits to encourage China to improve its treatment of dissidents. "He felt that the US was strong enough that we could basically leverage China into shifting its policies on things like human rights. I thought at the time that betrayed a substantial degree of ignorance," said Kenneth Lieberthal, a China expert who later joined Clinton's National Security Council staff.

Clinton discovered, as would subsequent presidents, that Chinese leaders jealously guarded their prerogatives on what they regarded as internal issues. No Chinese leader could be seen to be bowing to foreign pressure on human rights.

After repeated fruitless clashes with Beijing, Clinton eventually acknowledged he had been wrong and in May 1994 abandoned the formal linkage. From then on, Congress each year approved routine trade privileges for Chinese goods. Beijing had won an important battle without firing a shot.

Despite Clinton's concession, relations remained brittle. The Chinese were irked by several US policies, including post–Tiananmen Square economic sanctions and Washington's stance toward Taiwan, the self-governing island that Beijing claims as its sovereign territory.

In July 1995, former Secretary of State Henry Kissinger, fresh from a trip to Beijing, led a small delegation into a private Oval Office meeting.

"Where do you think we are in the relationship?" Clinton asked Kissinger, who was joined by Alexander Haig, another former secretary of state; John Whitehead, former deputy secretary of state; and Maurice Greenberg, chief executive of American International Group, which had major investments in China.

"I've been to China 25 times or so, beginning back in 1971. And in all that time, I've never seen such potential for disintegration of relations," Kissinger said. ". . . We were exposed to a litany of complaints."[21]

One month earlier, Clinton had allowed Lee Teng-hui, the Taiwanese president, to visit Cornell University for his class reunion. Chinese leaders were so agitated over Lee's trip that they might "invade or blockade Taiwan," Whitehead warned.

"It's not just that they think we've broken the 'Three Communiqués,'" Kissinger said, referring to the diplomatic agreements that governed the Sino-US relationship, including Taiwan's status. "When I met with Premier Li Peng, he was much more blunt. He asked me, 'Does the United States see China as our enemy?'"

Kissinger acknowledged that congressional Republicans had been "behaving very irresponsibly on this issue." A few days earlier, House Speaker Newt Gingrich had antagonized Beijing by calling for US diplomatic recognition of Taiwan as an independent country.[22] Haig volunteered that he had told the Georgia Republican to "get off this wicket." The visiting Republicans urged the president to take steps to ease tensions.

Caught between his political opponents on Capitol Hill and a hypersensitive foreign power, Clinton was exasperated. "We're making every effort to understand their domestic political situation and factor it into our policy. Why can't they do the same for us?" the president vented. Dealing with Congress, he added, was like being in "a funhouse."

With Chinese President Jiang Zemin scheduled to visit the United Nations in October, the president said he was "worried sick" about a downward spiral in the relationship. "We can't have him come here and get rained on," he said, alluding to China's congressional critics.

In the end, Clinton and Jiang met at New York's Lincoln Center, on the sidelines of the annual UN meeting. "Much of the discussion" was devoted to trade, *The Washington Post* reported.[23] At issue was a potential bargain that would pave the way for China to join the WTO: American products would get wider access to the Chinese market in return for an end to the annual US review of China's trade privileges or, in the official jargon, "permanent normal trade relations."

In June 1998, Clinton traveled to China for a nine-day trip that took him to Beijing, Shanghai, and Hong Kong. But he failed to make much progress on trade. Chinese leaders were worried about the tens of millions of workers who would inevitably lose their jobs at uncompetitive state-owned enterprises when China joined the WTO, he told reporters.

Nonetheless, Clinton was visibly buoyed by his time with Jiang. The two had not clicked when they first met at the 1993 Asia-Pacific Economic

Cooperation summit in Seattle, which Mickey Kantor called "the most stilted, awful meeting I've ever seen Bill Clinton have with anybody."[24] Both men had clung to their official talking points, resolving nothing.

But Clinton eventually charmed the older man. When Jiang accidentally dropped his papers on the floor during a joint press conference at a subsequent meeting in Washington, Clinton instantly bent and gathered them up, a courtesy that impressed the Chinese president.[25]

Asked at the end of his 1998 trip if he thought there could be a democratic China, Clinton enthused: "Not only do I believe there can be, I believe there will be." He went on to suggest that Jiang and Chinese Premier Zhu Rongji might be the leaders to bring it about.[26]

Four months later, Clinton—preoccupied by a fresh crisis in Iraq—dispatched his vice president to an Asian economic summit in Kuala Lumpur, Malaysia, for another meeting with Jiang. Gore began by quoting a Tang dynasty poet, prompting a smiling Jiang to correct his pronunciation. During a two-hour meeting in the Shangri-La Hotel, Gore complained that the US trade deficit with China was growing, and he criticized China for closing its markets for telecommunications, power generation, and retail sales.

But Gore had not flown to Malaysia to gripe. He extended an invitation for Zhu to visit Washington in the spring in hopes of finalizing a WTO deal, after more than a decade of talks under two US presidents.

"We are ready to do our part, but it does not depend on China alone," Jiang said. ". . . Both sides need to adopt a practical and flexible attitude."

Gore said the president would instruct his team to complete a deal before Zhu arrived in Washington, adding, "Without such an agreement, protectionist pressures are certain to mount."[27]

The American business community lobbied hard for an agreement. Importers told Congress the constant uncertainty over China's status put them at a disadvantage against foreign rivals who did not face the prospect of sudden tariff changes each year. Retailers complained they had to gamble that relations would not deteriorate in the time between ordering goods and receiving them.

The concern was well-founded. If China somehow lost its trade privileges, the average US tariff on Chinese goods would jump from

4 percent to 37 percent. Some products would abruptly face levies of up to 70 percent.[28] "While the risk that the United States would withdraw [normal trade relations] status from China may be small, if it did occur the consequences would be catastrophic for US toy companies," a Mattel lobbyist told Congress.[29]

Many companies also wanted changes in Chinese regulations that would only materialize if China won permanent trade status. Avon Products, for example, had been operating in the Chinese market from its base in Guangzhou since 1990. But in 1998, Beijing abruptly imposed a ban on direct selling, which sidelined the company's famed "Avon ladies" and dented its $100 million in annual China sales. Once admitted to the WTO, however, China would be required to permit door-to-door sales.[30]

Charlene Barshefsky, who replaced Mickey Kantor as the US trade representative in 1997, said the Chinese initially viewed the trade talks as a purely political transaction. She corrected them, explaining that the WTO worked by ensuring that trading partners had "compatible" systems, which meant that China would need to enact significant changes in its economy.

"China was going to have to do, not just what every other WTO member did, which is to agree to hundreds of rules and thousands of individualized market access commitments. They would also have to do more—because of the nature of their economy and because of its scale," she said.[31]

Already-low US tariffs, meanwhile, would not change. As a result, American officials believed that the biggest impact of China's eventual WTO entry would be a jump in US exports. Imports of Chinese goods were expected to rise by just 7 percent in the first year after a deal, according to the International Trade Commission.[32] The administration had "no reason to expect any substantial increases in Chinese imports at all," Barshefsky told Congress.[33]

Those assessments proved wrong. US imports from China rose by nearly 25 percent in the first year after WTO entry and by 50 percent in the first three years. The errant forecasts demonstrated that as Washington considered elevating its trade relationship with China, its focus was overwhelmingly on how expanded commerce would change China. Little thought was given to how it might change the United States.

A global struggle

The China talks, like NAFTA and the Uruguay Round multilateral negotiations before them, reflected Clinton's gut-level embrace of globalization. His presidential campaign had been based on the idea that a stagnant American economy needed to be revived after a dozen years of Republican rule. The combined effects of the Cold War's end and the telecommunications revolution were giving rise to a new world, one more complex and tightly integrated. "Economic growth," he said in his first address to a joint session of Congress, "depends as never before on opening up new markets overseas and expanding the volume of world trade."[34]

It was impossible for Americans to preserve the status quo, Clinton believed. But to maintain public support for trade deals that would involve painful adjustments for millions of workers, the government had to help those least equipped to reinvent themselves. Under his "Putting People First" campaign slogan, he had promised $200 billion in new domestic spending to help voters navigate the new environment.

Clinton's aides found it easier to describe his grasp of globalization than to explain how he had come by it. "He was seeing the connections between the economics and the politics, and between the domestic and the foreign, and was less limited to the boxes that we were all living in," National Security Advisor Anthony Lake said.[35] Strobe Talbott, the deputy secretary of state who had known Clinton since they were at Oxford University together in 1968, attributed the president's feel for this new era to his experiences as the nation's youngest governor. "His overarching intellectual passion, almost, was how you could elevate a poor, backward, remote southern state by plugging it into the global economy," Talbott said.[36]

During annual visits to Washington for the National Governors Association conference, Clinton found time for trade-themed embassy events. In 1979, he turned up at the Japanese embassy. One year later, he pitched his state's soybean crop at a dinner hosted by the Chinese ambassador.[37] In 1990, he rebutted complaints about the cost to tax-payers of his trade missions to Europe and Asia, saying they resulted in foreign companies opening facilities in the state and providing "hundreds of jobs for our people." Clinton spent nearly ten years wooing a company from Luxembourg before it opened an Arkansas plant.[38]

"When he was governor, he traveled more than you would expect a governor of Arkansas to travel outside the US," said Kantor, his first trade negotiator.[39]

During the 1992 campaign, Clinton flirted with criticism of Japan as "unfair." But he was friendlier to trade than rivals like Sens. Bob Kerrey of Nebraska, who said Washington should stop "begging" Tokyo to open its markets, and Tom Harkin of Iowa, who was "proud" to be considered a protectionist.[40] Clinton saw a global "struggle between the forces of integration and the forces of disintegration" with trade helping hold things together.[41]

Waldman, who wrote many of Clinton's speeches on the subject, said the president regarded globalization as "inevitable." Increased flows of goods and capital were an almost "organic" reality that could not be arrested by governments. Protectionist politicians who told voters they could insulate them from what was happening in the global economy were not telling the truth.

As a law student at Yale University, a Rhodes Scholar at Oxford, and a successful politician in state and national politics, Clinton moved easily among the elites who choreographed this new globalized age. But he did so mindful of having grown up among those who feared becoming worse off.

"Bill Clinton came from a lower-middle-class background. You can't ever escape the significance of that. He saw so much of his path politically as explaining the world he learned about at Oxford to the people he grew up with, who lived in trailer parks," said Waldman. "He was explaining Council on Foreign Relations economics to people who go to county fairs."[42]

From the first weeks of his presidential run, Clinton sounded themes that would resonate throughout his two terms in the White House. In a global economic competition, the United States was falling behind other nations that better prepared their citizens for the demanding new era.

With capital, goods, and technology free to move wherever they could most profitably be employed, individuals would thrive only if they continuously upgraded their skills. Government would facilitate this "lifelong learning" by funding the necessary education and job-training programs.

"If we offer these hard-working families no hope for the future, no solutions to their problems, no relief for their pain, then fear and insecurity will grow, and the politics of hate and division will spread. If we do not act to bring this country together in common cause to build a better future, [the neo-Nazi] David Duke and his kind will be able to divide and destroy our nation," Clinton told an audience at Georgetown University.[43]

Still, trade was not an end in itself. Expanded commerce with other nations meant greater prosperity, which would encourage a parallel expansion of liberty abroad. Having won the Cold War, Americans faced "the more subtle challenge of consolidating the victory of democracy," Clinton said.[44] And trade could help.

Americans listened. In 1992, when Detroit's Big Three automakers were struggling to match the "Toyota Way" and many voters were reeling from a Japanese company's purchase of Rockefeller Center, only 36 percent of Democrats saw trade as "an opportunity," according to Gallup. By 1994, after hearing Clinton repeatedly extol the virtues of greater openness, that figure rose to 52 percent and remained at or above that level for the duration of his presidency.[45]

Public sentiment was supportive but soft. For most Americans, trade was not a voting priority. Even workers who directly benefited did not always realize its significance. Kantor, the trade negotiator, visited a Texas company during a NAFTA roadshow and asked the workers if they supported the deal. Standing on the loading dock, the men were surrounded by giant boxes waiting to be shipped to customers all around the world.

"They all were going to China or Asia. Every one of them. Yet the guys I was talking to about their support for NAFTA, they said, 'No, of course not; it's going to cost us jobs.' I said look, look at where these [boxes] are going! They hadn't paid any attention to where they were going. All were going someplace else and creating jobs for them," Kantor said.[46]

40

The benefits and the burdens

With Clinton's 1996 reelection campaign looming, White House officials drafted a communications strategy to rebut attacks from economic nationalists like Ross Perot and Pat Buchanan, a former speechwriter for Richard Nixon, who was mounting a long shot bid for the Republican presidential nomination. Clinton's trade policies had won elite approval but remained a tough sell with some voters, including blue-collar, union households, the Reagan Democrats "who feel left behind by the changes in the global economy," according to an internal memo from Christopher Dorval, a communications aide on the National Economic Council.[47]

"There remains a deep skepticism among most ordinary Americans about the real benefits of trade to the lives of hard-working men and women of this country," Dorval wrote Don Baer, the White House communications director. "Fear of global trade is widespread in the country," but was particularly prevalent in electorally important states such as Michigan, Ohio, New Jersey, Pennsylvania, Georgia, and Wisconsin.

Clinton could take credit for creating hundreds of thousands of jobs via exports, reducing foreign trade barriers, and promoting further liberalization. But though he repeatedly tried, Clinton never felt that he had really closed the sale with voters.

"He was very frustrated that we were never able to find the language. Part of the problem is of course that while in the aggregate, globalization is good, its impact falls disproportionately. The benefits and the burdens are not equally shared. It may be good for the economy, but it may not be good for the tire manufacturer in Louisiana who then goes down to Mexico," said Sandy Berger, his national security advisor.

The problem was more than just language. Every Clinton paean to the benefits of globalization included a warning that government must do more for those who could be left behind. His NAFTA sales pitch acknowledged that there was "no use denying that many of our people have lost in the battle for change."[48] Speaking in Littleton, Colorado, on the eve of the Denver G8, he promised summit participants would "work to deepen and extend the benefits of the global economy and protect people more against its downsides."[49] In his second term, Clinton increasingly emphasized "how there has to be much more intervention by the government to smooth the bumps and reconcile the gaps between the winners and the losers," according to Berger.[50]

He had been talking like this since his first days as a national figure. Yet little was done. The domestic investment agenda that had been the heart of his campaign was eclipsed within weeks of his November 1992 election victory by concerns about the federal budget deficit. Clinton's economic team, led by Robert Rubin, the first head of the National Economic Council, argued that the only way to revive the economy was to first stem the flood of red ink from Washington. The deficit had nearly doubled between 1987 and 1992. And internal forecasts called for it to balloon further. Such unrestrained government borrowing threatened to drive up interest rates, depressing private sector investment and job creation.

When Congress finally approved the president's economic plan in August 1993, the public investments it contained were "just a tiny morsel of what we originally sought," said Labor Secretary Robert Reich.[51] Clinton agreed to reduce the cumulative deficit by $500 billion over the next five years, believing that only by satisfying investors that he was not a tax-and-spend Democrat could he win the market credibility to later proceed with his expansive domestic agenda.

But "later" never arrived. In September 1994, Reich warned the president that Democrats were in danger of losing the House because workers who lacked a college degree were defecting to the Republicans. Clinton's embrace of trade was part of the problem. "The higher-skilled and better-educated gain a global market for their services, while those with low skills or no skills have to compete with lower-wage workers around the world," Reich wrote.[52]

In seismic congressional elections two months later, Republicans gained fifty-two House seats, seizing control of the chamber for the first time since 1952. The GOP takeover effectively quashed Clinton's domestic ambitions. In April 1995, he accepted Republican budget cuts that left spending on education and job training below Bush administration levels from 1992.[53] Two months later, he called for a balanced budget within ten years. After Republicans shut down the government, he agreed to accelerate the timetable to seven years, requiring even deeper cuts in domestic spending.

Clinton recognized globalization's downside. He spoke often of plans to transform an outdated unemployment system into a "reemployment" program. In his first State of the Union address, he called for "special assistance to areas and to workers displaced" by unavoidable economic shocks. In 1995, he urged Congress to merge dozens of redundant job-training programs into a $2,600 voucher that workers could use for community college tuition or other training. Clinton called it a "GI Bill for America's Workers," but within months of highlighting it in a prime-time address, he was told by aides that it was "increasingly unlikely" Congress would pass such legislation.[54]

The political concern about the deficit was understandable, but excessive. A liberal Democratic president needed to establish his fiscal bona fides with the financial markets. But there was nothing sacred about a balanced budget. Neither Ronald Reagan nor George H. W. Bush had even come close. Incurring a modest annual deficit of, say, 1 percent of gross domestic product would have freed up tens of billions of dollars for needed social investments by the end of Clinton's presidency, just in time to cushion the blow from China's economic rise. One of the architects of Clinton's economic policies would later acknowledge their shortcomings.

"Trade benefits us. But it should have been accompanied by the training and social safety nets and all that sort of thing," Treasury Secretary Robert Rubin said. After losing the House, "we weren't able to follow through."[55]

After Clinton won reelection, he faced renewed calls to do more for the victims of economic change. On November 8, Joseph Stiglitz, the chairman of the Council of Economic Advisers, sent the president a twenty-six-page memo with proposals for second-term initiatives. "The increasing public concern about job dislocation highlights a real problem. If we are to encourage workers to accept changes—including those dictated by new technologies and global competition—we must also help them bear some of the costs," Stiglitz wrote. "While the evidence on whether there has been an overall increase in the rate of job dislocation remains ambiguous, it is clear that some previously unaffected groups now face significant risks of displacement."[56]

Stiglitz proposed a number of measures to help dislocated workers, including low-cost government loans to carry them while they searched for jobs or learned new skills. But his ideas were stillborn. After years of pressing, the president finally notched a success in August 1998 when Congress approved the Workforce Investment Act, which consolidated dozens of redundant federal job-training programs into the $2,600 voucher that he had sought. It was a rare safety net victory.

Globalization is irreversible

Concerns about the way that globalization created "winners" and "losers" grew during Clinton's White House years. In a 1997 book, *Has Globalization Gone Too Far?*, Dani Rodrik, a Turkish economist who taught at Harvard University, argued that reducing barriers to trade and investment helped some people—business owners, highly skilled workers, and professionals—and hurt others, notably the less educated and less skilled. Since the late 1970s, less-educated workers had seen their inflation-adjusted hourly wages fall by more than 20 percent while their hours and earnings had become less predictable, Rodrik wrote.[57]

Rodrik was bothered by the widespread triumphalism he saw among policymakers and mainstream economists. Their "Panglossian" consensus favoring market-based solutions and greater trade liberalization brooked little dissent. Questions about rising social tensions or globalization's disproportionate impact upon low-skilled workers were routinely dismissed as disguised protectionism.

To Rodrik, the lessons of history and economics suggested that the pro-globalization consensus would run aground. Previous eras of global integration, such as the years before the First World War, had produced sharp political reactions, including in the United States. Meanwhile, the same economic theories that said trade would bring nations a rising standard of living also warned it would deliver domestic conflicts about the distribution of those gains.

Rodrik agreed that automation, not trade, was responsible for the bulk of manufacturing job loss. But globalization was not an immutable fact like gravity. It was the product of specific public policy choices. And some of those choices were only getting harder. As capital became more mobile, it was easier for corporations and the wealthy to move their assets beyond the taxman's reach.

"If the tension is not managed intelligently and creatively, the danger is that the domestic consensus in favor of open markets will ultimately erode to the point where a generalized resurgence of protectionism becomes a serious possibility," Rodrik wrote.[58]

Clinton explained his ideas for addressing those social tensions and maintaining the pro-trade consensus at the Denver summit. But he did not press the point. In a memo written a few days before the meeting, Rubin, his treasury secretary, had advised the president to avoid saying too much about "the risks posed by globalization, as this could complicate our efforts to gain fast-track authority" in Congress to negotiate new trade deals.[59]

US officials identified other risks in a more integrated global economy. New computer and telecommunication systems enabled Wall Street traders to translate impulse into action in ways that could produce damaging swings in financial markets. Clinton and his summit guests hoped to "build international cooperation to meet the increased risks that have accompanied the faster pace of integration in global capital markets," reporters were told.[60] Allowing goods and money to move across borders unencumbered would only work if there were regulatory guardrails to prevent excessive risk-taking. And those guardrails, Deputy Treasury Secretary Larry Summers made clear, should carry a Made-in-the-USA label. "We are now in the process of trying to replicate at a global level the types of safeguards against risk that have been so important to growth in the United States," he said.[61]

On the summit's second day, Clinton led a discussion of a new US initiative on "infectious diseases." The same business travelers who brought cash, ideas, and technologies to overseas markets might just as easily carry novel viruses home with them. "Beyond the tragic loss of life, the diseases can have significant global economic and political consequences," Clinton's 256-page briefing book had noted. There had been a recent example with the outbreak of mad cow disease in Britain.

Such concerns received only secondary consideration. The US was superbly positioned to prosper from greater global integration, the president said. And the phenomenon should not become a "scapegoat" for any country's domestic problems. Globalization, Clinton averred, was "irreversible."[62]

The economic damage was brutal

That proposition soon faced a severe test. On July 2, ten days after the summit's end, Thailand unexpectedly devalued its currency, which had been tied to the US dollar. The baht lost 20 percent of its value in the first hours of trading, becoming the first victim of a financial contagion that would scorch multiple emerging markets, the fast-growing countries that represented the promise of the post–Cold War era.

The crisis had its origins in both government policy and investor sentiment. Thailand in the late 1980s began opening its markets by eliminating restrictions on foreign investments, foreign ownership of export industries, and, eventually, the amount of foreign currency that could be brought in or out of the country.[63] Freeing capital to move across borders represented the conventional wisdom at the time, encouraged by the US Treasury Department and the International Monetary Fund. Other nations, including Indonesia and South Korea, implemented similar reforms.[64]

Putting out the welcome mat for Wall Street had the desired effect. Money flooded Thailand and other developing economies, as top financial institutions swooned over rapid growth in places that until recently had been economic backwaters. In 1996, banks and investment houses pumped $190 billion into developing countries, almost four times as much as in 1990. Three-quarters of that total ended up in just a dozen markets.[65]

All that foreign cash helped drive economic growth for much of the decade. Skyscrapers sprouted in downtown Bangkok, and the city's bars filled with young investment bankers from New York and Hong Kong. By 1996, Thailand's economy was almost 60 percent larger than it had been just six years earlier.

That was the good news. The bad news was that the Thai economic miracle—and that of its neighbors—rested on sand. For starters,

Thailand was importing much more than it was exporting. To finance the difference, it needed to borrow huge amounts of dollars and yen. Thai banks then turned around and used those short-term loans to finance long-term projects, including in the booming local real estate market. In the mid-1990s, Thai bankers grew their provision of credit to the private sector nearly three times as fast as banks did in the United States.[66]

The government's decision to fix the value of the baht to the US dollar only made things worse, once the dollar began soaring in the mid-1990s. As the baht rose in lockstep with the greenback, Thais could afford to buy even more imported goods. But the stronger currency made Thailand's exports too expensive for foreign customers. More imports and fewer exports meant a wider trade gap, which required even more outside financing. Eventually, foreign investors decided the risks in Thailand exceeded the potential rewards and began selling Thai assets as fast as they once had bought them.[67]

More than $20 billion, an amount equal to 15 percent of Thailand's gross domestic product, headed for the exits.[68] Rubin, who spent decades in the markets with Goldman Sachs, marveled at how new technologies, such as fiber-optic cables, allowed traders to instantly dump their holdings.[69] Lightning-quick markets, and investors' herdlike behavior, were outpacing the ability of global policymakers to respond.

US officials were deeply involved in August when the IMF unveiled a $17 billion package aimed at stemming the bleeding. But congressional restrictions imposed in the wake of the 1995 Mexican bailout limited Washington's ability to contribute any American money, something Clinton later said he regretted. China, for its part, won US plaudits by avoiding the temptation to join the region's currency devaluations, which would have only intensified the economic plunge.[70]

The Thai bailout did not end the crisis. When currencies in Malaysia, Singapore, the Philippines, and Hong Kong plunged under pressure from investors, Americans felt more pain. More than half of all exports from California, Oregon, and Washington ended up in the region, and Asia's emerging markets now were buying less.[71] Concern over the likely hit to US corporate earnings sent the Dow Jones Industrial Average into a 554-point decline on October 27, 1997, further illustrating the stakes for Americans.[72] The market's 7 percent drop was its worst single-day performance since the 1987 crash, when the Dow lost nearly one-quarter of its value.

Yet the crisis spread. Indonesia required an IMF rescue at the end of October. And then, South Korea, the world's eleventh-largest economy and a key military ally of the United States, became investors' next target. Its problems were similar to Thailand's: the local currency, the won, had become overvalued because it was fixed to the dollar. Local banks had borrowed short-term money from foreign institutions and then loaned it to domestic industrial groups known as chaebols. South Korea's largest employers, the chaebols borrowed heavily in foreign currency, yet earned revenues in won. The sinking currency made it harder for them to repay their dollar or yen debts.

South Korean authorities burned through their foreign exchange reserves in an effort to preserve the won's link to the dollar. But foreign banks balked at rolling over their short-term loans. Troops in neighboring North Korea went on a heightened state of alert, adding to the tension.[73]

"Your financial situation is extremely grave," Clinton warned Korean President Kim Young-sam in a Thanksgiving Day call from Camp David. Unless agreement were reached soon with the IMF, South Korea would default on its foreign debt, sending shockwaves through the global economy. Kim was reluctant, saying no deal was likely before December 20 and asking instead for a bridge loan from the US and Japan.

"You know I would do anything to help you, but all of my advisers and I believe it will not work because no amount of official external support would be sufficient to compensate for the absence of a strong economic program and because it would only defer the tough decisions that are necessary to restore confidence," the president insisted.[74]

Kim kept pushing. But Clinton and his team believed outside financial support would be wasted if the Korean government did not implement sweeping economic reforms, including opening the banking sector to foreign competition. The Koreans eventually got the message and on December 3, Michel Camdessus, the head of the IMF, announced a $55 billion aid package.

Yet after a brief respite, the won resumed its plunge. At one point, Korea's foreign exchange reserves were down to $9 billion and were dwindling by $1 billion each day.[75] A new president, the veteran democracy activist Kim Dae-jung, was elected on December 18. He had speculated publicly on election day about renegotiating the IMF deal, leading Clinton to add a warning to his congratulatory call. "The markets are very shaky and volatile and we have to be careful what is said.... The reserves remain perilously low.... I just don't want this reserve crisis to be worse in the short run," Clinton said.[76]

To shore up the IMF package, Rubin got the big global banks to roll over their South Korean loans. The banks had been reluctant, fearing that the new government in Seoul would default. No banker wanted to be the last institution left holding Korean debt.[77] On Christmas Eve, Rubin issued a statement saying the IMF would speed up its payment to South Korea once the bankers came on board.[78]

Clinton recognized the crisis was crushing Asia's newly minted middle class. He spoke of doctors and nurses living in the lobby of a closed hospital and once-prosperous parents forced to sell their possessions to stay afloat.[79] In 1998 alone, Indonesia's economy shrank by 13 percent. "The economic damage was brutal, even when our interventions were successful," recalled Timothy Geithner, then a top Treasury Department crisis-fighter.[80]

In the United States, exporters saw Asian demand for their products evaporate. US exports to Thailand in April 1999 were half of what they had been in the same month two years earlier, before the baht was devalued. Similar losses were seen in sales to Indonesia and South Korea, though the latter recovered quickly. Overall, the economic impact of the crisis in the United States was "small and localized," an economist at the Federal Reserve Bank of New York concluded.[81]

The exception was the steel industry. Over a six-month period, cheap hot-rolled steel from Korea, Japan, Brazil, and Russia flooded the US market. Imports rose 70 percent in a year, as foreign producers claimed more than one-third of the US market, the highest level in more than twenty years. Six American steel producers were driven into bankruptcy, and thousands of workers were idled.[82]

When the contagion reached Russia in 1998, Yeltsin finally ran out of runway with his halting efforts to remake the Russian economy. A chronic failure to collect sufficient tax revenue left the Russian state with a yawning budget deficit, which it financed by selling bonds to foreign and domestic investors. Known as GKOs, these securities attracted speculators who could borrow foreign currencies at low interest rates and then invest the funds in short-term Russian bonds offering yields up to 66 percent.[83] The IMF had been providing a steady infusion of financial help in return for promised reforms, some of which materialized and many of which became victims of the infighting between Yeltsin and lawmakers. In late July, the fund agreed to a fresh $22.6 billion package, which included money from the World Bank and Japan.

But in Washington and other capitals, patience with Russia was nearing its end. On August 14, Clinton called Yeltsin to discuss his upcoming trip to Moscow. "I am concerned about the financial situation around the world," Clinton began. "I know you face a lot of pressure in Russia, both economic and political.... Markets are very volatile and still somewhat negative. I just called in part to get your feeling about what is happening and what needs to be done."

Yeltsin conceded he was "very worried" and pressed Clinton to help accelerate the IMF money and to have the US Treasury encourage American investment in Russia.

"An early release of funds from the IMF will only help if it lifts confidence," Clinton said. ". . . It's a question of taking moves that change the psychology of these markets.... You have to keep trying things to stop the slide until I get there in September."

Yeltsin broached a joint appearance before the Russian parliament to press recalcitrant Communist and ultranationalist lawmakers to back his program. Clinton said he would do "whatever has the most positive effect on them," but parried the suggestion of a buddy act in front of the Duma. Yeltsin ended the call by proclaiming their views "identical" and expressing his fondness for the American. "I hug you Bill. I give you a good warm hug," he said.[84]

Three days later, Russia devalued the ruble and defaulted on its domestic debt. It was a desperate bid to head off the collapse of the banking system. The ruble sank following the devaluation, eventually shedding almost three-quarters of its value. For the average Russian, a collaps-ing currency meant higher prices and a lower standard of living. The continuing impasse between Yeltsin and parliament prevented needed action on tax collection and fiscal reforms. On August 31, growing in-vestor alarm over Russia sent the Dow into a 512-point spiral, erasing the market's gains for the year.

The next day Clinton boarded Air Force One to see firsthand how Yeltsin was handling the crisis. Once in Moscow, Clinton found the Russian appearing much older than he remembered. "I'm not sure enough oxygen is getting up to his brain," Clinton told one confidant.[85]

Less than two weeks later, after Yeltsin had once again reshuffled his government, replacing his prime minister, central bank chief, and top financial negotiator, Clinton was back on the phone. This time, he warned that investors doubted the new lineup's commitment to economic reforms. "I think as a friend I owe it to you to say the ap-pointments you made raise concerns that Russia will return to the hy-perinflation Russia suffered in 1992," Clinton said. "The truth is no nation, including the US, can go it alone in today's global economy. We have to work together and restore growth, and we have got to have private investment, and IMF investment, and we have got to get inter-national investors. We've got to get money coming into Russia instead of flowing out of Russia."

The ruble's slide had been halted, at least temporarily, Yeltsin replied, adding, "There is no reason for you to feel worried in any way because there will be no backtracking away from reforms."[86] Annual inflation, already high, spiked to 95 percent the following year. And several more months of negotiations with the IMF were needed before a final aid package was agreed to in July 1999. The effort kept Russia's "nascent move to democracy alive—on life support, perhaps, but alive."[87] One month later, an exhausted Yeltsin named a new prime minister to handle the country's affairs, a former KGB officer named Vladimir Putin.

Rising tide of political liberty

Clinton returned from Moscow convinced that he needed to speak publicly about the crisis that had ravaged countries one after another for more than a year. The new global economy he often celebrated was displaying worrisome boom-and-bust attributes. Unfettered financial flows had lifted developing countries out of poverty and then plunged them right back into it. The financier George Soros had sent the president a pre-publication copy of his new book on globalization, proposing a global central bank. Clinton underlined numerous passages before recommending Soros's book to Gene Sperling, the head of the National Economic Council.[88]

On September 14, the president flew to New York to address the Council on Foreign Relations. Five days earlier, the independent counsel investigating the Monica Lewinsky affair had sent his 211-page report to Congress, which contained lurid details of the president's conduct. But Clinton remained focused. "This is the biggest financial challenge facing the world in a half century," he began. ". . . There is now a stark challenge not only to economic freedom, but, if unaddressed, a challenge that could stem the rising tide of political liberty as well."[89]

Clinton spoke of the links between nations that could spread instability as easily as prosperity, talked of an Asian middle class being impoverished, and warned against a return to protectionism. For fifteen months, world leaders had mobilized to contain the Asian crisis. But more action was needed, including in Washington, where Congress was dallying on IMF funding. Reform of the international financial system was imperative, the president said, if the democratic and market tide was to advance. In calling for global regulation, Clinton felt he had to be careful not to get "the black helicopter crowd stirred up," a reference to right-wing conspiracists.[90]

Less than a week after his New York speech, a fresh crisis arose. Financial fallout from Russia's default threatened to capsize Long-Term Capital Management, a giant hedge fund that was linked to many of the nation's largest financial institutions. LTCM was the brainchild of John Meriwether, the former vice chairman of Salomon Brothers, and included two Nobel laureates, Myron Scholes and Robert Merton, as partners.

Using billions of dollars in borrowed money, the fund made massive bets based on mathematical models devised from the historical relationships between securities. Meriwether had produced annual returns of more than 40 percent in the two years leading up to the Asian crisis, more than double the average hedge fund's performance. But in August alone, his portfolio shed 44 percent, or $1.8 billion.[91] Russia's default had ricocheted through global markets in so many unexpected ways that LTCM's models had gone haywire. Meriwether had anticipated a narrowing in the yield offered by US Treasuries compared with those of other bonds. Instead, yields had widened. Only if markets suddenly began behaving normally again could the fund avoid collapse. Otherwise, as LTCM's losses mounted, its creditors would demand it put up more collateral to backstop its bets. And the fund didn't have the money.

Normally, the failure of a single hedge fund would not have shaken global markets. But LTCM had entered into unusually large off-balance-sheet investments in derivatives that brought its total exposure to an astonishing $1.4 trillion. These positions were so large and so interconnected with other financial institutions that not even the savviest investors fully understood the implications.[92] Meriwether had borrowed fifty-five dollars for every dollar of capital the firm held to invest on behalf of foreign banks, wealthy clients, and sophisticated institutions.[93] If LTCM failed, it might take with it some of the big Wall Street banks it had borrowed from, including Citigroup, Goldman Sachs, and Merrill Lynch. Even firms that had never done business with it, but now held $3 trillion in similar trading positions, could become collateral damage.[94] At least seventeen financial institutions around the world had sizable exposure to LTCM.[95] If the hedge fund collapsed, all of its clients and creditors would rush to raise cash, dumping their holdings at the same time and triggering a global market rout.

"We shared the view that the collapse of Long-Term Capital would create chaotic financial markets around the world and that nobody could make a good estimate of what the likely damage would be," William McDonough, the president of the New York Fed, told the board of governors at a closed-door meeting.[96]

It took extraordinary action to avert disaster. On September 23, the Federal Reserve Bank of New York arranged for a group of fourteen banks and brokerage firms to invest $3.6 billion in the crippled fund. The cash infusion gave Meriwether and his team time to unwind their positions without engaging in a fire sale.

What began in Thailand before eventually rocking a sophisticated investment firm in Greenwich, Connecticut, illustrated how globalization was proving a double-edged sword. This fresh crisis came less than three years after the collapse of the Mexican peso triggered an economic emergency requiring an extraordinary US financial bailout. Asia's cataclysm led to a profound rethinking of how easy it had become for global finance to move money in and out of developing countries. It would not be the last time that policymakers were forced to reconsider their most basic assumptions.

2

—————

Whose Streets?

Growing up in a small town in northern Wisconsin in the 1970s, Lori Wallach belonged to one of the few Jewish families in the area. The antisemitism, at times, was far from subtle. Decades later, she still recalled an elementary school classmate chasing her through the neighborhood, hollering, "Jesus killer!"[1]

Wallach, whose grandfather fled the Nazis in 1938 for the United States, learned while still in grade school to speak her mind and to stick up for herself. "Fighting for one's principles became a necessity the moment we went to school and started getting picked on for being Jewish," she said.[2]

Outgoing and articulate, she was a natural advocate. By her senior year in high school, Wallach, the student body president and editor of the school paper, was leading the opposition to a planned merger of local high schools. In an early sign of her instinct for the performative, she organized a New Orleans–style funeral procession to mark the death of "quality education in Wausau, Wisconsin."[3]

In 1984, alarmed by what she saw as Ronald Reagan's bellicosity, she dropped out of Wellesley College to work for Walter Mondale's doomed presidential campaign. After his landslide defeat, she returned to campus and graduated with her class. Years later, after earning a law degree at Harvard—where her classmates included Barack Obama—she would credit those experiences with preparing her for a career battling the establishment.

She got her start in Washington working for Ralph Nader as a consumer activist specializing in food safety. But when she saw all the ways that arcane trade rules limited governments' ability to legislate on subjects such as pesticides or meat inspections, she switched roles. By the early 1990s, she was running Global Trade Watch, an arm of Nader's Public Citizen organization, devoted to defeating what it labeled "corporate-rigged" trade deals.

Wallach's rise illustrated the role of interest groups in shaping government policy. Corporations, labor unions, and organizations like Global Trade Watch that claimed to represent the public interest all circled lawmakers and executive-branch officials in search of allies. Washington had advocacy groups the way Pittsburgh had steel mills. They were part of the town's institutional landscape. Many left little mark on the public policies they aimed to shape. But Wallach's was different. The issues that she championed—labor standards, environmental considerations, and the rights of developing countries—and the political coalition that she helped assemble foreshadowed the eventual demise of the 1990s pro-trade consensus.

But that lay many years in the future and would come at some cost. It would be more than a decade before Wallach's full influence was felt amid a broad rethinking of globalization. And it would take a political earthquake that imperiled the progressive America that she had devoted her career to building. Wallach ultimately would have a prominent role in steering US trade policy in a fresh direction. She would enjoy the confidence of the nation's chief trade negotiator. But only by working in concert with a president who represented just about everything she abhorred in American politics would that prominence be possible.

Wallach parlayed a deep knowledge of trade law, sharp tongue, and thick Rolodex into influence with congressional Democrats—and eventually with a disruptive Republican president. Her critics in the corporate world said her rapid-fire monologues were often exaggerated or misleading, and, in the mid-1990s, she and her allies had a mixed record. Global Trade Watch in 1993 had opposed the landmark North American Free Trade Agreement, which passed the House 234–200 and the Senate 61–38. The following year, legislation to implement a global trade deal called the Uruguay Round, which lowered tariffs on industrial products, passed both houses of Congress by even wider margins. Later in the decade, however, she helped defeat Bill Clinton's request for renewed "fast track" negotiating authority, which would require Congress to approve or reject trade deals on a straight up-or-down vote without amendments. And she was instrumental in killing a planned global investment deal by publicizing a leaked copy of the negotiating text, which ignited an uproar.

Despite her efforts, globalization advanced. The Uruguay Round had created a multilateral body called the World Trade Organization to administer the rules for global commerce and to promote further trade liberalization. To Clinton, the WTO, founded on January 1, 1995, stood in a long line of US-created institutions designed to regulate international competition and to keep it peaceful. "America is committed to open trade among all nations," he said during a visit to its Geneva headquarters in May 1998. ". . . It will advance the free flow of ideas, information and people that are the lifeblood of democracy and prosperity. Globalization is not a policy choice—it is a fact."[4]

Revolutionary information and communication technologies accelerated that process. In the late 1960s, transatlantic telephone cables could accommodate just eighty calls between Europe and the United States at one time. By the time Clinton addressed the WTO, they could handle one million simultaneous conversations. Just four years earlier, fewer than three million people on the planet enjoyed internet access. As Clinton spoke, the number stood at one hundred million and was doubling every year.[5] Easier global communications allowed corporations to become more efficient by moving production offshore. Marrying first-world managerial talent to low-cost labor in the developing world boosted corporate profits, albeit often at the expense of American workers.[6]

For a half century, world leaders had worked together to regulate trade, believing that agreed rules would prevent a repeat of the protectionism that had deepened the Great Depression and paved the road to world war. First as the General Agreement on Tariffs and Trade (GATT), then as the WTO, the global community had bargained its way toward managed commerce. This new organization for the first time included a judicial forum for adjudicating trade disputes between nations.

The trading system had grown from 23 nations in 1948 to 132 WTO members. With the Cold War consigned to the past, world leaders wanted to bring into the fold the one-sixth of the world economy represented by the former Communist nations of the Soviet bloc, China, Vietnam, the Balkans, and the Middle East. Doing so would "strengthen peace by giving these nations greater interests in stability and prosperity beyond their borders," Charlene Barshefsky, Clinton's chief trade negotiator, told the Council on Foreign Relations. But it wouldn't be easy. Melding these nations into the global order was a challenge comparable to returning Japan and Germany to membership in the global economy following World War II.[7]

Though still in its infancy, the WTO needed to change, Clinton said. Few Americans understood its operations, usually conducted behind closed doors by anonymous global bureaucrats. Its meetings should be open to the public and future trade deals must include labor standards and environmental protections. New negotiations could not drag on for the seven years it had taken to conclude the Uruguay Round. "Without such a strategy, we cannot build the necessary public support for the global economy. Working people will only assume the risks of a free international market if they have the confidence that the system will work for them," he said.

The president saw the WTO as an imperfect vessel, albeit one that was pursuing laudable objectives. But to Wallach, the institution was "a monster" ensuring corporate control of political questions—on worker rights or environmental protection—that should be decided by voters. "It's 900 pages of rules that tell you how to run your whole damn government—federal, local, state, the whole thing," she said.[8] The distant bureaucracy with the final say over so much of modern life stirred an instinctual resentment in Wallach. "I just have never had a tolerance for bullying. For mean, stupid bossy stuff. That just has, my whole life, pissed me the hell off," she said. "And probably I just got a thick skin about fighting and standing up against the odds, by growing up in a kind of 'other' situation."

Globalize this

It was only natural that when the WTO scheduled its 1999 ministerial meeting in Seattle, Wallach was among the organizers of what became one of the most consequential American protests since the end of the Vietnam War. The stakes were high. The Clinton administration was pushing for new global trade talks that would build on the Uruguay Round. The notion of a new negotiation just a few years after the conclusion of the last one had originated with European officials. The president endorsed the idea in his State of the Union address earlier that year, saying a new round should encourage greater exports of goods, services, and farm products.[9] Barshefsky sketched a broad agenda that included the elimination of all subsidies for agricultural exports and deep cuts in domestic price support programs, further reductions in tariffs on industrial goods, and measures to address regulatory weaknesses that had contributed to the Asian financial crisis. Proposals for competition, investment, trade facilitation, and government procurement—a quartet known as the Singapore issues—also were on the table.[10]

But Barshefsky faced an uphill slog. Many developing country officials were resentful, believing major powers like the United States routinely overlooked or ignored their interests. Politicians in the United States and other advanced economies, meanwhile, confronted constituents who complained that insufficient attention was being paid to labor and environmental concerns. Despite the difficulties, she wanted the new negotiating round to be completed in three years, less than half what the Uruguay talks had required.[11]

The first step was to win approval from the Seattle ministerial to formally launch the talks. And it was this that Wallach set out to prevent. Even before Seattle edged out San Diego and Honolulu to win host-city status, she swung into action. Working with local allies in each city, Wallach's team had researched potential office and hotel locations that would be close to likely meeting venues in each city. And she had gathered credit card numbers from staffers, staffers' spouses, parents, friends, and allies, so they could quickly secure reservations once the host city was named.

In January 1999, when WTO officials gathered in Geneva to pick the winning city, Wallach had a contact waiting in the lobby coffee shop. A friendly diplomat inside the closed meeting had agreed to tip them off as soon as the decision came down. The diplomat alerted the staffer in the coffee shop, who called Wallach, setting in motion a telephone tree that spread the news among the groups planning to demonstrate.

Wallach's staffers and allies immediately snapped up blocks of hotel rooms close to the Seattle convention center where the WTO delegates would meet in November. The activists reserved Town Hall, a converted church, for several nights of musical entertainment. Another building that was slated for demolition was tapped to be the coalition's headquarters. Supportive unions provided manpower to bring the facility up to code and to outfit a radio studio where Jim Hightower, the populist former Texas state agriculture commissioner, would broadcast. "We knew we had to have a really broad showing. We had to have a mass mobilization. We had to show, even here in the belly of the beast, people would say 'no,'" Wallach said.

Eight months before the meeting, Public Citizen had four paid staffers in Seattle, coordinating six hundred volunteers.[12] Along with the Naderite group, the anti-WTO alliance included students, environmentalists, faith groups, socialists, and labor unions. Representatives of the AFL-CIO, the United Steelworkers, the Machinists, and the Teamsters played pivotal roles.

The mobilization was a blend of logistics, education, motivation, and activism. Budgets were drawn up, covering food, fundraising, "guerilla media," housing, first aid, legal, and communications expenses. With participants coming from multiple countries, translators were needed. One group promoting developing-country debt forgiveness planned a "10,000 person human chain around the opening reception." Another distributed pamphlets warning that the WTO spelled "the end of democracy."[13]

Organizers aimed to marry traditional lobbying with grassroots protest. Visible opposition to globalization outside the conference center would inevitably shape what happened inside. "We had a negotiating-suite strategy and then we had the streets strategy. And the idea was to basically have some synergy between the suites and the streets," Wallach said.

In September, a group called the Ruckus Society, which specialized in nonviolent acts of civil disobedience, held a weeklong "Globalize This! action camp" on a farm north of Seattle for about 160 activists. Instructors taught eager recruits how to climb buildings, so they could hang eye-catching anti-WTO banners, and brainstormed techniques to block movement through the city streets. Among the ideas that were rejected: filling parked cars with cement to block traffic.[14]

The Ruckus Society had advertised the camp all summer, billing it as an "advanced strategic and tactical skill share." Many who attended had been arrested during previous protests or were willing to go to jail. "The Ruckus Society is not interested in catalyzing another easily marginalized protest in which the left eats its own on international television," said one email from the group, which anticipated direct action against "an unprecedented meeting of corporate conquistadors from multinationals and governments all over the Earth."[15]

Seattle had seemed an appropriate choice for the WTO, given the city's thriving port, the presence of major exporters such as Boeing, and the city's experience hosting the Asia-Pacific Economic Cooperation summit several years earlier. But if the city showcased the nation's commercial links to the outside world, it also had a history of labor activism.

In February 1919, more than sixty-five thousand workers staged the first general strike in US history in support of local shipyard laborers. Seattle residents hoarded goods amid fears of economic collapse and political revolt. With memories of the 1917 Russian Revolution still fresh, a newspaper editorial warned: "It is only a step from Seattle to Petrograd." The labor action petered out after six days, but left a memory of worker power.[16]

Unions aimed to revive that spirit with the anti-WTO action. David Foster, who headed operations in a thirteen-state region for the United Steelworkers union, was among the earliest to sign on. A member of the union's executive board, Foster in late 1998 argued that the steelworkers needed to make the anti-WTO fight "our fundamental strategic initiative over the next year."[17]

At the time, the steelworkers were beginning what became a two-year lockout at Kaiser Aluminum, which Foster, who headed the negotiating committee for the roughly three thousand strikers, saw as an "example of what was going wrong with the global economy."[18] Kaiser, which had several plants in Washington state, had been bought and sold twice in the past dozen years, ending up in the hands of Charles Hurwitz, a prominent private-equity investor. The company and the union were at loggerheads over wages and benefits, possible job cuts, and the contracting out of work.[19]

In the months leading up to the protest, Foster dispatched a newly hired organizer to union locals throughout his territory to educate members about global trends that were hurting the steel industry. Foster saw Seattle as an opportunity to combine street protests with daily educational forums illustrating the impact of trade rules on working Americans, "not just to march and go home."[20] Ron Judd, leader of the King County Labor Council, said demonstrators explicitly wanted to disprove Seattle's trade-friendly image. "The whole world thinks that we're all neoliberal free traders here because we're so damn dependent upon trade. So what better message to send [than] to shut the entire city down... and tell the whole world that we all don't think like President Clinton," he said.[21]

Mike Dolan, the Seattle-based field director for Wallach's group, had begun wooing supporters in March, touting the WTO meeting as "the protest of the century" at an activists' meeting in Louisville, Kentucky. In late June, he arranged a dinner for protest organizers at Seattle's waterside Edgewater Hotel, known for hosting the Beatles during their 1964 US tour. About three dozen representatives of the Teamsters, Steelworkers, Longshoremen, and the AFL-CIO joined religious and community leaders, as well as Wallach, for a meeting that cemented labor's participation.

During the months leading up to November, Dolan acted as an intermediary between organized labor and the more rambunctious civil disobedience groups. The unions were planning a rally and downtown march for the first day of the conference and did not want agitators to spook the Seattle police beforehand.

Several mainstream protest participants sought to keep their distance, at least officially, from the more radical Direct Action Network (DAN), which was vowing to shut down the WTO meeting. Dolan had been asked to have Public Citizen sponsor the group but declined in order to preserve his relationships with the city and mainstream organizations, including the AFL-CIO and the Sierra Club. But behind the scenes, he was less reticent. "On the quiet, I gave money to DAN. Ultimately, around $6,000," Dolan said.

He also had preliminary meetings with police and city officials to apprise them of what was planned and to secure protest permits. At one point, municipal officials learned of plans for an opening night anti-WTO rock concert at a sports stadium right next to the host-committee reception for corporate executives and trade negotiators. When the city pushed for him to relocate the concert, Dolan succeeded in bluffing them into making available an alternative site at no cost with the county sheriff providing security. "They basically put $40,000 on the table and said, 'Will you please move your People's Gala away from the King-dome to the Key Arena?'" Dolan said.[22]

With little more than one month remaining before the WTO arrived, Dolan was inundated with requests for information, hotel rooms, office space, and money. One such missive, which came from the "Nepal World Legal Research Center," drew a sardonic reaction from a colleague: "Organizing would be so easy if it weren't for all these... people."[23]

Celebrity supporters drew special attention. In July, David Korten, head of the nonprofit People-Centered Development Forum, emailed Dolan that Anita Roddick, CEO of the Body Shop, a popular British cosmetics company, planned on joining the Seattle demonstration. "It isn't every day we get CEOs of major global corporations asking how they can work with us to get out the fair trade/not free trade message. I hope we can make full use of the offer," Korten wrote. The following week, Roddick wrote Dolan: "I'm extremely excited about working alongside you creating mischief at the WTO gathering."[24]

Filmmaker Michael Moore agreed to attend, hoping to shadow his namesake, the New Zealand politician who was the WTO's director-general. The filmmaker's goal was to contrast his outsider experience in Seattle with the insider activities of the globalist with the same name. While in town, the filmmaker also hoped to "throw a ball around with Fidel" Castro, the Cuban dictator who had once attended a Washington Senators tryout camp and was expected to appear.[25]

By August, Clinton administration officials were increasingly alarmed about the reception that awaited the trade ministers. The 1998 WTO ministerial in Geneva, after all, had drawn protesters who broke windows, sprayed graffiti on buildings, looted businesses, and clashed with Swiss police. Cars were torched within sight of the WTO headquarters.

The authorities in Seattle, however, viewed the Geneva unrest as a European phenomenon, at odds with a local tradition of peaceful protest. Plus, despite the tumult, the Geneva ministerial had proceeded more or less as planned, thanks to extensive security, including a secure official zone demarcated by concrete barriers, razor wire, and metal fencing, all patrolled by uniformed police.[26]

Oddly, Seattle officials rejected a White House request to establish a similar security zone that would be off-limits to everyone except WTO delegates.[27] Using physical barriers was seen as "inflammatory" by municipal officials, who were sensitive to merchants' fears that excessive security would disrupt the holiday shopping season.[28] City leaders also believed the trade conference would be easier to police than the 1993 Asia-Pacific Economic Cooperation leaders' summit, which had passed without incident.

Not everyone was so sanguine. Sen. Patty Murray, a Washington Democrat, wrote to Clinton voicing "deep concern" about potential protests and urging him to give a speech to head them off. All the energy and enthusiasm, however, seemed to reside with activists. Commerce Secretary William Daley drew anemic support from business groups for a pro-trade bus tour.[29]

The WTO's preparations also were falling short. Member nations had been mired for months in a distracting struggle over the selection of a new director-general to replace the retiring Italian diplomat Renato Ruggiero. Moore, the former New Zealand prime minister who ultimately won the job, did not take office until September 1, less than ninety days before the Seattle meeting. His four deputies had never met before they arrived in the Pacific Northwest. Barshefsky and the new European, Canadian, and Australian trade ministers also were unacquainted.[30]

As the autumn wore on, Barshefsky grew worried. The process of hammering out a unified negotiating document to serve as the basis for the ministerial was "a mess." She feared that negotiators could only produce a "heavily bracketed text," which would merely enumerate their disagreements rather than move the countries closer to agreement. (The version ultimately sent to ministers before the meeting contained 402 pairs of square brackets.)[31] About six weeks before the meeting, Barshefsky asked her chief of staff whether the government could back out of its contract with the city. But she was told that the cancellation penalties were too steep.[32]

The black bloc

Like an army preparing for battle, the protest organizers concentrated on logistics. They cobbled together a 1,500-vehicle volunteer carpool and arranged accommodations for ten thousand people in the homes of local residents, union halls, warehouses, university fraternities, and sororities.[33] The basement of a Methodist church was secured as storage for three hundred giant sea turtle costumes, which the Humane Society would use to protest a WTO ruling against US implementation of a ban on shrimp imports from countries that did not protect the marine creatures.[34]

In the final days of November, Seattle became a festival of anti-globalization activists, union members, environmentalists, journalists, corporate executives, government officials, and trade ministers from more than one hundred countries. Awaiting them were protesters engaged in street actions and panel discussions. Each day featured a specific theme: labor, the environment, health, human rights, or women.

Wallach had been laughed at earlier in the year when she spoke of drawing thirty thousand people to Seattle. Now that the downtown area was jammed with people, no one was laughing. On Monday, November 29, the day before the ministerial's scheduled start, five members of the Rainforest Action Network scaled a fifteen-story construction crane and unfurled an enormous banner assailing the WTO as antidemocratic. They were arrested as soon as they climbed down.[35]

These publicity stunts were an integral part of the protest. But something more worrisome was afoot. Wallach had picked up rumors months earlier about shadowy groups that were intent on attacking the capitalist system itself, even if their actions disrupted the planned peaceful demonstration. Several dozen anarchists, including "black bloc" squads from Eugene, Oregon, arrived in Seattle intent on mayhem. In August and September, Seattle police department intelligence officials detected increasingly frequent signs of planned disruptions. But officers struggled to distinguish rumor from fact in assessing the potential threat.

"Most of these reports were alarming and many were preposterous," a department report later concluded. The Federal Bureau of Investigation's final threat assessment, distributed less than two weeks before the opening ceremony, said that the "threat of violent protest activity directed at the WTO ministerial is low to medium." Yet, the interagency intelligence subcommittee preparing for the meeting warned that organized extremists were planning blockades, street theater, and civil disobedience leading to mass arrests in a bid to "shut down the WTO." [36]

Protesters' preparations, the city government's cheerful assumptions, and the WTO's organizational shortcomings all collided on Tuesday, November 30, the ministerial's opening day. Wallach awakened in her room at the Edgewater and, after a quick television interview, headed for the daily meeting at protest headquarters. On the way, she noticed a parking lot "chock-a-block full" of buses. "Oh my goodness," she thought to herself. "This is working!" [37]

Around 10 a.m., the labor rally kicked off at Memorial Stadium, near the city's best-known landmark, the Space Needle. Members of several unions, identifiable by the color of their rain ponchos—yellow for the Steelworkers, red for the Teamsters—stood in the late November chill, holding placards reading "No WTO" and "Fair trade not free trade." On the stage, Rick Bender, the head of the state AFL-CIO, greeted them with a shout: "Welcome to Washington! The first and probably the last state after today to host the World Trade Organization."

Waiting backstage for her turn to speak, Wallach peeked out at the massive crowd. Only at football games had she ever seen so many people. "This is fucking amazing," she thought. The rally was in its second hour when she crossed the stage to offer brief remarks. She was nervous. Attacking the WTO, she said in a singsong cadence: "It's got-ta be fixed or it's got-ta be nixed." [38]

Despite the gloomy Seattle weather, rally-goers were upbeat. Elsewhere, the mood was darker. Members of the direct action squads had begun gathering in a park near Pike Place Market before dawn. At 5:30 a.m., police reported individuals equipped with gas masks, carrying what appeared to be "chemical munitions."[39] Various "affinity groups" that composed the Direct Action Network had each been assigned to swarm an intersection near the conference. Protesters linked themselves with bicycle locks before inserting their arms into lengths of PVC pipe, which made it impossible for the police to safely cut the chains.

Others advanced on the conference site from multiple directions. Protesters set fires in the streets, chained themselves to manhole covers, and occupied fourteen downtown intersections, overwhelming police. Though most of those demonstrating were peaceful, a few hundred black-clad anarchists broke windows and sprayed cops with chemical irritants.[40] By 8 a.m., some police units already were reeling and exhausted. There was no time for rest or meal breaks, and the resupply of food, water, radio batteries, and other supplies was flagging.[41] Many delegates were trapped in their hotels. Nearby, roughly one hundred people were jumping on cars while others attacked moving vehicles. The police had lost control.

The activists' goal was to shut down the 135-nation conference and block any new trade talks. As the sun rose, the chaos downtown spread. Protesters blocked streets, sidewalks, and building entrances at the convention center where WTO delegates were scheduled to meet. The police knew that "criminal agitators" were planning to target the center and the nearby Paramount Theatre, where the opening ceremony was to occur. In response, the department improvised a corridor between the two venues by parking metro buses nose to tail.

But the intelligence reports were incomplete. Officers had not anticipated that activists would try to intercept delegates as they left their hotels several blocks away, where the police presence was thinner.[42] After negotiators trying to leave the Sheraton hotel were accosted by demonstrators, hotel security guards quickly locked down the structure. "These people do not understand the benefits of free trade," a flustered German negotiator told a reporter.[43] About twenty anarchists dressed in black, and with masks or bandanas obscuring their faces, heaved eight metal newspaper boxes into the street before being chased away by other protesters.[44]

Inside the Westin hotel, amid a faint scent of tear gas, Barshefsky, who was due to call the meeting to order, was trapped with Secretary of State Madeleine Albright. Their Secret Service details judged it unsafe to attempt to reach the Paramount. As some of the protesters broke store windows at Planet Hollywood, NikeTown, and Bank of America, the two women engaged in a bit of gallows humor, worrying aloud about the fate of the nearby Nordstrom's shoe department. But on the streets below, the situation was deteriorating.

Shortly before 9 a.m., a police commander at the Sheraton reported that he was losing control of the scene, as protesters assaulted delegates. Police in numerous spots over the next several hours began indiscriminately using tear gas and pepper spray on demonstrators, who responded by lobbing gas canisters right back at them. A violent minority, lashing out against symbols of corporate power, shattered windows at McDonald's and Starbucks outlets.

As about twenty thousand marchers set off from the labor rally for the one-mile walk to the convention center, the ministerial's opening ceremony was canceled. It was a humiliating public relations setback for the United States, with the president due to arrive in little more than twelve hours. As the news spread, the crowd cheered. "That was victory," Wallach said. "We had shut down the first day."[45]

Chaos

Labor officials had a permit to march from the rally site, through the downtown streets, to the convention center. Upon arriving, the marchers planned to chant anti-WTO slogans for a bit, before looping back to their buses to start for home. Wallach was near the front of the euphoric procession, at times running ahead to take photos. She knew what the authorities did not: Several thousand people in the crowd of forty thousand intended to break away from the approved route and besiege the convention center.

As the protests grew into running street battles with police, senior Clinton administration officials telephoned Seattle Mayor Paul Schell and threatened to cancel the ministerial if he could not reestablish control. The beleaguered Schell declared a civil emergency at 3:32 p.m. and ordered an overnight curfew. Washington Governor Gary Locke called up the National Guard.

Still the chaos raged. As she was making her way through the crowd to check on a young staffer who had been caught in the violence, Wallach was hit by a blast of tear gas. Belatedly pulling her silk scarf over her mouth, she stumbled, eyes streaming. A young protester doused her face with vinegar to ease the sting.

Police regrouped in the early evening and pushed the protesters east into the Capitol Hill neighborhood. America's thirteenth-largest city was convulsed: Clouds of tear gas billowed and sparks flew as police saws cut the legs of mailboxes to which protesters had chained themselves.

Throughout the tumultuous hours, administration officials were reworking the speech that Clinton was scheduled to deliver the next day at a luncheon meeting of trade ministers. Jeff Shesol, a White House speechwriter, had flown out ahead of the president, who was making a fundraising stop in California before arriving in Seattle. Tear gas had drifted through the open windows of the hotel suite where Shesol and other members of the White House staff were working. "It was surreal. I'd done a lot of traveling with Clinton. I'd never seen anything like this before," he said.[46]

Before leaving Washington, Clinton had gathered reporters in the Oval Office. When Helen Thomas of United Press International asked him what he hoped to achieve in Seattle, the president said he wanted to see a new round launched to reduce trade barriers. Then, he appeared to side with the protesters. "Since this has now become a global society with global communications, as well as a global economy, I think it was unrealistic to assume that for the next 50 years, trade could be like it's been for the last 50—primarily the province of business executives and political leaders. I think more people are going to demand to be heard, and I think that's a good thing," Clinton said.[47]

The president spoke before Seattle descended into anarchy. As Air Force One lifted off for San Francisco, the first of two California stops, Shesol and Gene Sperling, another Clinton aide, were in Seattle laboring over the president's speech. Sperling had rejected an early draft as "too defensive on protesters," according to the handwritten notes Shesol scribbled on White House stationery. The Friday speech should "set [a] vision for winning public support for" trade. The president had penned his own thoughts in a note to Sperling, commending a *Los Angeles Times* story about WTO rulings that had opened foreign markets to American products. "We need to address this issue in my speech," the president wrote, signing the note "BC."[48]

Perhaps because of the Thanksgiving holiday, Shesol had not had his customary advance meeting with Clinton to discuss the speech. Instead, the aide cribbed from ideas in a commencement address the president had given in June at the University of Chicago, devoted to "putting a human face on the global economy." Over the 29th and 30th, Shesol produced multiple drafts, tweaking each in response to edits from multiple presidential aides, including Sperling; Richard Samans, who handled international economic policy for the National Security Council; National Security Advisor Sandy Berger; and Berger's deputy, James Steinberg. "Everybody knew this was going to be a big, big speech.... Even if there hadn't been a single demonstrator in the streets, this was going to be a contentious set of meetings," Shesol said.[49]

After a day of fundraising—including a gun control reception in Los Angeles where he was introduced by the entertainer Whoopi Goldberg—Clinton landed at Seattle's Boeing Field at 1 a.m. He arrived at the Westin about thirty-five minutes later and watched local television news footage of the day's street combat before turning in.[50]

While still in San Francisco, however, the president had given an interview to a *Seattle Post-Intelligencer* reporter that threatened to blow up the talks. One of the most difficult issues facing negotiators involved the relationship between trade and labor. But dealing with it presented too many problems, political and economic, for both the advanced economies like the United States and the developing world. Before coming to Seattle, Barshefsky had told delegates that setting enforceable labor standards was only a long-term goal. The negotiating text did not even address the subject.[51]

But in a telephone interview earlier in the day, Clinton cast caution aside and called for sanctions on countries that failed to meet basic labor standards, a principal demand of union leaders. "What we ought to do first of all is to adopt the United States' position on having a working group on labor within the WTO, and then that working group should develop these core labor standards, and then they ought to be a part of every trade agreement," the president said. "And ultimately, I would favor a system in which sanctions would come for violating any provision of a trade agreement."[52]

Wednesday's *Post-Intelligencer* blared the headline "Chaos Closes Downtown" across the front page, which also featured the paper's exclusive account of Clinton's remarks. As the WTO scrambled to salvage the ministerial, the president's comments angered delegates who were already on edge from trying to navigate the battlefield that Seattle had become. Trade ministers from the developing world were furious. They had been reassured that labor standards were something for the distant future, and yet here was their American host saying they should be an immediate objective. Already suspicious of labor rules, seeing them as a tool to prevent poor countries from competing with countries like the United States, negotiators now feared they were walking into an American ambush.

When Clinton saw Barshefsky, he asked, "How are we doing?"

"Not too well," she replied.

"Why?"

Barshefsky said, "I'm not too thrilled with the newspaper today."

"How bad was it?"

"Not helpful, but I don't think this is going to go anywhere in any event. I just don't see this coming together," she said.[53]

Indeed, well before landing in Seattle, Barshefsky had been skeptical about prospects for a new round. A political scandal in Europe had brought an untested negotiator to the EU's top trade post. Many developing countries were preoccupied with implementing the requirements of the Uruguay Round and were not eager to take on additional commitments. And despite Clinton's public support, the United States itself was ambivalent. Vice President Al Gore, facing a presidential campaign in 2000, was wary of whatever US concessions would be needed to launch a new round.

Strange bedfellows

Once the ministerial began, Barshefsky's fears were confirmed. "It was clear that countries were not ready for this. You could feel it in the room. There was just no cohesion," she said.[54]

During his thirty-six-hour stay, Clinton toured the Port of Seattle, where he touted Washington state's apple exports, and gave a luncheon speech to about three hundred trade ministers and WTO delegates. The imposition of a broad no-protest zone had muted the unrest in the streets, allowing Clinton to discuss the ministerial in a larger frame. He had made a list of his goals upon becoming president, he said: supporting the expansion of the European Union and NATO; standing against ethnic and religious hatred in the Middle East; and promoting the integration of Russia, China, and India "into the large political and economic flows of our time."[55]

Liberalizing trade over the past half century had made the world more prosperous, Clinton said. The rules-based system established under the WTO would make it more secure. Clinton disavowed the violent protests but said those demonstrating peacefully should be heard. "What they are telling us in the streets here is, this was an issue we used to be silent on. We're not going to be silent on it anymore. We haven't necessarily given up on trade, but we want to be heard," the president said.

At the negotiating venue, Barshefsky maintained a brave face, telling reporters: "I am quite comfortable with where we are right now."[56] In fact, the talks were headed nowhere. Negotiators from several developing countries, cooling their heels while the larger powers haggled behind closed doors, watched television replays of the previous day's turmoil and saw it as evidence that the Clinton administration's trade stance lacked public support, Wallach said.[57]

In fact, Americans' views were nuanced. Nearly 60 percent of those surveyed in the most recent Gallup poll approved of Clinton's performance as president.[58] A healthy 54-percent-to-33-percent majority backed the administration's deal with China over WTO membership. A similar share of Americans favored trade in general, despite believing that workers would be hurt. The public was certain that US companies would prosper from expanded trade. But only a little more than one-third of those asked saw trade as benefiting labor; 59 percent said workers would suffer.[59] Unlike those thronging the streets of Seattle, most Americans seemed clear-eyed about the gains from trade in terms of lower prices, greater product availability, and enhanced economic efficiency—and their costs.

Before noon on Thursday, Clinton was gone. But negotiators staged a final bid for progress: eight hours of word-by-word bargaining over a four-paragraph agriculture clause. After sitting out most of the discussion, Pascal Lamy, the EU trade minister, returned to announce his opposition, prompting an exhausted Barshefsky to pull the plug. "That's it. We're done," she said.[60]

Wallach, who had lobbied foreign trade ministers behind the scenes as a credentialed observer, was certain the WTO had suffered a lasting blow to its legitimacy. The organization "has given every indication that it is an institution that will break itself by its inability to bend," she said. "Seattle was the wake-up call of all time."[61] By demonstrating the breadth of opposition to globalization, the protesters had stopped the WTO in its tracks, she said. The chaos in the streets—and Clinton's interview—also effectively increased negotiators' workload while reducing the time available to them. The protests had prompted the formation of an ad hoc labor-rights working group whose time-consuming meetings made some headway, but at the expense of frayed tempers. And the turmoil had delayed the start of the meeting, leaving less time to reach agreement.[62] Barshefsky acknowledged the protests had been "logistically inconvenient for the delegates" but insisted they "had no substantive impact on the outcome."[63] In the White House, James Steinberg, the number-two official at the National Security Council, felt "the prestige damage was very high." He blamed the trade team for mishandling the run-up to the talks.[64]

Robert Cassidy, a US trade negotiator at the time, said officials were "shocked" by what happened in Seattle. Being pinned in their hotel rooms by protesters rampaging through the streets left an indelible impression.

"That to me demonstrated that there was a disconnect between people and government officials," he said. "We were on a mission. We were on God's mission to open up markets, to make trade free and increase globalization. I mean, this was our mission and then to see that this was absolutely not what people wanted. I think that hurt Democrats from then on."[65]

Elsewhere, the fallout was swift. Seattle Police Chief Norm Stamper, whose officers were caught flat-footed before violently suppressing the protests, took responsibility and announced his resignation five days after the WTO left town. In 2001, Paul Schell became the first Seattle mayoral incumbent in sixty-five years to lose a primary election.

In an after-action report, the police department acknowledged "that, tactically, it was taught a hard lesson by a well-trained and equipped adversary." Initial planning and staffing were "inadequate," the department conceded.[66] Officers had expended 2,019 tear gas canisters, cans of pepper spray, and other "nonlethal" munitions as they struggled to regain control of Seattle's streets.[67]

While the majority of the protesters had been nonviolent, it was images of destruction and chaos that came to symbolize the WTO meeting. Police arrested 631 people, charging most with misdemeanors such as "failure to disperse" and "obstruction of traffic." Property damage to downtown businesses reached an estimated $3 million.[68] *New York Times* columnist Thomas Friedman labeled the demonstrations "ridiculous" and said the anti-WTO coalition was "protesting against the wrong target with the wrong tools."[69]

Shepherded by the WTO, trade was the solution to the protesters' irritations, not their cause, he argued. The global rules-making body was more likely to midwife higher labor and environmental standards than to become an all-powerful global government trespassing on national sovereignties.

The protesters were easy to mock, with their turtle costumes and drum circles and earnest social justice jargon. Yet, the proliferation of controversies surrounding the trade agenda would ultimately cause support for greater liberalization to wither. Trade negotiations were arduous enough when the primary concern was adjusting or eliminating tariffs. When the roster of negotiating items expanded to include intellectual property rights, cross-border regulatory harmonization, and competition policy, both the domestic politics and the required diplomatic logrolling eventually became too complex.

Wallach scoffed at Friedman's views. "We won. There was no WTO expansion. We won on the merits," she said.[70] The anti-globalization fires lit in Seattle also consumed other negotiations, such as George W. Bush's proposed Free Trade Area of the Americas, she said. Those talks aimed at expanding NAFTA throughout the region collapsed in 2003, after being mortally wounded by massive protests at an April 2001 summit in Quebec City.

Above all, Seattle highlighted issues that would dog trade liberalization for decades, such as labor rights, environmental protection, and developing-country debt burdens. The protesters had succeeded in assembling a broad anti-globalization coalition of church, labor, environmental, youth, consumer, public interest, and farm groups.

Especially noteworthy was the alliance with right-wing anti-trade elements that bore fruit in the streets of Seattle. While the men and women who filled the streets were overwhelmingly of the left, much of the money that paid for the protest organizing originated in the coffers of Roger Milliken, a prominent South Carolina textile magnate and avowed protectionist.

Dolan, Wallach's field director who called himself a socialist, had no illusions about his allies on the right. "It was a dirty little secret of the movement in those days.... This guy was a John Bircher. I'm taking John Birch money. It's getting kinda laundered through the Citizens Trade Campaign. [But] I'm taking that guy's money. Anti-union. Racist. Whatever that guy was. I'm taking that guy's money. And I'm giving it to the anarchists," Dolan said.[71]

The strange bedfellows alliance had its roots in a series of clandestine Capitol Hill dinners held in the early 1990s. Joined around the table were Democrats, Republicans, administration officials, congressional staffers, union and corporate lobbyists, and public-interest-group representatives. The political views of those attending ranged from the far left to the far right. To avoid awkward questions, the gatherings were secretive. Wallach likened them to Alcoholics Anonymous meetings; you could say that you had attended, but it was forbidden to disclose the names of other participants.

"We would all go to a restaurant on Capitol Hill and have dinner. And Roger Milliken paid for it. We would do this once a month," said Jock Nash, a former marine who worked directly for Milliken as his trade lobbyist. "There was this wealth of information that we shared with one another."[72]

Milliken had little in common with Wallach or Dolan other than opposition to free trade. The billionaire was so fiercely opposed to collective bargaining that he had abruptly closed one South Carolina plant after the workers there voted to unionize. To help build the conservative movement, he had funded *National Review* and the Heritage Foundation while backing politicians such as Arizona Sen. Barry Goldwater, the 1964 Republican presidential nominee. It was hard to imagine someone whose politics, apart from trade, were more at odds with Wallach's beliefs.

She viewed the gatherings as a "tactical alliance" that multiplied the anti-trade coalition's influence. Counting votes in Congress, she could track Democrats while Nash kept tabs on the Republicans. In that way, both sides of the anti-globalization coalition ended up better armed for legislative battles.

"Our biggest allies were Ralph Nader and Lori Wallach," Nash said. "We worked hand in hand, basically across the ideological aisle."

Nash was among those who went to Seattle. He brought along his sons, who spent the time snowboarding. But marching in the streets was not his thing. He visited Dolan's headquarters, reporting to Milliken by phone on what happened as the event dissolved into chaos. The anarchist violence was unfortunate. But without it, he believed, the press would barely have covered the debate.[73]

Nash respected the left's organizing ability, believing it superior to anything conservatives could muster. But mass mobilization had its limits. Wallach and her allies tried to repeat their Seattle success at the April 2000 meetings of the IMF and World Bank, but the protests fizzled amid much tougher security. The authorities, too, had learned from Seattle.

A horrible mistake

For all the public attention and notoriety, the events in Seattle were not the most consequential globalization development to occur in November 1999. Instead, it was Barshefsky's announcement from Beijing two weeks earlier that an agreement with the Chinese had been reached over the terms of their entry into the WTO. Barshefsky, Sperling, and Chinese negotiator Long Yongtu celebrated with a champagne toast, capping fitful negotiations that had stretched on for more than thirteen years.

The endgame began in April, when Chinese Premier Zhu Rongji traveled to Washington expecting to put the finishing touches on the deal, only to have Clinton balk. The president was under pressure from Republicans over testimony by a former Democratic fundraiser that $300,000 in political contributions for Clinton's 1996 reelection campaign had originated with the head of Chinese military intelligence.[74] With labor already opposing the China deal, some of the president's political advisers urged him to wait until the optics improved, according to Kenneth Lieberthal, the National Security Council's senior director for Asia.

On April 7, Zhu arrived for his White House meetings with the administration still divided over China's WTO bid.[75] The political challenge seemed daunting. Little had been done to boost support among congressional Democrats since the administration's failure to secure "fast track" negotiating authority one year earlier. Plus, Zhu had his own worries. Hardliners within the Chinese government were suspicious of the negotiations, believing that the Americans "really wanted to keep China 'down on the farm,'" the Chinese leader told the president.[76]

The next day, Clinton said publicly that Zhu's trip would not result in a deal, adding, "There is still work to be done." At a joint press conference, the Chinese premier blamed the breakdown on "the political atmosphere" in Washington.[77]

To make matters worse, Barshefsky made public the draft text that China had accepted. Publicizing Zhu's specific concessions put his political standing at home under threat. Any deal would require China to cut its tariffs on numerous products, exposing its lumbering state-owned enterprises to foreign competition that would mean massive job losses. The Chinese politburo in February had signed off on Zhu's strategy.[78] But powerful officials elsewhere in China's government remained in the dark until Barshefsky's revelations.

Clinton's abrupt rejection humiliated Zhu and left the talks over China's trade status adrift. Incredibly, less than one month later, things got even worse. Around midnight local time on May 7, a B-2 bomber fired five one-ton "smart" bombs into the Chinese embassy in Belgrade.[79] The aircraft was supporting NATO's war against Serbia for its repression of ethnic Albanians in Kosovo. Intending to strike a military procurement office three hundred meters away, the Air Force jet—relying on inaccurate targeting guidance—instead destroyed the Chinese facility, killing three diplomats and injuring twenty others.

The attack was a horrible mistake. An inexperienced intelligence officer at the Central Intelligence Agency, pressed into service because of a staffing shortfall at the Pentagon, misread overhead reconnaissance photos and relied on outdated maps in preparing the B-2's targeting package. Separately, officials failed to consult a US diplomat who had visited the new embassy and could have corrected the mistake. Another US diplomat who could have caught the error was out with the flu when the orders passed through his office. And the three Chinese individuals who were killed, though ostensibly journalists, were in fact intelligence officers working in China's largest signals-intelligence facility in Europe.[80]

Clinton in June dispatched Under Secretary of State Thomas Pickering to brief Chinese officials on what had gone wrong. No one in Beijing believed the American account of the tragedy. Plenty of Americans doubted it, too. Clinton aides entered the Oval Office one day to find the president shaking his head over a US intelligence report. "Can you believe that 94 percent of the Chinese think we deliberately bombed their embassy?" the president asked, visibly irritated. To which John Podesta, the White House chief of staff, quipped: "That's compared to like 50 percent of your White House staff."[81] Clinton glared at him in response.

For weeks, the future of the talks was unclear. But by late August, Chinese leaders had privately decided to resume the negotiations, according to the memoirs of former Premier Li Peng.[82] In September, Clinton met with Chinese President Jiang Zemin in Auckland, New Zealand, following an APEC summit, seeking his agreement to restart the talks. After a prolonged exchange, Jiang agreed. "That was a tough meeting," said the NSC's Lieberthal.[83]

The talks headed into the home stretch, following an October visit to China by Treasury Secretary Larry Summers. To clinch the deal, Barshefsky in early November invited Gene Sperling to join her for what she hoped would be a final bargaining round in Beijing. The White House aide was known to be close to Clinton and skeptical of the deal's domestic political consequences. Bringing him along would signal the Chinese that the administration was united, Barshefsky reasoned.

Chinese officials saw multiple benefits from WTO membership. The need to comply with foreign demands to lower trade barriers would give reformers like Zhu a powerful argument in their internal battles over China's economic policy. Cementing trade relations with the United States also would eliminate a source of uncertainty and potential coercion that American officials had held over Beijing for years.

China had enjoyed the same status in the US market as most other countries since 1992. But the annual ritual of congressional review discouraged long-term corporate investments in China. Chinese officials worried that the US could revoke normal trade status at any time, instantly subjecting imports from China to crushing tariffs.[84]

The WTO operated by consensus. In theory, US approval was needed for the country to join. At the same time, outright refusal was never really an option for Washington. If the US refused to make permanent China's trade privileges, it would have lost out on the tariff reductions that Beijing was offering in return. Chinese authorities then likely would have reached separate bilateral deals with European and other trading partners that would have left American companies at a disadvantage, US officials believed.

After Seattle, Mike Moore, the WTO's director-general, agreed with the principal negotiators that the organization needed a "time-out," Barshefsky said. But that's all the pro-trade forces thought was required to get back on track. In Washington, the president remained supportive. At the same time, Clinton insisted that globalization would not sell itself. A global economy that was growing more complex and interdependent by the day required agreed-upon rules coordinated by the WTO. "But trade could not survive on policy wonks and CEOs alone," Clinton told Taylor Branch, his biographer. "Broad public confidence was essential."

The test of whether the president could cultivate such popular support would come soon, once Clinton asked Congress to approve his China deal.

3

Sense of Menace

Tim Draper needed a win. A third-generation venture capitalist, whose grandfather had launched Silicon Valley's first investment firm in 1959, Draper by the year 2000 had earned a reputation in tech circles as a freethinker whose investment ideas were long on risk and short on return. Competitors disparaged him as "a bit of a hack."[1] True, he had scored big with an early investment in Hotmail, a free internet mail service acquired by Microsoft in 1997 for a reported $400 million. But he had a weakness for publicity stunts—billing himself as "the Riskmaster" at investment conferences where he sang his own songs—and he squandered time and money on long shot political ventures. A failed campaign for a California ballot initiative promoting school vouchers cost him $20 million.[2]

As a new century beckoned, however, Draper found himself at the intersection of American capital and Chinese innovation. China's economic opening was generally thought of in terms of its impact upon global manufacturing. But fueled by American cash, the flowering of Chinese technology proved equally consequential. China's rise, it showed, involved more than cheap labor and mammoth factories.

This informal innovation alliance would become a powerful engine of wealth generation on two shores while spawning new global technology leaders that would challenge American dominance of the industries of tomorrow.

Draper's good fortune in China—and the profits enjoyed by countless American corporations in this period—explained why so many people held on to their hopes for the Chinese market for so long. The Sino-US economic partnership seemed poised to generate enormous riches for all concerned.

In Washington, meanwhile, policymakers from both parties cheered the gains that US industry and finance were reaping in China. These early years of China's membership in the global trading system featured numerous disagreements between US and Chinese officials. But American officials, in general, were patient with their Chinese counterparts. The US government saw the rough spots in China's implementation of promised reforms as the expected difficulties in converting a state-led system to one governed by market principles rather than as deliberate resistance to change.

Still, there were a few dissenters. These individuals had personal experience dealing with the Chinese Communist Party and an economic system that—even as it changed dramatically—retained core attributes that were antithetical to liberal democracies. And those experiences gradually soured them on the likelihood that the future envisioned in Washington, Silicon Valley, and countless corporate boardrooms would be realized.

Draper, to this point, was not one of the dissenters. He was among a handful of risk-taking Americans in those early years whose ready cash and investing savvy earned them a place in China's embryonic tech scene. At first, the balance of financial power favored the Americans. The lords of Silicon Valley, after all, had accomplished what Chinese innovators could only aspire to achieve. But as the years passed, that balance would inevitably shift, unsettling business relationships and markets in ways that few could foresee.

Draper's family boasted a storied lineage. His grandfather, William Draper Jr., was born in Harlem in 1894. He earned two degrees in economics at New York University and, as a student delegate, joined industrialist Henry Ford's quixotic 1915 peace expedition, which sought to end the First World War. William Draper had a successful career as an investment banker, became an army general, oversaw the economies of occupied Germany and Japan after the Second World War, and served as the first US ambassador to NATO.[3] In 1959, he and two partners established the first venture capital firm on the West Coast, Draper, Gaither & Anderson, laying the groundwork for what would later be known as Silicon Valley.[4]

Tim Draper's father, William Draper III, also worked in the family firm before launching his own venture capital shop a few years later. Like the family patriarch, he too had a career in public service, helming the Export-Import Bank during the Reagan administration and running the United Nations Development Programme in the late 1980s. UNDP began working in China in 1979, less than a year after Deng Xiaoping launched the "reform and opening" that would drag the country out of Maoist isolation and poverty. Among the agency's first ventures under its new administrator was designing English-language textbooks for Chinese schools. UN specialists also helped Chinese reformers draft new laws governing trade, banking, and securities.[5]

As Draper's father jetted among the UN agency's 108 field offices, he was occasionally joined by Tim, who had taken over the family business. "I got a chance to see what other parts of the world were like," he said.[6] When he was about thirty years old, they visited China, a trip that left the younger Draper with memories of a poor land that radiated potential. His father left the UN in 1993 and launched a new venture fund that would invest outside the United States. Draper III and his partner considered basing their fledgling outfit in Shanghai, but decided "the lack of true freedom of ideas, democracy, and the rule of law" made it a "bad fit." They opted for India instead.[7]

At first, Tim Draper did not want to follow in his elders' footsteps. "I really wanted to cut my own path," he said.[8] He studied at Stanford University, ignoring his father's preference for Yale. After graduating from Harvard Business School, he took a job with Alex Brown & Sons, where he met his future business partner, John Fisher. Running the family venture capital business, Tim Draper adopted "anything is possible" as his mantra.[9]

In 1985, he founded his own firm, which eventually became Draper Fisher Jurvetson, and assembled a network of venture capital funds that were on the ground and thus considered "local" investors in several US cities. In the late 1990s, at a time when most tech investors were obsessed with Palo Alto's next hot idea, Tim Draper steered DFJ to markets outside the United States, where there was little tradition of investors gambling on entrepreneurs. "I invested in places a lot of people hadn't touched: Africa, South America," he said.[10]

At the time, DFJ had invested in six aspiring search engine providers in the United States. When Draper tried to interest his partners in a seventh, a start-up called Google, they balked. Draper later was glum about the missed payday, until he realized that other countries would need their own Google. China, with a distinctive character-based language and huge growth potential, seemed a good place to start.

In July 2000, as Congress moved toward final approval of permanent normal trade relations (PNTR) for China, Steven Walchek, an entrepreneur whom Draper had funded, introduced him to Robin Li, a young internet-search specialist. Draper and Fisher were both impressed with Li, who had worked at Infoseek before launching his own company called Baidu one year earlier. The Chinese entrepreneur had obvious technical chops, industry experience, and a clear vision: bringing internet search to China's fast-growing market. Draper and Li hit it off. Draper said later that the younger man seemed "thoughtful and open."[11]

Draper flew to China to conclude negotiations for an investment in Baidu. He met other Chinese entrepreneurs at the time, including Alibaba's Jack Ma. But Draper had trouble understanding Ma's accented English, so he backed Li instead.[12] Draper and Li hammered out the terms while riding in a taxi. DFJ put up about $7.5 million for a 28 percent stake in the company.[13] "It was one of the toughest negotiations ever 'cuz he was not moving. He was very, very tough. Finally, I got the deal done," Draper later said.[14]

On its first day of trading in August 2005, Baidu's stock quadrupled in value. Suddenly, Draper had a $1 billion hit on his hands. To Draper, China was a "free country," where the government had decided to get out of the way and let risk-takers make money. Expanded trade with the US and other countries "of course" would lead to political liberalization, he said. "I felt that once the country tasted freedom, they would never go back to government control," he said.[15]

Draper's investing approach relied on firsthand observation. His trips to China were a blur. Meetings with potential entrepreneurs began at seven in the morning and ran until late at night. In the evening, there would often be dinners with local government officials or karaoke sessions with Chinese reporters. "I have a horrible voice, but I'm very enthusiastic," he said.[16]

Traveling to China up to six times a year, Draper invested in several more Chinese firms. Once, on a drive from Shanghai to Hangzhou, he spied a handful of modern homes with paved driveways dotting a landscape that otherwise featured dirt roads and spartan structures. The more expensive properties were an early sign, Draper concluded, of a Chinese version of "keeping up with the Joneses."

Just two decades removed from abject poverty, China was visibly getting richer. Urban couples enjoyed consumer comforts their parents never knew, including private cars, home entertainment systems, fashionable clothes, and international travel. Foreign brands were coveted. In Shanghai, the Super Brand Mall opened, featuring Gucci, Christian Dior, and Montblanc stores along with Starbucks and McDonald's outlets. The economy was leaping ahead by 10 percent each year. In a country where private property was once outlawed, condos sold for more than $200,000 in developments complete with pool, sauna, and health club.

"Twenty years ago, everybody in my town had about the same income, so life was about the same for everybody. During recent years, some people are getting more and more rich while some people still have a hard life," said Chen Xiaowen, a marketing manager for a Chinese manufacturer of liquid crystal displays.[17]

Draper's excitement about the potential profits from China's development only grew. At one point, he broached with his wife the idea of moving to China. "It was so exciting. The entrepreneurs were so dynamic!" he said.[18]

His father ultimately talked him out of moving across the Pacific Ocean. But Draper's enthusiasm for Chinese investments reflected the Western euphoria that greeted economic reform in China and the post-Communist states in the former Soviet Union and Eastern Europe. At first, no financial bonanza seemed too extreme. No get-rich-quick scheme too outlandish. And the idea that things might go wrong was derided as naysaying. "The risks in China are overblown," he said in 2005.[19]

We will look back on this day and be glad

American venture capitalists had been dabbling in China since 1993, when Patrick McGovern, the head of Boston-based International Data Group, began taking stakes in Chinese start-ups.[20] By the late 1990s, Chinese graduates of American universities were returning home to capitalize on an emerging boom. Risk-averse Chinese banks, however, were leery of tech start-ups, and most established Silicon Valley venture funds saw China as too risky.[21] That left an opening for Draper, who billed himself as the first venture capitalist from the valley to invest in a Chinese company.

By demonstrating that Beijing was legitimizing individual wealth, China's WTO entry paved the way for venture financing to flourish. US funds invested less than $50 million in China in 2001. Five years later, annual venture financing was more than ten times that amount, according to Rhodium Group, a New York consultancy.

"What it impacted was the spirits of the entrepreneurs saying, 'It's okay for us to go start these businesses.... We're basically free to go and start our business, create this venture ecosystem.' WTO created the environment in which that could thrive," said Gary Rieschel, a former SoftBank executive who launched his own venture capital firm in Shanghai in 2006.

The first wave of Chinese start-ups involved local versions of business models that had already been proven in the United States, such as Baidu's foray into the search business popularized by Yahoo. The Chinese internet company Sohu in fact was initially known as Sohoo in homage to the American pioneer.

But venture capitalists from the United States brought with them more than cash; they introduced to China the American playbook for wealth creation. In a country where stock markets were little more than a decade old, employee stock options quickly became the standard form of compensation used to woo top talent.

Foreign financiers, however, needed to find creative ways to circumvent a Chinese legal system that lagged behind the changing economy. Under Chinese law, foreigners were not permitted to own many businesses, including those that operated websites. That left many venture capital investments in a kind of legal limbo. In 1999, Goldman Sachs invested $5 million for half of an embryonic online business called Alibaba. Strictly speaking, the bank's stake in what became China's best-known internet economy success, valued at $25 billion when it eventually went public, was illegal.[22]

Wall Street lawyers, however, devised a complex legal stratagem to get around that prohibition. A Chinese internet company could be re-organized under a corporate parent that was a shell company based in the Cayman Islands. Known as a "variable interest entity," this structure allowed foreigners to invest in Chinese companies that otherwise would be off-limits and to ultimately list them on stock exchanges outside China.[23] So long as regulators in Beijing continued looking the other way, the legal maneuver would enable foreign cash to flow to Chinese start-ups.

Within a few years, Chinese entrepreneurs began doing more than copying proven ideas. The outbreak of SARS in 2003 spurred Chinese tech development by encouraging text messaging and home shopping, according to Duncan Clark, chair of BDA China, a technology-investment advisory firm. Major Silicon Valley venture firms responded by establishing their own operations in China, where they could carry out the detailed due diligence that was difficult to accomplish from abroad.

In 2005, Sequoia Capital, best known for funding Apple, set up Sequoia China. Rieschel retired from SoftBank and launched Qiming Venture Partners in Shanghai, which became a leading investor in China's health care sector. Chinese entrepreneurs besieged the new arrivals with ideas for e-commerce and digital-payments companies. "You started for the first time to see relatively novel business ideas emerge in China. So the benefit of being on the ground was that you were much closer to what was happening. It wasn't just derivative of what had happened in the US moving into China. It was now business models and ideas and technologies being developed on the ground in China," Rieschel said.[24]

American money and expertise were central to China's efforts to develop technology companies that could challenge global leaders. Companies such as Alibaba, Tencent, and Sohu all drew funding from US firms.[25] Without American participation in the market, many of those innovators would have been starved of capital, according to BDA China's Clark. US investors evaluated entrepreneurs based on the quality of their ideas and the likelihood they could turn them into a river of cash. Chinese financiers were much more concerned about personal connections, or *guanxi*.

"In China they would never have raised [money] because there would have been too much focus on the near term or the fact that they weren't connected. So US capital has had a real impact, betting on the little guy sometimes or the not-connected guy," said Clark.

Draper's rosy outlook was mirrored in the White House, where the president sometimes evinced excessive optimism about China. Though Clinton was usually careful in his choice of words, the cumulative effect of his public statements suggested that China's economic transformation would spur political change. In March 2000, urging passage of the legislation needed for China to join the World Trade Organization, Clinton said: "By joining the WTO, China is not simply agreeing to import more of our products; it is agreeing to import one of democracy's most cherished values: economic freedom." The president said bringing China into the global trading system represented "the most significant opportunity that we have had to create positive change in China since the 1970s." He hailed the appearance of elections for local leaders in some Chinese villages, suggesting that the country's leaders would find that "the genie of freedom will not go back into the bottle." And he mocked those who said Chinese leaders could maintain a chokehold on the internet, likening such censorship attempts to "nailing jello to the wall."[26]

In April 2000, Kenneth Lieberthal, Clinton's top China hand on the National Security Council staff, wrote in an internal memo that granting PNTR would have political as well as economic consequences in China. Normalized trade relations would improve China's economic performance, "which will bolster the confidence of the Chinese leadership in ways that reduce their fears about political reform," Lieberthal concluded.[27] US exports to China also would increase faster than imports, "taking some of the animus out of our large current trade deficit with China." Over the next several years, exports did rise at a slightly faster pace. But because the US bought six times as much as it sold to

China, the overall effect was an ever-wider trade deficit, more than twice as large in 2005 as in 2000.[28]

Debate over granting China full trading privileges consumed much of 2000. Congressional Democrats were miffed at the White House for bringing another controversial trade measure to the floor in an election year, with bruises from the "fast track" and NAFTA fights still fresh.[29] The business community launched a lobbying blitz to overcome opposition based on job-loss fears, China's dismal human rights record, and its potential as a national security threat.

The chief executives of companies such as Boeing, Motorola, General Motors, Caterpillar, and Procter & Gamble had multiple goals in supporting China's bid. Many companies thirsted after China's enormous domestic market, full of customers that were steadily growing more prosperous. Others, such as insurer American International Group, would benefit from specific regulatory provisions of the agreement that Barshefsky had negotiated. Most CEOs anticipated that the addition of China would strengthen the rules-based trading system. And more than a few anticipated relying on low-wage Chinese laborers to perform work that was then being performed by Americans.

"I think it was $100-million-plus spent on lobbying. There's been no such effort since by the business community. There have been lobby efforts on behalf of trade deals, but never the size and breadth of work done on the grassroots. That would tell you something," said Myron Brilliant, a top US Chamber of Commerce executive who co-chaired the business coalition supporting the deal. "There was a lot at stake for business."[30]

Even as the two sides clashed on Capitol Hill, there was an unreal element to the battle. In theory, the United States could block the WTO consensus needed to admit China. But such a rejection would come at enormous cost. What was at issue in Washington's legislative fight was whether the US would grant China the same tariffs and trade status that it allowed all but six countries. If it did, American exporters would, in return, face much lower Chinese tariff barriers on their products. But if Congress said no, then China would exclude American companies from the planned tariff reductions. In that case, European and Japanese companies would enjoy an enormous competitive advantage over their American rivals.[31]

Economists of all stripes supported China's entry into the WTO, from monetarist Milton Friedman to liberal James Tobin of Yale University. Both men joined an open letter to the American public signed by 149 economists, including thirteen Nobel laureates, which said bringing China into the global trading system would "advance the rule of law" and "promote economic development and freedoms" there.[32]

Organized labor led the opposition, centered on China's suppression of independent unions and other human rights abuses. Prohibiting Chinese workers from bargaining collectively was a key part of China's business model and one that threatened the livelihoods of American unionists. Labor representatives were worried about competition from companies like Xin Qiao Electronics in Shenzhen, which produced can openers for Farberware, a US brand.

Xin Qiao paid its workers a base hourly wage of fifteen cents and required them to work fourteen hours each day, standing the entire time, seven days a week, thirty days a month, according to a report by China Labor Watch, a Hong Kong–based labor rights group. Mandatory overtime paid up to eighty cents per hour.

Conditions in the factory were brutal. Workers got no more than ten days off each year, including holidays. If they were too sick to work, they were fired. There were no medical or retirement benefits. In December 1999, a group of roughly one thousand workers staged an unauthorized strike with a single demand: no mandatory overtime on Sunday evenings after 6:30 p.m. "The factory fired them immediately and threatened to turn them over to police," the report said.[33]

The AFL-CIO, which had staged protests on Capitol Hill for months, arranged thirty thousand phone calls to thirty-two lawmakers' offices. The president of the United Auto Workers threatened to back Ralph Nader in the presidential race rather than Vice President Al Gore.[34] But in the final days before the House vote, the labor pressure backfired. Members of the Congressional Black Caucus grumbled about disruptive union vigils outside their district offices.[35] Clinton, meanwhile, worked the phones, wheeling and dealing to corral stragglers. In the end, PNTR passed 237–197, with seventy-three Democrats in support. That was a handful more Democrats than the White House figured would be needed, but roughly one-third fewer than the number who had supported NAFTA seven years earlier.[36]

Clinton appeared in the Rose Garden after the vote, praising it as "historic" and crediting it with advancing US economic growth, Chinese reform, and world peace. He revisited the arguments that he had made for months, with an eye on the upcoming Senate vote, which ultimately proved to be an easy win. Granting China normal trade relations would make it easier to sell American chemicals, computers, and farm goods to Chinese customers. It would promote the rule of law in China. "And 10 years from now we will look back on this day and be glad we did this," Clinton said.[37]

Don't leave the little guys out

A few prescient voices warned that it all seemed too good to be true. In *The Washington Post*, columnist Robert Samuelson, a respected and clear-eyed economic commentator, called the administration's sales pitch overstated. The US economy was chugging along fast enough to withstand new competition from China. But when the inevitable recession eventually arrived, a ballooning US-China trade deficit would make an irresistible political target. Plus, claims about the deal's political benefits had become excessive. "It has been merchandised so aggressively and loaded with such extravagant expectations—of how trade can democratize China and pacify our relations—that it seems doomed to disappoint," Samuelson wrote.[38]

The erosion in Democratic support for open trade, meanwhile, reflected a trend that Clinton had noted earlier in the year. Making his final appearance as president at the annual meeting of the World Economic Forum in Davos, he defended globalization against criticism that it ran roughshod over labor and environmental concerns or shortchanged developing nations.

Memories of the debacle in Seattle two months earlier were still fresh. More than one thousand protesters, some from the same groups that helped thwart the WTO meeting, trashed the Davos McDonald's before Clinton addressed an audience billed as the "1,000 most influential business leaders" in the world. The president repeated his call for a new round of global trade talks, but warned that protectionist sentiment in Congress was higher than ever.

Convincing the public to support further global integration, which "might require some of them, unlike most of us, to change what they do for a living, remains a challenge," Clinton acknowledged. Industrialized countries like the United States and developing nations needed to "ensure that the benefits of trade flow widely to workers and families." It was imperative that "the poor and those hard hit by changes are not left behind."

The unemployment rate in the US had been dropping more or less consistently since Clinton became president and was now just 4 percent. The federal budget, after years of red ink, was in surplus. "We have never had an expansion this long, and if we can't help our people now, we will never get around to it," he said.

Despite the boom, there remained parts of the United States, including rural areas, that were not sharing in the new prosperity. And they would be used, Clinton warned, as symbols of globalization's shortcomings by those who opposed greater global integration.

Few leaders spoke of globalization's multiple facets as fluently as Clinton. Few could explain how the interests of rich and poor nations and rich and poor peoples were connected as persuasively. Gazing out at the assembled crowd in the Davos conference center, he saw the chief executives of multinational corporations such as Nike, Microsoft, Coca-Cola, and DuPont. Lavishly compensated men and women who had arrived at the snowy alpine retreat via private jets and sleek black sedans. Globalization had been good to these people, Clinton understood. But if more were not done for those less fortunate, popular support for additional trade liberalization would evaporate.

He had been born in a town of just six thousand people, Clinton reminded his audience, in a state with an income that was barely half of the national average. He knew how this bewildering new world looked to people who worked with their hands and lacked the educational pedigree of the Davos elite. "None of us who are fortunate can any longer help ourselves unless we are prepared to help our neighbors," the president said. "Don't leave the little guys out."[39]

91

The president's remarks appeared heartfelt. But he offered no new proposals to address the problems he identified.[40] And Clinton's time in the White House was nearing its end. Later that year, Governor George W. Bush of Texas, son of the forty-first president, won a narrow victory over Gore, which was not final until the Supreme Court halted a recount in Florida five weeks after Election Day.

The failure to help those least equipped to handle global competition was already having political consequences. In West Virginia, one of eleven states that voted for Bush after having gone for Clinton in 1996, Gore was hurt by the plight of local steelmakers, the president believed. Workers at Weirton Steel blamed the administration for failing to protect them from the cheap Russian and Asian products that flooded into the country during the Asian financial crisis.

"The evidence indicated that the company had failed for other reasons, but the Weirton workers thought otherwise and Al paid the price," the president said.[41] With the state's five electoral votes, Gore would have been president, even without Florida.

The spread of freedoms in China

The new Republican president was a free trade enthusiast, seeing it as the key to both economic prosperity and political liberty. In a post-election meeting, Clinton recognized a kindred spirit. Both men, he told his biographer, were "free traders."[42] But Bush had criticized the Democrats for being soft on China, which he called "a strategic competitor" of the United States. The campaign rhetoric left Chinese leaders "deeply suspicious" that the incoming administration would treat China as its principal global adversary.[43]

Still, Bush backed China's WTO membership and was more explicit than Clinton in describing its likely political consequences. "My belief is by trading with an entrepreneurial class in China it will enhance the spread of freedoms in China," Bush said during the congressional debate.[44]

Unexpectedly, China became the new administration's first foreign policy crisis. Bush had been president for just ten weeks when a US EP-3 spy plane collided with a Chinese military jet over China's

Hainan Island. The US aircraft was badly damaged but managed to make an emergency landing at a Chinese military airfield. The pilot of the Chinese interceptor was killed. After the US government said it was "very sorry" for what had occurred, the twenty-four American crew members—after being detained for ten days—were released.

Though the episode only inflamed Chinese doubts about US intentions, it did nothing to disrupt economic ties. In a speech one month later, Bush detailed his "prosperity agenda" of tax cuts, education reform, skilled immigration, and trade agreements. He endorsed his predecessor's call for a new global negotiation and asked Congress to grant him the fast-track authority it had denied Clinton. Bush had expansive plans. Already, talks were underway on a free trade area of the Americas, which would spread the NAFTA model from the Arctic Ocean to Cape Horn. He also wanted new deals with Chile and Singapore.[45]

Later that summer, the new chairman of the Senate Foreign Relations Committee led a quartet of senators to the Chinese seaside resort of Beidaihe for meetings with the country's top leaders. Joe Biden had planned to make the trip in 2000, but canceled forty-eight hours before his scheduled departure after his daughter's sports team unexpectedly made it to the state championship. The trip had been months in the planning, so he visited the Chinese embassy to break the news to China's ambassador in person. "I am going to report to Beijing exactly what you've told me, and I have a prediction, senator. Your stock is going to go up in Beijing. A father has no more important duty than to his children," the ambassador said. "China has been around for five thousand years. We'll still be around when you're ready to visit."[46]

One year later, Biden finally made it to China. He was received by President Jiang Zemin, Premier Zhu Rongji, and China's defense and foreign ministers for talks about China's foreign sales of missile technology, the status of Taiwan, and prospects for developing the rule of law. This was Biden's first trip to China since his 1979 meeting with Deng Xiaoping, and he was amazed by how much had changed. On that earlier trip, at the beginning of the reform-and-opening era, everyone he met had worn the same standard-issue "Mao suit"; there were no private cars; and electricity supplies were limited. Now, cities like Beijing and Shanghai were full of traffic, skyscrapers, and blazing lights. "This was a totally different China. He was blown away," Frank Jannuzi, the Senate aide who accompanied Biden, said later.

Biden also wanted to see the part of China that prosperity had not yet reached. Jannuzi asked the US embassy to identify "a rural, hot, poor, dusty village" that the lawmakers could visit. With its unpaved roads and simple stone buildings, Yanzikou, about thirty miles outside the capital, fit the bill. Biden heard from villagers about local elections that, once every three years, chose a leader from among candidates approved by the Communist Party. After he and his Senate colleagues toured a local Catholic church, Biden said China needed to improve its human rights record. "The fair treatment of human beings is a universal right," he said. "China has to understand that to partake of the benefits of a global economy, they have to adopt the norms."[47]

Biden came away from the trip convinced that Chinese leaders, especially Zhu, the premier, were committed to economic reforms. But he was clear-eyed about the challenges that lay ahead. "Biden said to me, 'They've made remarkable progress, but they've got a long way to go. If I could be president of any country in the world, it wouldn't be China. That job's too hard,'" Jannuzi said.

Then, less than one month after Biden arrived home, on a crystal-line September morning, everything changed. The terrorist attack by al-Qaeda hit symbols of American financial power and governance, leaving 2,977 dead. Chinese President Jiang Zemin, watching the attacks on television, reportedly told aides that the coming anti-terror fight could unite the United States and China just as the joint stand against the Soviet Union had brought them together in the 1980s. Bush, meanwhile, impressed the Chinese leadership by attending the annual Asia-Pacific Economic Cooperation (APEC) leaders' summit, held that year in Shanghai, just a few weeks later.[48]

Al-Qaeda's lethal campaign showcased a previously unappreciated dark side of globalization. But it also jolted the US push for a new round of global trade talks. Two months after the attacks, amid extraordinary security precautions, diplomats meeting in the Qatari capital of Doha agreed to launch a new negotiation. The initiative would formally be known as the Doha Development Round, a nod to the notion that helping poor nations grow prosperous could starve terrorism of the deprivation that was believed to fuel it. "September 11 focused all our minds," said Pascal Lamy, Europe's top negotiator.[49]

The trade ministers in Doha succeeded where their predecessors in Seattle had failed. But the obstacles to a new agreement, including US resistance to reducing its agricultural subsidies, were daunting. The diplomats set an aggressive three-year schedule. Few expected them to meet it.

The worst bloodletting since the Great Depression

Bush was a strong believer in the virtues of unfettered trade. But he was also a politician. During the 2000 campaign, he had promised voters in West Virginia protection against the surge of imported steel that they had blamed on Bill Clinton and Al Gore. Now in office, it was time to deliver. Steel prices were at a twenty-year low and almost one-third of the US industry was in bankruptcy as Bush mulled his options. In March 2002, he imposed tariffs of up to 30 percent on steel imports in a bid to provide domestic producers time to restructure and become more efficient.

Tariffs were anathema to a free trader like Bush. In the nineteenth century, the US government raised most of its money by placing tariffs on imported goods. Tariff advocates supported them as a way to protect American companies by raising the cost of foreign products. But after the Hawley–Smoot Tariff of 1930 exacerbated the Great Depression, such trade restrictions fell out of favor. The 1947 General Agreement on Tariffs and Trade (GATT), the precursor to the WTO, began the process of lowering tariffs on a wide array of goods.[50] Over the ensuing decades, an elite consensus arose that the costs of tariffs to consumers of imported products outweighed the benefits for protected industries.

Robert Zoellick, the president's chief trade negotiator, tried to justify the president's decision to make an exception for the steel industry. "We all know that financial and information markets move with lightning speed. But some traditional manufacturing industries and the communities that depend on them cannot. Some may need a breathing space to regain competitiveness. And this includes the steel industry," Zoellick told reporters.[51]

Breathing space was a nice idea. But it was one with little relation to the steel industry's problems. Steelmakers traditionally were among the most protected companies in the United States. Their presence in states such as Ohio and Pennsylvania, which weighed heavily in Electoral College votes during presidential election years, gave them the political clout needed to routinely gain Washington's help.

Yet despite frequent rounds of tariff protection, the domestic steel industry continued to lag its foreign rivals in embracing modern technologies. There was little reason to think Bush's action would cause it to break with that pattern. New tariffs, while doing little to save chronically embattled US steel mills and steelworkers, would raise costs for carmakers and other manufacturers that used steel and employed millions more workers, thus leaving the country worse off.

Within the White House, Bush aides were split. His economic advisers, reflecting the president's laissez-faire instincts, opposed the tariffs. But Bush and his political team saw two reasons to act, according to Karl Rove, the president's senior adviser and chief campaign strategist.

Steel was a vital industry in states such as Ohio, Pennsylvania, and West Virginia that would be critical to Republican hopes in the November congressional elections. The president's chances of obtaining congressional support for fast-track negotiating authority and for several trade deals, including with South Korea, would be hurt if he failed to enforce existing US trade laws that prohibited foreign companies from "dumping" or selling products below their cost of production. The steel tariffs had been recommended by the International Trade Commission, which found that an import surge was damaging domestic producers.

"Our choice was being pure on this issue or enforcing the laws as written on the books and using it to gain credibility and votes on [fast track] and all these other agreements," Rove said.[52]

When reporters pressed Zoellick on the tariffs, he echoed Clinton on the imperative to preserve the domestic consensus that supported trade liberalization. Bush had long favored expanding US trade and had an extensive roster of potential deals he hoped Congress would approve. But public sentiment was souring. Amid the post-9/11 recession, more than 40 percent of Americans now viewed trade as a threat to the economy, up from 35 percent just a few years earlier, according to Gallup.[53]

Tariffs might offend economists. They might throw sand in the gears of an otherwise-efficient market economy. But for the moment, they were the price of keeping the public behind the administration's broader goals. "It's our strong belief that if we're going to promote a free trade agenda around the world and have support for it at home, we have to be willing to use the rules available internationally and domestically to help those industries that have really gotten flattened," said Zoellick.[54]

Bush put a three-year limit on the tariffs. But less than two years later, in December 2003, the WTO ruled them illegal, concluding that they exceeded rules allowing countries to defend themselves against sudden import surges. The WTO decision authorized retaliation by the European Union, which drew up plans to hit politically important industries in the United States, including by reducing imports of Florida oranges.[55] The US steel industry was far from good health, but the president lifted the protections that he had billed as necessary for its restructuring.

That summer, Bush called the economic team to his ranch in Crawford, Texas, to discuss the economy and mounting concerns about China. More than 2.5 million jobs had disappeared since his inauguration, vaporized by the brief post-9/11 recession and subsequent "jobless recovery." Among the culprits, many Americans believed, were rising volumes of Chinese imports.

Before leaving Washington for Crawford's triple-digit August heat, Treasury Secretary John Snow, a former railroad CEO with limited financial-markets expertise, called economist Fred Bergsten and asked for a quick tutorial on China's currency policy. Bergsten, the head of a Washington think tank, had testified recently before a House committee that the Chinese currency was artificially undervalued against the dollar. By intervening in foreign exchange markets, the Chinese were keeping the yuan below its fair market value. The result was to effectively put Chinese goods on sale, making them less expensive than American alternatives. Many American manufacturers complained they couldn't compete.

"One morning at 8 a.m., I had a call at home from John Snow when he was secretary of the treasury. And he said, 'Fred, I was in the Midwest yesterday going around defending Bush's tax program. And all anybody wanted to talk about was the Chinese currency. Can you come and tell me about that and what we ought to do about it?'" Bergsten recalled. "I stayed with him for four consecutive hours."[56]

The treasury secretary spent so much time on the nuances of the currency issue because of the complaints the administration was fielding from the business community. In Chestertown, Maryland, Dick Goodall, the CEO of Dixon Valve, faced unrelenting pressure from Chinese competition. The company for nearly a century had produced metal fittings and couplings that connected hoses to jackhammers, oil rigs, and tanker trucks. But now, Chinese companies were able to make competing products, often using designs copied from Dixon, and ship them thousands of miles to the United States for less than Goodall spent on his raw materials.

"There are subsidies going on over there or monetary manipulation," Goodall said. "What happens if Dixon Valve, in a little town like Chestertown, isn't here anymore? What if management decides it just isn't worth it anymore?" he asks. "What happens to the hundreds of people if they lose their jobs?"[57]

Questions about China's compliance with its WTO commitments were becoming too large to ignore. At the end of 2003, the office of Bush's trade negotiator warned that China's WTO implementation efforts had lost "a significant amount of momentum" and, in many areas, fell "far short" of its commitments.[58]

Among the US complaints was China's failure to provide an annual notification of the government subsidies it provided numerous industries, a concern that would ultimately prove more enduring than the question of currency valuation. WTO rules prohibited subsidies that were contingent on a company's exports or that favored domestic over imported products.[59] But China found ways to provide a wide range of special assistance to numerous Chinese manufacturers, including free or discounted land, cut-rate financing, and infrastructure improvements. Most of these benefits, which often encouraged excessive industrial production that weighed on global markets, were provided by public bodies at the provincial and local level. Yet China had failed to notify the WTO of any of this spending. It would be fifteen years before the first such reports made their way from Beijing to Geneva.[60] The omission reflected a pattern: The Chinese government generally complied with WTO rules that included specific numerical requirements. But the authorities in Beijing earned a reputation for stretching less precise rules to the breaking point.

Makers of industrial parts, gift wrapping, machine tools, and furniture trooped to Capitol Hill, pleading for lawmakers to act against what they called China's unfair trade practices. "Since 1997 we have closed more than 200 textile plants in the United States and lost more than 210,000 textile jobs. It is the worst bloodletting for this industry since the Great Depression. In fact, I can give you a whole list of companies that made it through the Great Depression, but have not survived the last years," said Cass Johnson, senior vice president from the American Textile Manufacturers Institute.[61]

Bush dispatched Snow to Beijing a few weeks later. The Chinese had pegged the yuan to the dollar since 1994. They had won plaudits, from the United States and other trading partners, for holding the currency steady during the Asian financial crisis when other countries cheapened theirs to boost their exports. But many economists now believed the yuan would rise in value by 30 percent or more if Chinese authorities allowed it to float freely, which would shrink the yawning trade deficit and ease the pressure on American industry. "It would have big implications if we could ever get China on a path to move, where over time the currency floated up," Snow said.[62]

When Snow met with Chinese President Hu Jintao and Prime Minister Wen Jiabao, he gave them a "sort of Economics 101 on currencies," trying to convince them that it was in China's interest to change. Pegging the yuan to the dollar made it more expensive for Chinese consumers to buy American products, effectively depressing living standards. It also raised the risk of inflation, the economic malady that had helped spark the Tiananmen Square protests. But the Chinese were unmoved. Leaving the yuan at the mercy of traders could destabilize China's fragile banking system and cause additional layoffs when tens of millions of workers at state-owned factories already were losing their jobs.

Press reaction also was skeptical. *The Economist* called the administration's arguments "misleading." *The New York Times* editorialized: "There are valid reasons for Beijing to fear a surging currency."[63] In their meetings with Snow, Chinese leaders agreed that they would eventually move toward a market-based system.

Almost two years later, in July 2005, China finally acted. The authorities lifted the yuan's value by just 2 percent, not enough to have a meaningful impact upon the politically sensitive trade deficit. But they also loosened the peg to the dollar, allowing the yuan to trade in a slightly wider band, which hinted at a greater revaluation ahead.[64] Washington welcomed it as a meaningful first step. But on Capitol Hill, Sens. Chuck Schumer (D-NY) and Lindsey Graham (R-SC) proposed legislation that would apply a 27.5 percent tariff on all Chinese imports unless Beijing allowed the yuan to float free. The lawmakers thought their "bad cop" act might help the administration's "good cop" make further headway with Beijing. But Snow feared the Chinese would simply call the lawmakers' bluff, leading to a costly trade war.

To head off a clash, Snow invited Schumer and Graham to dinner at Mr. K's, a popular Chinese restaurant located on the capital's lobbying avenue, K Street. Snow enlisted as an ally Alan Greenspan, the chairman of the Federal Reserve, whose reputation was then at its peak. "Alan, we've got to stop this," he told Greenspan on the phone beforehand. "We've got to give them a way to back down from this because they are way out on a limb here."

After entering the restaurant via a back door, the four men gathered in a private room and began chatting over appetizers. Then Snow asked Greenspan to describe the likely outcome if the Schumer–Graham bill became law. "We'll rue that day. It will be the collapse of the equity markets, the collapse of the bond markets. It would send shivers through the financial markets around the world. One of you will go down in history as Smoot and one of you will go down in history as Hawley," Greenspan said, alluding to the authors of the 1930 tariff that economists blamed for exacerbating the Great Depression.

Having conjured up the specter of financial ruin, however overstated, Snow then paved an exit ramp for the lawmakers. He asked Olin Wethington, a Treasury representative at the US embassy in Beijing, to arrange meetings for them with Zhou Xiaochuan, China's central bank governor, and Jin Renqing, the finance minister. Graham and Schumer spent a week touring Beijing, Shanghai, and Hong Kong before announcing on March 28, 2006, that they would delay a vote on their bill. To Snow, the lawmakers' decision to recognize economic reality was "statesmanlike," but the trade imbalance would only get worse.[65]

The Bush administration's handling of the yuan issue illustrated the shortcomings of Washington's approach to China and the complexity of the challenge. During the first decade of China's WTO membership, the undervalued yuan provided real benefits to Chinese exporters and caused real damage to American manufacturers.

But the United States was slow to press for real change, and its public statements on the issue also ignored the trade-offs that were involved. Convincing the Chinese to allow the yuan to rise in value would certainly have helped American companies. But by making imported Chinese products more expensive, it also would have undeniably hurt American consumers.

Our assumptions had been misplaced

The yuan was far from the only economic irritant between the United States and China. In June 2005, the state-owned China National Offshore Oil Corporation (CNOOC) made an unsolicited $18.5 billion takeover bid for Unocal, an American oil major. The offer came two months after Unocal had agreed to be acquired by Chevron for $16.5 billion. While Unocal shareholders could be forgiven for preferring the higher sales price, the CNOOC bid prompted months of controversy in Washington.

Monitoring the fallout in Beijing was Matt Pottinger, a twenty-seven-year-old reporter for *The Wall Street Journal*. When CNOOC ultimately bowed to what it called "unprecedented political opposition" in Washington and abandoned its takeover bid, Pottinger's account landed on the *Journal*'s front page.[66] The boardroom drama was one of the last stories he covered in China, as his seven years there drew to an unexpected close.

Like Draper, Pottinger had a larger-than-life father who had succeeded in multiple careers. J. Stanley Pottinger, a Harvard graduate, ran the Department of Health, Education, and Welfare's civil rights office in the Nixon administration before becoming assistant attorney general for civil rights at the Justice Department. "It was such a bizarre balancing act, trying to do liberal work in a conservative administration," he said later.[67]

After leaving government, he practiced law and went to Wall Street, where he opened a boutique investment bank that made him millions of dollars in the 1980s. That windfall gave him the freedom to pursue his dream of becoming a writer. He penned several novels, landing on the bestseller list with his first offering. During an unrelated 1976 federal court case, J. Stanley Pottinger also managed to deduce that FBI official Mark Felt had been "Deep Throat"—the government source who helped Bob Woodward and Carl Bernstein bring down Richard Nixon. The elder Pottinger earned Woodward's gratitude by keeping the explosive secret to himself for nearly thirty years.[68]

His son Matt first became interested in China in high school, when a planned stint as an exchange student was derailed by the violent crackdown at Tiananmen Square. Stranded stateside, he spent the summer of 1989 reading *The Boston Globe* to keep tabs on what was happening in China. Those stories sparked an interest in news, which he nurtured as a student at the University of Massachusetts in Amherst. Pottinger spent his junior year at Beijing Normal University, polishing his Mandarin and devoting most weekends and breaks to traveling by train all over China. Sometimes alone, sometimes with classmates, he roamed to Harbin in the northeast, Kunming near the border with Vietnam, and central Wuhan. In those pre-internet days, he devoured copies of *Time*, *Newsweek*, or *Far Eastern Economic Review*, many missing pages that government censors had excised by hand. "That got me hooked on the idea of becoming a journalist," Pottinger said.[69]

He graduated with a degree in Chinese studies and began his journalism career at States News Service, a perennially cash-strapped outfit that served as journalistic boot camp for generations of Washington reporters. States reliably produced talent for papers like *The Washington Post* and *The New York Times*. But it was also the sort of place where reporters rushed to the bank each Friday to cash their $300 paychecks, knowing that the last one to reach the teller might end up empty-handed.

At States, Pottinger unearthed local angles on Washington news for papers in Arkansas and New Jersey. He covered congressional hearings and tracked regulatory developments at the Federal Communications Commission, earning bylines in publications as varied as the *Chicago Tribune* and *The Hollywood Reporter*. He did not consider himself a business journalist. But an article he wrote about toilet maker American Standard's China business helped him land a job with the Reuters news agency in Beijing.

He started in the summer of 1998, shortly after Clinton's visit. As a junior reporter, he was thrown into every type of story. He wrote about the WTO negotiations, business developments, and the spread of technology, including cell phones and the internet. It was a fabulous time to have a front-row seat to China's transformation. Tens of millions of rural Chinese were flocking into the cities, drawn by the ready availability of factory work. The entire country seemed alive with promise and possibility. At first, like so many foreign observers, Pottinger was optimistic that expectations of continued liberalization would be born out.

Many foreign publications still considered China a hardship post for reporters. But that label was becoming outdated. Technically, foreign journalists required government approval to make reporting trips outside the capital. But it was not difficult to get around those rules. Journalists also were no longer required to live in diplomatic housing compounds in the center of the capital. "China at that time was like 'the good China.' It was China becoming part of the global economy. Now, certainly at the *Journal*, because we were covering economics, I always felt that the government was like, 'Well, you guys do your thing. You're not talking to dissidents like the bad *New York Times*.' And so we had a fair amount of freedom. The story was, frankly, pretty optimistic at that point," said Jonathan Kaufman of *The Wall Street Journal*, the editor who hired Pottinger in 2001.[70]

In the close-knit circle of foreign reporters in China, meanwhile, Pottinger was well-liked. He quickly made his mark at the business paper of record. When he called the office, the local staff members who answered the phone often would not recognize him as American. His pronunciation was that good. He also impressed Kaufman, the *Journal*'s Beijing-based China bureau chief, as having a classic journalistic curiosity and drive.

On one occasion, amid rumors that a Chinese businessman had been arrested in Hong Kong, reporters and editors were on a meandering conference call, puzzling over what had happened. As is often the case with breaking news, the journalists were trading more speculation than fact. Exasperated, Pottinger left the bureau in the middle of the call and walked several blocks to the man's office, where he was told the executive no longer worked for the firm, effectively confirming that the man had been detained.

Within a few years, the hopeful mood began to ebb. For Pottinger, it was a pair of high-profile assignments in 2003 that reshaped his view of the Chinese system. The first involved a flu-like illness that had appeared in southern China late the previous year. The Chinese government initially played down its severity and disclosed little real-time information. State-run media ignored the situation, and when unofficial accounts surfaced on the internet, government officials insisted they had the situation under control.

But in March, the World Health Organization issued a rare global alert, warning of an outbreak of a "severe form of pneumonia."[71] At the end of the month, Pottinger wrote a front-page story describing Hong Kong "as a city suddenly gripped with fear."[72] Residents began wearing surgical masks. The Rolling Stones canceled a concert, and business travelers vanished. With the government mum, no one was sure how the disease spread or how it could be stopped. He visited southern China's wild-animal markets, where exotic creatures lived and died in close contact with people, allowing germs to spread between species.[73]

As the outbreak of severe acute respiratory syndrome (SARS) filled hospitals, the government tried to cover up the truth. Pottinger profiled Jiang Yanyong, a prominent Chinese doctor, who revealed that official estimates of the number sickened were ludicrously low.[74] He also tracked a subsequent flare-up the following year, which was traced to a laboratory mishap in Beijing. A twenty-six-year-old graduate student working in the China Center for Disease Control's Institute of Virology, where

SARS-related research was conducted, was hospitalized after falling ill. A nurse at the hospital became infected, as did the graduate student's mother. A second lab researcher also developed SARS. In the *Journal*, Pottinger wrote that it cast "an uncomfortable spotlight on safety standards and practices at laboratories that handle the virus."[75]

Beijing's response to SARS revealed China's rulers to be incompetent as well as untrustworthy. More than 8,000 people worldwide ultimately were infected and 774 killed before the epidemic was brought under control. His reporting experiences convinced Pottinger that China had no intention of changing in the ways that many American policymakers expected.

Shortly before he left China, Pottinger was approached by a whistleblower with information about a uranium mining operation in China's far west that had been polluting a local river. The central government ordered the mine closed, but corrupt local officials quietly made a deal to reopen it for a tidy profit. When Pottinger met the whistleblower at a Beijing Starbucks, he was accosted by a thug working for the Ministry of State Security. "A guy who'd been hovering behind me punched me and said in English: 'You need to leave China now,'" Pottinger recalled.

It was not an isolated event. Chinese authorities quashed Hong Kong's freedoms, despite having promised to respect them for fifty years following the 1997 end of British colonial rule. Pottinger witnessed protesters in Tiananmen Square beaten by plainclothes police and was himself arrested just for doing his job.

In 2004, he was detained by local police in a village called Weicun, about a three-hour drive from Nanjing, where he had spent two days interviewing villagers about a planned steel mill. Developers had bought the farmers' land, promising to house them in modern apartments as part of the project. But when the development stalled amid a corruption probe, the apartment blocks were never built.

The policemen bundled Pottinger into an unmarked sedan and drove him to their rural headquarters for an interrogation that lasted several hours. During the commotion, he had stuffed his notebook inside the waistband of his pants. When the Chinese cops asked him to surrender his interview notes, he convinced them that they were back in his hotel room. They drove him there, and when Pottinger and his captors reached his room, he opened the door, rushed inside without turning on the lights, and swapped his Weicun notebook with another containing notes from an unrelated story. To the Chinese policemen, who could not read English, one page of notes looked the same as another. As they stood watch, Pottinger ripped the unrelated notes into pieces and flushed them down the toilet.

The Weicun steel project was a tale of local corruption. But it had global relevance. China already produced one-quarter of the world's entire steel output. The central government in Beijing, under fire from China's trading partners, was trying to curb construction of additional steelmaking capacity that would further depress global prices. But the architects of the Weicun plan found ways around the central government's edicts, dividing the project into twenty-two pieces and reclassifying state-bank construction loans as working capital. This local scandal highlighted how the nature of the Chinese system affected markets far from China.

Investors like Draper might think China was "free." Those who lived there knew better. By 2004, Pottinger had concluded "that China was not really going to converge with the liberal order in the way we hoped it might. The party was biding its time until it was powerful enough to influence the world on its own terms." Years later, Pottinger added: "My experiences reporting in 2004, 2005, convinced me that Beijing had the will and the tenacity and commitment to their system and to the single-party state. That basically this experiment of liberalization was really going to sort of peter out. I left Beijing with the feeling that this experiment was not working. That our assumptions had been misplaced."[76]

Finally, one afternoon, Pottinger walked into Kaufman's office in the Full Link Plaza in Beijing and closed the door. The bureau chief thought his star reporter was about to tell him of a job offer from a rival newspaper. Instead, Pottinger shocked him with word that he planned to join the US Marines.

He had seen an internet video of an Iraqi jihadist beheading an American hostage. A mixture of revulsion, fear, and anger started him thinking of getting in the fight rather than continuing to watch from the sidelines. Then, covering the US military relief effort during the

2004 Asian tsunami, Pottinger had something of an epiphany. The marines he saw helping desperate people in Thailand convinced him that, at its best, no other country could do what the US could.

The world faced a choice between free and non-free models, he felt. Seven years in China had left him with no illusions about authoritarianism. The American system was worth protecting from its enemies, foreign and domestic.

"What impresses you most, when you don't have them day to day, are the institutions that distinguish the US: the separation of powers, a free press, the right to vote, and a culture that values civic duty and service, to name but a few," he wrote in an essay in the *Journal*.[77]

In Washington, officials were preoccupied with other foreign challenges, in Iraq and Afghanistan. There was little appetite for a confrontation with China over its foot-dragging on economic reform. But the systemic shortcomings that were playing out in places like Weicun, and their implications for the global economy, were being felt in manufacturing communities across the American heartland.

By September 2005, Pottinger had made it official. Troubled by what he saw in China—and the mishandling of the US war in Iraq—he quit journalism and headed for officer candidate school in Quantico, Virginia. The thirty-one-year-old soon-to-be Marine lieutenant left China with mixed feelings. "It was a heady time. It was a fun time to be there," Pottinger said. "But lurking in the background was always this sense of menace."[78]

4

China Shock

Kent Greer went to work in the Goodyear tire plant in Obion County, Tennessee, in 1989. The work was hot and hard, and he was glad to have it. Hefting hundred-pound loads. The constant roar of machinery that could be heard and felt through earplugs. Wearing on his face and in his hair the soot from a substance called carbon black, which gave tires their distinctive color. Goodyear had been the rural county's largest employer since the plant opened in 1969, making car and truck tires for tens of millions of American vehicles. Every Corvette produced in the Chevrolet factory in Bowling Green, Kentucky, about two hundred miles away, rode on tires made by Greer and his coworkers.

Located on the outskirts of Union City, Goodyear's sprawling two-million-square-foot facility offered the best-paying jobs in the area. Men—and the workforce in those days was nearly all men—could graduate from high school and walk into a job that paid more than enough to support a family. By the early 2000s, annual pay of $80,000 was not impossible. With overtime, some workers pulled in $100,000 a year.

Obion County took its name from an Indian word meaning "many forks," a reference to the river that courses through this corner of the state. The county is part of a region in Kentucky and western Tennessee that Gen. Andrew Jackson purchased in 1818 from the Chickasaw nation. Among its early residents was Davy Crockett, who represented the local Scots-Irish settlers in the US House of Representatives. Those first arrivals were farmers from the Carolinas and Virginia. The coming of the railroad helped turn Obion into a manufacturing and commercial center.[1]

Greer had grown up in nearby South Fulton, a town of about 2,500 people that straddled the Kentucky-Tennessee state line. His mother worked in a local factory, and his father was a clerk in an electrical store. "Goodyear was the premium job for this area. I was tickled to death," he said. "I really felt like there was a personal connection between Goodyear and myself, that as long as I showed up for work and did what I was supposed to, and really cared, that Goodyear was going to reciprocate that same thing. They were going to pay me well; they were going to give me good benefits; and, they were going to look after my best interests also. I foolishly thought that for a long, long time."

What happened each day inside the Goodyear plant was the sort of basic manufacturing that China targeted in the first wave of its capitalist opening. As China prospered, the effects were felt in the American heartland. People in places like Obion County found themselves in intense competition with a rising manufacturing power, one that many Americans felt played dirty. China had assured American officials that it embraced the market. But its growth was fueled by generous state subsidies, an undervalued currency, and a low-wage labor force that enjoyed few rights.

Obion County's experience over the first decade of the twenty-first century showed the complexity of the economic changes roiling the American manufacturing belt. The federal government on two occasions formally concluded that Goodyear's travails were the result of foreign trade. But in truth, automation and decisions by both management and labor probably played as big a role as Chinese competition in killing off the local tire plant.

Yet parsing the specific causes of the job loss was almost beside the point, particularly for those affected. Whether because of technology, trade, or management blunders, almost two thousand relatively well-paid men and women were put out of work. Similar episodes played out in other manufacturing-dependent communities across a wide swath of the United States, even while the nation as a whole prospered. And the

US government did not so much struggle to respond to the challenge as fail to try.

China's economic rise began long before it joined the WTO in 2001. From almost nothing, trade between the United States and China began a steady climb in the late 1980s before quadrupling in the 1990s. In 2000, China's last full year outside the global trading body, the United States for the first time imported more than $100 billion worth of Chinese goods.

Then, trade really took off. By 2005, more than $243 billion worth of toys, furniture, electronics, and industrial parts made in China was showing up in American homes and factories. American exports to China also had increased, but by a much smaller amount, leaving the US with a yawning trade deficit that was to have far-reaching consequences.

As Beijing's WTO entry became a certainty, more than eighty corporations announced they were moving production from the United States to China. Among them were the US subsidiaries of companies such as Mattel, International Paper, General Electric, Motorola, and Rubbermaid. Lexmark, a printer manufacturer, closed its production site in Lexington, Kentucky, eliminating nine hundred jobs, and relocated the work to third-party contractors in China and Mexico.[2]

US investment in China had increased through the 1990s, rising especially quickly after Clinton delinked trade and human rights in 1994, according to Commerce Department figures. But once China joined the WTO, the flow of corporate cash more than doubled in just six years. No longer did CEOs thinking of making products in China to sell in the United States have to worry that an American president would ruin their plans by hiking tariffs on Chinese imports. By 2008, US companies were investing more in China in one year than they had during the entire 1990s.[3]

In blue-collar towns all over the country, in places like Dalton, Georgia; Lynchburg, Virginia; and Barnwell County, South Carolina, factories felt relentless pressure from low-wage Chinese competition—what economists David Autor, David Dorn, and Gordon Hanson dubbed the "China shock."[4] Their groundbreaking research highlighted the American jobs lost as China's economic reforms and its WTO entry put it at the center of global supply chains. Between 1999 and 2011, in what the trio called "a conservative lower bound" estimate, a total of 2.4 million US jobs were eliminated by Chinese competition.[5]

Measured against the 130 million or so Americans who were employed in that period, the losses did not seem crippling. But manufacturers and their suppliers tended to cluster in specific places. So a blow to one company often became a blow to all. "It wouldn't be a large number if it were evenly distributed. But it's not," Autor said of the resulting job destruction. "It's the linchpin employment in a limited number of places. And so that's why it's so much more devastating. These are very, very concentrated shocks."[6]

In Obion County alone, imports were responsible for the loss of hundreds of jobs at Plastech, which made injection-molded auto parts; Keneric, a maker of men's jackets; Crown Manufacturing, which made headgear; and Liggett, a producer of athletic uniforms, the US Labor Department concluded.[7] Over the first seven years of the century, the number of manufacturing businesses in the county stagnated before plunging by almost one-third, twice the statewide decline, as the Great Recession took hold in 2008. And while the state as a whole eventually recovered what it had lost and resumed growing, Obion County never did. As late as 2023, the number of county manufacturers remained stuck at its 2001 level.[8]

Incredible and inexcusable

Union City's Goodyear plant felt the pressure, as imports of Chinese passenger car tires between 2004 and 2008 tripled to more than forty-five million.[9] The Chinese tires sold in the United States for not much more than it cost American companies to buy the rubber and chemicals needed to produce theirs.[10] At least four US tire plants closed, including another Goodyear facility in Tyler, Texas.

In 2006, a retired Goodyear maintenance supervisor named Benny McGuire was elected mayor of Obion County. He had started work in the tire factory in February 1970 when they were still pouring concrete for the foundation. As his thirty-six years on the job drew to a close, he noticed that the managers Goodyear sent to Union City were fresh from closing other company plants. "I saw the handwriting on the wall. The union didn't believe me," he said.[11]

China was a competitor like none before it. But the Union City plant had other issues. As customers adopted just-in-time manufacturing systems, they wanted their tires delivered by truck rather than rail, a change that increased shipping costs. When demand was strong during the late 1990s boom, Goodyear ordered continuous twelve-hour shifts. The long days meant higher pay but led to fatigued workers getting injured more often and driving up workers' compensation claims. The local union, United Steelworkers Local 878, had a reputation for obstinacy, rejecting contract proposals that workers at other plants approved. Hiring in the Union City plant's final years was challenging: To find one new worker, the company typically had to screen seven applicants for drugs.[12] There was even a minor scandal once when a worker was caught selling pornographic tapes to coworkers. "Union City was a thorn in Goodyear's side," said Jerome Leath, who worked there for eleven years.[13]

Old-timers joked that the tiremaker's motto was "round, black, and out the back." In fact, the Union City workers took pride in their work. The plant delivered five million tires to customers like Ford and General Motors in 2006 without a single one being returned as defective.[14] Workers bragged that only Union City employees could get certain balky Goodyear machines to work. They "could take a problem tire that the company was struggling to get quality in and they could produce it in Union City. They could move that tire to Union City, and Union City could develop the tire and have it marketable in a short period of time," said Ricky Waggoner, president of USW Local 878.[15]

Goodyear invested what was needed to keep the Union City plant up to date. In 1998, the facility got new gear for the final finish and component preparation stage, the first step in a $60 million renovation. Factory modernization continued in each of the next two years, according to Goodyear securities filings.[16]

But industry trends were working against Union City. US producers were specializing in more complex tires that offered larger rim diameters, new technology, and features like greater fuel efficiency. The industry had "consciously moved away from producing simpler, less expensive designs" like those made in Union City.[17]

The recession that followed the terror attacks of September 11, 2001, only intensified the financial strain. With the unemployment rate near 6 percent, Americans bought fewer cars. In 2002, Goodyear laid off 450 workers in Union City. Bob Keegan, the company's president and chief operating officer, told Wall Street analysts the company had shifted some production to Latin America. "Increasing utilization of these low-cost supply sources in other parts of the world is going to be a very serious consideration as we try to offset some of the negative factors," he said.[18]

Six months later, the Union City body count rose to nine hundred; seven hundred mostly white-collar workers at Goodyear headquarters in Akron also received pink slips.[19] Jerome Leath was among those let go. He had been hired under an arrangement that paid him 70 percent of the union wage for three years before elevating him to full pay. When the layoff notice arrived, he was just one month shy of qualifying for a significant pay increase. Instead, he was given the option to move to another Goodyear factory in St. Mary's, Ohio, almost five hundred miles away, which he reluctantly accepted. It took eighteen months before he was called back to his old job in Union City. "The funny thing is, when I left that plant in Ohio, I told my wife one of two things are going to happen when we go home, I'm either going to get laid off again or they're going to close the plant," he said.

Goodyear faced unrelenting cost pressures. The company's stock, which had traded around seventy-five dollars per share in 1998, sank below five dollars. Keegan launched a turnaround effort in 2003, rethinking the company's cost structure, brand strategy, product development cycle, and manufacturing footprint.[20] As management tightened the purse strings, workers in 2006 went on strike over their health care coverage and job security. After an eighty-six-day walkout, the union and Goodyear agreed on a new three-year contract, which delayed the closure of the plant in Tyler, Texas, until 2008.

The financial crisis that erupted that year made a tough situation even tougher. The US unemployment rate soared to 10 percent in the fall of 2009, its highest level in more than a quarter of a century. Goodyear's revenues shrank by nearly one-fifth while its losses ballooned to $375 million.[21] Keegan's annual letter to shareholders somehow struck a positive note: Despite the global crisis, Goodyear had successfully cut costs. The company was deliberately shrinking to survive. Since 2003, Goodyear had eliminated factory space that could produce thirty million tires each year. An additional fifteen to twenty million units of "high-cost capacity" were on the chopping block, as the company sought $1 billion in fresh savings, Keegan wrote.[22]

Goodyear was not alone in shrinking its domestic footprint. In 2004, Continental Tire closed a plant in Mayfield, Kentucky, eliminating almost one thousand jobs. Two years later, Continental shuttered its site in Charlotte, North Carolina, vaporizing an additional one thousand paychecks. Bridgestone that same year closed its 1,400-worker Oklahoma City facility. And Michelin in 2009 discontinued production at its BFGoodrich factory in Opelika, Alabama, sending nearly 1,100 men and women into unemployment.[23]

In April 2009, the United Steelworkers union, which represented the workers in Union City and most other Goodyear plants in North America, petitioned the federal government for help. Surging Chinese imports had disrupted the US market, the union said, leading Goodyear and its competitors to shutter plants and eliminate thousands of jobs. The steelworkers asked the Obama administration, in office just ninety days and battling a global financial meltdown, to cap Chinese shipments at their 2005 level of twenty-one million tires, less than half the 2009 volume.

The union's bid for help took advantage of a special safeguard provision that Charlene Barshefsky, Clinton's trade negotiator, had secured from China in the WTO deal. Unlike in conventional trade disputes, the union was not required to demonstrate that the Chinese had violated their trade commitments. The special safeguard measure allowed Washington to impose protective tariffs in response to any surge of Chinese imports that disrupted the US market. China had agreed that those terms would apply for twelve years, far longer than any other developing country had accepted.

The safeguard mechanism was designed to provide breathing room for US industries to adjust to a sudden influx of Chinese goods. It was also a central plank in the Clinton administration's sales pitch for the China trade deal. Officials such as Barshefsky repeatedly cited it as evidence that American workers would not be left undefended.

But when Chinese products started flooding American markets, the safeguard went unused. On four occasions, the International Trade Commission (ITC) concluded that imports of Chinese goods were rising so quickly that tariffs or quotas were needed to protect American companies. Each time, President George W. Bush turned it down, saying such measures would just raise prices for US consumers or encourage importers to buy from other foreign countries, leaving the economy as a whole worse off.[24]

None of the products at issue—such as wire coat hangers or waterwork fittings—were central to the US economy. But watching from her Washington law office, Barshefsky was baffled by the administration's stance. "It is both incredible and inexcusable to me that this tool was not used. We put the safeguards measure in the deal because of China's scale and because it had already become something of a manufacturing hub. China's low costs and large manpower reserves had already benefited from Asian capital and technology, making China *the* go-to country for low-end manufacturing," she said later.[25]

Bush had made a political calculation, she thought, that in the aftermath of 9/11, with wars raging in Afghanistan and Iraq, he could not afford another foreign headache. The diplomatic benefits of a cordial relationship with China outweighed the potential economic gains from confronting Beijing over its surging shipments to the United States. In a relationship as important and complex as that between Washington and Beijing, there was always a strategic consideration that took precedence over trade complaints. Along with seeking China's backing for its war on terror, the Bush administration was eager for Chinese help in curbing North Korea's nuclear weapons ambitions.

Bush aides were largely unsympathetic to the industries seeking a respite from Chinese competition. Robert Zoellick, Bush's trade negotiator, thought Barshefsky's argument was "overstated." Safeguard tariffs, in certain limited circumstances, might have some utility as a "safety valve," he thought. But the benefits were more political than economic and simply were not relevant in the specific cases brought to the ITC.

Zoellick also distinguished the handful of China-related cases from the Bush administration's controversial imposition of steel tariffs in 2002, which he said were needed to win congressional support for the president's trade agenda.

"I would not have pushed for the steel safeguards, except I needed the votes. That's the real world, though I also hoped the industry would use the breathing space to restructure," he said. "If I were going to get Congress to enact negotiating authority for all the trade agreements, I needed the votes to get started. The other safeguards were just pure protectionism."[26]

Zoellick also was mindful of the impact of any US tariff offensive on the political debate within China. The Chinese government did not approach its WTO commitments with a single mind. The vast internal restructuring that was required created bureaucratic winners and losers within the Chinese system. Inefficient state-owned enterprises resisted the job cuts and market reforms that were required. Provincial officials often disagreed with their counterparts in the central government over how to proceed while officials at the local level were protective of industries threatened by foreign competition.[27]

"Despite single-party rule, China's policy responses to WTO entry depend on much more than just the preferences of the top leadership," concluded Yeling Tan, the author of a comprehensive study of the Chinese implementation debate.[28]

Rather than impose safeguard tariffs, Washington at this time should have confronted Beijing with fresh demands for the swifter implementation of promised reforms, Zoellick said. China was doing a good job meeting quantitative targets, such as reducing tariffs. But it was falling short in areas where the requirements could not be specified numerically, such as with enforcement of intellectual property rights or its promise to stop requiring foreign companies to transfer their technology to Chinese partners as a condition of market entry. The United States also should have pressed China on its currency policies earlier than it did.

"After the first five or six years of China's WTO implementation, the US should have worked with other countries to push for additional [market] openings," Zoellick said. "We should have warned China of the risks of protectionist reactions to its rapidly growing exports. By urging additional steps, we would have strengthened the hand of Chinese reformers who favored opening and who were pushing against resistant ministries and local interests."[29]

China's progress toward becoming a genuine market economy began to notably slow by 2006, Zoellick's successor as trade negotiator, Susan Schwab, told Congress. US industry associations reported troubling signs that Chinese policymakers were growing less enthusiastic about "foreign participation in the economy." Some officials advocated a greater role for the state in directing the economy. Schwab warned that the United States and other trading nations would need to be on guard against China retreating from the progress it had made toward opening up its economy.[30]

The business community's complaints about China, of course, extended well beyond the half dozen safeguard cases that were brought to the federal government during this period. Yet affected companies were reluctant to file cases with the ITC. Preparing a petition was costly, time-consuming, and likely to invite Chinese government retaliation against the complainant. Plus, Bush had made clear his reluctance to impose tariffs. "So why bother?" said Scott Paul, who was a lobbyist for the AFL-CIO in 2004, when it sought action over China's lack of labor rights.[31]

The Steelworkers union hoped for a different outcome from Bush's successor, President Barack Obama. As the union's safeguard bid made its way through the Washington bureaucracy, Goodyear closed what it called "high-cost" plants in the Philippines and Amiens, France. The tiremaker also reduced production in Union City and offered buyouts to 550 workers "to align North American production capacity with weak industry demand."[32] In return for the exit packages, the union agreed to contractually designate the Union City plant as "unprotected," meaning it could be closed at any time.[33] It was an ominous sign.

In June 2009, the ITC voted 4–2 to recommend to Obama that he restrict Chinese tire imports. Unlike his predecessor, Obama accepted the panel's recommendation. With the economy in its worst shape since the 1930s, the administration was reluctant to sit idle while domestic manufacturers fought to survive. The president ordered three years of tariffs, starting at 35 percent and dropping to 30 percent and 25 percent in subsequent years.

The union cheered. But Goodyear insisted the measure was irrelevant. "The tariffs didn't have any material impact on our North American business," Keith Price, a Goodyear spokesman, said at the time. "The stuff coming in from China is primarily low end. We got out of that market years ago."[34]

Obama claimed the tariffs saved more than one thousand American jobs.[35] But tire sales mostly switched from Chinese companies to other foreign makers, not domestic manufacturers. An independent analysis concluded the protection had been expensive: Each job saved had cost taxpayers roughly $900,000 in higher tire prices. American farmers also lost about $1 billion in export sales after China retaliated by imposing its own tariffs on US chicken parts.[36] For Obama, the Goodyear case was the exception that proved the rule. Unlike Bush, he had used the safeguard tool. But even as he said, "We need to do more," this would be the only time he used it.[37] Far more often, he tried to enforce China's trade commitments by filing cases with the WTO, which took years and rarely led to dramatic change.

Goodyear's sales recovered in 2010 as the economy slowly healed. But the company remained unprofitable, losing $216 million that year. On February 10, 2011, the company announced plans to close Union City.

The move, scheduled to occur by year's end, was expected to produce annual savings of $80 million. It would also eliminate 1,900 jobs, sending Obion County's unemployment rate to nearly 17 percent in August. "All of our plants must be cost competitive and be able to demonstrate sustainable world-class productivity. That is not the case with this plant and, as a result, the market has moved beyond what the factory is able to build," CEO Richard J. Kramer said in a statement.

The problems this country has with trade

There had been signs for months, if not years, that the plant's days were numbered. But the news landed like a physical blow. Security guards walked workers to their lockers to collect their personal effects and then ushered them out. Greer was hurt and furious. He had once been such a company loyalist that he insisted on replacing the tires on a brand-new car after discovering they were not Goodyears. But Kramer's insinuation that Union City was a lost cause stung. When he was informed of the closure, Greer marched straight to his office and emailed the CEO. Labeling the plant unprofitable was "a lie," Greer wrote the boss. "I expected more out of Goodyear and its leadership."[38]

In his late forties, Greer was too young to retire. But with more than two decades of seniority, he was eligible to transfer to another Goodyear plant in Gadsden, Alabama, roughly three hundred miles away. "My wife and I made a decision. She's a schoolteacher. She had 21 years in the state of Tennessee. And so we decided she would stay here with the kids and work on her retirement while I was working on mine. And that way I wouldn't have to pull the kids out of school because one of them was going to be a senior when I first left. And the other one was going to be a freshman. So we made that decision. And yeah, it was tough," he said.

Greer worked twelve-hour shifts at the nearly century-old Gadsden plant. He typically labored for eleven straight days before piling into his car at 7 a.m. on Friday to begin the five-and-a-half-hour drive back to Union City. After enjoying a weekend with his wife and kids, he would leave for Alabama at 7 a.m. and clock in that night for another long shift. He kept that up for nine years, until Goodyear closed the Gadsden plant in 2020.

"I almost got where I could drive it blindfolded," Greer said. "There was a couple of people that would do the same thing. And there was people that would fall asleep and have wrecks on the way home. But that's just how it was."[39]

Goodyear initially planned to close the Union City plant by the end of 2011. But right after the July 4 break that year, it abruptly ceased operations. The relocation of manufacturing to other plants had gone faster than anticipated, Kramer said. Keith "Squizz" Roberson, who had spent thirty-two years at the plant, including a full quarter century on the overnight shift, received eight weeks' severance pay and then retired.

Roberson had hoped to make it to his fortieth anniversary at Goodyear, which he figured would be long enough to get both of his daughters through college. To supplement his pension checks, he took a job as a high school janitor making eight dollars an hour, less than one-third of his Goodyear pay. Some of his coworkers went back to farming soybeans, wheat, or corn.

When Roberson looked for a villain in the plant's closure, he found several. Over the years, the company had automated parts of the tire-making process, which cut jobs. Low-cost competition from China put pressure on the bottom line. And company executives were better compensated with each passing year. Kramer, who became CEO in April 2010, saw his total compensation increase from $10.1 million that year to $19.2 million in 2013.[40]

"Goodyear's trying to save every penny they can to fill their pockets. Why not ship it over to China for cheap labor?" Roberson said.

Some of Union City's work was shifted to a Goodyear plant in Chile, according to Waggoner, the head of the USW local and a thirty-three-year company veteran. But he placed the ultimate blame elsewhere. "I think Union City would still be open and so would Gadsden, were it not for the influx of Chinese tires. I'll just say it like that," Waggoner said.[41]

The Goodyear plant's demise caused lasting damage to the local economy. The shutdown eliminated roughly $2 million in payroll every week and put at risk an additional two to four thousand jobs at local tool-and-die shops and other suppliers. The county's manufacturing employment had been in a slow retreat for a decade before Goodyear pulled the plug. But the plant's demise accelerated the decline.

By 2017, one out of every three jobs that had existed in Obion County in 2001 would be gone. Three-quarters of the county's factory jobs vanished, a much steeper toll than the statewide decline of about one-third. And workers who found new jobs—like Kent Greer—ended up earning less. As late as 2014, the county's average manufacturing wage was lower than it had been in 2001. More than a decade after Goodyear closed, the county's jobless rate remained nearly a full percentage point higher than the statewide figure.[42]

Many factors contributed to the plant's ultimate demise. But since the federal government certified that trade policy was responsible, Goodyear workers qualified for special retraining assistance through the federal Trade Adjustment Assistance (TAA) program.

Jackie Starks, a longtime Goodyear employee, was among them. To reduce expenses, he and his wife, Lauree, sold their camper and a lakeside vacation property. He signed up for TAA benefits. But after attending welding school, he was unable to find a job. Finally after two years out of work, he was hired by a steel-wire producer in neighboring Kentucky for $10.25 an hour, less than half the $24.76 Goodyear had paid him.

"At one point, my 10-year-old son asked me if he should get a job. This was the first time I had been without work since I was 15 years old. It sucked. It takes a toll on you," Starks said. "If you could rewind it, and put everything back where it was, it would be awesome. But for that to happen, somebody's got to fix the problems this country has with trade."[43]

Winners and losers

President John F. Kennedy launched the government's main program to help workers who lost their jobs as a result of trade at the end of his first year in the White House. In a special message to Congress, Kennedy called for a new approach to trade policy. For nearly three decades, the United States had pursued a policy of reciprocal tariff cuts with its trading partners, negotiating levies on a product-by-product basis. In the rare cases where subsequent import surges harmed domestic manufacturers, the president could exercise an "escape clause" and impose protective measures.

Now, as part of his request for trade negotiating authority, Kennedy proposed active efforts to help workers find new jobs. The Trade Adjustment Assistance program would provide affected workers income support for one year, vocational training, and relocation aid. Only a tiny slice of the American workforce—less than one-half of 1 percent—would likely require the help, the president said. But such direct aid would be more efficient than protecting their jobs with tariffs, which would force everyone to pay more for imported goods.

"When considerations of national policy make it desirable to avoid higher tariffs, those injured by that competition should not be required to bear the full brunt of the impact," Kennedy told Congress. "Rather, the burden of economic adjustment should be borne in part by the Federal Government."[44]

TAA would encourage people to move to more productive parts of the economy rather than languish in declining industries girded by tariff walls. Kennedy had seen industrial decline in his home state of Massachusetts, where mill towns like Holyoke were steadily fading. Taxpayers had "an obligation," the president said, to help workers hurt by national policy, through no fault of their own.[45]

Kennedy's proposal swung George Meany, the head of the AFL-CIO, behind his request for trade negotiating powers, which passed the House over Republican opposition in June 1962.[46] The Senate followed suit in September with a bipartisan 78–8 margin, and Kennedy signed the bill on October 11, calling it "the most important" legislation affecting international economics since the Marshall Plan.[47] It was an early sign that presidents would value TAA as a bargaining chip to win support for further trade liberalization rather than as a mechanism for helping workers navigate an economic transition.

To obtain aid, a group of three or more workers, a union, or a state workforce official could petition the US Department of Labor for help. Once the government verified that imports were responsible for a layoff, benefits would flow. But the program soon proved a disappointment. From its inception until 1969, eighteen petitions were submitted on behalf of workers or entire industries. None were approved.[48] Over more than a quarter century, only 10 percent of eligible workers received benefits.[49] Amid complaints over a cumbersome application process, and continued failure to provide promised relief, the AFL-CIO by 1972 had given up on the program, withdrawing its support in congressional testimony.[50]

Union leaders rarely acknowledged it publicly, but they had little incentive to help workers transition into new jobs in other industries. For one thing, workers who left their current employer usually left their current union. John Sweeney, then-head of the AFL-CIO, once privately acknowledged his institutional imperative: "My job is not to care about future jobs for American workers. My job is to keep the jobs that my workers have now."[51]

Union leaders disparaged the meager TAA aid as "burial insurance." They feared that backing a program meant to take the sting out of new trade agreements would undermine their efforts to defeat them.[52] Lawmakers might feel free to back such deals if they believed affected workers would get help finding new jobs. Instead, union leaders argued that trade deals should proceed only if other countries agreed to raise their labor standards. If foreign workers could organize and bargain collectively, and if their governments required safe workplaces, the difference between US and foreign wages would narrow. And the argument for offshoring American jobs no longer would look so compelling.

Whatever its logic, labor's new approach seemed designed above all else to prevent further liberalization. After all, the United States could, on its own, establish programs to help American workers adjust to the new economy. Getting developing nations to improve labor conditions, which would erode their competitive advantage and thus slow their economic development, was a much heavier lift. Labor's shift also meant that TAA now had political problems in both parties.

"TAA is poorly funded, is hard to access, and reaches few displaced workers. In principle, Washington could improve it. In practice, however, Republicans don't like the program and organized labor sometimes scoffs at it," Alan Blinder, former vice chair of the Federal Reserve Board, wrote. ". . . Unions prefer jobs to 'welfare.' This attitude, however understandable, creates an insuperable barrier to creating a better policy. A pro-labor program that organized labor won't support will get nowhere politically."[53]

Lawmakers repeatedly tinkered with the program but refused to grapple with the nation's fundamental lack of adequate labor market protections. They relaxed eligibility criteria in 1974 and streamlined the application process. Demand for aid soared amid the early 1980s double-dip recession. But the growing tab led Congress to shift the emphasis from costly income support to retraining, which had a spotty track record. Additional changes were introduced in 1994, when a special program for workers hurt by NAFTA was added, and in 2002 when the Bush administration expanded coverage to workers who had been indirectly harmed by trade and added a health insurance tax credit.

The program's inadequacies were evident even before China joined the WTO. Less than two-thirds of workers displaced by trade found new jobs, and the fortunate ones who did saw their annual earnings shrink by 13 percent, according to a 2001 assessment.[54] After the 2002 reforms, one study concluded that the program cost more than it was worth.[55]

Touring a North Carolina community college in late 2003, Bush lampooned traditional job training. "I remember the old days in Texas. There would be job training programs—they really didn't care whether the jobs actually existed. All they want to do is make sure you're trained," the president said to laughter. "So you end up with, like, 1,500 hairdressers for 25 jobs."[56]

There was a grain of truth to the president's gibe. But the remark was also evidence that official Washington found it easier to find fault with efforts to help workers than to develop new measures that might prove more effective.

TAA, meanwhile, remained a mixed bag. When Goodyear closed in Union City, 1,900 workers were dumped simultaneously into the job market. Some were too old to start a new career. Others moved or took whatever work they could find. Even so, the number of people seeking training overwhelmed local schools. It took Jerome Leath more than a year to get accepted into a program to learn solar energy installation and electronics. "I lost a year sitting at home 'cuz the classes filled up so fast, I couldn't get in," he said. "You just had two thousand people get laid off. Well, the schools, the trade schools around here, weren't prepared for that. They couldn't handle that. We're rural. They were probably expecting, you know, thirty or forty kids a year."[57]

Leath eventually found a job, working as director of electrical and mechanical facilities at Discovery Park of America, a local tourist attraction. But twelve years after the plant closed, he still earned just half of his twenty-five-dollars-an-hour Goodyear salary.

He was one of the luckier ones. Overall, little more than one-third of the workers who completed TAA-funded training managed to find jobs in the field for which they had trained.[58] An evaluation funded by the US Labor Department concluded that workers were better off seeking new jobs on their own. There was "strong evidence" the program was particularly ineffective for older workers, who most needed the help, the report said.[59] A 2008 study concluded that TAA was "of dubious value in terms of helping displaced workers find new, well-paying employment opportunities." Workers retrained thanks to TAA ended up making 10 percent less in their new job than they would have if they had skipped the program entirely.[60]

"If you look at the evaluations, most of them show that the impacts on earnings and employment of dislocated workers—that there's no impact of the programs. It's just zero or close to it," said economist Burt Barnow, former director of the Office of Research and Evaluation in the Labor Department's Employment and Training Administration.[61]

To be sure, meeting dislocated workers' needs is difficult. Those left stranded by a factory that's moved offshore or closed typically cling to hopes of regaining their lost job or at least staying in the same occupation or industry. That is frequently not possible. But retraining programs often misfire, equipping workers for jobs that do not exist. Government forecasters have a poor record predicting future employment trends, Barnow said.

Presidents of both parties, along with mainstream economists, recognized that trade liberalization would create "winners" and "losers." In theory, the winners' gains would be so great that they would compensate the losers, leaving everyone better off. But by the mid-2000s, several years after global competition accelerated with China's economic rise, and despite growing public concern about the impact of globalization on blue-collar workers, the United States devoted a smaller share of its economic resources to education and training than it did at the time of the Berlin Wall's collapse.[62]

Retraining "is doable," said Robert Rubin, the former treasury secretary. "But it was never done well at the federal level."

Both Democratic and Republican administrations were guilty of devoting insufficient focus, effort, and cash to helping those affected by globalization transition to new jobs. But the Bush administration was also philosophically opposed to government intervention in the market, even in the face of China's unprecedented competitive challenge. In 2003, the president proposed spending $3.6 billion to create reemployment accounts of $3,000 for individual workers.[63] The plan was well-intentioned, but paltry; the total price tag was equivalent to about three weeks of Pentagon spending in Iraq that year, and the measure stalled after passing the House.[64] In mid-2006, Treasury Secretary Henry Paulson called for "thinking more creatively" about helping those hurt by globalization. Bush batted down that notion, calling existing programs adequate.[65]

"The United States has not had a coherent workforce development program since the GI Bill strategy. Instead, what we do is we administer programs, which end up being manipulated to score political points," said Howard Rosen, a former Democratic aide on the Joint Economic Committee who helped formulate the 2002 legislation.

Indeed, the GI Bill showed what was possible when a nation invested in its people. The legislation, which FDR signed into law two weeks after D-Day, was uncommonly generous to those who served in the wartime military. Veterans received free university educations, low-cost mortgages, business loans, and up to a year of unemployment benefits to ease their transition to civilian life. The Servicemen's Readjustment Act of 1944, the bill's formal name, was the rare initiative that truly reshaped US society. It helped avert a feared postwar depression and put millions of returning veterans on the path to a better life. Within seven years, eight million ex-soldiers were educated thanks to the GI Bill, more than doubling the number of college graduates in the United States and equipping the economy for its postwar boom.[66] For decades afterward, the GI Bill would stand as evidence that the US government was capable of transformative achievement.

In the globalization era, however, other advanced economies devoted far more time, attention, money, and effort to the fate of their workers. After controlling for differences in national unemployment rates, France and Germany spent roughly five times as much as the United States, according to a broad measure of active labor market programs, such as wage subsidies, job search assistance, and training.[67]

Tiny Denmark's workforce program was renowned for its ambition and effectiveness. Relative to the size of its economy, Denmark devotes twenty times as much as the United States to active labor market policies, such as individualized job counseling, retraining assistance, and work practice. Participation in these programs is mandatory for those receiving unemployment benefits, which themselves are remarkably generous and available for up to two years.[68]

Danish officials also repeatedly tested novel ideas in randomized controlled experiments, so that their policies would be "based on high-quality empirical evidence."[69] As a result, officials adjusted workforce initiatives to require jobless individuals to meet early and often with their government caseworkers.

There were myriad weaknesses in the US approach: chronic funding inadequacy, administrative shortcomings, and the failure to cover workers in the services sector, even as their jobs were outsourced to nations such as India. The economy, meanwhile, produced few new jobs in the first years of the twenty-first century. The bursting of the internet stock bubble in early 2000 was followed by the post-9/11 recession and a "jobless" recovery.

The market for blue-collar workers improved in 2003 as a housing boom took hold. But the boom became a bust and the surge in housing-related hiring proved unsustainable. Rapid growth in construction jobs only "masked" the erosion in manufacturing, which was especially devastating for older workers who lost their jobs amid China's rise.[70]

There were occasional proposals to do more to equip Americans for an economy that was continuously changing. In Washington, Democrats launched an initiative called the Hamilton Project, which was backed by Robert Rubin and then-Sen. Barack Obama of Illinois, who spoke at its April 2006 launch. "We have all known for some time that the forces of globalization have changed the rules of the game—how we work, how we prosper, how we compete with the rest of the world," Obama said. "Unfortunately, while the world has changed around us, Washington has been remarkably slow to adapt twenty-first century solutions for a twenty-first century economy."[71]

Addressing a Brookings Institution audience, Obama dismissed the standard political remedies. Workers in Illinois, he said, had lost their jobs, health care, and retirement security because of globalization. When they appealed for help, the government's response was insufficient. "How do we, in fact, deal with the losers in a globalized economy? There has been a tendency in the past for us to say, well, look, we have got to grow the pie, and we will retrain those who need retraining. But, in fact, we have never taken that side of the equation as seriously as we need to take it," Obama said.[72]

He was right. But little changed. Hamilton convened panels and issued policy papers, largely as a dress rehearsal for the next Democratic presidency. But with Republicans in control of Washington, the group's proposals got little traction.

Popular disquiet over the collateral damage from trade, however, was growing. In an April 2006 poll, only 30 percent of respondents agreed that global trade "mostly helps" American workers; 65 percent said it "mostly hurts."[73] Greater trade flows were benefiting the economy but also fueling income inequality. The Bush administration struggled to win congressional approval for new trade agreements, including a deal with six Central American nations that squeaked through the House on a 217–215 vote. The Doha Round of global trade talks, which had begun with high hopes after 9/11, was going nowhere.

The erosion of public support stirred a reaction from prominent supporters of global integration. Don Evans, the head of the Financial Services Forum, an industry trade group, commissioned three studies to make the case for continued trade liberalization. The analyses by Grant Aldonas, a former top Commerce Department official; Matthew Slaughter, who had worked for the Council of Economic Advisers in the Bush administration; and Robert Lawrence, a trade specialist at Harvard, recognized that the failure to address worker concerns about involuntary job loss threatened prospects for increasing economic openness. "You needed an answer both in terms of economic policy and in politics to the changes that were going on in the American economy," Aldonas said later. "Ultimately, what they feared was a backlash against globalization."[74]

While trade drew most of the public's attention, economists insisted that technology eliminated far more factory jobs. Some prominent globalization enthusiasts dismissed concerns about job loss as exaggerated or merely the predictable defense of self-interest by organized labor. But the forum report described the fears "as real, widespread and legitimate."[75]

In response, it recommended a major expansion of adjustment assistance to cover all workers, not just those displaced by trade. Workers at least forty-five years old would receive wage insurance, to make up 50 percent of their lost income if they took a new job for less than their original salary; continued health insurance coverage; the ability to withdraw money from their retirement accounts without penalty; and expanded retraining benefits. A new tax of 1.32 percent on all wages would pay for it.[76]

The proposal met the moment. But its estimated annual cost of $22 billion—more than twenty times TAA's budget—made it overly ambitious. If some Democrats on Capitol Hill were intrigued, the onset just weeks later of the global financial crisis obliterated any chance that the expensive new initiative might be pursued.

Later, as the Obama administration pursued a trade deal with South Korea, Congress finally expanded TAA to include service workers—but only for two years. Corporations that would benefit from the new agreement would do so forever. Workers who lost out would be helped only temporarily. Few policymakers took seriously what Rosen called "the downside" of globalization, the risk that untreated economic injuries could have material and unpredictable consequences.

"The issue wasn't that economists didn't understand there would be winners and losers. I think there was a feeling somehow that would work out very quickly. And indeed, if you think about political elites instead of economists, whether they're center right or center left, there wasn't a lot of attention to this problem," said Glenn Hubbard, who chaired Bush's Council of Economic Advisers. "We usually think of policies like technological change and globalization as speeding up the boat. But maybe we need to step back and make sure everybody is in the boat first. . . . We need to put more weight on making sure that everybody has an opportunity to benefit."[77]

They don't talk the way we do

Manufacturing employment had been declining in the United States for decades, both in total and as a percentage of all jobs. In 1979, about 19.5 million Americans clocked in each workday at a factory. By 2000, that number had fallen to 17.3 million, a gradual decline of 2.2 million jobs over twenty-one years. Then, starting in the summer of 2000, the number suddenly plunged by an additional 3 million in just three years.

A portion of the accelerated job loss between mid-2000 and mid-2003 was certainly caused by an eight-month recession that began in March 2001. Much of the decline, as always, could be attributed to the introduction of new technologies that enabled fewer workers to produce more goods. Productivity in US factories rose over the period as manufacturers learned amid the economic downturn to get by with fewer workers.

But it was hard to see what technological change could explain the large and abrupt drop in factory employment between 2000 and 2003. Some economists blamed the US trade deficit, which grew steadily over this period, ultimately reaching a historic high relative to the size of the economy in late 2005. Trade and globalization was "the major factor behind the large and swift decline of manufacturing employment in the 2000s," one expert concluded.[78]

These years ignited a fierce debate over the relative roles of trade and technology in reducing American factory employment. Economists generally agreed that technology was the dominant factor. But their public certitude was at odds with studies that produced a wide array of specific estimates: Trade was culpable for anywhere from just 12 percent of long-run factory job loss to more than half.[79] The conclusion of the China shock researchers that competition from Chinese imports was responsible for about one-quarter of the manufacturing job losses between 2000 and 2007 was probably as good an estimate as any.[80]

But the debate indulged a false dichotomy. Trade and technology are intrinsically related, not entirely distinct. Technological process permitted and indeed fueled globalization. Over the past few decades, as the United States has promoted lower tariffs and liberalized trade, it also has imported steadily rising volumes of industrial automation. Factory robots. Process controls. Motors and generators. Switchgears and switchboards. Tens of billions of dollars' worth of equipment designed to replace individual workers poured into the country each year from suppliers in Mexico, Germany, China, Canada, Japan, and the United Kingdom.

Was this technology at work or trade? It was both. And for those who lost their job as a result of these intertwined forces, the distinction between them blurred. These Americans cared less about the specific villain to blame and more about what they would do next. "Automation had a big negative impact on the Midwest. The China shock, for sure, exacerbated that by hitting some of the same people," said Simon Johnson, former chief economist of the International Monetary Fund.[81]

Joining the WTO turbocharged China's internal economic reforms and thus contributed to the economic growth that made it an increasingly formidable competitor. China, not the United States, had opened its market starting in 2001. But the country's emergence as a manufacturing power was having a greater-than-anticipated impact on the United States. And there was no separating the issue of China's WTO membership from its remarkable economic performance. "This economic expansion was a massive shock to world markets," wrote Douglas Irwin in his history of US trade policy.[82]

The Autor, Dorn, and Hanson conclusion that competition from China had destroyed up to 2.4 million American jobs was disputed by subsequent studies. Yes, there were job losses at US companies that directly competed with Chinese imports and at the companies that supplied those firms, these studies said. But taking into account "downstream" companies that benefited from the availability of less expensive Chinese products, from laptops and smartphones to industrial parts and components, trade with China actually led to a small increase in total US employment.

Between 1995 and 2011, increased US exports—made possible in part by cheaper parts and materials from China—resulted in a net increase of 1.7 million jobs, according to a paper by Robert Feenstra and Akira Sasahara.[83] Three-quarters of workers in a typical region enjoyed wage increases, thanks to trade with China, according to research by a team of economists from George Mason University, Columbia University, and the University of International Business and Economics in China.[84]

The gains from trade and globalization were spread across the entire country. Everyone benefited from cheaper goods and the ready availability of more capital for mortgages and business loans. But the losses were concentrated among particular groups—those with the least education and skills—and in particular places, those that were the most dependent upon manufacturing. Nationwide, about one in every ten

American workers was employed in a factory. In Obion County, the share was closer to one in four.

Even if three-quarters of the US workforce experienced higher wages, the one-quarter that did not lived in places like Obion County, where the median household income was about one-third lower than the national average. As economic conditions got tougher, the effects were felt in the quality of life. In the years after Goodyear closed, marriage rates in Obion County were below the state average, and divorce rates rose above it.[85] The local population shrunk by 6 percent between 2000 and 2016, as residents died off and the young felt little pull to remain. Of nine counties in the state's northwest corner, Obion's decline was the most pronounced.[86]

Nationwide, most of the impact from greater trade with China was felt by large multinational corporations. And even as they reduced their factory payrolls, they added non-manufacturing jobs. This reorganization by countless individual companies typically involved keeping their research, design, engineering, and corporate headquarters jobs in the United States while shifting the actual production of goods offshore.

Whether that was a good thing or a bad thing depended on where a person lived and what work they did. Residents of areas with large numbers of college graduates, which tended to be on the coasts, prospered. Those living in places where fewer people had gone to college suffered.[87] In those places, factories simply closed. Few new opportunities appeared. For workers without a college degree, the China shock meant declines in their inflation-adjusted weekly wages each year for almost a decade.[88]

The economist Janet Yellen headed Bill Clinton's Council of Economic Advisers as China prepared to enter the World Trade Organization and later served as Federal Reserve chair and secretary of the treasury. Like most in her profession, she had supported conventional trade liberalization. Years later, she looked back on the China shock with some regret.

"I don't think all the consequences were really anticipated. And you know there was the view that we have strong export industries. Yes, some import-competing industries are going to suffer losses. But this is going to be good for US exports, and they tend to have high-paying jobs and probably better jobs. But these are two distinct groups of people with different education and skills. And the winners in those industries are not the same people," she said. "I think a lot of people like me look back on this and think this was a development that actually resulted in a lot of people being made worse off in a way that has had a highly adverse effect on American society, broadly speaking, and politics."[89]

Indeed, between 2000 and 2007, the most common landing place for laid-off factory workers was in administration and support jobs. Those who found work in that sector saw their earnings drop by 22 percent, leaving them by the end of the period with paychecks that were 40 percent smaller than their counterparts who had been lucky enough to remain in manufacturing, according to one study.[90]

Trade, with China and other countries, undoubtedly created plenty of new American jobs. But it did not do the tiremakers of Union City much good when companies in Silicon Valley hired more software designers or banks in New York added quantitative analysts or investment advisers. "Chinese trade redistributed jobs from manufacturing in lower income areas to services in higher income, high human capital areas," another study concluded.[91]

The winners and losers in this round of globalization were different people in different places. Economists had always assumed that those who lost their jobs because of trade would move to new opportunities created by trade. But in the China shock years, that simply did not happen as often as it once had. Young or old, high earners or just getting by, Americans moved significantly less than in the past, according to a comprehensive review of Social Security Administration data. Economists attributed the change to any number of causes: an aging population, the rise of the two-income household, a convergence in regional wage rates, even a growing attachment to "home." The decline in mobility was especially pronounced after 2004.[92]

In Union City, Waggoner, the union official, was surprised by how few workers agreed to move to other Goodyear plants. An outsider might look at this part of Tennessee, see as many dollar stores as churches, and wonder at the hold it had on its residents. Local people, however, had put down deep roots, and family was the center of their lives. Keith Roberson had worked the punishing third shift for decades so he would be free in the afternoon to coach his daughters' softball and soccer teams. Jerome Leath said he knew he could make more money if he traveled. But he didn't want to be away from his young family.

The prospect of uprooting from rural Obion County to start over at another Goodyear facility in Danville, Virginia, or Topeka, Kansas, or Buffalo, New York, held little appeal. "They don't talk the way we do," Waggoner said, only half-kidding. "You got to get up at 4 a.m. and shovel snow. We don't do that here."[93]

Workers affected by rising import competition also had varying degrees of success moving from the shrinking manufacturing sector to the growing services sector. One 2023 study found that black workers more readily switched occupations than did white workers.

But this was not due to a lack of initiative on the part of white workers; it was the result of economic incentives and circumstances. Even before the China shock, black employees moved more frequently between jobs and thus were less likely to be attached to any single employer.[94] Black workers were also overrepresented in some of the fastest-growing services sectors, such as education and health services, and thus may have found them more attractive or welcoming.[95]

The factory jobs typically held by black workers, on average, paid less than what white workers earned. So blacks moving into a service industry job could do so without accepting as large a pay cut or perhaps any pay cut at all. The typical white factory worker, whose higher pay was linked to greater longevity on the job, was "less willing to shift into the non-manufacturing jobs that opened following the China shock," the study concluded. To do so would have meant a much lower salary.[96]

The implosion of local housing markets around the country also helped cement workers in place. Rural Tennessee did not experience the worst of the national housing bubble. In communities like Maricopa County, Arizona, or Miami-Dade County, Florida, home values plunged from their 2007 peak by more than half. But even in Obion County, falling prices made it harder for some homeowners to leave for better job prospects elsewhere. The typical home peaked in value in the spring of 2008 and then slid 12 percent by 2012.[97]

For the economy as a whole, rising imports were not the only problem. The job-creating export boom that Clinton and his successors had promised also failed to materialize.[98] Between 2000 and 2007, as China grew and grew, Americans' purchases of foreign goods increased more than twice as fast as their sales to foreign customers. Relative to the size of the economy, the US trade deficit had never been larger. And the flip side of this lopsided trade relationship was an unusual river of capital flowing not in the customary direction—from rich countries to poor ones—but in reverse.

China, and other developing countries, were financing Americans' way of life.

5

Sleepwalking Toward Disaster

After his second try for the White House crashed and burned, Joe Biden returned to the place where he was most at home as a public official: the United States Senate. Biden may have failed as a 2008 presidential candidate. But on Capitol Hill, he remained the powerful chairman of the Senate Foreign Relations Committee, filling a post held by lions of the Senate such as Henry Clay, John Sherman, Arthur Vandenberg, and J. William Fulbright. As he took up his gavel, among his first acts was to convene a searching examination of US policy toward China.

With each passing year, China loomed larger in American thinking. Trade between the two nations had more than tripled since China entered the WTO; American complaints about unfair Chinese trading practices grew just as quickly. Washington's early efforts to press Beijing to abide by global trade rules met with mixed success, presaging diplomatic strains that would only worsen. Yet even as they did, more American corporations designed their supply chains with China at the center. Little attention was paid to the risks if something were to go wrong.

The lopsided trade relationship had financial consequences. As China sold more goods to the United States than it bought, Beijing was left with a surplus of dollars that it invested mostly in Treasury securities, eventually becoming the largest single holder of US government debt. All that Chinese investment capital flooding into the United

States effectively kept borrowing costs low for Americans, which seemed like a good thing at the time. A river of money cycled among the United States, Europe, and China as Biden prepared to begin his inquiry into "United States–China relations in the era of globalization."[1]

From Capitol Hill to the White House, the United States was grappling with the implications of a more powerful China. Many experts still believed that integrating the Asian giant into the US-led global order would deliver the promised results. But in corners of the bureaucracy and the commentariat, the first tremors of a revisionist assessment of China's rise were emerging.

As Biden opened his first hearing in May 2008—expressing condolences for the victims of a massive earthquake in Sichuan Province—a cataclysmic financial crisis was building. Weeks earlier, the Federal Reserve had convened its first emergency meeting in thirty years to deal with the wobbly US economy. Chinese authorities, who had long been on the receiving end of American lectures about the virtues of the free market, noted that Washington's crisis response leaned heavily on state power.

The 2008 crisis—aggravated by torrents of global capital—revealed the risks that the United States had been running with its unbridled approach to globalization. The subsequent damage to household finances only compounded the sense of alienation and resentment that had been growing in blue-collar America since the China shock began.

It would be years before these grievances forced their way to the center of American politics. But when they did, they would challenge traditional thinking on both economics and foreign policy.

The China fantasy

Biden made his first visit to China in 1979, meeting Deng Xiaoping four months after the normalization of relations between the two nations. In Beijing's Great Hall of the People, Biden—one of five senators to make the trip—asked the Chinese leader if he would allow the United States to locate intelligence-gathering systems in China.[2] "You and other high officials in China have indicated repeatedly what we can or might consider doing to harness the polar bear," Biden told Deng, referring to the Soviet Union. ". . . Would China consider US monitoring stations on Chinese soil?"

Deng replied first by discussing prospects for US arms sales to China and then opening the door to a remarkable example of how Washington and Beijing could operationalize their common antipathy toward Moscow. "If you provide monitoring technology and the sovereignty belongs to China, China will accept. I will not do it if the US comes to China to set up monitoring bases. If China uses monitoring technology, we can provide you with intelligence and information," Deng said, according to a declassified State Department transcript.[3]

One year later, the US and China established two joint bases in the western Xinjiang region where electronic eavesdropping systems gathered data on Soviet nuclear and antiballistic missile launches. The listening posts in Korla and Qitai, located along ancient Silk Road caravan routes, were outfitted with American monitoring devices and staffed by Chinese technicians. The sensitive information gathered there helped Washington verify Soviet compliance with key arms control treaties.[4]

But by 2008, the USSR was gone and anti-Russian animus no longer bound the US and China. Biden hoped the hearings would illuminate prospects for fresh US-China cooperation now that economics had become the principal global battlefield. For nearly three hours, Biden and his colleagues quizzed a panel of scholars about China's trade practices and its global ambitions. Sen. Ben Cardin, a Maryland Democrat, complained that the Bush administration had been passive in handling China's undervalued currency. Republican Sen. George Voinovich said his Ohio constituents were "livid" about China. "They feel that China is walking all over us, that it is fixing its currency, that it's violating intellectual property rights, that its human rights record is very bad," he said. After listening to one expert describe the complexities involved in managing relations with China, Biden quipped: "You make me feel very good that I dropped out of the race."[5]

Turning serious, Biden said the United States and China had much to gain by cooperating and everything to lose by falling into confrontation. Some in Washington believed the two powers were destined for a great ideological clash. "In this view, the great struggle of our time will be between liberal democracies like the United States and autocracies like China and Russia," Biden said. "But I believe this view is mistaken."[6]

As George W. Bush neared the end of his second term, the US attitude toward China blended frustration and hope. In 2005, Robert Zoellick, the deputy secretary of state, had called on China to become a "responsible stakeholder" in the international system. After decades spent encouraging China to participate in organizations such as the WTO, IMF, and United Nations, Washington now wanted Beijing to work with the United States to shape the international system. Some voices even called for the United States and China to run the world as a "G2." US officials had sought to contain the Soviet Union during the Cold War, Zoellick noted in a major address. There would be no similar effort to quarantine China, even if it remained nominally Communist.

While careful to treat China with respect, Zoellick insisted that it abandon the mercantilist trade practices—such as brazenly copying and stealing American product designs—that were inflaming protectionism. "The United States will not be able to sustain an open international economic system—or domestic US support for such a system—without greater cooperation from China," he warned.[7]

Two years later, the United States filed a series of trade complaints with the WTO accusing China of using government subsidies to help its manufacturing firms battle foreign competitors and violating American companies' intellectual property rights through rampant counterfeiting. As Americans gobbled up ever-greater volumes of low-priced Chinese products, they also rediscovered that "you get what you pay for." Suspect Chinese ingredients were blamed in 2007 for lethal pet food that sickened and killed some cats and dogs. Health inspectors that same year found that toothpaste made in China contained a poisonous substance used in antifreeze; Chinese seafood was laced with potentially unhealthy antibiotics.[8]

In the global marketplace, the Chinese earned a reputation for fighting dirty. China's security services were mounting a comprehensive spying campaign to copy or steal blueprints, corporate plans, product formulas, and anything else that would allow it to narrow the gap with advanced countries. By 2007, one-third of the Federal Bureau of Investigation's economic espionage investigations were linked to China.[9]

Chinese spies vacuumed up military secrets about nuclear missiles and state-of-the-art Pentagon weaponry via the standard espionage campaigns that every great power conducted. But they also wormed their way into little-known industrial companies that represented the backbone of the US economy. Only two companies in the world, for example, could turn powdered metal into high-performance auto engine components. One was Metaldyne, an auto parts maker located about thirty-five miles west of Detroit. In 2004, Anne Lockwood, its former vice president for sales, cooked up a scheme with a Chinese metallurgist in the company's Shanghai office to steal Metaldyne's trade secrets and establish a Chinese company that could replace it as a key supplier for General Motors and Ford.

Lockwood had already left Metaldyne when she concocted the plot. But her husband, Michael Haehnel, still worked there. He used his position as a senior engineer to access "hundreds of confidential" computer files, which he copied to compact discs and gave to his wife. Lockwood and Fuping Liu, the Shanghai metallurgist, negotiated with potential Chinese partners to set up the new Metaldyne competitor. The trio was indicted in 2006, subsequently convicted, and sentenced to prison.[10]

Amid a drumbeat of such stories, public opinion soured on China. More Americans held an unfavorable view of the country than a favorable one in 2006, a marked change from just two years earlier when the public, by a margin of nearly two to one, held a positive assessment.[11]

In 2007, James Mann, a former Beijing bureau chief for the *Los Angeles Times*, challenged the conventional wisdom on China with a book called *The China Fantasy*. US officials, business executives, and academics, he wrote, were wrong that greater trade and engagement with China would eventually lead the country to become more democratic. In fact, its repressive one-party state might endure for decades. If that proved true, he wrote, US policy toward its fast-rising challenger would have been sold to American voters on the basis of "a fraud."[12]

Mann was an established journalist and the author of several fine histories. After returning from Beijing, where he had covered the Tiananmen Square crackdown, he spent the 1990s specializing in American policy toward China. But *The China Fantasy* bucked a powerful intellectual consensus on the likelihood that greater economic engagement with China would encourage the liberalization of its authoritarian political system. Many of his Washington sources seemed to regard the book as an act of betrayal. One leading China scholar lambasted it as "more an expression of frustration than analysis" in a review that rejected Mann's argument in its entirety.[13]

"I became sort of persona non grata. One person literally walked across the street to avoid me," Mann said.[14]

On a US military base on Okinawa, however, a young Marine Corps officer devoured Mann's book. Matt Pottinger, the former *Wall Street Journal* reporter, was now a Marine second lieutenant, preparing for his first deployment to Iraq. *The China Fantasy* helped him make sense of his kaleidoscopic experiences in Hong Kong and Beijing. "It crystallized for me all these things that I had observed but had not fully accounted for or organized in my mind. That book was like a thunderbolt to my head," Pottinger later recalled. "I just said, this is the truth. This is the predicament we now find ourselves in: They are not going to liberalize. And we have actually been playing into the party's interests, not against it."[15]

A cascading set of problems

One month after Biden's hearing, American and Chinese officials convened the fourth meeting of the US-China Strategic Economic Dialogue (SED). A twice-yearly set of high-level talks that was the brainchild of Henry Paulson, Bush's secretary of the treasury, the SED gathered in June 2008 at the US Naval Academy in Annapolis, Maryland.

Paulson, the former CEO of Goldman Sachs, had accepted an offer from Bush to join his cabinet on the condition that he be granted top billing in managing the nation's economic relationship with China. As one of his first initiatives, he had sold the Chinese on regular discussions between the two governments' top officials. For Paulson, the idea was to surmount the stovepiped nature of the Chinese system, which lacked a mechanism for routine policy coordination across agencies. In the United States, the national security advisor and the head of the National Economic Council were charged with getting multiple cabinet-level officials on the same page. China had no such arrangement.

Paulson believed that bringing Vice Premier Wang Qishan and eighteen top Chinese officials together with their American counterparts for regular talks would fill the void.

Publicly, the Bush administration said the Chinese had embraced the idea of regular talks with "surprising fervor." At the previous session in December 2007, Paulson had appealed to Vice Premier Wu Yi to permit the Chinese currency to rise against the dollar, a key US demand. Since then, the yuan had risen by more than 8 percent, a significant move in such a short period.[16] The White House credited the dialogue with accelerating China's timetable for action. "But it is not entirely clear that China views the SED as more than a method to stem Congressional angst and stave off protectionist legislation," Dennis Wilder, the head of the NSC's East Asian affairs directorate, concluded in a classified memo.[17]

As the novelty wore off, some of Paulson's colleagues chafed at the time and travel involved in the multiday gatherings. Each meeting produced a lengthy list of agreed items: The Treasury Department claimed twenty-four separate agreements on energy, insurance, and food safety from the June 2008 SED. Though Paulson was especially proud of the product safety measures, public opinion in the United States remained suspicious of China.[18] Over time, it became clear the Chinese and Americans brought different mindsets to the talks. "We want deliverables. And for them, the process is the deliverable," said one former Bush administration official who was directly involved in the meetings. "So it's often a set of miscommunications and mis-expectations about what comes out of it."[19]

The Annapolis talks took place amid a rapidly worsening financial crisis. For almost a year, Paulson had been grappling with fallout from the bursting of a mammoth, debt-fueled housing bubble. As housing prices roughly doubled between 1999 and 2006, American mortgages—many approved for borrowers with sketchy credit histories—were packaged into securities that were sold to banks and other investors around the world. When the bubble burst, the damage spread from one market to the next.

US officials had long lectured, scolded, and encouraged the Chinese to embrace the free movement of money across borders. Markets—not the state—should rule, the Americans said. And for years, the Chinese had resisted, fearing the instability that could result from unpredictable capital flows. Now those Chinese officials watched as the Americans embraced state action to stem the deepening crisis.

In March 2008, Paulson had pushed for and applauded the sale of Bear Stearns, an investment bank drowning in bad mortgage bets, to JPMorgan Chase. As US and Chinese officials gathered in Annapolis three months later, Paulson was distracted by the plight of mortgage giants Fannie Mae and Freddie Mac.

To the Chinese, the financial crisis—coupled with the military quagmires in Iraq and Afghanistan—showed that US power was "seriously weakened" and the American economic model deeply flawed. "It has shown the negative consequences of blind faith in market and laissez-faire economy, compelling the United States and Europe to reexamine the relationship between state intervention and market," one Chinese diplomat concluded.[20]

During a break in the meetings, Wang Qishan, the newly minted vice premier who had replaced Wu Yi as head of the Chinese delegation, took Paulson aside. The two men had first met more than a decade earlier when Paulson was a Goldman Sachs investment banker and Wang ran China Construction Bank. Paulson considered him a friend, but Wang carried a sobering message.

"You were my teacher, but now here I am in my teacher's domain, and look at your system, Hank. We aren't sure we should be learning from you anymore," Wang said.[21]

The crisis provided ammunition for Chinese opponents of further economic reform. As policy debates continued in Beijing, Chinese conservatives cited the American debacle as evidence of the superiority of a more cautious, state-led approach. But at a press conference following the meeting, Paulson put the best face on the situation, saying: "They want to learn from our mistakes."[22] His dealings with the Chinese leadership had convinced him, he said, that they were determined to "get to a totally market-driven economy."[23]

In fact, Chinese leaders felt vindicated by the American-made crisis. At a global summit later that year, Chinese President Hu Jintao said China had been able to support the global economy with a $586 billion stimulus program only because it had followed its own path. "I bet you're glad we didn't move the currency faster than we did. I hope you now understand why," he told Paulson privately. "Some of the things you wanted us to do would have been dangerous. Now we're stable and can stimulate the economy, and that's helping us and the whole world."[24]

Chinese officials channeled the stimulus spending through their state-owned enterprises, continuing a turn toward greater intervention in the economy that had begun with the 2006 five-year plan. State sector employment as a share of all jobs had fallen by half between 2001 and 2006, an indication that the promised economic restructuring was underway. But then the drop abruptly stopped and plateaued for several years.[25]

The hit to US prestige lingered. In May 2009, Beijing University students laughed when Paulson's successor as treasury secretary, Timothy Geithner, insisted in response to a question that US government bonds remained safe. He later called the incident "a pretty remarkable show of how far the United States had fallen."[26]

The Chinese at first had viewed the financial crisis as an investment opportunity. American banks were suffering huge losses on their holdings of subprime-mortgage-backed securities and needed to rebuild their financial defenses. Cash-rich Chinese institutions stepped up. In October 2007, CITIC Securities bought 6 percent of Bear Stearns for $1 billion after the investment bank's stock fell by one-quarter. Two months later, state-owned China Investment Corporation (CIC), China's first sovereign wealth fund, put up $5 billion for almost 10 percent of Morgan Stanley, its second major US investment following a $3 billion stake in Blackstone, a private equity firm.

CITIC's deal with Bear Stearns lasted less than six months before the investment bank collapsed into JPMorgan's arms. CIC's stake in Morgan Stanley lost half its value in just weeks, and its Blackstone shares fell by 70 percent.[27] On China's popular social media sites, bloggers criticized the country's leaders for gambling on failing American institutions.[28]

Beijing's concerns were far broader than the multibillion-dollar stakes in some American banks. China had more than $1 trillion parked in US Treasury securities and the debt of Fannie and Freddie, the government-sponsored mortgage giants that looked set to be the next dominoes to topple. "I remember getting calls from Chinese officials: 'Can you help us understand? How bad is this? And how bad is it going to get?'" recalled one senior Treasury official. "Whatever capacity we had to sort of lecture and tell them how the world works and how to do policy—that's all gone."[29]

US officials were desperate to keep China from dumping its holdings, a move that Paulson worried could ignite a mass financial markets sell-off. If Fannie and Freddie themselves failed, the result might be a global meltdown.[30]

At one point, Chinese banks began unloading some of their US holdings. Capitalizing on the relationships that he had nurtured for years, Paulson quickly contacted Zhou Xiaochuan, the head of China's central bank. "It worked," Paulson recalled. "He got to them and put it out right away, and they stopped selling immediately. And that stabilized the market. We would have had a totally different outcome, and it could have been much worse, if we didn't have the relationship with the Chinese."[31]

Later, while Paulson was in Beijing attending the 2008 Olympic Games, he learned that Russian officials had approached the Chinese about coordinating a joint sale of their Fannie and Freddie holdings to put pressure on the US government. But the Chinese refused.[32]

China's massive holdings of US securities were effectively the flip side of its trade relationship with the United States. Americans bought much more from China each year than the Chinese bought from the United States. That left the Chinese with a mounting pile of dollars, which they plowed into the perceived safety of Treasuries and agency debt. (The principal agency debt was issued by Fannie and Freddie, which transformed mortgages into securities that carried a Triple-A safety rating.)[33]

In layman's terms, Americans spent too much and saved too little. Living beyond their means, they needed to borrow money from China and oil-exporting nations, where there was a surplus of savings and lower consumer spending. The gap between US savings and spending showed up in something called the current account deficit, the broadest measure of the nation's trade balance. Such deficits once were rare and modest. At the end of the Cold War, they hovered around 1 percent of the economy. But amid China's emergence as an export powerhouse, the deficit soared to more than 6 percent in 2006. The American and Chinese economies were each distorted in their own way, mirror images of one another. And these global imbalances "created massive and destabilizing cross-border capital flows," according to Paulson.[34]

Domestic considerations—weak regulations, lax lending standards, and bank management errors—were the primary drivers behind the early 2000s housing bubble. But extraordinary amounts of foreign capital flowed into the American economy in the years preceding the global crisis, making the bubble worse than it otherwise would have been.

Two rivers of money poured into the United States. One came from Asian countries that were investing their trade surpluses into US assets. Indeed, purchases by foreign investors accounted for all of the new Treasury and agency securities issued between 2003 and 2007.[35] The global demand for safe investments was greater than the market could bear; there literally were not enough available to satisfy all who wanted them.

All that money stimulated the US economy by keeping borrowing costs low for consumers and businesses. The yield on the ten-year Treasury bond, which influences mortgage rates, was almost a full percentage point lower than it otherwise would have been thanks to the surge of foreign money.[36] For someone borrowing $200,000 to buy a typical home that year, that discount was enough to cut their monthly mortgage payment by $100. Low rates also triggered a rush for homeowners to refinance their mortgages. Many Americans used the opportunity to extract money from their increasingly valuable homes to support their spending. Such "cash-out" refinancings totaled nearly $80 billion annually in mid-2003, or almost 4 percent of disposable income.[37]

But when money is cheap, people tend to get a little reckless. As Asian reserve managers' demand for a safe place to put their money drove down the return on Treasuries and similar securities, investors moved into riskier products that they mistakenly regarded as nearly as safe. European banks in just four years pumped nearly $500 billion into private-label mortgage-backed securities.[38] Issued by banks, these investments lacked the credit guarantee of mortgages backed by Fannie and Freddie. But they carried Triple-A ratings from Moody's, Standard & Poor's, or Fitch, which reassured investors that they were safe.

This European demand was the era's second main source of foreign capital and helped convince US banks to continue churning out investment products that converted risky subprime mortgages into Triple-A securities.[39] European banks funded these deals by effectively borrowing dollars from US money market funds or Middle Eastern oil producers, flush with cash thanks to triple-digit oil prices. These trades made sense so long as the banks could roll over their short-term borrowings when they matured. If that ever became impossible, the whole financial system could seize up.

"I honestly don't think you can understand the US side of the global financial crisis without looking at foreign inflows," said economist Brad Setser, who worked in the Obama Treasury Department. ". . . It directly contributed to the buildup of risk that led to the crisis."[40]

Lax regulation on both sides of the Atlantic was to blame for the steady accumulation of risk in the global financial system. Starting in 1996, as European banks increasingly moved into investment banking, a global arbiter of banking standards known as the Basel Committee agreed not to dictate how much capital they should hold in reserve as a buffer against potential losses on the securities they owned. Instead, regulators would trust banks to use their own internal risk models to decide. It was like letting drivers choose their own speed limit on the highway.

Large European banks chose to hold less capital in reserve than regulators preferred, seeking a competitive advantage over their smaller rivals. This gamble meant higher profits for Europe's biggest banks but left the financial system vulnerable to unexpected losses. In 2007, for example, Germany's Deutsche Bank booked €6 billion in profits, fifteen times what it had earned just five years earlier.[41] Allowing banks to grade themselves on the riskiness of their holdings reflected an excessive faith in the ability of market forces to restrain damaging financial behavior.

"This was largely driven by views coming from the United States," concluded Tamim Bayoumi, a deputy director at the IMF. ". . . The US anti-regulatory philosophy was exported to the international banking system."[42]

Throughout this period, deregulatory enthusiasm on one side of the Atlantic encouraged corresponding actions on the other shore. The libertarian influence of Federal Reserve Chair Alan Greenspan was felt in Basel and in London, where authorities in 1997 established a new Financial Services Authority. Mimicking the US model, the FSA promoted a "light touch" approach to regulation. "Firms' managements—not their regulators—are responsible for identifying and controlling risks," the agency's head said as the housing bubble inflated.[43]

On the continent, banks were regulated by national governments, not the European Union. With leading banks in Germany or France vying to dominate Europe's financial services market, regulators in those nations faced pressure to go easy on their "national champions."

Financial authorities also believed the industry's innovative new products were making the system safer. Greenspan celebrated the growth of securitized bank loans as a way to spread risk across a wider pool of institutions, creating a more resilient global financial system and avoiding "cascading failures that could threaten financial stability." In a 2002 speech in London, Greenspan acknowledged the "remote possibility" of disaster, but concluded blithely: "So far, so good."[44]

Even as the mortgage market began melting down in the summer of 2007, the IMF praised the packaging of mortgages into securities for sale to global investors. Such innovations allowed Americans to finance their lifestyles, despite inadequate national savings. The "originate-to-distribute" system—with banks packaging mortgages into securities and selling them to investors rather than holding them on their books—was a key reason for the US economy's strength. Securitization had proven "highly resilient, including to recent difficulties in the subprime mortgage market," the fund concluded.[45]

The IMF's praise landed as the first cracks in the mortgage market widened. In June, Bear Stearns had disclosed that two of its hedge funds were near collapse because of bad bets on subprime mortgages. July saw major credit rating agencies downgrade such asset-backed securities, citing an increase in their delinquency rates. And in August, a pair of German banks required government rescues after their mortgage-related investments soured.

"Foreign purchases of [asset-backed securities] ensured that when the bubble finally burst, the financial crisis would not be confined to the United States but would spread throughout the world," four Fed economists later wrote.[46]

European banks for years had funded their purchases of mortgage-backed products by selling short-term securities known as commercial paper to money market mutual funds. By 2007, European banks such as Barclays, Deutsche Bank, and HSBC had raised a total of $1.2 trillion through such short-term borrowing.[47]

On August 7, BNP Paribas, a French bank, refused investor requests to withdraw their money from three mutual funds, saying it was unable to calculate the value of the funds' mortgage-related holdings. The decision kicked off a panic. Managers of money market funds abruptly stopped buying commercial paper from European banks. With their principal source of funding cut off, the banks were unable to continue investing in the American mortgage market. They now faced major losses.

Germany's Landesbank Sachsen Girozentrale was one of the first European institutions to require a government bailout after being blindsided by heavy losses on mortgage securities.[48] The bank, known as SachsenLB, had backed its commercial paper with credit guarantees, which made them risk-free for the money market funds that bought them. But the bank overdid it, assuming gigantic risks. The amount of short-term debt that it ultimately guaranteed was worth three times its equity capital or the financial buffer that would absorb any losses. That gamble left it at risk of collapse when sentiment turned.

SachsenLB illustrated the European dimension of the global financial crisis. It used the money raised by selling commercial paper to invest in longer-term mortgages and mortgage-backed securities, mostly in the United States and United Kingdom. Like many European institutions, SachsenLB dramatically reduced its capital requirements by setting up off-balance-sheet vehicles known as conduits to manage its subprime investments.

Under German regulations, using a conduit rather than holding the assets on its books enabled SachsenLB to eliminate the need to set aside any capital against its subprime holdings.[49] And SachsenLB held an enormous amount of assets off its books: €25 billion, or more than one-third of the assets it held on its balance sheet.[50] Holding less capital in reserve meant there was more available for lending or investing, which translated directly into higher profits. The results were dramatic. In 2003, the bank's Dublin unit, which generated the off-the-books ventures, accounted for two-thirds of SachsenLB's profits.[51]

A typical example of the way this strategy worked involved a vehicle called Ormond Quay, which held $11.4 billion in securitized residential and commercial loans. SachsenLB funded Ormond Quay, named for a dock near the bank's Dublin office, by selling short-term commercial paper. It also guaranteed repayment of the commercial paper when it matured, which satisfied money market funds' need for ultra-safe assets.

When spooked investors stopped buying banks' commercial paper, it marked the beginning of the end for the boom. Unable to roll over their short-term borrowings, SachsenLB and other European banks abruptly stopped investing in new mortgages or mortgage-backed securities. In late August, the bank—on the brink of insolvency—was taken over by the biggest German regional state-owned bank, Landesbank Baden-Württemberg.

Starved of demand, mortgage-backed securities plummeted in value. That created problems for the banks that owned them, as well as for other investors who had bet on their value through sophisticated derivatives. "From then on, we're just in a cascading set of problems," said Setser.

We believed in markets too much

Subprime losses migrated through the global financial system in unexpected and cataclysmic ways. At the start of 2007, the world's largest insurance company, AIG, seemed to be in enviable condition. Its AIG Financial Products subsidiary in London sold enormous volumes of credit insurance to European banks such as Société Générale in Paris, as well as Goldman Sachs and other Wall Street giants. The transactions appeared to benefit both sides. AIG earned lucrative fees for selling credit default swaps, a form of insurance that would protect the banks against defaults on their subprime mortgage securities and other debt.

Paying AIG to assume that risk was another way banks reduced the amount of capital they needed to hold in reserve; instead of needing a backstop equal to 8 percent of their investments, they got away with just 1.6 percent. By 2007, AIG had written $379 billion worth of protection, mostly for banks in Europe.[52] Though it was selling an insurance-like product, AIG did not set aside any of its own capital to absorb potential losses. Its internal models showed little chance of a market decline, and no regulator required it take such precautions.

Their sudden inability to roll over commercial paper left European banks desperate to find an alternate source of dollars. To meet the unprecedented demand, the Fed established currency swap lines with foreign central banks, including the European Central Bank and the Swiss National Bank, enabling them to obtain dollars for banks in their jurisdiction. The Fed subsequently expanded the swaps to include twenty additional central banks, as the American institution effectively became the world's dollar lender of last resort.

Battling alongside Paulson to quell the financial chaos, Federal Reserve Chair Ben Bernanke presided over a major expansion of the central bank's role and responsibilities. The Fed lowered its benchmark interest rate to near zero and held it there for seven years. And it purchased trillions of dollars in government securities in a further effort to spur growth. At the same time, the Treasury pumped an estimated $500 billion into banks, automakers, and the Fannie and Freddie takeover.[53] In September 2008, with AIG unable to raise fresh capital and facing multibillion-dollar losses on its credit default swap business, the government reluctantly rescued the firm from bankruptcy. The bailout would ultimately cost a staggering $180 billion. But officials feared they had no choice: The insurer had such complex links with every major bank in the United States and Europe that its failure would capsize the global financial system.[54]

The financial rescue likely prevented a second Great Depression. Saving the nation's banks saved the economy, even if it also benefited wealthy bankers and their creditors. But at a time when millions of Americans feared the loss of their homes or jobs, it also reinforced the division between winners and losers that had deepened with the China shock. However necessary, the rescue's most visible consequences disproportionately benefited owners of stocks and bonds, the wealthiest people in the nation. As of late 2007, the richest 10 percent of Americans owned more than $11 trillion in stocks and mutual funds, eighty-six times the total holdings of the bottom half of American society.[55]

The crisis was often viewed as a morality tale, pitting the interests of Wall Street against those of Main Street. But it held implications for globalization as well. Foreign central bankers poured more than $2 trillion into long-term US government and agency securities between 2000 and 2008.[56] Much of that cash had originated in the lopsided US trade relationship with China and Middle East oil producers. If the US had pressed China sooner to revalue the yuan or act on its other trade complaints, that flow—and thus the demand for mortgage-related securities and the scale of the crisis—would have been smaller.

Fallout from the housing implosion also could have been minimized by a more gimlet-eyed approach to regulation. Counting on bankers to police their own risks was asking for trouble. And trouble is what it delivered. Light-touch regulation imported from the United States produced "the most disastrous episode in the history of financial globalization," according to a leading European think tank.[57]

This epic failure cost American households $11 trillion in lost wealth. Roughly nine million workers lost their jobs while nearly four million Americans lost their homes.[58] The consequences were similarly severe in Europe.

Barely a decade had elapsed since unrestrained capital flows ignited financial mayhem in the emerging markets of Asia. Now the largest economy in the world was feeling the effects of free-moving finance. "The United States, like some emerging-market nations during the 1990s, has learned that the interaction of strong capital inflows and weaknesses in the domestic financial system can produce unintended and devastating results," Bernanke later wrote.[59]

The era of hyper-globalization was making financial crises more common and costly. A decade earlier, China and its neighbors lacked the financial reserves necessary to be an important source of demand for US government debt. Now decisions made in Beijing and other Asian capitals reshaped American financial markets and reverberated throughout the global economy.

Global living standards had risen thanks to the tide of investment capital that surged across national borders. Financiers had profited mightily. But whatever the tangible gains, the increased flows of money sloshing around the world also had produced a more volatile system whose periodic seizures were enormously costly. "International capital is getting more mobile over time and there's more of it as deregulation really takes hold. And so you end up with these bigger and bigger crises," said Bayoumi, the former IMF official. ". . . We believed in markets too much."[60]

The bargain has been breached with the American people

The political consequences of the financial crisis were nearly immediate. As the economy sank into the worst downturn since the 1930s, the Bush and Obama administrations—along with the Federal Reserve—took necessary actions that nonetheless left millions of Americans fuming at the perceived unfairness of the financial rescue. Protesters at one point even besieged Bernanke's home.[61]

On February 19, 2009, Rick Santelli, a reporter for CNBC, the financial news network, stood on the floor of the Chicago Mercantile Exchange and began ranting about the Obama administration's newly announced housing bailout. The $75 billion program was aimed at allowing up to nine million homeowners to refinance their mortgages, as a rising tide of foreclosures threatened to swamp an already depressed market.

Santelli depicted the initiative as an unfair government plan to "subsidize the losers" who had bought more home than they could afford. "This is America. How many of you people want to pay for your neighbor's mortgage that has an extra bathroom and can't pay their bills?" Santelli asked the floor traders as a chorus of boos swelled. "President Obama, are you listening?"

Pivoting back to the camera, Santelli added: "We're thinking of having a Chicago tea party in July. All you capitalists that want to show up to Lake Michigan, I'm gonna start organizing."[62]

With that spark, a nationwide "Tea Party" movement was born. Supporters organized a September march on the US Capitol, with seventy-five thousand people, including some wearing Revolutionary War–era cocked hats, coats, and breeches. Marchers carried American and Gadsden ("Don't Tread on Me") flags and called for action to address the ballooning national debt.

Among the movement's animating principles was a belief in "an unapologetic US sovereignty," one sympathetic analyst wrote.[63] A Tea Partier's greatest pejorative was to label someone "a globalist," meaning a supporter of unfettered immigration or multilateral action on climate change and trade. These right-wing populists were deeply skeptical of experts and elite opinion, "believing that the credentialed and the connected are trying to advance their own class agenda," including on issues like trade.[64]

The backlash against the financial rescue, however, was not limited to the right. On September 17, 2011, more than one thousand left-wing protesters aiming to "occupy Wall Street" ended up in nearby Zuccotti Park after the authorities blocked access to the Financial District. Initial press coverage was dismissive. *The New York Times* focused on a female demonstrator named Zuni Tikka, who had stripped down to her underwear before starting a topless dance.[65]

But as several hundred people camped in the park for weeks, the movement's complaints about inequality and corporate power began to draw attention. "We are the 99 percent that will no longer tolerate the greed and corruption of the 1 percent," the organizers said.[66]

Like the Tea Party, the Occupy crowds were mostly white. A blend of college-educated leftists and veterans of the Seattle anti-globalization demonstrations, they inspired copycat campouts in several other cities, including Washington, Boston, Chicago, Los Angeles, Wichita, Nashville, and El Paso.

Lori Wallach made a handful of appearances at one of the Washington sites, speaking about globalization. She also briefed some of the more prominent speakers who addressed the main Occupy site in New York, such as actor Mark Ruffalo, on Obama's trade policy. (Barred by the police from using megaphones or a public address system, the speakers relied on the crowd to echo their remarks so that those in the back could hear them.)

But she spent the bulk of her time working behind the scenes to generate opposition in Congress to the administration's trade strategy, which was centered on the proposed Trans-Pacific Partnership. The largest trade pact since China's WTO entry, the twelve-nation accord would have reduced tariffs, set new rules for digital commerce, and linked countries accounting for 40 percent of global trade. US officials saw it as a critical tool to cement American leadership in the Pacific at China's expense. To Wallach, the proposed TPP was just more of the same corporate-friendly trade policy. And she was determined to stop it.

"What I realized over time is actually my probably greatest value added was to be able to do much more of the strategy, the analysis, the talking to people, talking to members of Congress," she said. "I'm much more effective if I'm able to help support, educate, inform, you know, thirty members of Congress versus me running around doing [public speaking]."[67]

Almost two months after Zuccotti Park was occupied, New York Mayor Michael Bloomberg ordered it cleared. As the leaderless left-wing movement wound down, it was more popular than the Tea Party.[68] Obama adopted its language in a December 2011 speech in Osawatomie, Kansas, inveighing against an inequality he said sapped the nation's economic vigor and undermined its democracy.[69]

Yet it was right-wing populism that produced more tangible political consequences, fueling a Republican drive for austerity economics that hobbled the US economic recovery. The Tea Party pulled the Republican Party to the right and contributed grassroots energy that gave the GOP control of the House, with a sixty-three-seat pickup that was the biggest gain since 1948.

Wallach, however, detected a favorable shift in popular sentiment. In the months after the New York protest fizzled, her organization conducted focus groups around the country, to shape their campaign against Obama's Asian trade deal. The traditional arguments—that a NAFTA-style deal would cost US manufacturing jobs—no longer dominated public concern.

"The one thing that cut across was corporate power. People were in a hot rage over corporate power. Part of the reason that Occupy Wall

Street took off the way it did is because people needed a place to channel that anger about how could it be, like, all my neighbors lost their house, my pension is gone, and not a single bankster went to fucking jail? What is this?" she said. "People were in a real rage about that."[70]

On October 5, 2011, Biden, who was now the vice president, traveled a few blocks east of the White House for one of the capital's frequent public events. On a stage at the Newseum, he was quizzed by NBC's David Gregory about the Occupy movement's significance.

"What is the core of that protest? And why is it increasing in terms of the people it's attracting?" Biden asked. "The core is: The bargain has been breached with the American people. The core is the American people do not think the system is fair or on the level, that is the core of what you're seeing on Wall Street. By the way, there's a lot in common with the tea party. The tea party started why?...They thought it was unfair we were bailing out the big guys. Look guys, the bargain is not on the level any more in the eyes of the vast majority of the American people."[71]

Globalization was not supposed to work this way

The violent shaking began at 2:46 p.m. on March 11, 2011, and continued for three full minutes. Two ancient tectonic plates located roughly eighty miles off the Japanese coast had slipped, moving more than fifty feet in some places and causing an earthquake that registered 9.0 on the Richter scale and sent a wall of water racing toward the city of Sendai.

The remorseless fifty-foot-high tsunami pushed inward, sweeping before it cars, buildings, boats, and bodies. An area of approximately 140,000 acres, extending six miles from the coast, was inundated. More than twenty thousand people were killed and one million buildings damaged or destroyed.

About seventy miles south of Sendai stood the Fukushima Dai-ichi nuclear power plant. When the tsunami swept past the site's defenses, it quickly disabled the power supply and cooling equipment. Three reactor cores melted down, resulting in a release of radioactivity that was the most serious nuclear accident since Chernobyl in 1986. More than one hundred thousand local residents were evacuated as a precaution.[72]

As well as the obvious human tragedy, the Great East Japan Earthquake and tsunami represented a stress test of the global economy.

Technology, politics, and the profit motive had come together in the rise of global supply chains. Instead of producing everything they needed in one place, corporations increasingly divided their operations. An American company might put most of its manufacturing in China. Parts would arrive at the Chinese factory from suppliers elsewhere in Asia, be soldered and screwed together by Chinese workers, and then be loaded into metal shipping containers for the six-week ocean voyage to the United States.

Ever-larger container vessels transformed the economics of shipping, making it attractive to send items large and small all over the world. In 1956, the first container ship, a converted oil tanker called the *Ideal X*, carried just fifty-eight containers on her maiden voyage from Newark to Houston.[73] Now a single vessel held the equivalent of up to fifteen thousand 20-foot metal boxes, linking factories in Asia to customers in the American heartland.

The proliferation of personal computers and inexpensive telecommunications allowed distant managers to keep track of their parts and finished products as they moved around the world. The early post–Cold War years also were marked by a certain relative stability in global affairs, which further encouraged the development of production chains that spanned national borders. By 2011, nearly six hundred million shipping containers were moving through the world's ports each year, more than six times as many as when the Berlin Wall came down.[74]

Fukushima interrupted all of that. Manufacturers, especially in the automotive and electronics industries, relied on dozens of Japanese suppliers to provide critical parts, such as microcontrollers, overlay glass, and silicon wafers. Under the just-in-time approach pioneered by Toyota, companies reduced their costs by holding only limited inventories of the components they needed. General Motors, for example, kept only enough parts at some assembly plants for eight hours of production.[75]

Manufacturers counted on parts arriving at their factories "just-in-time" to be used on the assembly line. Any interruption in regularly scheduled deliveries would quickly cause problems. When newly strict US customs inspections slowed cargo movements following the 2001 terrorist attacks, it took only three days for Michigan auto factories to run out of supplies.[76]

In the aftermath of the earthquake, Japanese manufacturing output sank by 15 percent and remained depressed for five months. The weakness quickly spread to the United States, where companies relied on Japanese suppliers for highly specialized components and materials. The only plant in the world that produced Xirallic pigments, which give auto paint its glitter, belonged to Merck and stood in the shadow of the Fukushima reactor.[77] Another Japanese plant in the affected area produced more than 20 percent of the global supply of a type of silicon needed to produce computer chips. Other critical auto parts, lithium-battery chemicals, flash memory, and a film used in flat panel displays also originated in the region.[78] Alternative suppliers could not be located overnight.[79]

Intel feared radioactive dust from the crippled reactor would contaminate its sensitive computer chips. Chemical giant BASF, which produced a lipstick ingredient for Procter & Gamble, used Geiger counters to inspect its output. And General Motors identified 30 suppliers and 390 parts that had been affected by the quake. On March 21, ten days after the disaster, a shortage of airflow sensors caused GM to shut its plant in Shreveport, Louisiana, for one week.[80] That closure, in turn, triggered brief layoffs at a plant in Tonawanda, New York, which made engines for the Shreveport facility.[81]

For Flextronics, a multinational contract manufacturer, the episode was disruptive but not catastrophic. The company had two sites in Japan: a manufacturing operation in Ibaraki and a services facility in Koriyama, about forty-five miles inland from the reactors. Neither suffered physical damage. But both were out of action for about a week because of the difficulty of moving around. "We still can't say with certainty what the ultimate impact will be," CEO Mike McNamara told investors seven weeks after the tsunami.[82]

One reason for the uncertainty was that Flextronics had only limited information about the condition and, in some cases, even the identity of the smaller vendors that supplied its major suppliers. As it struggled to maintain its delivery schedules, Flextronics had "hundreds if not thousands of risk items associated with Japan," McNamara said. In some cases, the company faced higher prices once it identified an alternative source. In others, Flextronics needed to quickly reduce its orders for parts as some of its Japanese customers throttled back their own operations.

The disruption proved fleeting for Flextronics. By July, the company reassured investors that it had "not experienced any material effects to our revenues or operations."[83] But just as the crisis appeared to have passed, a new threat arose: A historic monsoon caused widespread flooding in Thailand that disrupted production of computer hard drives and other electronics. More than one thousand Thai factories were affected. Major manufacturers Seagate and Western Digital saw their market value fall 40 percent in just four months after the flooding.

This time, Flextronics did not escape unscathed. The initial reports were that dozens of factories—responsible for producing two thousand components—had been swamped. The company ultimately whittled that estimate down to a manageable list of one hundred high-priority parts that were needed to make high-dollar items.[84] Despite such rapid industrial triage, Flextronics lost $100 million in sales, and profits in the last quarter of 2011 fell by half compared to the same period one year earlier.[85]

The one-two punch of natural disasters in 2011 exposed the vulnerabilities of global supply chains that were optimized for low cost and high efficiency. Less expensive and more capable communications and transportation had facilitated the development of longer supply chains. But they also promoted greater concentration of risk as manufacturers gravitated to the same low-cost suppliers, often located on the other side of the globe.[86]

In the aftermath of the Asian calamities, the corporate response was uneven. Toyota took steps to protect itself against future disruptions. It standardized parts so that they could be used in several different vehicles, which permitted greater sharing of inventory among its factories. The automaker compiled an exhaustive database of its suppliers and redesigned its supply chain around regional operations, rather than the global model that was more vulnerable to single-point failures. And it asked its suppliers to diversify their own supply networks.[87]

Manufacturers such as GM also sought more detailed information about their suppliers' suppliers: the unheralded companies whose output was critical to the automaker's ability to keep producing cars and trucks. "Most of the time we didn't even know who the Tier 2 and Tier 3 suppliers were, and that became so, so obvious when we got into this situation," said Bill Hurles, GM's global supply chain lead at the time.[88]

In a few cases, GM tweaked its parts inventories and bolstered its internal communication plans. But there was no wholesale redesign of supply chains at GM or most other corporations. After all, global value chains had helped lift corporate profits as a share of the economy to an all-time high, roughly double the figure at the Cold War's end.[89] Questioning the wisdom of the just-in-time philosophy was just a "knee-jerk reaction," one expert said.[90]

In Washington, DC, Barry Lynn had watched the Asian crises unfold with a strong sense of "I told you so." A former journalist turned think-tank analyst, Lynn had been warning about the nation's fragile supply chains for nearly a decade. In publications like *Harper's Magazine* and the *Financial Times*, he had decried the cumulative effects of industrial mergers, outsourcing, and the wholesale embrace of just-in-time production, saying they had left the global economy vulnerable to natural disasters, wars, revolutions, or even a pandemic.

"Globalization was not supposed to work this way," he wrote.[91]

While Fukushima was an extreme case, there had been earlier close calls. A 1999 earthquake in Taiwan, home to most of the world's semiconductor production. A 2002 dockworkers strike on the US West Coast. Hurricane Katrina in 2005. And a previous Japanese earthquake in 2007, which closed the factory that produced half of the piston rings needed by Japan's auto industry.

Over the years, Lynn found occasional kindred spirits in the electronics industry, who understood the chokepoints of resins and pigments and metals that could paralyze entire assembly lines. But these like-minded analysts did not know the right door to knock on in

Washington. No single government official or agency had responsibility for managing the nation's supply chain. No one was in charge.

Other warnings went unheard due to a failure of imagination. A viral pandemic, akin to the 1918 Spanish influenza, was almost certain to erupt at some point, experts agreed. And when it did, the consequences in deaths and disruption of daily life would be severe, Michael Osterholm, a professor at the University of Minnesota's School of Public Health, warned in a prescient 2005 article in *Foreign Affairs*. Global business, he wrote, was sleepwalking toward disaster. Most companies' contingency planning accounted only for "localized disruption," such as the closing of a single plant, not the global shutdown that would result if a lethal virus spread along the channels carved by trade.

"There would be major shortages in all countries of a wide range of commodities, including food, soap, paper, light bulbs, gasoline, parts for repairing military equipment and municipal water pumps, and medicines, including vaccines unrelated to the pandemic," said Osterholm, who had recently concluded a stint as a special adviser on public health preparedness to the secretary of homeland security. Many countries, including the United States, would lack the capacity to produce the medical supplies needed to fight the contagion. "Virtually every piece of medical equipment or protective gear would be in short supply within days," Osterholm concluded. Ventilators and respiratory masks would be especially scarce.[92]

That same year, Lynn—by then ensconced at the New America Foundation in Washington—secured an audience with the Treasury Department's leadership. Over a three-hour lunch in the secretary's dining room, he briefed department officials on his findings. They were receptive and promised to follow up. But within a month, they all had been replaced as Henry Paulson supplanted John Snow.

Still, Lynn kept at it, writing books and articles, speaking to economists and journalists. But he got little traction. His claims were dismissed as protectionism—sophisticated protectionism, perhaps, but protectionism all the same. "I assumed I would just put my case before the elites. Their minds will be crystallized in a different way; they will see every implication and they will go fix it," he said later. "And that didn't happen."[93]

A warning

Barack Obama had come to the presidency convinced that the nation's policies and institutions needed an overhaul before the average American could count on getting "a fair shake" from globalization. But the all-consuming nature of the global financial emergency blew away any possibility of such reforms. After little more than one hundred days in the White House, beset by illiberalism at home and abroad, the new president worried that "the hopeful tide of democratization, liberalization, and integration that had swept the globe after the end of the Cold War was beginning to recede."[94]

As Obama's secretary of state and his vice president jockeyed to succeed him, they sketched contrasting economic visions. Hillary Clinton, unsurprisingly, harkened back to the market-friendly approach of her husband's eight years in office. Joe Biden, on the other hand, sounded more like the sort of Democrat that had been popular before Bill Clinton steered the party to the right.

"I have a basic disagreement," Biden told one journalist, "with the underlying rationale that began in the Clinton administration about the concentration of economic wealth to generate economic growth." To address rising inequality, and working-class discontent, "significant change" in the country's policies was needed, Biden added.[95]

But in October 2015, after months of agonizing, Biden decided he would not run in 2016, after all. He was still grieving the loss of his son, Beau, to brain cancer, and much of the party had coalesced behind Hillary Clinton. His decision appeared to mark the end of four decades of presidential ambition. It also deprived the country and the Democratic Party of a debate over the need for an economic course correction. The stage seemed set for a Clinton restoration and the election of the country's first woman president—even if millions of Americans found themselves drawn to populist candidates on the left and the right.

Appearing in the Rose Garden on a bright fall day, flanked by his wife, Jill, and Obama, Biden bowed out with a warning. "It isn't just a matter of fairness or economic growth, it's a matter of social stability for this nation," he said. "We cannot sustain the current levels of inequality that exist in this country."[96]

6

No More Money into China

Tim Draper had seen modest bets pay off big before. In the 1990s, his firm's $1 million stake in Hotmail eventually generated $1 billion for Draper's investors.[1] Baidu, which was billed as China's answer to Google, was that kind of win. Shares of the Chinese search engine, which went public in 2005 at $27, topped $100 in 2010, hit $150 the following year, and soared past $200 in 2014. Fresh from that success, Draper went looking for other potential Chinese stars.

He thought he'd found one in YeePay, a Beijing-based payment services company. Unlike established competitors like PayPal, YeePay allowed businesses to make and receive payments via traditional phone lines as well as mobile devices and the internet. In a country where most consumers paid for goods with cash on delivery, YeePay's focus on old-fashioned telephones was deliberate. In 2006, Draper invested $1.5 million in the company through Draper Fisher Jurvetson; his affiliate fund DFJ Dragon committed an additional $1 million.[2] Within a few years of its 2002 launch, YeePay claimed five thousand corporate clients and seemed positioned to be a significant player in China's emerging third-party payment industry.[3]

Then, its fortunes abruptly changed. In 2014, Chinese regulators repeatedly fined the little-known company before a state-backed private equity firm suggested the penalties would stop if executives agreed to sell YeePay at a fraction of its market value. "All of a sudden, one of my companies started getting all these fines. And I thought, what's going on? And nobody could really tell me," Draper said.

What eventually transpired with YeePay would ruin Draper's romance with China. His disillusionment was part of a broader change of heart among foreign investors and business executives, as a new Chinese leader turned his back on market reforms, doubled down on state capitalism, and challenged US interests. China's turn inward was mirrored by a rising populist tide in the United States, which questioned globalization's benefits and hinted at political upheaval in the world's largest economy.

As Draper dug into the details of YeePay's plight, the situation grew only murkier. There was talk of repeated visits to company headquarters by local police and possible missed payments for employee health care. Finally, YeePay executives told Draper they had an opportunity to take the company public. Listing a company's shares on a stock market is the ultimate goal for entrepreneurs and their financial backers, allowing them to cash out their initial investment and realize a big windfall.

But in this case, there was a wrinkle. If YeePay listed on the NASDAQ exchange in the United States, the company would be valued at $1.5 billion, Draper said he was told. But if it listed on China's over-the-counter market, the valuation—and thus the payday for investors—would be three times as large. That seemed odd.

Draper's suspicions soon deepened. As a step toward listing on the Chinese market, YeePay was required to change its corporate structure. Like many Chinese companies with global ambitions, the company had been organized with a parent holding company based in the Cayman Islands. Now, Draper was told, YeePay had to become a Chinese corporation, which would legally make it less friendly to foreign investors.[4] "I wasn't too happy about that," he said.

Meanwhile, the fines accelerated. That's when a state-backed private equity operation approached YeePay with an offer it couldn't refuse: Sell the company for roughly one-sixth of its value, and the fines would stop. Draper was baffled. But the YeePay executives told him they really had no choice. In the end, the private equity group acquired a three-year option to purchase the company without actually handing over any money, Draper said.[5] The confused outcome convinced him to head for the exits.

"I just went to all of our investors and I said, 'No more money into China.' And I started telling a bunch of other people, 'No more money in China,'" he said.

Not just commercial institutions

Draper blamed China's new leader for what he interpreted as a major shift in China's economic climate. But there was more to it than that. Xi Jinping became general secretary of the Chinese Communist Party in November 2012. The son of Xi Zhongxun, a revolutionary hero, Xi and his entire family were politically persecuted during the Cultural Revolution after Mao turned on his father.

Given that experience, some American observers expected Xi to be a reformer. But he had drawn surprising conclusions from his suffering at the hands of unchecked state authority. Rather than reject the Communist Party, he sought to revitalize it, to save it from the fate of its counterpart in the Soviet Union. Xi chose, one colleague later said, "to survive by becoming redder than the red."[6]

His nationalistic and authoritarian leanings were not immediately apparent. As party secretary of coastal Zhejiang Province, Xi had helped foreign corporations such as Federal Express, Citibank, and Motorola expand their Chinese operations and boasted of the region's growing wealth. He charmed American officials at a dinner at the US ambassador's residence in Beijing, saying he was a fan of Hollywood World War II movies, including the blockbuster *Saving Private Ryan*.[7] Still, Xi was fixated on rooting out the chronic corruption that sapped the party's public standing, and he was said to be "repulsed by the all-encompassing commercialization of Chinese society."[8]

Draper's souring on China coincided with the maturation of its domestic venture capital industry. Not so long before, China had thirsted for Western capital and Western expertise. Now, Chinese VC specialists nurtured local entrepreneurs, and Chinese investment bankers took them public. Foreigners like Draper—who was respected for having been an early investor in companies like Tesla and Skype—were still welcome. But they were no longer essential. "An American outsider could no longer add much to China's venture industry."[9]

Draper saw the YeePay episode—and similar experiences with other Chinese companies he had invested in—as evidence of political gamesmanship emanating from the top. From his vantage point, flying in several times a year to meet with entrepreneurs and attend industry conferences, China had appeared "free." Now it no longer did, and he blamed Xi.

"He is a weak leader. He's trying to control his people. He's trying to control everything. He's controlling speech. He's 'wokeism' times fifty," said Draper, whose own politics tilt Republican-libertarian.

In fact, Xi had nothing in common with American progressives, let alone any "woke" tendencies. Draper's conviction that China was "free" reflected a blinkered view of the country's development. Yes, business executives and investors were permitted to meet, speak openly, and place their bets on future growth. And China's emerging middle class was empowered to make decisions about their daily lives in ways that would have been unimaginable to their parents' generation.

But that was the limit of China's freedoms. Public criticism of the Communist Party's hold on power or advocacy that conflicted with its priorities remained forbidden, as dissidents like Hu Jia could attest. The human rights activist had first come to prominence several years earlier for his advocacy on behalf of AIDS victims whose plight was being covered up by the government.[10] In late 2007, he was arrested and later sentenced to three and a half years in prison after pleading innocent to charges of "inciting subversion of state power" for his support of peasants protesting government abuses. While jailed, and deprived of routine medical care, Hu became seriously ill with suspected liver cancer. His wife's petition for his early release on medical grounds was denied. In 2008, the European Parliament awarded him the Sakharov Prize, praising him as one of China's "most vocal and respected democracy activists."

A clearer view of Chinese realities would have anticipated that foreign investors in essential parts of China's financial infrastructure might eventually encounter trouble. The amount of money moving through the new payment channels grew year by year, until it became important enough to attract the attention of government authorities. By 2014, Yee-Pay, just one of dozens of private payment companies, alone processed

$77 billion of payments, double the figure from one year earlier.[11] Altogether, third-party payment firms handled more than $1.25 trillion in transactions.[12]

Chinese regulators had moved slowly at first to control the new companies that battled over this river of money, but they had moved. In a 2009 crackdown on internet pornography, the Ministry of State Security threatened to prosecute third-party payment companies if they provided services for customers of illicit websites. Police in Hebei said the owners of the Love City porn video website made 800,000 yuan, or roughly $100,000, by selling eight thousand memberships through YeePay, PayPal, and Alipay, the market leader.[13] In mid-2010, China's central bank, the People's Bank of China (PBOC), issued regulations discouraging e-payment companies from allowing foreign investors to hold a controlling stake in their business.[14]

When the central bank began granting licenses for third-party payment services in 2011, YeePay was among the first batch of twenty-seven recipients, which also included giants like Alipay and Tenpay. In March 2014, the PBOC ordered YeePay and seven other payments firms to stop adding new businesses to their networks. The payment companies had inadequate risk controls, often failing to ensure that new merchants registered for their service using their real names, the central bank said.[15] Four months later, China's state-backed bank-card association, UnionPay, slapped several payment companies, including YeePay, with monthly fines of more than $1.6 million apiece for charging users less than the industry's agreed-upon fees.[16] The central bank followed up by ordering YeePay and three other payment firms to stop doing business in fifteen provinces amid reports that the companies had helped merchants circumvent the regulations.[17]

As Chinese consumers increasingly moved online, regulators followed. In 2015, the central bank proposed a daily limit on individual transactions of 5,000 yuan—less than the price of the latest iPhone.[18] In 2016, the PBOC fined YeePay roughly $8 million, reportedly for violations of anti-money-laundering regulations, the largest such penalty imposed between 2011 and 2016.[19] Chinese authorities even arrested one payment industry executive, accusing him of facilitating capital flight.[20]

Funds deposited with innovative payment companies were not covered by deposit insurance, leaving consumers at risk of big losses. Amid an epidemic of financial scams, Chinese authorities feared the impact of unexpected financial setbacks on social stability. Rare public protests erupted in multiple Chinese cities after the Fanya Metal Exchange in Kunming bilked 240,000 retail investors of more than $6 billion.[21] The apparent Ponzi scheme promised mom-and-pop investors across China annual returns of 14 percent, but investors ended up with their Fanya accounts frozen.[22]

Regulators' actions reflected official concern about the potential for non-bank payment companies to threaten the Communist Party's control of the financial system. Chinese officials allocated capital through the "big four" state banks. Whatever threatened those institutions ultimately imperiled the party's interests. Even after the big banks went public in the late 2000s, in some of the largest share offerings in history, they were "not just commercial institutions," journalist Richard McGregor wrote in *The Party*. "They were instruments of national economic policy."[23] Bank managers were not focused exclusively on profit maximization. The party committees at each of the big state banks made sure that they supported the party's goals. If the party wanted capital to flow to state-owned enterprises, as it did during the 2008 crisis, the banks' party secretaries would make that happen.

"YeePay, payment systems, things like that, started to come under a lot of scrutiny because the government, frankly, screwed up, and they became terrified when they realized that Alipay and Tenpay were taking 95 percent of all the new account formation. And that was money that was not going to a traditional bank," said Gary Rieschel, the Shanghai venture capitalist.[24]

Like many businesses in China, YeePay also was targeted by local officials who had no obvious regulatory authority over it. At the end of 2019, police from Qitaihe, a city in Heilongjiang Province in northeast China, suddenly appeared at the company's Beijing headquarters and accused executives of facilitating gambling and prostitution in their jurisdiction.

The company denied the charges and called the Beijing police, which dispatched officers in response. But when challenged, the Qitaihe police responded by quoting Xi Jinping's official statements on fighting corruption. The Beijing officers advised YeePay to cooperate.

Instead, the company alerted the Communist Party's powerful Central Commission for Discipline Inspection, a top party organ, which discovered that the company was one of several that the Qitaihe officers had visited. The raid came at a sensitive time for YeePay with the company months away from filing for an initial public offering.

The Qitaihe police took six YeePay employees into custody and held them until one of the company's co-founders personally traveled to Heilongjiang and appealed for their release. Three were set free at that point. The other three were detained for nine months before being released after an unsuccessful ransom demand, according to a source with knowledge of the affair.[25] The episode came at a time when Qitaihe, like countless municipalities across China, was debt-ridden and cash-strapped. Its annual interest payments in 2019 jumped to nearly $50 million, up more than three-quarters from the prior year. Facing mounting bills, officials in cities across China sought to increase revenue by hitting private companies with various fines and penalties.[26]

Support for a constructive relationship with China will disappear

From the 1990s to the early 2000s, external pressure on China to change encouraged Chinese leaders to follow Deng Xiaoping's path of reform and opening. As it prepared to join the WTO, China reduced its average tariff on imported goods from 44 percent in 1991 to roughly 15 percent in 2001.[27] Chinese authorities were shifting their economy's orientation from state-led to market-led, a positive change that nonetheless meant real pain for many people. The number of workers employed by state-owned businesses fell by one-third in little more than three years. More than thirty-six million men and women who had earned their living in 1998 working for the state no longer did so by mid-2001.[28]

Beijing fulfilled many of its commitments under its WTO accession agreement, revising thousands of regulations, enacting scores of new laws, and retraining officials throughout the massive bureaucracy. Regulators revised or abolished more than half of China's roughly twenty-one thousand domestic technical standards to comply with WTO requirements.[29]

No centrally planned nation had ever been a full participant in the global economy. Within a few years of entering the WTO, China arguably was the most open large developing economy in the world. Its average industrial trade barriers were just one-third or one-quarter as large as those of countries such as India and Brazil.[30] Private companies that previously had been allowed to trade with foreigners only by working through a handful of approved state intermediaries were freed to buy and sell directly in global markets.

But the domestic impetus for reform soon ebbed. In 2002, Hu Jintao replaced Jiang Zemin as the country's top leader. Zhu Rhongji, the reformist premier who impressed every American official who met him, also retired. Pressure from abroad became less intense as China met its initial WTO commitments and the US government grew preoccupied with the wars in Iraq and Afghanistan. The collapse of the Doha Round of global trade talks, followed by the financial crisis that emerged from the United States housing market, further weakened pro-market voices within China. As hardliners in the bureaucracy mobilized against further reforms, Hu and Wen Jiabao, Zhu's successor, lacked the "political strength to discipline the state" and drive reforms to completion.[31]

Barack Obama entered the White House convinced that the cooperative elements of the US-China relationship would outweigh the competitive aspects, according to Jeffrey Bader, his chief White House adviser on China. The president publicly welcomed an increasingly prosperous China as good for the United States and, during his first year in office, spoke with Hu Jintao four times.[32]

By 2010, the amount of merchandise moving between the United States and China each year had quadrupled since 2000. China was increasingly important both as a market for US goods and as a supplier of products desired by American consumers and businesses. WTO membership was supposed to mean abiding by a rules-based global trading order. But China was earning a reputation for cheating and unfairness in global trade. Washington's initial optimism about the relationship faded.

Obama's team searched for tougher measures that could push China to change. Larry Summers, director of the White House National Economic Council, and Treasury Secretary Timothy Geithner drew up a list of options, including getting US allies to support a full-court press on the currency issue; imposing safeguard tariffs; and sanctioning Chinese companies that violated US intellectual property rights.[33]

Most of the measures were discarded as provocative or unlikely to succeed. But the administration intensified efforts to hold China accountable at the WTO, filing and winning sixteen cases. Though the Chinese government had a good record of complying with adverse WTO rulings, some US complaints were never really resolved.

In February 2015, for example, the United States complained that China was subsidizing exports in seven industries—including advanced metals, specialty chemicals, agriculture, and textiles—in violation of global trade rules. The US charged China with using 150 separate government measures to funnel cash grants and discounted services to exporters. After several rounds of talks, China agreed to scrap the programs, which the Obama administration hailed as "a win for Americans...who will benefit from a more level playing field on which to compete."[34]

It was a fleeting triumph. The Chinese shuttered the specific programs the United States had identified, but industrial subsidies remained embedded throughout the Chinese economy. "They realized that it was a violation. They shut it down right away, but then they opened up something else that was somewhat different but had the same result," said Michael Froman, Obama's chief trade negotiator.[35]

The Obama administration played Whac-A-Mole with China until its last days in office. In January 2017, the United States accused China of improperly subsidizing its aluminum industry, resulting in excess production that depressed global prices and hurt American producers. The endless battles, which often took years to traverse the sluggish WTO process, took a toll on the business community's enthusiasm for China. Aluminum shipments remained a source of trade friction years after Obama left office.[36]

Following the global financial crisis, relations fell into a negative cycle. By 2014, some 55 percent of Americans had an unfavorable opinion of China, up from 36 percent in 2011, according to the Pew Research Center.[37] Millions of Americans were suffering economically and growing more agitated about China's mercantilist trade practices at a time when Chinese officials were less awed by their American counterparts. US economic performance coming out of the crisis was unimpressive, Washington relied on China to buy US government debt, and the American military was mired in a war in Afghanistan that had entered its second decade.

"We'd bring up these economic issues, and we'd say you really need to take these seriously because you don't understand that people are getting increasingly angry at what they view to be an unlevel playing field—China, violating or exploiting the rules-based trading system at the expense of Americans and others around the world," Froman, the trade negotiator, said. "And that if we don't make progress on these issues, that the foundation of support for a constructive relationship with China will disappear. That's exactly what happened."[38]

Ugly gorilla

China's economic miracle was the result of decades of hard work by countless Chinese citizens and domestic economic reforms that reversed Maoist idiocy. But to many Americans, Chinese growth appeared to rest on exploitation of its trading partners.

Generous subsidies to promote domestic manufacturers. An undervalued currency that made its prices impossible to match. Rampant counterfeiting of American goods, from DVDs and computer software to clothing and even industrial hardware. American executives stewed over their Chinese partners' demand that they surrender valuable technology before being allowed to operate in China while the US government fought a brazen campaign of state-backed espionage that was responsible for an estimated 50 percent to 80 percent of global intellectual property theft.[39]

Just how brazen started to become clear in the fall of 2010, thanks to a chance encounter between David Hickton, the new US attorney in Pittsburgh, and two of the city's most prominent figures. Hickton one day crashed a monthly 7:30 a.m. breakfast that brought together the

CEO of US Steel, John Surma, and Leo Gerard, the head of the United Steelworkers union, seeking help with a mentoring program for at-risk youth.

Over bacon and eggs at the downtown Hilton, Hickton quickly obtained their agreement to help his charitable venture. But then Surma and Gerard steered the conversation in another direction. They told the federal prosecutor that China was hacking into their computer networks and the US government wasn't doing much about it. The FBI had installed devices to record intrusions. But no one ever told them what the bureau learned. Meanwhile, inexpensive Chinese copies of American innovations, such as a special type of pipe used in oil and gas projects, were appearing on global markets, taking sales from Surma and costing Gerard's members jobs.

A Pennsylvania native, Hickton could see the consequences of China's actions across the state, in places like New Castle and Donora and Uniontown, once-vital communities that were deteriorating as manufacturing employment dried up. But with just fifty lawyers, he ran a small office by Justice Department standards.

Before proceeding with a China hacking probe, Hickton leveraged his local connections to get an appointment with FBI Director Robert Mueller. Mueller's wife, Ann, had grown up in Sewickley, about a dozen miles northwest of Pittsburgh along the Ohio River. One of Hickton's sons worked for the FBI and played hockey with Mueller after work. Those Pennsylvania ties got Hickton face time with him. "What do I need to know?" he asked the director.

Mueller told him there was more than enough work to justify a special focus on computer crimes and national security. The director himself already had zeroed in on the cyber threat, distributing to FBI trainees copies of a book called *The Cuckoo's Egg*, which detailed a costly hack of Lawrence Livermore National Laboratory in the late 1980s.

Hickton quickly established a special computer crimes unit. In doing so, he was bucking Justice Department resistance to prosecuting such cases. The FBI chief might be alert to the danger of hostile governments and criminals breaking into American computers. But Hickton's bosses across the street from the fortress-like FBI building regarded cyber cases as a dead end.

It was notoriously difficult to demonstrate that a specific hacker was responsible for an intrusion. Corporate victims often balked at going public for fear of shareholder lawsuits or reputational damage. And any case that surmounted those obstacles still needed to navigate the Justice Department bureaucracy, where senior political appointees had an infinite number of reasons to shy from indicting hackers affiliated with a foreign government. Plus, there was always the chance that if a US attorney like Hickton did steer a potential indictment past those shoals, a higher-profile office like the Southern District of New York would swoop in at the last moment and take it over.

"No US attorneys wanted to do cyber cases. Everybody felt that if you did those cases, they were going to derail at some point," Hickton said.[40]

The China case, in fact, already had been turned down by the much larger US attorney's office in Sacramento. FBI Agent Keith Mularski, who was based in Pittsburgh, approached Hickton and told him the bureau had an orphan investigation, involving state-sponsored Chinese hackers that had targeted numerous US corporations. It was much larger than just the steel industry. "I said, 'Grab it,'" Hickton recalled.

The sheer scale of the apparent wrongdoing and the technical complexity of the computer violations made the probe challenging. As the investigation proceeded, it became clear that a special unit within the People's Liberation Army (PLA) had been carrying out an ambitious campaign to plunder the trade secrets and intellectual property of some of the United States' top corporations, as well as its largest industrial union.

Based in Shanghai's Pudong district, Unit 61398 had used "spear-fishing" emails to trick recipients into downloading malware that gave the Chinese hackers free reign in their computer networks. The spies also took over unrelated computers, which they used to mask their operations. Using online aliases such as "UglyGorilla" and "KandyGoo," the hackers stole the equivalent of seven hundred thousand pages of email messages and attachments detailing Westinghouse's negotiating strategy in talks with a state-owned Chinese company to build four nuclear power plants in China. When SolarWorld, a German company, filed trade complaints against state-owned Chinese solar manufacturers,

Unit 61398 hacked into the company's US subsidiaries and made off with thousands of emails detailing its financial position, business strategy, and cost structure. Three weeks after Alcoa announced a joint venture with a Chinese state-owned aluminum maker, Unit 61398 targeted senior Alcoa managers with spearfishing emails.

Much of the digital thievery seemed aimed at enabling China to skip costly research and development by copying American products, like the special pipes made by US Steel. The spies vacuumed up enough internal information—cash-flow spreadsheets from SolarWorld's chief financial officer and detailed manufacturing metrics—to equip Chinese enterprises to outcompete American companies.

In the fall of 2012, Hickton drove to Washington and convinced Lisa Monaco, head of the department's national security division, to temporarily assign two additional lawyers to his office. He promised to have a draft of the indictment ready in several months. The hackers had been cocky to the point of sloppiness, especially in the beginning, failing to cover their tracks online and even leaving their own photos easily discoverable on the internet.[41] One thing was clear: The hackers worked for the Chinese government. This was not some rogue group of Chinese criminals.

Fearing a diplomatic rupture, the Obama administration had confined its complaints about Chinese hacking to private demarches. That began to change in early 2013. In March, Tom Donilon, the president's national security advisor, went public in a speech to the Asia Society in New York. Concerns about protecting trade secrets and intellectual property had moved "to the forefront of our agenda," Donilon said. "Increasingly, US businesses are speaking out about their serious concerns about sophisticated, targeted theft of confidential business information and proprietary technologies through cyber intrusions emanating from China on an unprecedented scale," he added. "The international community cannot afford to tolerate such activity from any country."[42]

The truth was that it had tolerated such activity—and had done so for years. Companies often knew they were being victimized by Chinese hackers, but they effectively treated the resulting financial losses as the cost of admission to China's lucrative market. Their governments, balancing the irritation and financial toll of chronic computer theft against more pressing priorities, such as cooperation in dealing with North Korea or Iran, had played down its significance.

Hickton, a former scholastic basketball player, saw himself as the captain of an FBI–Justice Department team. He led weekly meetings with bureau agents and Justice attorneys as the case progressed while focusing his personal efforts on outreach to the victims. Hickton's local ties paid off again when he asked the targets of the Chinese hacking to go public. He and Surma had overlapped at Penn State. The Westinghouse general counsel was a classmate from Catholic school. Hickton was on a first-name basis with the steelworkers' Gerard, with whom he traded good-natured profanities. "There was no way that those people would trust anyone from Washington, DC, of any political persuasion," Hickton said.

The prosecutor was heartened by Donilon's speech and by an executive order that Obama issued calling for greater information sharing between business and the government to thwart cyberattacks on critical infrastructure, such as power grids, dams, and the air traffic control network. In April, Hickton sent a draft indictment of the Chinese hackers to his superiors in Washington and waited. "We had tons of evidence, but there was a lot of pushback by the NSC, the White House, and primarily the CIA," said William Evanina, who was chief of the CIA's counterintelligence division at the time.

Some administration officials worried that Beijing would retaliate against US companies or executives working in China. There were countless meetings in the White House, involving officials from Justice, the FBI, the intelligence agencies, the Commerce Department, and the State Department, all battling over the pros and cons of an unprecedented indictment of state-sponsored hackers.

After Attorney General Eric Holder signed off, the case was set to go in early 2014. But then Russia invaded Crimea, a geopolitical earthquake that prompted a brief postponement. Finally, on May 16, 2014, Hickton brought all of the victims to the FBI office in Pittsburgh, ushered them into separate rooms, and disclosed the scope of the case. "I had no idea how they were going to react to what we were telling them.

It turned out that it became comforting to them to know that they were part of a larger case because as far as they knew, they were the only victim," he said.

Three days later, Holder—flanked by Hickton and other senior FBI and Justice Department officials—announced the thirty-one-count indictment at a press conference in Washington. Five members of the PLA—their photographs included in the court documents—faced six charges, including economic espionage, theft of trade secrets, and conspiracy to commit computer fraud and abuse.[43] It was the first time the United States had charged members of a foreign military with cybercrimes.

The Chinese government denied the allegations, withdrew from cybersecurity talks with the United States, and threatened unspecified actions against US technology companies operating in China. In the United States, the reaction was mixed. *The New York Times* called the indictments "pointless and perhaps counterproductive," noting there was no chance the indicted Chinese military officers would ever see the inside of a US courtroom.[44] Tom Ridge, a former secretary of homeland security, dismissed the case as "a public relations stunt."[45] Hickton also drew criticism for overstating the causal link between Chinese hacking and steel plant closures in the United States.

The prosecutor insisted that even if the indictment never resulted in a trial, it would be a success. The Treasury Department might sanction Chinese personnel or institutions tied to hacking. Trade negotiators could translate the criminal charges into a formal WTO complaint. Whatever actions the US government ultimately took—and Treasury did sanction Chinese state-sponsored hackers in 2024—Beijing's computer intrusions continued apace.[46] But in the episode's wake, corporate America betrayed a new willingness to acknowledge the vulnerability of its computer networks. "Just a tsunami of companies came out of nowhere saying the same happened to me," said the CIA's Evanina. "We were just inundated in the counterintelligence community."

In their complaints about Chinese behavior, US officials distinguished between traditional spying and hacking designed to provide specific companies with a commercial edge. Washington, like many other countries, engaged in the former but insisted the latter was verboten.

China called the American stance hypocritical, citing documents made public in 2013 by Edward Snowden, a former contractor for the National Security Agency (NSA), which suggested the US did not observe such a clear distinction between commerce and national security in practice.

In 2010, for example, the NSA drew up plans to surveil the Chinese telecommunications company Huawei. The clandestine program was aimed at determining whether the company carried out electronic spying for the Chinese government. But answering that question required a deep dive into the company's organization, leadership, and commercial operations, according to agency briefing documents. "If we can see how Huawei is marketing itself, and working to expand this will help us to understand the company's plans and intentions," said an NSA PowerPoint justifying the operation. "If we can determine the company's plans and intentions, we hope that this will lead us back to plans and intentions of the PRC."[47]

The indictment marked a turn in the Obama administration's attitude toward Chinese hacking. US officials for at least two years had been trying, with little success, to get China to take their cyber complaints seriously.[48] As the Justice Department considered whether to proceed with the indictment Hickton had prepared, Obama personally raised the hacking issue with Xi during their June 2013 summit in Rancho Mirage, California.

The American president made little progress. As the next Xi–Obama meeting approached in September 2015, administration officials drafted a package of economic sanctions to punish the Chinese beneficiaries of the commercial spying program.[49] Such action could effectively sever some Chinese individuals and businesses from the US dollar and the global financial system.

With the threat of crippling punishment looming, Xi arrived in Washington for his first state visit. US and Chinese negotiators raced to reach agreement on a joint disavowal of commercially motivated hacking before he left town. On September 25, the two leaders appeared in the Rose Garden, where they announced an agreement to prohibit spying for commercial gain.

Obama was blunt: "I raised once again our very serious concerns about growing cyber-threats to American companies and American citizens. I indicated that it has to stop." After welcoming the agreement—which involved information sharing between American and Chinese law enforcement authorities—he indicated that his concerns were not entirely resolved. "What I've said to President Xi and what I say to the American people is the question now is: Are words followed by action?"[50]

The answer, at least initially, was yes. In the spring of 2016, Admiral Michael Rogers, the NSA's director, said that Chinese business-related hacking was "somewhat lower" since the Rose Garden agreement.[51] The CEO of FireEye, a private cybersecurity firm, said that none of the twenty-two Chinese state-sponsored hacking units it had identified remained active against US companies.[52] Hickton thought the process for US-China consultations over cyber spying was working.

But the computer intrusions soon resumed. Hickton began working on another Chinese hacking case before resigning at the end of the Obama administration. Months after he quit, a grand jury in Pittsburgh returned an indictment of three Chinese men, accusing them of breaking into computers belonging to three US companies "for the purpose of commercial advantage and private financial gain."[53] They were charged with conspiracy to commit wire fraud, conspiracy to commit trade secret theft, wire fraud, and aggravated identity theft. It was as if the Rose Garden agreement had changed nothing.

Operating from offices in Guangzhou in southern China, the men hacked into networks belonging to Siemens, Moody's Analytics, and Trimble, a maker of Global Positioning System software. From 2011 until May 2017—twenty months after Xi had pledged a halt—they stole trade secrets and confidential business plans, including for a precision navigation system that Trimble had spent three years and millions of dollars developing.

Justice Department officials contacted their Chinese counterparts while investigating. But after receiving "no meaningful response," they proceeded with the indictment.[54] Prosecutors made no explicit statements about any Chinese government links to the affair. But they seemed to doubt the commercial bona fides of the hackers' employer,

Guangzhou Bo Yu Information Technology Company Ltd., or Boyu-sec, saying it "purported" to be a Chinese cybersecurity company.

The alleged hackers, including one who used the online alias "Christ Wu," used similar techniques to those employed by the PLA officers charged in 2014. They tricked email recipients into down-loading malware that allowed them access to the companies' net-works and commandeered other computers to mask their activities. In fact, Boyusec was likely a front for China's Ministry of State Secu-rity (MSS).[55] "You have to see that case as connected to the PLA case," Hickton said.

The state security ministry's growing role reflected fallout from the Chinese military's blown hacking operation and a sweeping PLA reor-ganization that occurred at the same time.[56] For years, Chinese military hackers had hired themselves out to state-owned businesses in order to supplement their meager government salaries, according to Dennis Wilder, who at the time was a top China analyst for the Central Intelli-gence Agency.

From 2006 to at least 2009, for example, Unit 61398 assigned one of its members "to perform programming work" for a state-owned iron and steel company in Shanghai. His job was to create "a 'secret' data-base . . . designed to hold corporate 'intelligence' about the iron and steel industries, including information about American companies," prose-cutors alleged.[57]

"Everybody in the military tries to make money. That would have irritated Xi Jinping," said Wilder, referring to the Chinese leader's anti-corruption campaign, which accelerated shortly after the indictments were made public.[58]

At the time, Xi was reorganizing the PLA to create a modern war-fighting force. The plan involved reducing the uniformed head count by three hundred thousand while professionalizing the ranks and im-proving the military's ability to fight joint or multiservice operations. The reshuffle reassigned the PLA's Third Department, including Unit 61398, giving it a cyber assignment more narrowly focused on military objectives, according to Wilder.

Xi almost certainly had not been aware of the PLA operations cited in the 2014 indictment, said Evanina of the CIA. Amid a global burst of bad publicity, Xi regrouped and tapped the powerful MSS to take over from the PLA and lead an expanded hacking campaign. "The Chinese are really upset. What do they do? They double down," said Evanina. "In late 2014, he tells the MSS: 'You're now in the game.'"[59]

We'll dispose of Donald Trump

In October 2011, Congress by solid margins approved trade agreements— with South Korea, Colombia, and Panama—that had been stalled for years. Even the largest deal, with South Korea, would have only a "negligible" impact on US employment or output, according to the International Trade Commission.[60] But 84 percent of House Democrats voted against the most controversial of the three, the pact with Colombia, underscoring the erosion of Democratic Party support for trade liberalization.[61]

Two decades after NAFTA, which had passed with 102 Democratic votes, trade was unpopular with Democrats.[62] But the Democrat in the White House was pursuing a twelve-nation Pacific trade accord as the centerpiece of a strategic effort to "pivot" to Asia and shape the Asian economy before China could do so. The Trans-Pacific Partnership would join the United States, Australia, Brunei, Canada, Chile, Japan, Malaysia, Mexico, New Zealand, Peru, Singapore, and Vietnam in a pact that would lower trade barriers and set standards for digital trade, labor, and the environment.

Secretary of State Hillary Clinton, in an article in *Foreign Policy* magazine, explained the need to rebalance the US global footprint, arguing that after a decade of bleeding resources in the Middle East, the United States needed to "lock in a substantially increased investment— diplomatic, economic, strategic, and otherwise—in the Asia-Pacific region."[63]

It was a sensible, even vital strategic goal. But proposing the largest trade deal in history, one that would have knit 40 percent of the global economy into a single commercial zone, defied political reality. Obama pursued the Pacific trade deal over the objections of Summers, who argued that the economic gains would be modest while the political fight would be painful, according to an administration official. To Lori

Wallach, who was trying to stir up congressional and labor union opposition, the new trade deal was "NAFTA on steroids." Along with the scope of a traditional free trade agreement, TPP included e-commerce provisions, limits on nations' ability to require that companies store their digital data locally rather than in a distant headquarters, and intellectual property rules for a new class of drugs known as biologics. Many lawmakers complained that the administration was not listening to their concerns.

"It was clear they were totally ignoring everything the Democrats were saying. They'd been at it for a bunch of years; it was really heading in a bad direction," Wallach said. "All of these members of Congress who we're working with on the negotiations, each of whom cares about a different part of it, are getting more and more upset."[64]

The trade initiative was hobbled almost from the start. In November 2013, some 151 House Democrats wrote Obama opposing his request for fast-track negotiating authority, which would allow him to bring the proposed Pacific deal to Congress for a straight up-or-down vote, no amendments allowed. Without fast track's approval, the other nations in the negotiations would refuse to close a deal, fearing Congress could rewrite the terms and press for additional concessions.

In the 2014 State of the Union address, Obama appealed for negotiating authority. But Senate Majority Leader Harry Reid, a Nevada Democrat, quickly shot him down, saying the president would be "well-advised just to not push this right now."[65] Obama's decision to name Senate Finance Committee Chairman Max Baucus ambassador to China also hurt the fast-track push by depriving it of an experienced legislative quarterback. By April 2015, Richard Trumka, the president of the AFL-CIO, was complaining that the administration's labor consultations were "fundamentally inadequate."[66]

With the clock ticking, Obama went to the House in June 2015 to plead with Democrats for fast track. But just hours after the president's personal appeal, lawmakers rejected the first part of the administration's trade package. Obama's team had paired fast track with a separate measure reauthorizing Trade Adjustment Assistance for workers who would be hurt by TPP, and it was that TAA bill that failed. It was a "staggering" setback.[67]

"They made the mistake of not paying attention to the House, of being arrogantly dismissive.... They had the president come up. To come to the Democratic caucus. And he was rude. He was insulting. He's like, how dare you not give me an authority every other president has had?" Wallach said.

By the end of June, after separating the two bills, the administration finally secured fast-track powers, formally known as Trade Promotion Authority. The Pacific trade deal's sheer scope complicated the domestic politics surrounding the negotiations. The legislation that finally passed Congress in June 2015 contained fifteen single-spaced pages of deal objectives, including new rules governing trade in goods, services, and agriculture; foreign investment; digital products; state-owned enterprises; labor and the environment; anti-corruption efforts; and currency values.[68] "We loaded on more and more topics into trade agreements. That, in my mind, probably made it even more difficult. We created more opponents as we expanded the coverage," said Wendy Cutler, a top USTR negotiator.[69]

The delay in approving the fast-track measure meant that final congressional action on TPP would occur during the 2016 election year.[70] At the time, that seemed to the administration like a problem, but not an insurmountable one. As secretary of state, the Democratic front-runner, Hillary Clinton, had celebrated the proposed Pacific deal as "the gold standard in trade agreements," and that month's NBC News poll showed former Florida Governor Jeb Bush, who held traditional pro-trade views, leading the Republican primary pack.[71] An avowed protectionist, businessman Donald Trump, who had declared his unlikely candidacy two weeks earlier, was drawing just 1 percent of the vote.[72]

At the White House, the president's economic and trade teams gathered in the Roosevelt Room for a discussion of the outlook for TPP. David Simas, the White House director of political affairs, had detected important shifts in public opinion on trade in extensive polling and focus groups of swing voters that he had conducted. Republican and Republican-leaning voters—especially non-college-educated whites—had suddenly soured on trade. A solid majority of the Republican electorate now flatly opposed trade deals.

Democrats and Democratic-leaning independents, especially those with college educations, were far more supportive. The most enthusiastic were younger voters and Democrat-supporting Hispanics. Adding Obama's name to the polling polarized the findings, with Democrats embracing a deal that bore the president's brand and Republicans shunning it. About the only way that Republicans could be convinced to support a potential Obama trade deal was if it were billed as an anti-China measure.

Obama had carried Michigan, Wisconsin, Ohio, and Pennsylvania, pillars of the industrial Midwest, in both of his election wins. To make TPP palatable to the working-class whites who had backed him, he would need to emphasize its value in preventing China from establishing the commercial rules in the fast-growing Asia-Pacific region.

"This is a really different picture than the debate on the Hill, where the most pro-free-trade party were the Republicans and the most anti-trade were the Democrats and, at least at that moment, were completely not representing their bases," said Simas. "It's less that Republicans were changing their minds and more that the composition of the parties had been changing," he added. "This is a new battlefield."[73]

The sharp anti-trade swing among Republican voters was bad news, Simas told the men and women gathered just steps from the Oval Office. But the good news was that there remained a path to passing the Pacific trade deal: Pro-trade Republican leaders had not yet recognized that their voters had rejected the party's traditional pro-trade stance. The administration could pilot the Pacific trade deal to approval before Senate Majority Leader Mitch McConnell and House Speaker John Boehner recognized the disconnect.

The meeting broke up on that cheery note. But the populism that animated the Republican base was not so easily overcome. As the Republican presidential contest entered the fall, Trump, the brash reality television star, steadily surged. By October, when Froman and his counterparts announced agreement on a tentative deal, Trump was in first place.

Behind the scenes, Republican leaders assured Froman that their voters' flirtation with the disruptive outsider who swore he was "totally against" the deal would not last.[74] "The word we get from Republican leadership is don't worry, as soon as we have a pro-trade nominee, we'll move ahead with it. And the view was we'll dispose of Donald Trump. We'll get Jeb Bush nominated. It'll be clear by February or March that Bush or somebody like Bush will be the nominee and we can proceed," Froman said.[75]

Antiestablishment politics had taken over

If many Americans were unwilling to accept Washington's assurances about the new trade deal, their prolonged economic stagnation might explain why. Adjusted for inflation, the median household income in 2015 of $71,000 was almost unchanged from 1999.[76] Millions of American families had basically been running in place for the better part of two decades.

Obama himself had famously recognized the political consequences of chronic economic disappointment. Campaigning in the 2008 Democratic primary, he was captured on tape explaining the party's difficulties with working-class voters to a crowd of wealthy contributors in San Francisco.

"You go into some of these small towns in Pennsylvania, and like a lot of small towns in the Midwest, the jobs have been gone now for 25 years and nothing's replaced them," Obama said. "And they fell through the Clinton Administration, and the Bush Administration, and each successive administration has said that somehow these communities are gonna regenerate and they have not. And it's not surprising then they get bitter, they cling to guns or religion or antipathy to people who aren't like them or anti-immigrant sentiment or anti-trade sentiment as a way to explain their frustrations."[77]

When the housing bubble popped, the economic fallout was the most serious since the Great Depression. The government response initially was swift and creative, as the Bush and Obama administrations managed to stave off a repeat of the 1930s.

But the $787 billion stimulus program that Obama signed into law during his first full month in office filled less than half of the economic hole. An estimated $1.8 trillion over two years would be needed to return the economy to full employment by early 2011, Christina Romer, head of Obama's Council of Economic Advisers, had calculated.[78]

The inadequate stimulus was made worse by ill-timed austerity. By May 2009, under pressure from Republicans, Obama was touting minor budget cuts and calling for the government to cut back, just like everyday Americans. "We can no longer afford to spend as if deficits do not matter and waste is not our problem," the president told reporters at the White House.[79] Obama's rhetoric recognized political reality, but it was the opposite of what the economy needed.

Driven by the populism of the Tea Party, congressional Republicans insisted on additional cuts. Traditional Keynesian economics argued for the public sector to spend money until the private sector could get back on its feet. Instead, driven by a wrong-headed obsession with federal belt-tightening, the United States did the opposite. As a share of the economy, the deficit fell for six consecutive years. By mid-2016, federal spending had fallen more during the recovery from the Great Recession than during any previous postwar rebound.[80] Government—even as the economy remained badly damaged—acted as a brake on activity rather than as a spur. Not until a subsequent global crisis several years later would the nation's leaders demonstrate that they had learned their lesson.

It took the economy until May 2014 to recover all the jobs that had been lost in the 2008 crash. Even then, the labor market remained severely bruised. The share of Americans in their working prime who were employed never recovered to its pre-crisis level throughout Obama's time in office.[81] In 2015, an unexpected slowdown in China caused a mini-recession in manufacturing, which depressed US blue-collar employment at a politically sensitive time. After growing steadily since the spring of 2010, factory hiring flatlined in the eighteen months before the 2016 election.

The weakest recovery since World War II aggravated the impact of the China shock, which was starting to fade as the 2008 crisis began. Between 2001 and 2016, the economy grew in inflation-adjusted terms by just one-third, well below the 61 percent gain during the previous fifteen years.[82] Job growth in Pennsylvania, Michigan, and Wisconsin, politically vital states in the industrial Midwest, occurred at no better than half the national average in the years leading to the 2016 election.[83]

While blue-collar workers struggled, others flourished. Shareholders, for example, enjoyed stock prices that by the end of 2016 had more than tripled since their March 2009 low. Luxury goods retailer LVMH saw its annual sales nearly double to more than $51 billion over the same period, as consumers snapped up Louis Vuitton bags, bottles of Moët & Chandon champagne, and TAG Heuer watches.

Even some of globalization's greatest enthusiasts belatedly recognized that it was contributing to a societal divide. In 2015, Obama's treasury secretary, Larry Summers, acknowledged that the growth in US trade with low-wage countries like China had shifted mainstream economic thinking. "The consensus view now is that trade and globalization have meaningfully increased inequality in the United States by allowing more earning opportunities for those at the top and exposing ordinary workers to more competition, especially in manufacturing," he wrote.[84] Indeed, the richest 10 percent of Americans received more than half of all national income each year, up from about one-third in the late 1970s. That was the highest percentage since 1917.[85]

Still, as the 2016 election approached, Obama officials felt good about the economy. Output was expanding. Real wages were growing at their fastest pace since the Great Recession. And roughly 160,000 new jobs were being created each month.

Yet the public mood was downbeat: More than three-quarters of those polled told Gallup they were "very" or "somewhat" dissatisfied with the way things were going in the country.[86]

In 2015, Bill Clinton's Oxford classmate, and former labor secretary, hit the road. Robert Reich was working on a book and documentary film to be called *Saving Capitalism*. He wanted to revisit people he had met during his official travels to see how they had fared. Traveling to states like Wisconsin, Michigan, North Carolina, and Missouri, he held informal focus groups designed to take the temperature of popular opinion.

Even in the early 1990s, before NAFTA and the rise of China, many workers in these communities had been struggling. Their struggles were aggravated by a sense that the governing class did not understand or care about their problems. More than two decades later, that sense of betrayal had only deepened. Conventional wisdom expected Hillary Clinton and Jeb Bush to face off for the presidency in 2016. But Reich kept encountering voters who were in thrall to Bernie Sanders, the US Senate's lone socialist, or Donald Trump, the disruptive outsider. For many Americans, the electoral choice was no longer between Republican and Democrat or even right and left. It was between different flavors of populist rebellion.

"The Washington establishment was completely out of touch with what was happening in the heartland," Reich said. "I became convinced by the end of my travels in 2015 that the heartland was in revolt and that antiestablishment politics had taken over."[87]

7

Everything Wrong with Globalization and Trade

The Big Dog was back. Fifteen years removed from the White House, Bill Clinton was campaigning in Indianapolis for his wife, Hillary, who was making her second try at the Democratic Party's presidential nomination. Well ahead in the 2016 delegate race, she seemed destined to become the party's choice. But she was locked in a tight Indiana primary battle with Sen. Bernie Sanders.

The former first lady had been having trouble shaking Sanders for months. In March, the self-professed socialist stunned Clinton by winning Michigan. Sanders had drawn blue-collar voters by blistering corporate CEOs for their greed. Michigan's working class "cared about trade, trade, and trade." White primary voters, in particular, were focused on the Trans-Pacific Partnership (TPP), which Clinton belatedly opposed after hailing it as the "gold standard" of trade deals.[1]

In the aftermath of her Michigan loss, Clinton concluded that she had spent too much time campaigning in minority districts in cities such as Detroit and Flint at the expense of white working-class communities where her support was soft. Her aides, meanwhile, bemoaned her refusal to highlight trade policy as a contributor to blue-collar discontent.[2]

Across the country, voters were angry, and Clinton struggled to understand why. The sluggish recovery finally seemed to have found its footing. Employers were creating more than two hundred thousand jobs each month. And the stock market was climbing. Yet many Americans were furious at the political establishment—and there seemed no greater representative of that establishment than Hillary Clinton.

Volatile issues of trade and globalization were at the center of the 2016 election. After decades of an American-led global order that promoted open commerce, long-established truths suddenly were up for grabs. The volume of goods and people crossing US borders had provoked a reaction among supporters of both parties. The campaign's shock conclusion would have many causes and many consequences. But one thing was clear: The populist tide that crested in November 2016 rejected more than the eventual Democratic nominee. It also repudiated the global economy that Bill Clinton, among others, had labored to build.

For Hillary Clinton, the irony was that working-class whites in Ohio and Pennsylvania had been her salvation in her losing 2008 effort. But now the choice was not between Clinton and Barack Obama, an African American; it was between Clinton and a rumpled figure who inveighed constantly against "millionaires and billionaires." Eight years after the worst financial crisis since the 1930s, the public welcomed attacks on the financial and political elite. The surprising support for unconventional candidates such as Sanders and Trump, both broadcasting a relentless anti-trade message, "showed how much the Great Recession had radicalized significant parts of the electorate."[3]

From the start, Bill Clinton had pushed his wife's advisers to seek out rural and working-class votes. One week before the May 3 Indiana primary, the former president was dispatched to Evansville, a blue-collar city of almost 120,000 people about 170 miles southwest of Indianapolis. He spoke at a union office a few blocks from the Ohio River. A crowd of eighty union members, some with stickers reading "Hard Hats for Hillary" on their headgear, listened as he touted her economic plan.[4]

The appearance was vintage Bill Clinton: equal parts Southern charm and policy substance. Both in Evansville and at a later stop at campaign headquarters in Indianapolis, Clinton's focus was an episode that had emerged as a potent symbol of working-class resentment.

Back in February, at a time when candidates in both parties were occupied elsewhere, a three-minute-thirty-two-second YouTube video went viral and reset the political agenda. The clip showed the scene inside a Carrier Corp. plant in Indianapolis, where Chris Nelson, president of Carrier's North American HVAC unit, had gathered workers for an announcement.

"It became clear that the best way to stay competitive and protect the business for [the] long term is to move production from our facility in Indianapolis to Monterrey, Mexico," Nelson told employees. As he uttered the word *Mexico*, what had been a low rumble of discontent exploded into a howl of rage that drowned out his next words.

"Listen, I've got information that's important to share as part of the transition," continued an exasperated Nelson. "If you don't want to hear it, other people do. So let's quiet down."

A total of 1,400 jobs at the plant and a nearby distribution center were headed to Mexico. The first to leave would go in mid-2017, roughly eighteen months away. The full relocation would play out over three years. "I want to be clear: This is strictly a business decision," Nelson said.

One of the workers could be heard wondering "how long it takes before people start tearing shit up." As Nelson urged workers to continue producing high-quality products during the transition, another worker yelled, "Fuck you."

"We are committed to treating you with respect throughout this transition," Nelson lamely concluded. "Thank you for your attention."[5]

The February 10 announcement had been in the works for months, as United Technologies, Carrier's corporate parent, sought to reduce costs. Many of Carrier's competitors already had relocated south of the border, lured by lower Mexican wages. Company executives told union representatives that they would be paying Mexican workers an average hourly wage of three dollars rather than the twenty dollars that Americans earned.[6] The Indianapolis plant also suffered from chronic absenteeism due, in part, to a two-tier wage system that left newer hires, who earned less than veterans doing similar work, feeling unappreciated. On any given day, as many as one out of every five workers failed to appear. In Mexico, fewer than one out of every hundred were no-shows.

Announcing a plant relocation in the middle of a presidential election was certain to attract unwanted attention, company executives realized. To his credit, Nelson had insisted on delivering the news personally, despite knowing he would be running into a buzzsaw.[7] Indeed, populist criticism came from both ends of the political spectrum. Three days after the video appeared on YouTube, Trump attacked Carrier during a Republican primary debate. He threatened to put a tariff on any Carrier products exported to the United States from Mexico, ordered the company to "stay where you are," and complained that "we are killing ourselves with trade pacts that are no good for us and no good for our workers."[8] A few days later, Sanders called Carrier's move an "example of how NAFTA and other trade policies have been a disaster for American workers."[9]

The United Steelworkers Union Local 1999, which represented the Carrier workers, staged a protest outside the plant several weeks later. Hundreds of employees and retirees gathered along the road out front, holding American flags and signs reading "Fighting for American jobs" and "Free trade isn't free—ask the unemployed."[10] In April, the union endorsed Sanders for president.

With the Indiana primary looming, the Clinton campaign made a push for the blue-collar vote. Standing against an American flag backdrop at his wife's Indianapolis headquarters in late April, his voice raspy from weeks of campaigning, the former president cited Carrier as an example of corporate greed. "Carrier explains a lot of the inequality that's happening today," he said.[11] Bill Clinton painted the decision to leave Indiana as inexplicable. "The company, the division, was making $2.9 billion a year.... Why would anybody leave the number-one manufacturing state in America, that would be you, you have the highest percentage of your jobs in manufacturing, with a wildly productive workforce, at a time when every year labor costs were a smaller percentage of the total and materials, energy and transportation are a bigger percentage of the total, when we're bringing back manufacturing jobs to America," Clinton said.[12] The sign on his podium read: "Fighting for us."

Clinton was promoting his wife, but he was also defending himself. Robert James, the president of the USW local, had linked Carrier's exit to the North American trade deal that the former president had pushed through Congress. "I place the blame on Bill Clinton. I don't place the blame on Hillary Clinton," James told a reporter.[13] At a rally in Fort Wayne, when Bill Clinton began speaking about Carrier, someone in the crowd bellowed, "Repeal NAFTA!"[14]

Greed may have been a politically potent diagnosis. But it was economically unsound. Corporate chieftains were no greedier in 2016 than they had ever been. In moving low-skilled work to Mexico, Carrier was responding to the incentives that policymakers—including Clinton—had created. Why should the company pay someone twenty dollars to do an hour's work in Indianapolis if they could get someone in Mexico to do it for three dollars?

NAFTA had created a unified economic jurisdiction encompassing the United States, Mexico, and Canada. That was the treaty's entire raison d'être. For commercial purposes, the imaginary line on a map that separated Mexico and the United States was no more meaningful than the one that divided Indiana from Illinois. Carrier was far from alone in capitalizing on the rules that Washington had written. Numerous companies, such as Stanley Black & Decker, Johnson Controls, and Dometic, also shifted work from the Hoosier State to Mexico.[15]

Indiana was fertile ground for an anti-trade message. Since the Great Recession ended in mid-2009, the state had recovered all the jobs it lost during the financial crisis and added thousands of new ones. But factory employment remained thirty thousand shy of its pre-crisis peak.[16] Economists might shrug at what they viewed as an irreversible long-run decline. But voters were less sanguine about the absence of good-paying work for those without college degrees. That discontent lifted Sanders to another upset victory; he defeated Hillary Clinton by a 52.5 percent to 47.5 percent margin. The results would do little to stop her march to the nomination. But they were a klaxon warning of the former secretary of state's weakness with working-class voters.

Too much globalization going on

Trump, meanwhile, was using trade and globalization as a cudgel against the Clintons. "NAFTA has been a disaster, right? Disaster. What it's done to New England, what it's done to New York state, what

193

it's done here, what it's done everywhere," he said at an Indianapolis rally. "Bill Clinton signed it. Bill Clinton. It was [a] Clinton deal. Bill Clinton signed it. It's been horrible."[17]

At the end of June, Trump went to a battered steel town outside of Pittsburgh to detail his platform of economic nationalism. Monessen, Pennsylvania, in some ways was an ideal emblem of American industrial decline. The steel mills that once produced the cables for San Francisco's Golden Gate Bridge were long gone. The city, embraced on three sides by the Monongahela River, was dotted with hundreds of derelict buildings. Young people routinely fled for opportunities elsewhere.

But it was an odd place to bemoan the effects of trade liberalization. Monessen had fallen on hard times long before NAFTA, at a time when Deng Xiaoping had barely begun China's program of "reform and opening." The city's population had been declining since the 1940s. Its largest employer, Wheeling-Pittsburgh Steel, closed its local operations in 1986.

None of that bothered Trump. Standing in front of a mountain of crushed aluminum, he sketched a remarkably dark view of recent American history. The nation's elites, he said, had rigged the system to line their pockets while decimating proud communities all across the country. "Globalization has made the financial elite who donate to politicians very wealthy. But it has left millions of our workers with nothing but poverty and heartache," he said.[18]

Those who governed the United States had prioritized the interests of shadowy globalist figures and allowed foreign powers to impoverish Americans, he said. Trump quoted George Washington and Alexander Hamilton in support of his plan to block imports and to promote domestic production. He identified himself with nationalists in the United Kingdom, where voters had just endorsed withdrawal from the European Union. And he called out, by name, both of the Clintons for their roles in this ongoing national tragedy. After all, they had supported NAFTA, "the worst trade deal in history," as well as China's entry into the WTO, which produced "the greatest jobs theft in history," he said.

Worse, the Clintons were planning a new abomination, the TPP, which "would be the death blow for American manufacturing." Hillary Clinton had belatedly opposed the Pacific trade deal just to match him,

Trump said. But if elected, she would again betray American workers by negotiating a cosmetic change and reversing her position for a second time.

Trump concluded by itemizing a seven-step program to revolutionize US trade policy, including scrapping TPP, renegotiating NAFTA, and mounting a full-fledged assault on what he described as China's mercantilist cheating. Vowing to put "America First," Trump said: "Under a Trump Presidency, the American worker will finally have a president who will protect them and fight for them."[19] Peter Navarro, one of Trump's closest White House advisers, would later describe the speech as the "Rosetta stone" for understanding Trump's worldview.

The battle between Donald Trump and Hillary Clinton was a bizarre, whirlwind campaign like no other. She had enjoyed a mammoth polling lead over Trump in the spring. The gap closed, opened, and closed again by the end of July, even as most prognosticators gave the disruptive challenger little chance of winning the White House.[20]

Yet out in the country, Trump was taken more seriously. His loud complaints about foreign trade and foreign people, even if not always in accord with the facts, were striking a nerve. On Maryland's eastern shore, the local economy depended upon immigrant labor to staff poultry farms, seafood-processing facilities, and beach resorts. But many local residents saw migrants as a potential source of disease, terrorism, and competition for jobs, concerns that blended with a more inchoate animus. Some worries edged into the type of conspiratorial worldview that would increasingly come to dominate Republican thinking in the Trump era. "There's too much globalization going on," said Grant Helvey, a retired telecommunications engineer and the Republican party chairman in Worcester County, Maryland. "I resent some of the stuff coming out of the United Nations and becoming policy in my neighborhood."[21]

In late September, the two candidates met for their first debate. Trump went on the offensive, criticizing NAFTA, highlighting Clinton's past support for TPP, and citing the trade deficit as proof that the United States was being exploited by its trading partners.

"We have to stop our jobs from being stolen from us. We have to stop our companies from leaving the United States and, with it, firing all of their people. All you have to do is take a look at Carrier air conditioning in Indianapolis. They left—fired 1,400 people. They're going to Mexico. So many hundreds and hundreds of companies are doing this," Trump said.[22]

The campaign's final weeks were roiled by a series of shocks: Trump was caught on tape making vulgar comments about sexual assault; Wikileaks released hacked emails belonging to John Podesta, the Democrat's campaign manager; and FBI Director James Comey abruptly reopened the investigation into Hillary Clinton's use of an unauthorized email account while serving as secretary of state.

Bill Clinton had urged his wife's campaign team to devote more time and attention to working-class areas. But Robby Mook, her campaign manager, was a believer in data analytics, not the instincts of a veteran campaigner. During the primaries, he had concluded that it was more efficient to send the candidate and her surrogates to delegate-rich and vote-rich cities such as Detroit. But the legacy of that strategy was that the "Reagan Democrats" of places like suburban Macomb County felt neglected.[23]

In the campaign's final weeks, the former president was dispatched to small towns in Ohio. Places like Niles and Youngstown that were full of the white voters with high school degrees who felt that Trump was saying what they believed. When Bill Clinton made the case for his wife across the Mahoning Valley, Ohio's industrial heartland, he warned voters against being led by their "resentments," and he promised that his wife would do something about the unfair economic system that was leaving them behind.

"Look, there's a reason for the road rage today. People have gone fifteen years without a raise and they're mad," he said in Youngstown. For some groups, the situation was even worse than that. Workers who lacked a college degree, roughly half of the labor force, were earning less per hour than in 1979.[24] At another stop, he told a crowd that Trump was "the best I've ever seen at rubbing salt in open wounds."[25]

The problem with Clinton's appeal was its familiarity. Working-class voters in the Midwest had been listening to politicians, including both Clintons, promise them a fairer deal for two decades. From the vantage point of manufacturing-dependent communities in this part of the country, little progress had been made. Indeed, many people felt they were slipping back, not moving forward. And they were tired of being ignored.

The Clintons faced an uphill fight. Among likely male voters without a college degree, Trump led Hillary Clinton by 76 percent to 17 percent, according to an October *Washington Post*–ABC News poll.[26] These blue-collar laborers once had been reliable Democratic votes. Now, they were siding with a populist billionaire. After Comey reopened the FBI probe into Clinton's emails, her team detected a late shift toward Trump in Michigan, Wisconsin, and Pennsylvania.[27]

Early on election night, when Florida went for Trump, it became clear that Clinton would fall short. Trump had performed especially well in Pasco County, north of Tampa, which was known for attracting retirees from the industrial Midwest.[28] Later, as the Democrats' defenses in Michigan, Wisconsin, and Pennsylvania collapsed, Bill Clinton saw his wife's disappointment as part of a global populist phenomenon. "It's like Brexit," he said. "I guess it's real."[29]

Burn it down

Initial explanations of Trump's shock win paid particular attention to his success in mobilizing working-class voters angry over manufacturing job losses, even those unconnected to the trade deals that he routinely castigated. *The New York Times* highlighted workers at a General Electric plant in Erie, Pennsylvania, who backed Trump because their factory had moved thousands of thirty-four-dollars-per-hour factory jobs to nonunion Texas—not Mexico or China.[30]

"Few Americans knew the voters who rejected Hillary Clinton better than her husband," the journalist David Maraniss, a Clinton biographer, wrote in *The Washington Post*. ". . . One explanation for the stunning political demise of the Clintons might be the extent to which they moved away from a middle-American sensibility into the realm of the coastal elite, from McDonald's to veganism, to put it in symbolic terms, making it harder for Hillary to bridge the nation's yawning social divide. This rendered her vulnerable even to the most unlikely opponent, a wealthy Manhattan real estate developer who had nothing in common with many of his voters except his uncanny ability to speak their language of discontent."[31]

Indeed, Trump's appeal defied conventional political logic. His supporters overlooked all sorts of behavior that would have disqualified other politicians. Even individuals who had personal experience with the candidate's habitual dishonesty remained in his corner. Richard Morrison was among them.

The chief executive of Molded Fiber Glass Companies in Ashtabula, Ohio, had produced the colorful onion bulb domes for Trump's Taj Mahal casino and resort in Atlantic City. But when it came time to pay the bill, Trump stiffed him. MFG was one of more than one hundred contractors involved in the project that Trump failed to pay, according to Martin Rosenberg, whose small business provided the hotel's windows, doors, and mirrors.[32] It took an extended back-and-forth, including a forty-minute meeting at Trump Tower, plus legal action, before Morrison eventually received partial payment. "We got two-thirds" of the tab, Morrison said. "It was sort of an interesting experience. We were the first ones to sue him."

Despite Trump's efforts to avoid paying him what he owed, Morrison still voted for him. On a shelf in his office, Morrison kept a signed copy of Trump's book, *The Art of the Deal*. On an inside page, Trump had scrawled: "Richard... Thanks for the great work. Best wishes, Donald Trump."[33]

The businessman acknowledged that Trump's political style made him "uncomfortable." And MFG's shipments to a customer in Mexico could be adversely affected by Trump's plans to quit NAFTA. But Morrison was willing to ignore all of that. "He's on the right track. Some of these trade deals are out of whack," Morrison said. "They should be fair."

For most of 2016, Democrats had confidently planned for a Hillary Clinton presidency. Her loss drew bitter criticism of her shortcomings as a candidate. She had failed to secure the Democrats' "Blue Wall" across the upper Midwest before dabbling in long shot states like Georgia and Texas. She had misread the public mood, and after more than a quarter century in the public eye, she was burdened by establishment credentials that repelled voters.

Eight years later, Bill Clinton remained irked by his wife's defeat. She had lost, he said, "because the press decided to cover the emails as if they were the most important issue since the end of World War II, and then Jim Comey pulled that stunt at the end, something even J. Edgar Hoover didn't do, that violated seventy or eighty years of bipartisan policy."[34]

In truth, Trump's incredibly narrow victory made conclusive analysis of the reasons for his win—and its implications—difficult. He won the presidency in the Electoral College while losing the popular vote by 2.9 million votes. If roughly forty thousand of the nearly fourteen million voters in Wisconsin, Michigan, and Pennsylvania had chosen Clinton rather than Trump, she would have been president.

Trump won 46 percent of the overall vote. But among white, non-college voters, he thrashed Clinton 58 percent to 36 percent. His gains relative to previous Republican nominees were especially strong in counties with the highest percentage of such voters, who "tend to be dependent on low-skill jobs and vulnerable to structural economic change."[35]

Most analysts agreed that working-class voters delivered Trump the Midwestern states that made victory possible. But *why* had those voters selected a Manhattan businessman and reality television star as their tribune?

Analysts generally fell into two camps: those who saw Trump's rise as largely fueled by economic discontent and those who instead blamed cultural or racial concerns.

It was a mistake, however, to seek a single, all-encompassing explanation of Trump's triumph. His win had been so narrow, and accompanied by so many unprecedented features—Comey's intervention, Clinton's flaws as a candidate, state-sponsored Russian hacking—that it was tempting to conclude the entire affair had been a historical accident.

Yet dismissing this political earthquake as some sort of glitch also would have been an error. Someone like Trump should never have come close to the White House. Yet he had drawn almost sixty-three million votes. His was a narrow win, but it was no accident. And any fair analysis would land on multiple interrelated factors. Economics, race, class, immigration, anti-elite rage—all of it had lifted this unusual figure to the White House.

The first in-depth look at the Trump phenomenon, by the Democracy Fund Voter Study Group, involving two dozen experts from across the political spectrum, came down squarely on the side of racial resentment as an explanation. Eighty-three percent of 2016 voters backed the same party's presidential candidate they had supported in 2012, it said.[36] Among 2012 Obama voters who chose Trump in 2016, changing views of "immigration, Muslims, and black people" played the biggest role, according to surveys of the same eight thousand voters conducted in both election years. The Voter Study Group said that anti-trade sentiment was not "highly correlated with party switching."

But it was not that simple: The study made clear that long-term economic dissatisfaction had paved the way for a candidate like Trump. Voters who were negative about the economy in 2012 were more likely to favor restrictive immigration policies four years later. And while the authors played down trade's significance, 68 percent of Trump voters said trade deals would cost US jobs compared with 50 percent of Clinton's supporters. Among Obama-to-Trump voters, the two most salient motivations were the beliefs that minorities consumed too many government services and that trade deals eliminated too many American jobs.[37]

"Voters who experienced increased or continued economic stress were inclined to have become more negative about immigration and terrorism, demonstrating how economic pressures coincided with cultural concerns to produce an outcome that surprised most of us," wrote Henry Olsen, the Voter Study Group's project director.

The 2018 book *Identity Crisis*, by political scientists John Sides, Lynn Vavreck, and Michael Tesler, also linked Trump's victory to racial sentiments. Citing Trump's history of racist comments, the authors framed the election as a "debate about whether White Americans were being unfairly left behind in an increasingly diverse country."[38] The shrinking white share of the population, growing societal attention to African American civil rights and police brutality, and lingering terrorism concerns made group identity, not economics, white voters' priority, they wrote.

The same year, Diana Mutz, a political scientist specializing in communications studies, weighed in with a psychological analysis. In Mutz's view, "less-educated white males supported Trump because they felt threatened by the changing nature of America."[39] The common narrative that Trump had capitalized on Rust Belt voters' ire over unjust trade deals and runaway globalization was simply wrong, she said. Years of political science research demonstrated that voters rarely, if ever, held politicians accountable for their individual economic experiences. "It would be a mistake for people to understand the 2016 election as resulting from the frustration of those left behind economically," Mutz wrote.[40]

The study, which provided the foundation for Mutz's later book, *Winners and Losers: The Psychology of Foreign Trade*, received widespread press attention. But other scholars questioned her methodology.

Mutz compared voters' views using data from surveys conducted before the 2012 and 2016 elections. She argued that voters do not have long memories and that it was thus unlikely that they would choose a president in 2016 based upon the impact on themselves or their communities of the China shock, which had ended years earlier. Voters do not form their views of trade policy based on its impact on their own livelihoods, she wrote, focusing instead on "symbolic, status-related beliefs."[41]

But Mutz acknowledged that 2016 was the first election that presented anti-trade voters with an appealing choice. In 2012, certainly, they saw little difference between Obama and Romney. Four years later, however, Trump offered a sharp contrast with Clinton on NAFTA, China, and TPP. Indeed, Jake Sullivan, her top policy adviser, saw the Clinton–Trump contest as "the deferred debate of 2008."[42]

In reality, working-class voters' economic and racial motivations could not be separated. Voters who were angry over the perceived effects of global trade deals often grumbled about immigration as well, and they jumped at their first chance to back a candidate who shared their grievances.

"Most sociologists believe that people make decisions for mixed motives and have a hard time disentangling them," said Stephen L. Morgan, a professor of sociology and education at Johns Hopkins University.

"People are voting not based on the last few years on this matter. People are voting on 1982 onward. I'm from Ohio; I know what people are pissed off about."[43]

Morgan publicly critiqued Mutz's use of panel data and said she had drawn conclusions from her research that were not supported in the data. Based on her own results, it was just as likely that economic self-interest explained Trump's voting strength as the "status" explanation she favored, he said.

"Mutz's data do not support her overly strong conclusions. Material interests and her measures of status threat are sufficiently entangled among white voters, especially those in the working class, that it is impossible with her data to estimate their relative importance with any clarity," Morgan wrote.[44]

Other researchers also cast doubt on the racial resentment theory, concluding that Trump received fewer votes from voters with the highest levels of racial resentment than Romney did four years earlier. Stanford University political scientists Justin Grimmer and William Marble said that earlier analyses had failed to adequately consider who actually turned out to vote, focusing instead on what motivated voters to choose a particular candidate. Examining only those Americans who voted for Obama in 2012, Trump attracted relative moderates on immigration, not hardliners, they said. And he gained among whites of lower socio-economic circumstances.[45]

The 2012 Obama voters who chose Trump in 2016 were distinctive, according to a separate study using data from the American National Election Studies, a source of high-quality voter data since 1948.[46]

First, compared to other Obama voters, those who switched to Trump were both more hostile to racial equality and more financially insecure. They were also "significantly more anti-trade and anti-immigration."[47] These voters were equally likely to dislike trade agreements and immigration. But unlike other Trump voters, they also supported tougher regulation of giant banks.

"Switchers, in other words, view their economic and social status very differently (and as much more precarious) compared to run-of-the-mill Republican voters for Trump," wrote Dani Rodrik, the study author.[48]

One weakness in the studies that compared the 2016 election to the voting four years earlier was the short time frame. Resentment over globalization, whether related to trade, immigration, or a loss of national sovereignty, had been building in manufacturing-dependent communities for decades. When the 2008 financial crisis hit, it aggravated both the suffering and the political aftershocks. "Populism found its principal support in areas where the recovery was slower, and where economic decline had been underway for a long time," concluded political scientists J. Lawrence Broz, Jeffry Frieden, and Stephen Weymouth.[49]

Globalization had effectively sorted American communities into high-growth areas whose future prospects were bright and "hope deserts" that had been battered by waves of economic change and left to rot. Decline fed on itself, as counties with the highest share of manufacturing employment in 1970 performed worst in the first two decades of the twenty-first century.[50] As economic change accelerated, Americans also moved less frequently in pursuit of a better life than they had in the past—and less frequently than economists had assumed they would—which cemented the opportunity divide.[51]

The economy had improved in the two years before the election; the jobless rate was below 5 percent as voters went to the polls. But that didn't erase the damage that had been done to working- and middle-class families by the one-two punch of the China shock and the subsequent financial crisis. In 2010, median household wealth fell to its lowest level since 1969—erasing the fruits of more than four decades of labor. Despite a subsequent recovery in stock and housing values, the typical household's wealth in 2016 remained more than one-third lower than its 2007 peak.[52] As they weighed the choice in 2016 between a quintessential outsider and a consummate representative of the governing class, many voters were quite literally poorer than they had been in previous years.

There was ample evidence that views on trade policy had affected voting. In the Republican primary campaign, Trump won eighty-nine of the one hundred counties most affected by trade with China, according to a *Wall Street Journal* analysis.[53] The authors of the original China shock research conducted a subsequent study, which found that districts most exposed to rising imports became more politically polarized.[54] Majority-white districts shifted toward conservative Republicans, while majority-minority districts gave more votes to liberal Democrats. In both cases, moderate Democrats were the losers.

The shift toward Trump in these trade-exposed areas was decisive. If the China shock had been only half as destructive, it "would have tipped the narrow Republican voter majority in the states of Pennsylvania, Wisconsin, and Michigan, leading to an Electoral College victory for Hillary Clinton, instead of a victory for Donald Trump."[55]

Though Tennessee was not one of the contested swing states in presidential elections, other factory towns in Ohio, North Carolina, Wisconsin, Michigan, and Pennsylvania also were affected by rising imports. The China shock left its mark on electorally important areas, giving it an outsized importance in US politics.

"Geography matters because of politics. It matters where jobs are gained or lost, if you think about how we elect a president," said Glenn Hubbard, George W. Bush's top economic adviser.[56]

Trade did not start the process of political polarization in the United States. But trade's effects were concentrated, falling disproportionately upon less-educated workers in specific manufacturing-dependent communities. Tennessee's Obion County was no exception. Local political views became more extreme as the Washington establishment failed to effectively counter the loss of all those jobs in the Goodyear tire plant. In the 2000 presidential election, Obion County voters had split almost evenly between Bush and his Democratic opponent, Vice President Al Gore, a Tennessee native. But in 2016, Obion County warmed to Trump's "America First" platform of heavy tariffs and immigration restrictions, giving him almost 80 percent of its vote.[57]

Those who were actually in the arena were more likely to see Trump's rise as the outgrowth of multiple, related issues. Few people had done more to highlight or inflame popular sentiments on matters of trade, immigration, and race than Stephen K. Bannon, executive chairman of *Breitbart News*. In the years before the Trump–Clinton showdown, Bannon regularly populated the *Breitbart* home page with stories of foreigners taking advantage of the United States by overstaying their immigration visas, spreading disease, or taking American jobs.

Bannon, who joined the Trump campaign in August 2016, described Trump's hot rhetoric on trade and immigration as threads in a broader critique. "Trade was a proxy for 'unfair': The towns are gutted. The manufacturing jobs are gone. The high-value-added manufacturing jobs that you could support a family on. All the service businesses, the little restaurants and everything. Once the jobs went, the towns are never the same," he said.

Trump's supporters cheered his frequent promises to "build a wall" along the country's southern border. But Bannon said Trump's trade complaints held an even broader appeal. "People think 'Build-the-Wall' was up there. For people at those rallies, it was bringing back jobs from China. You say that and, man, the roar would overwhelm you," he said. "Yes, they want 'Build-the-Wall.'... But the thing that resonated was jobs, trade, and China. And I tell people, if you go to a rally in Dayton and go up there and say jobs and trade, you get a standing ovation."[58] Trump himself later said that trade was "one of the main reasons" he had defeated Clinton.[59]

Hillary Clinton had little in common with Bannon. But her assessment of Trump's working-class appeal was similar. She saw the debate between economics and culture, race and class, as a false choice. In the two decades before the 2016 election, Americans had been buffeted by astonishing waves of change: the China shock, the September 11 terror attacks, wars in Iraq and Afghanistan, the 2008 financial crisis, a sharp increase in the share of the population that had been born abroad, and rapid societal acceptance of gay marriage. Many Americans welcomed change and adapted. But millions struggled or refused to adjust.

"All these different strands of anxiety and resentment are related: The decline of manufacturing jobs in the Midwest that had allowed white men without a college degree to provide their families with middle-class lives, the breakdown of traditional gender roles, anger at immigrants and other minorities for 'cutting in line' and getting more than their 'fair share,' discomfort with a more diverse and cosmopolitan culture, worries about Muslims and terrorism, and a general sense that things aren't going the way they should and that life was better and easier for previous generations," Clinton wrote in her campaign memoir. "In people's lives and worldviews, concerns about economics, race, gender, class, and culture all blend together."[60]

She was right. In the weeks after the 2016 election, as shattered Democrats struggled to make sense of what had happened, Obama's political director, David Simas, conducted two nights of listening sessions with voters in Iowa. Participants had voted for the president in 2008 and 2012, approved of the job he had done—and yet voted for Trump.

One place in particular highlighted this extraordinary shift. In 2012, Obama had trounced Mitt Romney in Howard County by a margin of 59 percent to 38 percent. Four years later, Trump took 56 percent of the vote to Clinton's 36 percent, virtually a mirror image of the 2012 outcome. In an electorate of about 4,500 people, Trump topped Romney's total by 816 votes.

When the focus group moderator asked participants who had voted for both Obama and Trump to explain how the two men were alike, there was no hesitation. The Iowans said they saw both men as outsiders, not members of the Washington club. Both were pragmatic, devoted to outcomes not ideologies. And both were expected to shake up a complacent capital. One woman said she saw "hope and change" and "drain the swamp" as two sides of the same coin. For years, Washington had catered to everyone else, from Wall Street banks to newly arrived immigrants, rather than help these average Americans. Now their patience was exhausted. With Trump, they were ready to burn it all down.

Patient zero

Within days of his improbable November triumph, Trump was on the phone to Gregory Hayes, CEO of United Technologies, Carrier's parent company, asking him to reconsider Carrier's planned exit from Indianapolis. The president-elect promised that his tax and regulatory policies meant the company would be "printing money" if it stayed put, Hayes later told CNBC.

The economic logic behind Carrier's decision to relocate to Mexico had not changed, despite the political furor. But with roughly 20 percent of United Technologies' $57 billion in annual revenue dependent upon government contracts, Hayes did not want to be at odds with the new president.

Hayes suggested that he and Mike Pence, Trump's running mate, work something out. The two men were acquainted from Pence's time as governor of Indiana, and Hayes knew that Trump was just looking for an outcome that could be pitched as a political win.

On Monday, November 28, Hayes went to Trump Tower in Manhattan to meet with Pence, who was in his final weeks as governor, to hammer out a $7 million package of state incentives. Trump wanted to personally announce the job-saving deal at the Carrier plant, Pence told him.

Three days later, Hayes welcomed Trump and Pence to the factory where ten months earlier workers had cursed the executive announcing the Mexico move. Backstage, a mirror and a large can of hairspray awaited the guest of honor. Pence introduced Trump as "a man of action and a man of his word." Smiling broadly, flashing his signature thumbs-up, Trump walked out to shouts and applause. "I love that red hat," he said, pointing to someone in the crowd wearing a "Make America Great Again" cap. He began by praising himself for picking Pence as his running mate, saying he was "something special." He bragged about his Indiana victories in the Republican primary and general election, blasted China, overstated the number of jobs saved by almost 40 percent, and mistakenly said that the plant, which produced gas furnaces, made air conditioners. He derided NAFTA as a "total and complete disaster," sparking whoops and cheers from the assembled workers. It was a rambling, exhausting seventeen-minute monologue of the type that was becoming familiar to Americans.

"Companies are not going to leave the United States any more—without consequences," he said.[61]

But Carrier wasn't leaving on a whim. Labor costs in Mexico were roughly 80 percent lower than in Indiana. Trump himself noted that six of the eight largest players in its industry, companies like Lennox and Trane, already had established manufacturing sites in Mexico. If Carrier wanted to remain competitive, it needed to join them. Most of the industry's supply chain was based there.

Trump's performance that day, putting into action the grievances and instincts that had fueled his electoral triumph, drew a mixed reaction. The columnist Peggy Noonan, writing in *The Wall Street Journal*, called the president-elect's intervention with Carrier "a very good thing" and likened it to President John F. Kennedy's 1962 showdown with the steel industry over price increases.[62] Elsewhere, business executives worried about how they would deal with an unpredictable new president and "an agenda grounded as much in emotion as economics."[63]

For the moment, the episode was a political triumph, if ultimately a hollow one. It showed the president-elect as a man of action, determined to protect workers from the predations of footloose corporations. Trump billed Carrier's decision to modify its relocation plans as an inflection point in corporate America's generation-long shift of manufacturing from the United States to lower-cost foreign venues. It was far from it. Companies kept leaving.

As time passed, the deal's substantive heft dwindled. Hayes a few weeks later told CNBC's Jim Cramer that Carrier would invest $16 million to automate the plant, meaning "there will be fewer jobs."[64] The company also remained committed to producing its products outside the United States. In April 2017, Carrier broke ground on a $95 million manufacturing facility in Shanghai, which would produce compressors and light commercial-HVAC systems for China and the region.

One month later, Trump called Hayes, furious over news that Carrier had notified state officials that it was planning to lay off 632 workers in Indianapolis.[65] In a May 19 letter to the state's dislocated worker unit, a Carrier human resources executive said the company was moving fan-coil production out of the country. Those affected included maintenance associates, precision inspectors, truck drivers, group leaders, and production workers. "The separations," the letter concluded, "are expected to be permanent."

The president accused Hayes of lying to him about his plans to retain workers. The CEO and Pence, who was listening on a speaker phone, tried to mollify Trump, explaining that the move was consistent with their December agreement. Though Trump had bragged about saving "a minimum" of 1,100 jobs, the agreement had always guaranteed just 800. Trump groused that it was a "bad deal," but eventually calmed down.

His handling of the Carrier episode set the tone for his dealings with corporate leaders. Rather than develop a coherent plan and stick to it, Trump's approach was a blur of improvisation. He promised a man-ufacturing renaissance that would recapture the millions of factory jobs lost during the age of hyper-globalization. But his tax and trade policies were at odds, with the former encouraging the moves offshore that the latter were intended to discourage. By the time he left the presidency, there would be fewer people working in American factories than when he first entered the Oval Office.[66]

Hayes wryly referred to himself as "patient zero," the first CEO to be drawn into a PR scrap with Trump. He would not be the last. In the months ahead, titans of American capitalism such as General Motors, Harley-Davidson, and Amazon all would be singled out in presiden-tial tweets and interviews for displeasing the country's chief executive. CEOs learned that they needed to avoid drawing the president's gaze.

But if Trump was quick to anger, he also proved quick to forgive. When United Technologies and Raytheon in 2019 announced plans to merge, Trump at first complained that such defense industry consol-idation would make it harder for the Pentagon to negotiate favorable contracts. United Technologies, fearing that the comment suggested the president was looking for revenge after what had happened in In-dianapolis, sought a phone call with the White House to explain. But Trump instead invited Hayes and Raytheon's Thomas Kennedy to the Oval Office for a sit-down, which went well.

After the companies agreed to divest some overlapping businesses, the Justice Department approved the deal. "Once he got the informa-tion, it was a very positive meeting," Raytheon's Kennedy said of the president.[67]

The world was changing

All that lay ahead as Trump made his way out onto the west front of the US Capitol building on Friday, January 20, 2017, to take the oath of office as the forty-fifth president of the United States. Protesters braved a cold rain to fill the streets. Even before Trump appeared, an orga-nized group armed with hammers and crowbars smashed windows at a Crowne Plaza hotel and local Starbucks and Au Bon Pain outlets. Later, police engaged in a running battle with an anti-Trump mob gathered along K Street, the avenue populated by Washington's lobbying corps. By day's end, police had arrested more than two hundred people in the worst inaugural unrest since Richard Nixon's 1969 swearing-in during the Vietnam War.[68]

Three days later, Trump took aim at the Pacific trade deal that Obama had described as the centerpiece of his pivot to Asia. In one of his first acts as president, Trump called reporters to the Oval Office to witness the United States withdrawing from the twelve-nation agreement, which Congress had not yet ratified. "We've been talking about this for a long time," he said, as he signed the official paperwork.[69]

Ironically, Bannon, Trump's consigliere of economic nationalism, had once described Obama's Trans-Pacific Partnership as a "genius" move. "The concept of doing something like that to box in China is smart," he said, before lamenting what he described as a triumph of business lobbying that had spoiled the idea.

The man Trump picked to be his chief negotiator had no such mixed feelings. To Robert E. Lighthizer, a veteran trade attorney, TPP was symptomatic of everything that was wrong with the bipartisan consensus on doing business with the rest of the world. Officials from both parties saw TPP as a way to knit together a regional bloc to limit Chinese influence. Lighthizer thought the deal was predicated on "the foolish notion" that giving those other nations better trade terms would convince them to side with the United States against China.[70]

In the agreement's fine print, he detected provisions that would encourage the loss of American auto industry jobs. The issue involved "rules of origin," which determine how much of a product needs to be made within a member country to qualify for duty-free treatment. Negotiators had agreed that 45 percent of a vehicle would need to be sourced within a member country. To critics like Lighthizer, that meant that a new car made up of 45 percent Vietnamese components and 55 percent Chinese materials could be shipped to the United States without encountering a tariff.

"I was always against TPP. It was kind of the last heartbeat of the wrong 1990s notion. . . . It wasn't like it was something you could change this or that term about. The fundamental idea was wrong," he said.

Some Trump aides had an even darker view. One official said the deal was the corporate world's backup plan in case anything went wrong with the US-China trade relationship. In that event, this official said, multinationals would have an alternative low-wage base for their operations in Vietnam or Malaysia. It would be "the end of most US manufacturing," this official said.

The notion of a pan-Asian trade zone held genuine appeal with or without the United States. After Trump quit the deal, the remaining eleven nations continued the accord under a slightly different name—after first dropping several provisions that US negotiators had insisted upon, including a requirement for countries like Vietnam to permit independent labor unions. The economic costs of the withdrawal for the United States were modest; Lighthizer would go on to negotiate a separate deal with Japan, the largest TPP nation, which he said captured most of the promised gains.

But the strategic costs were real. At a time when many Asian countries already wondered about the US commitment to the region, Trump had given them fresh reason to doubt American staying power. China was happy to fill the void, establishing its own trade pact, the Regional Comprehensive Economic Partnership, with many of the same countries. Several years later, Beijing would even apply to join the very deal that the United States had intended would act as a curb on Chinese power. Trump's successors would struggle to cobble together an alternative arrangement to achieve the same foreign policy goals without triggering domestic political opposition.

Time had run out on TPP during the Obama administration. Froman had expected Obama to push ratification through in the lame-duck congressional session that would follow Hillary Clinton's expected victory. When that possibility evaporated late on the night of November 8, Wendy Cutler began hoping that Trump, once in office, would follow Obama's earlier example. The Democrat had criticized a proposed trade deal with South Korea in the 2008 primaries, then secured some improvements to it upon being elected and ushered it into law.

In truth, the Obama administration had been out of sync on the timing of the Pacific deal from the start. But beyond the political

211

calendar, there was a broader concern. Administration officials had pursued TPP believing it would advance the nation's foreign policy and economic interests. It turned out, however, that they had neglected to sell voters on the idea. "We lost sight of the public sentiment on trade and globalization. The world was changing," said Cutler, one of the key negotiators.

Indeed, it was. Political and economic fallout from the 2008 financial crisis had compounded the China shock. What happened to Obama's trade deal with a stroke of Trump's pen proved the point. Patience with the traditional approach to trade policy had evaporated. In a meeting with union leaders in the Roosevelt Room, when Trump announced he had just withdrawn from the Pacific agreement, the men and women of labor applauded.[71]

"It didn't matter what was in TPP," Cutler said. "It was just the poster child for everything that was wrong with globalization or trade."[72]

8

One of the Most Significant People in the Entire US Government

Matt Pottinger spent five years in the Marine Corps after leaving *The Wall Street Journal*. From a US military base in Japan, he deployed to Iraq and Afghanistan for three tours as an intelligence officer before returning to civilian life. He was awarded the Bronze Star for tracking down Taliban units that produced roadside bombs.[1]

The war in Afghanistan brought him into contact with Lt. Gen. Michael Flynn, the senior intelligence officer for the Marines and his superior officer. As a captain, Pottinger co-authored a report that recommended sweeping changes in US intelligence operations on the battlefield, arguing that they had been "unable to answer fundamental questions about the environment in which US and allied forces operate and the people they seek to persuade."[2] The report's critical tone won few converts in the Pentagon, but drew widespread praise when it was published by a Washington think tank.

Though it was not immediately apparent, the report suggested a future for Pottinger in shaping government policy. The journalist turned military officer in coming years would emerge as a White House adviser to an unconventional new president, parlaying his national security and

China credentials into genuine influence over a revolution in the US approach to the world's second-largest economy.

In particular, Pottinger's disillusionment with the Chinese government fueled the Trump administration's drive to preserve a US technological edge over China. This more assertive policy toward China was part of a broader rethinking of globalization that emerged in the wake of the 2016 election, prompting second thoughts among some advocates of the traditional approach and opening new possibilities for longtime critics of US policy like Pottinger and Lori Wallach. What at first seemed just a pause in the process of global integration would blossom into a true break with decades of US policy.

Pottinger left active duty in 2010 and moved to New York, where he established a small research firm called China Six LLC, which performed due diligence on Chinese companies. "I wasn't sure what I was going to do with myself. I was sort of decompressing from five years of combat deployments and just sort of getting reoriented in American life. It was kind of a hard year," he said.[3]

After hiring a small team of Chinese journalists to conduct research, he made several trips back to China. What he found surprised him. The go-go mood of the early 2000s, when everyone in China seemed to be on the make, had soured into a grim realization of the inherent flaws in the country's state-capitalist system. Life was getting better for the typical Chinese person. But some—often government insiders or those with connections to them—were obtaining fabulous wealth.

"It was like greed run amuck. A lot of my Chinese friends had made a lot of money but were unhappy and they didn't want to raise their kids in Beijing. They just said that the system is corrupt. Even the ones who'd done well in that system," he said. "And I found that a lot of my Chinese friends and former colleagues were all moving abroad. They moved to Australia and the United States. So it felt kind of lonely."

One of Pottinger's investigative targets was Evergrande, China's largest property developer. By analyzing commercial satellite photos and visiting the company's high-rise apartments, Pottinger learned that Evergrande was overvaluing its properties to support its borrowing from a state bank. The company included swampland and garbage dumps in its valuations and listed half-built apartments on its books as if they were completed properties.

Visiting a massive development made up entirely of unsold units, Pottinger raised alarms by asking too many questions of an Evergrande salesman. "They started to get suspicious of what I was doing there. And so they put a tail on me. I got back in the car and they tailed me all the way back to Beijing," he said. Pottinger wrote a prescient report for his investors concluding that Evergrande was a "house of cards" that might take a decade to collapse, but collapse it inevitably would.[4]

After several years, Pottinger was hired by one of his clients, the hedge fund Davidson Kempner Capital Management, to expand his due diligence work beyond China. He was doing that when Flynn called after the 2016 election to ask for his help educating Trump about China and North Korea.

In early December, Pottinger made the short walk from his office to Trump Tower. It was the first time he had met Trump, and he quickly discovered that he ran meetings nothing like a military officer. The session began with Trump talking about random issues, before gradually finding his way to the subject at hand. The meeting went well and shortly thereafter Keith Kellogg, a senior Trump adviser and retired three-star army general, asked Pottinger to join the administration.

Pottinger quickly agreed, but he was apprehensive about assuming the role of senior director for Asia on the NSC staff. It was a big job and Pottinger had never worked in government. Apart from the Trump Tower briefing, he had no relationship with the president-elect. And the policy stakes were high: Trump had assailed China's trade strategy throughout his campaign, and North Korea was approaching its sixth nuclear test.

Pottinger rented a house in Washington for his wife, Yen, and their eighteen-month-old son. But in February, Flynn resigned after administration officials concluded he had lied to Vice President Mike Pence about his contacts with the Russian ambassador during the transition. Flynn's implosion cost Pottinger his closest supporter and raised questions about his own future.

"I remember I went home that night and just said, look, this may have been a real detour into a cul-de-sac, and I'll see if I can figure out, you know, what to do with my life if I'm only in this job for another few days," he said.

But one week later, when Trump named another general, H. R. McMaster, to replace Flynn, the new national security advisor decided to retain Pottinger. For much of that year, he developed the administration's strategic framework for the Indo-Pacific region. The ten-page document addressed the threat from North Korea and the need to promote "a liberal economic order" in the region while blunting Chinese influence.[5]

Pottinger was unsentimental in describing Chinese ambitions. Gone were the Clintonian hopes for integrating China in a US-led global order. In their place was an expectation of "strategic competition" based on the "divergent nature and goals of our political and economic systems." China aimed to "dissolve" US alliances and would violate international norms and rules whenever it saw advantage in doing so.[6]

These blunt conclusions were among fourteen assumptions that guided the new strategy. Pottinger had secured interagency approval of them only after clashing for weeks with intelligence officials who argued that China had no ideological agenda, was content for the United States to remain the world's sole superpower, and was focused on economic development. Trump's team held a much darker view.

The Indo-Pacific strategy was a guide to the trade-and-technology war with China that Trump's advisers were planning. "China seeks to dominate cutting-edge technologies, including artificial intelligence and bio-genetics, and harness them in the service of authoritarianism," the strategy said. Chinese success would "pose profound challenges for free societies." Drawing on a classified game plan for "countering China's economic aggression," Pottinger called for preserving US technological supremacy and promoting an international consensus that China's behavior was damaging the global trading system. "Counter Chinese predatory economic practices that freeze out foreign competition, undermine US economic competitiveness, and abet the Chinese Communist Party's aspiration to dominate the 21st century economy," the document said.[7]

If there was agreement among the president's advisers on the goals of their new China strategy, there was dissent about how to achieve them. The administration was divided between traditional Republicans and MAGA populists determined to overturn conventional policies on trade, immigration, and foreign affairs.

As the NSC's Asia director, Pottinger was a rung below the principals, the president's closest advisers. The traditionalists included a pair of former Goldman Sachs bankers—Gary Cohn, the director of the National Economic Council, and Treasury Secretary Steven Mnuchin—who sought to preserve as much of the status quo on international economics as they could, despite the president's thirst for disruption.

Working in sometimes uneasy harness with the traditionalists were several unorthodox protectionists. Bannon, Trump's chief strategist, acted as the president's id on trade and immigration. Peter Navarro, a former university professor and unsuccessful political candidate who had authored an alarmist book entitled *Death by China*, sought a wholesale makeover of US trade policy. Commerce Secretary Wilbur Ross, a former steel industry investor, was an enthusiastic supporter of tariffs. But he was also a wealthy art collector and owner of a Manhattan penthouse, hardly a tribune of the common man.

Trump's chief trade negotiator, Robert E. Lighthizer, was a veteran trade attorney who had represented domestic steel producers seeking protection against foreign imports. Lighthizer had grown up in the northeast Ohio town of Ashtabula, a Great Lakes port that suffered from the steel industry's decline. While his family remained well-off—his father was a doctor—the social erosion he saw all around him forged an antipathy toward US trade policy. "For thirty years, he was a voice in the wilderness," said his older brother James. "He's emphatic about it. He really believes we've given away the store." [8]

The wilderness years ended with Trump's 2016 triumph. A partner at a prominent Manhattan law firm, Lighthizer had been anticipating retiring to his oceanfront condo, about three miles north of Mar-a-Lago, when Trump called. Now he would be the field general for Trump's multifront trade war.

Relations between the two camps ranged from cordial to antagonistic. Lighthizer and Mnuchin held very different views on trade. But both realized that Trump was the one who had been elected, and they cooperated to implement his goals. Navarro, an abrasive figure who alienated numerous colleagues, corporate executives, and congressional Republicans, was less collaborative. During an early round of trade negotiations in Beijing, Navarro and Mnuchin held a profanity-laced shouting match on the lawn outside the Diaoyutai government compound in the heart of the city.[9] As astonished Chinese diplomats watched from a nearby building, the two American officials hurled "f-bombs" at each other. Navarro also frequently telephoned Washington journalists to disparage Mnuchin as overly accommodating to China.

"In the White House, the nastiest, and I mean almost punch-outs, the nastiest fights we had were about trade policy [with] Gary Cohn and Mnuchin and [Jared] Kushner, kind of what I call the finance capitalism guys," Bannon said.[10]

This is a crisis

Trump's own views on trade had been remarkably consistent for thirty years. Even as he had changed parties and switched his stance on abortion rights, gun control, universal health care, tax cuts for the rich, and Hillary Clinton, Trump held fast to a belief that the United States was getting screwed by its trading partners.[11] In the late 1980s, as he first flirted with a presidential run, he directed his ire against Japan, which he accused of "taking advantage of the United States." In a full-page ad that appeared in both *The New York Times* and *The Washington Post*, Trump argued that Japan, and other US allies, had prospered while Americans bore the cost of their defense.[12]

In the years before he entered politics, two of Trump's favorite information sources were nightly viewings of cable television's *Lou Dobbs Tonight* and the alt-right Breitbart website, which gave prominent coverage to immigration, trade, and anti-Muslim stories. Dobbs was a distinctive cable news voice in the first years after China joined the WTO, railing against trade deals and corporations that moved American jobs overseas to cut costs. "We are outsourcing American jobs. We're killing middle class American jobs, high value jobs and we're not creating new ones. Isn't it time for people to get belligerent?" he demanded of one guest.[13]

Asked by *Washington Post* reporters what issue had first inflamed his political ambitions, Trump responded: "I would say in my case, more than anything else, the stupidity of the trade deals that we have with China, with Japan, with Mexico, with other... Because that's something that I see. And I didn't know that it would hit such a chord."[14]

In reality, Trump had one foot planted firmly in both the traditionalist and populist camps. He wanted to put an end to what he saw as decades of foreigners getting the better of Americans by imposing on China the highest tariffs in decades. At the same time, he coveted the approval of New York's financial class. To the president, the Dow Jones Industrial Average was a running report card on his economic stewardship. He was prepared to confront China right up to the point at which it alarmed investors and no farther.

This duality had been reflected in Trump's earlier approach to Japan as a private businessman. Even as he publicly assailed the Japanese as unfair traders who exploited their American ally, he eagerly sought Japanese customers and Japanese financing for his casino and real estate ventures.[15] In early 1990, as his debt woes mounted, he visited Tokyo hoping to refinance the Plaza Hotel and to find buyers for his yacht, the *Trump Princess*, and the Trump Palace condo development. Japanese investors bought roughly three-quarters of the Palace units, even as some bristled at his anti-Japanese rhetoric.[16]

Trump had not been a conventional political candidate, and he was not a conventional president. Less than a week after his inauguration, a team of Mexican diplomats arrived at the White House to discuss trade and the pending visit to Washington of Mexican President Enrique Peña Nieto.

They were shown to Jared Kushner's office and left there, unsupervised, literally just steps from the Oval Office. In past administrations, the foreign visitors would have been escorted continuously. But over the next few hours, a parade of top administration figures came to meet them: Bannon, the president's chief strategist; Treasury Secretary Steven Mnuchin; and Vice President Mike Pence. At one point, Ildefonso Guajardo Villarreal, Mexico's economy minister, stepped out to find a bathroom.

As he wandered the hallway, Guajardo encountered a startled Secret Service agent. "The security guard says, 'You know that you are not supposed to be wandering around in the White House.' And I look at him and say, 'And that's my responsibility or your responsibility? I'm wandering around because somebody left me here,'" he said.[17]

The disorganization extended beyond security protocols. On the day that the Mexican delegation arrived, Trump signed an executive order to begin construction of a wall along the US-Mexico border and to hire thousands of new Border Patrol officers to speed the deportation of unauthorized migrants.[18] The timing suggested an astonishing insult to the Mexican president, who was due to arrive in days. If a traditional American president had taken such actions, Guajardo said, the Mexican government would have seen them as a deliberate negotiating ploy. But Trump was not that carefully choreographed. "It was just complete chaos," Guajardo said.

China, meanwhile, had capitalized on Trump's embrace of protectionism. Chinese President Xi Jinping appeared at the World Economic Forum in Davos, an annual gathering of the global elite, where he posed as a defender of the free trade system that the United States once had championed. "Just blaming economic globalization for the world's problems is inconsistent with reality, and it will not help solve the problems," Xi intoned to rapturous applause.[19]

While in Davos, Xi spoke at a private luncheon with a group of Chinese and American executives. Billionaire Stephen Schwarzman, CEO of Blackstone, brought up working-class resentment over the US trade deficit with China, which he said had fueled Trump's rise. Xi said he was prepared to execute "a major economic reset with the United States," a message Schwarzman carried to the White House.[20]

In early April, the president hosted Xi at his Mar-a-Lago resort in Florida for an informal summit that began over a dinner of dry-aged steak and whipped potatoes. While Trump later claimed to have developed an "outstanding" relationship with Xi during the twenty-four-hour affair, the meeting's principal outcome was a new "Comprehensive Economic Dialogue," essentially Henry Paulson's high-level channel rebranded for the Trump era. "Progress has been made," the president claimed.[21]

Palm Beach introduced Xi to the splits within the administration. At the long golden table in the Mar-a-Lago dining room, Bannon, the White House strategist who always looked like he had just finished a multiday bender, was seated alongside the urbane Chinese foreign minister, Wang Yi. Commerce Secretary Ross, who had made his fortune buying and selling steel companies, rounded out the protectionist faction, while the so-called globalists were represented by the Goldman Sachs veterans, Mnuchin and Cohn. Navarro was present, after initially having been excluded from the delegation. "You had a split in the camp. I had to force to get Navarro down there. They left him off the list," Bannon later recalled.

Trump tapped Ross and Mnuchin to co-chair the first trade talks and set a hundred-day deadline for an agreement. Ross obliged within a few weeks, claiming he had reached a deal that represented "a herculean accomplishment."[22] It was nothing of the sort, and in July, the talks sputtered to an inconclusive end. The Chinese had dangled an apparent concession on American beef sales in China, which Ross saw as a breakthrough. In reality, Beijing had discussed opening its beef market for years. At a climactic White House meeting to discuss the potential bargain, Trump disparaged Ross's negotiating prowess and ordered him to cancel a scheduled celebration with the Chinese.[23]

Lighthizer, a longtime China skeptic, was among those who told the president that the deal was weak. A few months before the 1997 Denver G8 summit, Lighthizer, who had advised Clinton's Republican opponent in 1996, wrote in *The New York Times* that China wanted to join the WTO in order to gain "a dominant position" in global trade. "If China is allowed to join the WTO on the lenient terms that it has long been demanding, virtually no manufacturing job in this country will be safe," wrote Lighthizer.[24]

But if Ross had stumbled, his Chinese counterparts also misread the situation. Xi and his team emerged from the Mar-a-Lago summit believing that Trump was a transactional figure who simply wanted a deal that he could tout for domestic political advantage. That conclusion reflected a broader misunderstanding of the new president. Trump made no secret of his desire to revolutionize US trade policy, particularly insofar as it related to China. But Chinese leaders were slow to recognize the extent of his ambitions, his willingness to shatter long-standing diplomatic norms, and his reliance upon an unfamiliar corps of advisers.

Chinese officials at first tapped American contacts they had worked with for years, such as Henry Kissinger and Paulson, in hopes of fathoming the unusual new president. Months later, they turned to figures closer to Trump, including casino magnate Steve Wynn and Bannon.[25] The president's son-in-law, Jared Kushner, who had been named to a top White House post, also opened a back channel with Cui Tiankai, the Chinese ambassador to Washington.

Beijing initially viewed Ross as the most important Trump trade official, largely because his advanced age impressed Chinese officials accustomed to a hierarchical system based on longevity. They eventually recognized Lighthizer's importance, as he launched new initiatives affecting almost half of the nation's $3.6 trillion in annual trade. In August, he welcomed negotiators from Canada and Mexico for talks aimed at renegotiating NAFTA, telling them that Trump sought far-reaching changes, not "a mere tweaking of a few provisions and a couple of updated chapters."[26]

Those talks almost never happened. A few weeks after the Mar-a-Lago summit, Trump—looking to repeat the immediate gratification of withdrawing from TPP—prepared to kill NAFTA rather than renegotiate it. On the morning of April 26, Bannon marched into the Oval Office with a draft withdrawal order. The plan called for Trump to announce the move at a rally in Pennsylvania three days later, which would coincide with his hundredth day in office.[27]

When the news leaked, financial markets wobbled. The leaders of Canada and Mexico desperately phoned the White House and Capitol Hill, trying to forestall an impulsive move that could have crippled more than $1 trillion worth of annual trade. The message, said one diplomat who was directly involved, was: "This is a crisis; you have to stop this."[28] Prominent members of Congress, including Senate Majority Whip John Cornyn and Sen. John McCain, publicly urged the president to reconsider.[29] After Sonny Perdue, Trump's agriculture secretary, showed him an annotated map demonstrating that his farm-state voters would be hardest-hit by an exit, the president reversed himself and agreed to negotiate a new treaty.

Acting at cross purposes

A handful of officials in Ottawa and Mexico City had anticipated Trump's ascent. At a Canadian cabinet retreat in Ontario in August 2016, David MacNaughton, Canada's ambassador to the United States, warned colleagues in the Trudeau government that Trump might win. It was unlikely, MacNaughton said, but far from impossible, given the mood among Americans. Just to be safe, officials should stay mum about Trump, who was notoriously thin-skinned and would undoubtedly remember any slights, he added.

In Mexico City, Secretary of Finance Luis Videgaray Caso was alone in forecasting a Trump victory. To pave the way for a productive relationship, Videgaray reached out to Jared Kushner that summer and invited Trump to visit the Mexican capital. President Enrique Peña Nieto's decision to host Trump, who had been disparaging Mexico for months on the campaign trail, was viewed by Mexicans as a "colossal failure."[30] A few days later, as outrage mounted over what the public saw as a national humiliation, Videgaray resigned.

Still, both governments understood that Trump was not entirely an aberration. His electoral triumph grew out of a mismanaged globalization that had contributed to a perception of a hollowed-out middle class and a rising tide of political polarization. "Think of Trump as a consequence of something deeper that is going on in the United States," one of Peña's advisers told him shortly after the inauguration. "He understood that those forces were there and very intelligently managed them to win an election. But there are underlying forces in the United States that made that possible."[31]

Those forces were sufficiently strong that the Mexican leader overruled aides who believed the country could weather NAFTA's collapse and negotiate a new agreement with Trump's successor. Instead, Peña sided with advisers who understood the loss of US support for trade liberalization was bipartisan. Updating the existing trade deal was the only way to preserve the lucrative $1 trillion–plus regional market.

Trump approached the renegotiation convinced that, given its size, the United States had leverage. Access to the world's largest economy was a prize that should be granted only in return for concessions, he believed.

But Mexico and Canada were not without leverage of their own. And their diplomats exerted it whenever they could, either to rebut US demands for better terms or to showcase what Americans would lose if the talks failed. When Sen. Ron Johnson, a member of the Senate trade subcommittee, championed Wisconsin farmers' desire to sell more dairy products in Canada, for example, MacNaughton informed him that Canada was the largest export market for Epic Systems, a maker of hospital software that employed about ten thousand of his constituents. "I could shut down that market in Canada with three phone calls," he told Johnson, referring to the provincial leaders of Ontario, Quebec, and British Columbia.

Both the Mexican and Canadian negotiators regarded Lighthizer as a straight shooter, a knowledgeable professional who genuinely wanted a deal so long as it met the president's objectives. Kushner, described by one foreign official as "a deal junkie," also played a constructive role.

During a January 2018 negotiating round in Montreal, Canadian negotiators sought to break a deadlock over the rules governing duty-free treatment for automobiles. The Trump team originally had concentrated on requiring a certain percentage of auto parts to be made in the United States. The Canadians instead proposed requiring a percentage of parts to be made in factories that paid an hourly wage of sixteen dollars, high enough to discourage further outsourcing to Mexico, where workers earned far less.

Lighthizer immediately disparaged the proposal as "the stupidest idea I ever heard," according to a Canadian official. But after the United Auto Workers weighed in, the US negotiator had a change of heart. In practice, the requirement could address labor's core complaint about NAFTA, that the deal encouraged American companies to relocate to Mexico, where wages were lower.

Welcoming negotiators to the United States Trade Representative (USTR) headquarters a few weeks later, Lighthizer began by referencing the wage-based proposal. "Someone said it was a stupid idea. I don't know who it was," he said with a mischievous look. "But it seems to me like it's a really good idea." To his counterparts, the remark demonstrated that—for all his hardline instincts—Lighthizer was a pragmatist. He would take a good idea wherever he found one.

But Trump was a wild card, capable of saying or doing anything at any moment. The president was living proof of the adage that it's not what you don't know that will get you in trouble; it's what you know for sure that just isn't true. He frequently boasted, for example, of using tariffs to make other countries "pay."

Multiple studies indicated that the burden of US tariffs did not, in fact, fall on foreign nations.[32] But no matter how many times aides pointed out that tariffs were effectively a tax paid by American importers, Trump clung to his view.

"There's no philosophical or factual underpinning to the views," said one diplomat familiar with the trade talks. "And therefore, you know, on the one hand, you kind of shake your head. On the other hand, it's not a bad thing in the sense that it's easier to deal with somebody where it's so transparent that it's a game of making sure it looks as if he won, right? And, you know, the worrisome thing about that is we're not the only people in the world who figured that out."

The Canadians and Mexicans shared an interest in managing the mercurial American leader. But their negotiating interests were not identical. The Mexicans saw the sixteen-dollar hourly wage requirement as a way of stacking the deck in favor of the United States and Canadian auto industries. The number of Mexican autoworkers earning that much rounded to zero.

So in the summer of 2018, when the opportunity arose for the Mexicans to cut a separate deal with the Americans, they took it. "We understood at some point that [the] Canadians were with us only to some extent and that we could not count 100 percent on them working side by side with us," one Mexican diplomat said. "There was a point, and that became public, that Mexico said, 'We have a deal and we're ready to take it forward.' The Canadians took that, with some resentment, naturally."

Even as the North American trade talks made progress, Trump was taking action on his other trade priorities. The president had been pushing his aides for months to bring him tariff proposals. Finally, in early 2018, he would wait no longer. On March 1, the president abruptly imposed a 25 percent tariff on imported steel and a 10 percent levy on aluminum.

The decision only highlighted the president's erratic policymaking. Aides and congressional Republicans that day briefly talked Trump out of proceeding with the tariffs, which he had previewed with an early morning tweet. But a few hours later, in an unrelated meeting with industry executives at the White House, he went ahead and blurted out his plans, saying the tariffs were needed to protect national security and sending the stock market into a nosedive. European, Canadian, and Mexican leaders struggled to understand how relying on its allies' steel mills could put the US at risk. On Capitol Hill, startled Republicans blasted the move, as White House officials conceded the hasty announcement had been made before they had even finalized the list of affected countries.

As a trade-war general, Trump now was engaged on three fronts: steel, NAFTA, and China. Starting shortly after his bombshell steel announcement, Trump began imposing tariffs on most of what Americans bought from China. For decades, US consumers and businesses had grown dependent upon Chinese factories for low-cost products. Now Trump was putting all of that at risk.

His tariff war also increased the government's role in the economy, as Commerce Department bureaucrats got the authority to grant or reject companies' requests to be excluded from the import levies. If a manufacturer could demonstrate that a specific type of specialized steel or aluminum was unavailable in the US, it could win the right to continue importing the foreign product tariff-free. But the process was understaffed—with thirty inexperienced officials reviewing up to twenty-one thousand complex industry requests.[33] An equally irksome system governed the China tariffs and was used by the Trump administration to reward companies that had made campaign contributions to the Republican Party or employed Republican lobbyists, according to one study.[34]

Trump's international economic policies often worked at cross purposes. His tariffs on Chinese imports were intended to punish Beijing for its rampant theft of American companies' trade secrets and intellectual property. But they raised costs for US manufacturers that relied on foreign-made components.

Among those affected was Carrier, whose Indianapolis operations the president had personally tried to save. In December 2018, Carrier sought exclusions from Trump's 25 percent tariffs for several Chinese-made parts, including an electrical motor the company used in its residential gas furnaces, and air-conditioner parts.

Forcing Carrier to pay more for the Chinese motors would hit consumers with "a material increase in the price of a new furnace," the company told USTR.[35] The Chinese supplier, Zhongshan Broad-Ocean Motor Co. in Guangdong Province, customized the motors for Carrier's requirements. Substituting generic American-made alternatives was impossible, and qualifying a new supplier for these "safety critical" components would take up to three years, Carrier said. Its Chinese supplier was in the process of moving production to Vietnam to satisfy its US-based customers. But that shift would take a year.[36]

Likewise, imposing a tariff on Chinese-made air conditioner equipment would only raise costs and threaten jobs at the company that Trump had pressured to remain in the United States, executives testified.[37] Five months after asking the government for relief, Carrier learned that its request had been denied.[38]

Michael Strain, an economist with the American Enterprise Institute, said Carrier's experience reflected the inherent contradictions in Trump's economic philosophy. Traditional Republican priorities—such as lower taxes and deregulation—often conflicted with the president's populist trade policies, which themselves were inconsistent.

"There's this acting at cross purposes in administration economic policy that is really quite striking," said Strain, a former Federal Reserve economist.[39]

Reducing the trade deficit—which Trump repeatedly cited as a measure of the nation's economic health—was one of his core goals. Yet his 2017 tax cut effectively increased the trade gap, by increasing the federal budget deficit, which stimulated the economy and sucked in more imported goods.

The legislation also introduced changes, including a special tax regime for global profits on intangible income, which were billed as reducing the incentive for companies to move profits and jobs offshore. But they were poorly designed and ineffective. They amounted, said Kimberly Clausing, a noted tax expert, to an "America Last" policy.[40]

For years, many of the United States' most innovative and profitable firms had found ways to legally avoid paying income taxes in line with their profits. By producing in low-tax foreign jurisdictions or assigning their intellectual property to subsidiaries there, pharmaceutical companies and semiconductor manufacturers could dramatically slash their tax obligations.

The strategy required corporations to make some fairly brazen claims about their operations. In 2017, for example, US corporations reported nearly $30 billion in profits on their sales in Ireland, one of Europe's smallest markets, more than they earned in China, the world's most populous nation, according to Internal Revenue Service data.[41]

At the individual company level, the results were nothing short of stunning. In 2018, Applied Materials, a maker of semiconductor equipment, cut its effective tax rate from the 35 percent US statutory rate to just 8 percent, largely by booking profits overseas.[42] The tax cut had been sold to voters as a means of increasing job-creating business investment. And such spending did tick up for a period, growing at its fastest pace in almost four years.

But the increase was modest and short-lived. Trump's multifront trade war, with its near daily threats of new tariffs on China, Mexico, Canada, the European Union, Brazil, Argentina, and who knows what other trading partner, created so much uncertainty that corporate executives soon pulled back. Relative to the size of the economy, business investment in new buildings, equipment, and land merely returned to its late-Obama-administration level before falling back to where it had been before the tax cut.[43]

Trump's scattershot approach culminated in the G20 summit in Buenos Aires in December, where he signed the new trade deal with Mexico and Canada and agreed with Xi on a cease-fire. Over a two-hour dinner with their advisers, the US and Chinese leaders agreed to restart talks in hopes of reaching a deal early in 2019.

The new United States-Mexico-Canada Agreement (USMCA) rewrote regional trade rules to encourage more production in American plants. But economists expected it to have only a minor impact. The US economy would grow by a negligible amount while creating fewer total jobs than employers were adding in a typical month, one study concluded.[44]

While trade consumed much of the president's attention, officials elsewhere in the White House were taking decisions that carried far-reaching implications. In May 2018, a pandemic preparedness unit within the National Security Council was disbanded. Some of its members were reassigned to other offices while others were sent packing. Among those leaving the administration was Thomas Bossert, a homeland security adviser who had argued for "a comprehensive biodefense strategy against pandemics."[45]

We're not going to just sit here and whine about it

Lori Wallach was no fan of Donald Trump. A self-described progressive, she was appalled by "all the crazy, antidemocratic, racist, just like, Nazi-sounding things" he had said.[46] In the final weeks of the 2016 campaign, she had taken two weeks of vacation to work on election canvassing for Wisconsin Democrats. She spent several days knocking on doors in labor neighborhoods and grew more concerned each day. In neighborhoods where the residents should have been Clinton voters, they either were not going to vote at all or, worse, they were voting for Trump. In solidly Democratic areas, where people had pulled the lever twice for Obama, canvassers found they needed to sell people who already should have been sold. "I started to realize, actually, that at least in Wisconsin, he could win," she said later. "That was an eye opener."[47]

After the election, it took a while for her to see that trade policy could become the silver lining of this new populist administration. Trump himself was "just so full of bluster" that it was hard to know how seriously to take anything he said. His emerging White House team was also full of Wall Street figures whose trade preferences lay very much with the status quo that she abhorred.

On January 3, 2017, that changed when Trump selected Lighthizer for the USTR job. Lighthizer and Wallach had developed an unlikely friendship years earlier, bonding over their shared opposition to NAFTA. Appearing on a panel at the end of a conference one day, the Naderite leftist and the Republican corporate lawyer discovered enormous overlap in their views. Both were big personalities who appreciated a well-turned phrase or quip. And while they occupied opposite ends of the political spectrum, neither saw themselves as a reflexive partisan.

Early in her career, Wallach had blistered Bill Clinton for his business-friendly trade policies, which she thought no better than those of his Republican predecessors.[48] And she had joined with Roger Milliken, a staunch rightist, in congressional trade battles. Likewise, Lighthizer, who had worked alongside union leaders in his efforts to win protection for the steel industry, was happy to criticize Republicans who favored liberalized trade.

When Trump began his presidency by pulling the United States out of Obama's Trans-Pacific Partnership, Wallach praised the president for burying "the moldering corpse" of the trade deal.[49] But even as she applauded Trump's goals, she had no intention of surrendering political ownership of the issue. "No way we're gonna cede the trade reform mantle to Donald Trump," she said.[50]

Adherents to the traditional trade-and-globalization consensus, meanwhile, struggled to make sense of the backlash that Trump symbolized. His success was painful for top aides to Hillary Clinton, who had expected to be working in the White House and were instead marking time in the private sector.

Jake Sullivan had been a likely national security advisor in a Clinton administration. Instead, he divided his time between a Carnegie Endowment for International Peace office in Washington and a teaching gig at Yale Law School, his alma mater. Sullivan was a quintessential establishment creature: Rhodes Scholar, Supreme Court clerk, and Clinton's closest adviser during her tenure as secretary of state. If he had any doubts about the bipartisan consensus on trade before 2016, he kept them to himself.

As Clinton's policy chief during the campaign, he had battled the protectionist challenge, first from Bernie Sanders and later from Trump. Occasionally, he glimpsed firsthand its animating spirit. During a campaign event in Ohio, he once made a passing defense of the "liberal international order," only to find it had annoyed one of the voters he was trying to court.

"Someone came up to me afterwards and said, you used this phrase 'liberal international order.' I don't know what that is, but I don't like any of those three words," Sullivan recalled. "That really stuck with me."[51]

Across Washington, traditionalists grappled with the meaning of Trump's win. Sullivan sought funding from a number of liberal foundations for a project he called "US Foreign Policy for the Middle Class." But he repeatedly struck out. The rethinking of trade and globalization that he had in mind was regarded as a sort of flat-earth heresy. Eventually, he arranged funding through Carnegie and assembled a fourteen-person team of specialists drawn from both parties.

Fanning out to Ohio, Colorado, and Nebraska, they interviewed local officials and voters, finding a profound disconnect between what policymakers thought they were achieving through open trade and what average Americans experienced.

Trade was "a proxy for discussing a broader set of socioeconomic challenges arising from structural changes in the global economy," the group said. By itself, trade accounted for no more than one-third of the manufacturing job loss in Ohio, less than the average factory worker probably assumed. But minimizing its importance would be a "serious mistake," given the collateral damage the job losses caused individual communities, the group concluded.[52]

Less than a mile from Carnegie's headquarters, the International Monetary Fund also had felt the Trump shockwave. The organization was a centerpiece of the Bretton Woods arrangements that had established the international economic order following World War II, a sort of Vatican for the globalization faithful. For decades, its experts had promoted the elimination of barriers to trade and capital flows, arguing that markets were best placed to determine economic outcomes. This was more than just friendly advice; the fund often conditioned its financial assistance to troubled countries on their agreement to implement such policies.

Three weeks after Election Day, the IMF's flagship quarterly, *Finance & Development*, appeared with a searching look at the populist challenge to globalization. The magazine acknowledged what was by then obvious: Economists and policymakers had misread the distributional consequences of trade liberalization. "Chinese exports really have displaced millions of US manufacturing jobs," wrote Paul Krugman of Princeton University.

Bill Clinton's insistence that the winners from trade should compensate the losers had been ignored. Maurice Obstfeld, the IMF's chief economist, warned that without "decisive government action to support those who suffer" from globalization's disruptive effects, support for further trade liberalization would wither—even if technological change was responsible for most of the upheaval.

One year later, Obstfeld organized a daylong conference on "managing globalization's challenges," which featured IMF Managing Director Christine Lagarde and twenty other speakers. Appearing by video, Larry Summers agreed that the integration of advanced economies with low-wage populations in places like China and Mexico had made it "inevitable" that less-skilled American workers would be hurt. Elites, he said, "have oversold global integration and, in particular, have oversold trade agreements."

Proponents' hyping of the economic gains from trade deals was matched by critics' tendency to exaggerate the pain caused by such accords. But Summers warned that trade negotiators were making a mistake by prioritizing issues such as intellectual property protection that were almost entirely of concern to multinational corporations rather than voters—and by overlooking questions of global tax avoidance, which directly threatened governments' ability to invest in needed social programs. The growing populist backlash in the United States, United Kingdom, Germany, and elsewhere made clear that a new approach was needed.

"There is an anger and resentment and desire... that is present in all of our countries," he said. "And unless leaders show that they are hearing these voices, crafting strategies that respect these interests, I think the political developments we have seen are only the beginning of what is to come."[53]

Around this time, Catherine Novelli launched her own attempt to address the same questions. She had spent thirty years working on trade issues, including as chief negotiator for the US free trade agreement with Jordan and later as Apple's head of global government affairs, where in 2009 she secured approval to introduce the iPhone to China—after battling with Chinese regulators over their demand for one hundred separate changes in the product's design. In the Obama administration, she served as under secretary of state for economic development.

Novelli was a believer in globalization. But she detected what she called a "giant chasm" between the way Washington and the American public understood it. Dispatched during the Obama years to her home state of Ohio to promote TPP, she found a near-universal belief that it would facilitate the offshoring of even more American jobs, a view that she felt was wrong.

Trump's victory only cemented her belief that policymakers had lost touch with the people. In September 2017, she created Listening for America, a nonpartisan organization that conducted focus groups on trade issues in an effort to close the gap. Over two years, Novelli organized roundtables in thirty-seven cities in thirteen states, finding generally positive views of globalization, deep unease about lost manufacturing jobs, and an "absolute hostility" to corporate America.

She also found glimmers of hope in communities such as Greenville, South Carolina. The end of global textile quotas and China's entry into the WTO had devastated Greenville's mills, putting tens of thousands of people out of work.[54] But the city had reinvented itself by leveraging its trade schools, universities, and skilled workforce.

The German automaker BMW selected Greenville as the site of its North American factory, which opened in 1994, kick-starting a virtuous circle of development. Abandoned textile mills were converted to loft apartments. Restaurants and bike paths flourished. Foreign manufacturers such as Bosch and Electrolux joined BMW, keeping factory employment above the national average. Financial, management, and engineering jobs followed.

Greenville's experience convinced Novelli that initiatives designed to rescue individual communities, which economists referred to as "place-based" policies, bore promise.

"Some of them are still going to be devastated, but not all of them have to be that way," she said. "When I saw what they did in

Greenville... They were like, okay, this bad thing is going to happen to us or has happened to us. But we're not going to just sit here and whine about it. We're going to figure out what cards do we have to use, and then we're going to start playing them."[55]

It just doesn't get any better than this

Over their steak dinner in Buenos Aires, Trump and Xi reached the outlines of a tentative settlement of their trade war. In return for a Chinese offer to buy what the White House called a "very substantial" amount of US energy, agricultural products, and industrial goods, Trump canceled plans to raise tariffs to 25 percent on $200 billion in Chinese goods.

The United States and China also agreed to "immediately" begin talks over Chinese industrial policies, including coercive licensing of US technology, trade-secret theft, and nontariff trade barriers. These were the structural issues that had bedeviled US-China trade relations for years. Lighthizer, in particular, was insistent on addressing them rather than settling for a Chinese promise to buy more American products.

The White House said the two sides would finalize a deal in ninety days. But only three days later, US and Chinese officials disagreed about what had been decided in Buenos Aires. On Wall Street, stock prices fell more than 3 percent in one day as investors puzzled over the gap between US and Chinese accounts of the meeting. At issue were the deadline for the talks, the schedule for Chinese purchases of American products, and Beijing's plans to reduce its tariffs on US goods.[56]

As the talks approached the nominal March 1 deadline, Trump backed down a second time on his tariff threat. He also repeatedly teased the idea that an agreement was imminent, hyping negotiators' progress and telling reporters that he expected Xi to attend a signing ceremony at Mar-a-Lago within weeks.[57]

But when Lighthizer visited Beijing at the end of April, the feedback he received from Chinese Vice Premier Liu He was "highly discouraging." Chinese leaders were insisting that Trump's punitive tariffs be dropped as a condition for signing a deal. And there were other concerns about the draft accord in Zhongnanhai, the Chinese leadership compound.[58]

After returning to Washington, Lighthizer received a formal response from Beijing that made clear just how extensive the Chinese second thoughts were. A marked-up copy of one of the proposed chapters in the agreement, dealing with intellectual property, "was a sea of red lines," Lighthizer said. Trump was livid, tweeting on Sunday, May 5, that he would more than double the existing tariffs on $200 billion in Chinese goods at the end of the week and would impose new 25 percent tariffs on all other goods, worth about $300 billion.

In a rare joint press conference with Mnuchin the following day, Lighthizer accused the Chinese of "reneging" on their commitments.[59] Liu and his team traveled to Washington at the end of that week for one more attempt to close the gap. But they made no progress, and Trump went ahead with the additional tariffs.

In May 2019, less than one week after the talks ran aground, Trump's irritation with Chinese backsliding opened the door for his national security team to win presidential approval for a step that had been in the works for months. The US-China battle for global technological supremacy took center stage.

Looking to retaliate for Beijing's hesitancy to cut a deal, Trump approved a Commerce Department proposal to blacklist telecommunications giant Huawei, perhaps China's most prominent global firm, as a national security threat. Pottinger, one of the administration's most influential China hawks, helped drive the decision to place the company on the department's "entity list," effectively starving it of the American parts it needed for its servers and routers.

Months earlier, Canadian authorities, acting on a US warrant, had arrested Meng Wanzhou, Huawei's chief financial officer and the daughter of company founder Ren Zhengfei. Incredibly, Meng's arrest, as she changed planes in Vancouver, came as Trump and Xi were meeting for dinner in Buenos Aires. In January 2019, federal prosecutors in the Eastern District of New York indicted Meng and the company in connection with "a long-running scheme by Huawei, its CFO, and other employees to deceive numerous global financial institutions and the United States government regarding Huawei's business activities in Iran."[60]

Blacklisting Huawei marked the second time that Trump had struck at a prominent Chinese technology company. The technology war had gotten off to a rocky start about a year earlier when Commerce barred US companies from supplying Chinese telecom giant ZTE with essential computer chips and other advanced hardware. The move, which threatened to cripple ZTE, came after the United States accused the company of breaching an earlier settlement of civil and criminal charges for doing business with Iran and North Korea in violation of US sanctions.

US officials at the time told reporters that ZTE executives had brazenly and repeatedly lied about their actions. "ZTE misled the Department of Commerce. Instead of reprimanding ZTE staff and senior management, ZTE rewarded them. This egregious behavior cannot be ignored," Commerce Secretary Wilbur Ross said in a statement.[61]

Yet Trump decided to do just that. After Xi asked him to go easy on ZTE, which employed almost seventy thousand people, the president reversed course. "President Xi of China, and I, are working together to give massive Chinese phone company, ZTE, a way to get back into business, fast," Trump tweeted. "Too many jobs in China lost. Commerce Department has been instructed to get it done!"[62]

The move stunned White House aides and congressional Republicans, who received no advance notice of Trump's change of heart. The president's abrupt shift was aimed at paving the way for the trade deal he coveted and demonstrated that national security was a secondary consideration. But his sudden expression of concern over Chinese job losses and celebration of collaboration with Xi struck even some of his closest aides as odd.

Pottinger, who by this point was described by Bannon as "one of the most significant people in the entire US government," was disappointed.[63] "I was pretty stunned that we had reversed ourselves," he said. He rationalized it as Trump's attempt to gain leverage that he could use in the trade talks. Xi had personally lobbied the president to lift the ban on ZTE. In Trump's mind, granting the Chinese leader this favor created a chit that he could cash in later. Alternatively, the fact that Trump could be so easily swayed on an issue of US national security raised questions about his understanding of the issues.

Technology was an unfamiliar battlefield for the president. Trump had reached adulthood in the mid-1960s, long before the age of the

personal computer and internet. As late as 2007, he said in a legal proceeding that he did not use email.[64] "President Trump in many ways
inhabits the 1980s when most trade issues dealt with tangible goods
such as automobiles," Pottinger said. "We all struggle on the technology
front in ways that tend to leave us at least two or three steps behind
Beijing."[65]

Indeed, China had been fighting the technology war for some time
before the US government awoke to the challenge. The origins of the
conflict lay in a Chinese government program called "Made in China
2025." The successor to a 2006 effort to promote "indigenous innovation," it was introduced in 2015 and set specific market share goals for
China in ten high-tech sectors, such as advanced information technology, robotics, aeronautical equipment, and new materials. By 2025, for
example, 80 percent of China's electric vehicles and batteries were to
come from domestic manufacturers.

US officials regarded the web of industrial policies developed to
achieve these aims as doubly troubling. Washington had welcomed
China to the global trading system, believing that it would rely on
market forces to shape its economy. Instead, China was intensifying its
reliance on state action, and its successes would explicitly come at the expense of foreign—particularly American—companies. "Real structural
change is necessary. Nothing less than the future of tens of millions of
American jobs is at stake," Lighthizer had said.[66]

US officials had expected China to steadily become more market-
oriented as living standards rose. Instead, Beijing was demonstrating
that some things—such as the party's survival—were more important
than the market.[67] Plus, under a strategy known as "military-civilian
fusion," the resulting technological advances would be used to help the
People's Liberation Army achieve its goal of becoming a world-class military by 2049, making clear the link between China's objectionable economic policies and US national security.[68]

The money for this technology offensive came from "industrial
guidance funds," which drew resources from all levels of Chinese government, private and state-owned companies, and global venture capital
funds. Xi had revived the Communist Party's economic influence and
blurred the dividing line between state enterprise and the private sector.

Chinese leaders saw the "Fourth Industrial Revolution," a phrase referring to the marriage of digital technologies, data, and manufacturing, as an opportunity to overtake the United States once and for all.[69] And after two decades of exhausting foreign wars, financial crisis, and political disunion, the United States was ripe for the taking, Chinese leaders believed. Advanced technology was the battlefield where global leadership would be decided.

After US officials raised alarms about the Made in China 2025 program, Beijing dropped the phrase from its public statements. But the program continued, and others soon followed, promoting artificial intelligence, quantum computing, and 5G telecommunications networks. By 2019, China's spending on quantum research was more than ten times what the United States devoted to the task. Chinese officials also took a more active role in global bodies tasked with setting technology standards, shaping them to facilitate public surveillance, censorship, and control.[70]

Though few in Washington made the point, there was reason for skepticism about the imminence of the threat. China had been trying for decades to produce a commercial jetliner capable of competing with Boeing and Airbus and had little to show for it. One academic study of the welter of subsidies and preferences contained in the Made in China 2025 program found little "evidence of productivity improvement or increases in R&D expenditure, patenting and profitability." Considering the mammoth expenses involved, the program's benefits had "been limited at best," the researchers concluded.[71]

The May 2019 decision to blacklist Huawei damaged the US-China relationship. In Beijing, officials viewed it as a sign that US officials wanted to do more than recalibrate trade ties; they sought to block China's rise. Xi conspicuously went on a public tour of production sites for Chinese rare earth materials that the US required for its high-tech industries and weaponry. While there, he called upon citizens to prepare to endure a "new Long March," a reference to Mao's legendary five-thousand-mile fighting retreat in 1934.[72]

US concerns over the danger Huawei network gear posed had simmered since 2012, when the House Intelligence Committee said the company's links to the Chinese government, and those of ZTE, posed a national security risk.[73] The next year, the Obama administration restricted imports of Chinese-made gear by several government agencies. The US complaints got Huawei's attention. Some of the company's senior executives hesitated before traveling to New York in June 2014 for an all-day investor conference at the Waldorf Astoria, fearing they might be detained or arrested, according to a person familiar with the company's planning.

Pottinger, who had written about Huawei two decades earlier as a reporter, was familiar with the company's Janus-like reputation. Started in 1987 by Ren, a former Chinese Army officer, Huawei had grown to become a global player. But its alleged links to the Chinese military, and aggressive efforts to vacuum up foreign technologies, made it radioactive in Washington.

"The stories were legion about how Huawei does things like they'll hire a senior engineer from Ericsson and sit him in a room and have him write for the whole day. They give him a laptop and say, 'Write everything you know, everything you've ever worked on. Just unload your brain into this thing.' And they would lure these people in with money. Just squeeze them dry and then discard them," Pottinger said.[74]

In January 2020, Pottinger was dispatched to London to persuade British officials to abandon plans to use Huawei gear in the country's 5G telecommunications network. Using Chinese components in UK communications networks, he told his British counterparts, would be akin to Ronald Reagan and Margaret Thatcher allowing the KGB to install telephone networks in Washington or London during the Cold War.[75]

The Trump administration kept Huawei gear out of US telecommunications networks and those of some key allies, including the United Kingdom, Australia, Canada, and Poland. But if the goal of severing Huawei's access to US components was to cripple the company, it was something less than a success. In September 2019, Ren said that Huawei had begun producing 5G mobile base stations that contained no US parts. The announcement came as a "symbolic middle finger to the United States," according to Ryan Hass, who had worked in the Obama White House.[76] In 2020, the company's $137 billion in revenues were 4 percent higher than before the US blacklist.

In mid-January 2020, Trump staged a ceremony in the East Room of the White House to commemorate the signing of a trade deal with China. The president welcomed dozens of Wall Street figures and corporate executives, crowing: "It just doesn't get any better than this."[77]

In fact, the agreement represented only a partial triumph. Instead of the sweeping overhaul of Chinese mercantilism that he had promised, Trump settled for a limited accord that committed China to sharply increase its purchases of American products. The hardest fights, over China's subsidy-rich state capitalism, were left to future negotiations.

Trump claimed to be fighting for the common man. But no labor representatives were in attendance. On stage in the East Room, the president praised the agreement as "historic" and "remarkable." He looked relaxed, gently ribbing Lou Dobbs and Steve Schwarzman, who were in the audience along with Henry Kissinger. For Trump, the seventy-five-minute gathering was a welcome distraction from the imminent start of his Senate impeachment trial.

Even as he celebrated, a storm was gathering on the other side of the world. Japanese health officials that day confirmed that a man in his thirties, who had visited the Chinese city of Wuhan earlier in the month, was infected with a novel coronavirus.[78] His flu-like symptoms had forced a brief hospitalization, though he was now on the mend. More worrisome, this was the second confirmed case outside China involving person-to-person transmission of the disease.

Five days later came official word that the respiratory illness designated covid-19 was in the United States.

9

These Stupid Supply Chains

Two days before Trump's White House ceremony celebrating the China trade deal, Revathi Advaithi presided over a less exuberant gathering in Silicon Valley. The CEO of Flex, a global manufacturer, had just returned from a family holiday in India and was eager to catch up with her deputies, including François Barbier, the company's operations chief. Barbier, who joined the conference call from Europe, was headed to China later in the week.

His January 2020 trip came amid growing concern about the situation there. Chinese officials had just reported the first death from the coronavirus, triggering alarm about the potential for the unfamiliar illness to spread. Chinese scientists had isolated the genomic sequence of the virus, but that was just the first step on a long road to a solution. Developing treatments or a vaccine against the new virus could take years.[1]

In the meantime, Advaithi had a business to run. Few Americans had heard of the company, but Flex—formerly known as Flextronics, the company that had grappled with supply challenges in Japan and Thailand nearly a decade earlier—was a truly global player, making consumer and industrial products for brand names such as Apple, Ford, and Johnson & Johnson. What Flex experienced during the pandemic's first months accelerated a rethinking of globalization that began during the US-China trade war and would only intensify in later years.

For decades, US policies that promoted global economic integration, combined with new technologies that enabled executives to command distant factories, fueled the rise of cross-border production networks like those managed by Flex. As multinationals focused on reducing their costs, these global supply chains grew to account for roughly half of all world trade.[2] The pandemic would test their resilience.

Advaithi's biography showed globalization's promise. She had been born in India; her father was a chemical engineer and her mother a homemaker. One of five sisters, she was educated at one of the country's premier educational institutions, the Birla Institute of Technology and Science in Rajasthan. "I was the odd one out who went into engineering while the others went into other sciences," she said. "But I got that from my dad, and it turned out to be a very good choice."[3]

She started her career in the mid-1990s as a shop floor supervisor at a factory in Shawnee, Oklahoma, making hydraulic pumps and motors. Advaithi gravitated toward a hands-on approach, even learning how to operate a lathe. While working at another plant in Hutchinson, Kansas, she met her husband, Jeevan Mulgund, also a native of India.

Advaithi moved between jobs in the United States, the United Kingdom, and China before reaching the C-suite. As she prepared for what she would later describe as "probably the most difficult time in my thirty years of working," Advaithi commanded one hundred facilities in thirty countries. In China alone, Flex had twenty-one factories and roughly fifty thousand workers producing semiconductor equipment, telecom gear, and medical products like CT scanners.[4]

The rise of global value chains was among the developments that distinguished the post–Cold War era of globalization from what had preceded it. Traditionally, merchandise trade had involved finished goods moving from where they were made to where they were used. But as multinational corporations divided their operations among different locations, seeking to capitalize on local advantages in cheap labor, good infrastructure, or business-friendly regulation, trade increasingly involved items that were used to produce other goods. Over half of all US imports between 1992 and 2022 were industrial supplies or capital goods.[5]

Among the industries that capitalized on these international manufacturing alliances were autos and airplanes. The production of passenger cars for the North American market saw major assemblies and subassemblies move back and forth across the US borders with Canada and Mexico multiple times before resulting in a finished vehicle. Boeing's 787 commercial aircraft was an amalgam of parts from all over the world: The wings came from Japan; horizontal stabilizers were made in Italy; wingtips originated in South Korea; and the engines hailed from the United Kingdom.[6]

Many corporations embraced the philosophy known as "just-in-time," meaning that parts were supposed to arrive just as they were needed on the assembly line. Toyota's plant in Georgetown, Kentucky, for example, the automaker's largest production facility, kept just two hours' worth of car seats on hand.[7]

The logic seemed unassailable. Large stockpiles of raw materials cost money, as did the warehouses and the workers needed to manage them. The just-in-time approach, on the other hand, kept costs down and stock prices up. But this carefully calibrated strategy was unforgiving. Any interruption of the smooth flow of inputs could cripple production.

Inevitably, such snafus arose. Trucks broke down. Floods or fires disabled factories. In 2002, a West Coast dockworkers strike interrupted US-Asia trade and cost the economy $2 billion a day before presidential intervention finally brought it to an end.[8] But the problems were rare enough to be regarded as a cost of doing business.

A global pandemic was different—as Flex soon discovered. The illness racing around the world upended production webs that spanned borders, oceans, and political systems. Suddenly, the vulnerabilities that had been glimpsed years earlier when earthquakes shook Taiwan, a nuclear accident threatened Japan, and historic floods inundated Thailand produced global economic chaos.

At the same time, years of inadequate investment in US ports, railroad-industry labor practices designed to goose profits, and a chronic failure by supply chain participants to share information left the freight-delivery system with little surge capacity. When demand rose well above customary levels, the supply chain buckled.

243

As executives scrambled to cope with a once-in-a-century crisis, they began rethinking long-standing assumptions about the optimal way to organize their operations. In thrall to the just-in-time philosophy, manufacturers had slashed inventories by nearly one-third between 1992 and 2005.[9] The inherent risks of operating so close to the edge had been masked during a relatively benign era. The pandemic meant they were masked no longer. Executives realized they had taken just-in-time too far.

They had done so by ignoring the teachings of the company that pioneered the lean manufacturing doctrine. When Toyota developed its famous Toyota Production System beginning in the late 1940s—the model spread to other countries four decades later—a central tenet was that suppliers should be colocated with the main factory in an industrial cluster.[10] "More than any other automaker, Toyota has assembly plants that are geographically close to one another and to suppliers."[11] Its Kentucky plant, for example, could get away with holding just a two-hour supply of car seats because the company that produced them was located less than an hour's drive away. That wasn't the case for the American manufacturing work that other companies had offshored to China and Mexico.

The supply chain crisis that began in 2020 and lasted for more than two years also changed the thinking at the top levels of the US government. As shortages mounted, Trump invoked the 1950 Defense Production Act to order private companies to switch to producing vital medical supplies. But a subsequent congressional audit questioned the White House handling of several contracts and in one case found that the federal government had overpaid for ventilators by $500 million.[12]

The pandemic's unique mix of panic buying and disrupted production had consumers howling from the start. On March 15, 2020, Trump held a conference call with top grocers and retailers to discuss supply concerns. He emerged at a subsequent White House press conference to tell Americans to "relax." People were buying three to five times their normal amount of products, the president said. But the CEOs from companies such as Walmart, Costco, Target, and Albertsons were doing their best to keep up.

"We're doing great. It all will pass," Trump said.[13]

In fact, serial shortages of products, including personal protective equipment, bikes, furniture, laptops, auto parts, and cereal boxes, continued for months. Eventually, the political cost of rising prices made the state of the US supply chain an issue for Trump's successor, Democrat Joe Biden, in a way that it had been for no chief executive before him. Shortages of goods from medical gear to computer chips contributed to the highest inflation that Americans had seen in forty years.

Biden would struggle to gain control of the supply chain, which was almost entirely a private sector creation and responsibility. He could jawbone retailers, port officials, and freight specialists to work harder or smarter. And he could set in motion policies aimed at strengthening resilience in the long run, even at the expense of efficiency and low costs. But he could not deliver the instant gratification of reliable deliveries that the American consumer for years had taken for granted.

A false sense of security

Flex operated at enormous scale: It boasted roughly one thousand customers, including Google, HP, Xerox, Ford, and General Motors. Roughly sixteen thousand suppliers fed its factories. Each day, Flex supply chain specialists were responsible for tracking inventories of one million items, from tiny screws to sophisticated computer chips.

The crisis caught the company at a moment of transition. Under Advaithi, a mechanical engineer who had worked in executive posts for Eaton and Honeywell, Flex had abandoned some low-margin consumer products to concentrate on the more profitable medical market. But the company had yet to realize the expected financial payoff. The $24 billion in revenue Flex reported for its most recent fiscal year was unchanged from four years earlier, while profits were down by 80 percent.[14]

The shift in strategy—and changing customer preferences—also was reshaping the company's global footprint. Five years earlier, more than one-third of Flex's property and equipment was based in China. Operating "in low-cost geographic areas" was among the company's competitive advantages, Flex told investors.[15]

But by the time the pandemic erupted, Flex had cut its China presence in half while increasing its Mexican operations by roughly the same percentage.[16] The change was "a deliberate result" of the increased emphasis on the medical business. Flex manufactured a wide range of medical goods, including hospital beds, imaging systems, and drug-delivery devices, for customers that wanted their suppliers to be close at hand, Advaithi said.[17]

Barbier and his operations team had been through SARS and were not easily spooked. But the early weeks of the pandemic felt different. There were rumors that the Chinese government would order factories to remain closed after the annual break for the Lunar New Year cel-ebration, which was less than two weeks away. Hundreds of millions of Chinese workers would be traveling from coastal factories to their hometowns in the country's interior. The traditional holiday migration seemed ideal for spreading the pathogen.

Advaithi was surprised by what she heard at the mid-January meet-ing. Her subordinates were drafting emergency plans for securing masks, gloves, and hand sanitizer for Flex facilities in the affected area. "There was a lot of concern on the ground about the situation that was devel-oping in China. . . . Even then, I really didn't understand the magnitude of it," she said.[18] Speaking with Wall Street analysts at the end of the month, she played down the likely impact on Flex. "We don't have any factories in the Hubei province, where the bulk of the issue is," she said.[19]

It quickly became clear that there would be no escaping the virus. On January 23, Chinese authorities imposed a lockdown on Wuhan, the city of eleven million people where the outbreak had originated. Other cities quickly followed suit. The Lunar New Year break ended on February 10, but many workers who had journeyed home refused to re-turn to their faraway factories, fearing they would be infected en route.

Advaithi, who had been CEO for less than a year, launched a hundred-day blitz to pilot Flex through an unprecedented crisis. Un-certainty was the initial enemy. "This is like nothing before that we have seen because you can understand and predict sometimes economic downturns. But if you can't predict how significant the scale of this pan-demic is going to be, how do you deal with that?" she said.[20]

Still, in one respect, Flex was fortunate. Companies in China that stopped working during the annual holiday were required to pass a time-consuming government health audit before resuming operations.

But Tony Wang, the general manager of Flex's Shanghai and Suzhou plants, had kept about four hundred workers on the job to meet urgent customer demands and to allow him to resume production more quickly than his competitors. In contrast, Foxconn, a Taiwanese company that produced Apple's iPhone, said in mid-February that it would not have even half of its facilities reopened by the end of that month.[21]

Advaithi's early decision to tap suppliers in India, Malaysia, Mexico, Singapore, and Poland for masks and other personal protective equipment (PPE) also paid off. By the end of January, half of a three-million-mask order had arrived in China.[22] Wang had so many masks that he was able to equip his suppliers, enabling them to quickly reactivate their assembly lines.

Flex typically built up its raw-materials stockpile in the weeks before Lunar New Year to guard against possible shortfalls if vendors were slow to resume production following the holiday. But as the pandemic lockdowns disrupted normal operations across the economy, inventories soon blossomed into a major concern.

By the end of 2021, Flex was carrying $5.2 billion worth of raw materials and half-finished products on its books, 60 percent more than before the pandemic. Yet the numbers kept climbing: At the end of the following year, inventories were more than twice the pre-pandemic figure.[23]

In the first weeks of the crisis, even as Flex was drowning in supplies, it was simultaneously running short of key components. The shortfall peaked on February 22 when Advaithi learned that her factories lacked sufficient supplies of eight thousand items, roughly five times what Flex managed on a typical workday. Just one missing part could bring an assembly line to a halt.

"We had a pretty serious problem on our hands," she said.[24]

At the company's Silicon Valley headquarters, Lynn Torrel, the senior supply chain executive, kept tabs on the situation using a data analytics tool called Pulse. The system vacuumed up data from eighty-eight separate sources, fusing it into a comprehensive readout that was projected on a wall-mounted display comprised of twenty-two video screens.

The proprietary system allowed executives to check the status of every part in Flex's inventory using a desktop, laptop, or cell phone.

Among Torrel's first crisis moves was to tag every part coming from China on Pulse and then reconfirm with both her customers and suppliers that the parts were being produced and were still needed.

As covid rippled across the world, the situation in each of the company's six product markets changed by the day. In early February, a Hyundai auto plant in South Korea shut down after running out of Chinese parts. One week later, a Nissan plant in Japan did the same. The Big Three automakers closed on March 18. Consumers, stuck at home, stopped buying cell phones while ramping up purchases of coffee machines and floor-care products.

Just weeks earlier, the coronavirus had seemed like one more exotic feature of life in China. Troublesome. Fascinating. But a Chinese problem, nothing more. Now the global implications were coming into view, highlighting the dangers of having concentrated so much manufacturing in a single nation. The regions that the Chinese government had locked down contained nearly fifty thousand Chinese branches or subsidiaries of foreign corporations, including 9,500 American operations, according to Dun & Bradstreet. As China quarantined provinces that were home to sixty million people—more than the population of Spain—every member of the *Fortune* 100 felt the effects. Nike alone relied upon 110 Chinese factories.[25]

In the pandemic's initial weeks, Flex searched for alternatives to Chinese suppliers in countries such as South Korea and Japan. When a Chinese factory that produced a critical electronic component known as a resistor went dark, Torrel's team found a Malaysian supplier that could fill in.

Flex was essentially on a wartime footing. For Advaithi, the back-to-back Zoom meetings were so relentless that she finally ordered a mandatory fifteen-minute interlude between calls. Torrel, who was in the middle of moving her family from Arizona to California, presided over daily 5:30 a.m. conference calls with supply chain managers all over the world. At the end of one especially brutal day, she realized she was still wearing the pajamas that she had slept in the night before.[26]

All things considered, China returned to something approximating normal operations fairly quickly. By February 16, more than half of the company's Chinese workforce was back on the job; more than

90 percent of its employees were working in early March. "I think that gave us a false sense of security," Advaithi said.

Indeed, just as conditions in China began improving, Advaithi was confronted by a new hot spot. She was visiting a Flex facility in Romania in late February when she learned of the first coronavirus deaths in Italy, which confirmed her worst fears. Unlike the 2011 natural disasters in Japan and Thailand, covid-19's effects were not geographically confined. "This is going to be a global issue," she realized.

On March 9, the Italian government ordered a nationwide lockdown. The extraordinary decision shuttered Flex's medical design center in Milan, one of three company facilities in the country. It could not have happened at a worse time.

Three of Flex's top medical industry customers had asked if the company could produce ventilators for them. As the number of covid cases rose, hospitals everywhere were suddenly desperate for the lifesaving machines. No one could wait the typical twelve to twenty-four months to get a new design approved and produced. Advaithi gave the Flex specialists in Milan thirty to sixty days to rethink the ventilator designs and make them easier to manufacture.

As Italy locked down, some Flex workers took testing equipment home to continue brainstorming new designs with customers. In the United States, meanwhile, workers at a ventilator factory in Pennsylvania filmed each step along their assembly line using an augmented reality system. Flex used those images to replicate the line in a new facility in Juarez, Mexico. Racing the clock, the Flex team converted a 1.2-million-square-foot auto parts warehouse into a ventilator factory by mid-April.

The pandemic posed an extraordinary management challenge for a global company like Flex. As the disease hopped borders, the requirements for the company to operate safely could change overnight. Advaithi's team had developed an operations playbook based on its experience in China. But each country presented its own peculiarities, based on local government requirements and cultural norms.

Routine temperature checks at the factory gate were sufficient in China. But in India, workers first were required to answer questions about their health before traveling to the factory.

Employee views on working from home also differed. In advanced economies, including the United States, people wanted to stay home, either for personal safety, for convenience, or because they felt more productive. But in developing countries, working from home was not a respite; it was a chore. Many workers had tiny apartments, crowded with family members. Getting work done amid those conditions was unrealistic.

By the end of March, Flex had spent $52 million on pandemic-related expenses, including health measures and labor incentives. In the subsequent three months, the tab would double.[27] To conserve cash, Advaithi in March ordered a 20 percent pay cut for senior executives while cutting her own $1.1 million annual salary by half.

At a moment when the imperative to coordinate across borders had never been greater, the ability to move from one country to another had never been more constrained. Top executives like Barbier normally lived on the road, traveling 80 to 90 percent of the time. Flex executives as a group averaged up to eight hundred business trips in a typical month. Now, they were taking perhaps a dozen. Only members of the company's medical products division continued to travel regularly.

What replaced that firsthand experience was the ubiquitous Zoom call. Before the pandemic, Flex employees took part in sixty-three thousand video calls per month. By April, the number had nearly quadrupled. Information technology, which had facilitated the post–Cold War burst of globalization, was shaping its next iteration.

Advaithi recalled with some wistfulness a trip she had taken to a factory in Timişoara, Romania, right before the pandemic put an end to business as usual. "I personally miss the human aspect of it a lot," she said. "I do miss being in a factory."

By early May, the pandemic was far from over. But Flex had navigated the worst crisis in its half-century history. Advaithi had started and stopped production lines in China, Europe, Mexico, and the United States, redeploying workers from stagnant businesses to those that showed life. And despite all the trauma and turmoil, Flex in the end eked out a tiny profit.

As the immediate crisis eased, the long-term consequences for global supply chains remained a subject of debate. Executives had been scarred by the sudden difficulty in moving their goods from distant factories to the doorsteps of American consumers. Many spoke of redesigning their production systems to bring work back home or at least closer to home, even if it cost a bit more.

"There's a reason supply chains migrated to Asia over the past few decades," said Torrel. "But I think we will see a change."[28]

Palm reading

If Advaithi was expecting applause from the White House, she was in for a surprise. Trump was not a fan of global production networks. His idea of a supply chain ran from one American factory to another American factory. The early weeks of the pandemic—with their rolling shortages of masks, gloves, hand sanitizer, and bleach—only confirmed the president's instinctive aversion to globalized manufacturing.

As corporate executives scrambled to hold their operations together, Trump took a victory lap. In an interview with Fox Business, he criticized corporate America for "these stupid supply chains" and said the retail shortages proved him right.

"We have a supply chain where they're made in all different parts of the world. And one little piece of the world goes bad and the whole thing is messed up," he fumed. "I said we shouldn't have supply chains. We should have them all in the United States."[29]

Some of Trump's advisers spotted an economic silver lining in the pandemic. Commerce Secretary Wilbur Ross said that, after SARS and covid-19, businesses would reconsider China's place in their operations. The pandemic "will help to accelerate the return of jobs to North America," he added.[30]

Peter Navarro, a top White House trade official, said that by exposing the United States' dependence on foreign sources of medical goods, the crisis demonstrated the need to repatriate key supply lines. "If we learn anything from this crisis, it should be: Never again. Never again should we have to depend on the rest of the world for our essential medicines and countermeasures," Navarro told a White House briefing.[31]

Such views flew in the face of decades of management practices that American executives were reluctant to abandon. Indeed, as Flex itself demonstrated, if supply chains were shifting, they were moving from China to places like Mexico, not the United States. But where things were being produced was not the immediate priority. The economy was nosediving; more than seventeen million jobs disappeared in April and May. The stock market lost more than one-third of its value in just five weeks.

Then the gloom abruptly lifted. The US economy followed its worst quarter in history with its best. The sudden about-face caught many companies off guard. Major airlines, believing the March plummet would last, had mothballed their fleets and were caught short when travel rebounded.

The economy's unprecedented volatility made business forecasting about as accurate as palm reading. Peloton thought the work-from-home boom would mean permanently high orders for its exercise bikes. Less than a year after announcing plans for a $400 million factory in Ohio, the company pulled the plug as covid-19 vaccines allowed Americans to return to their local gyms.

Out of whack

The US economy ended 2020 smaller than it had been at the start of the year. Coupled with Trump's erratic handling of the health emergency, and the general air of chaos that surrounded his presidency, the economy's wobbly footing contributed to his November election loss to Biden.

Little more than a week after the election, a renewed wave of coronavirus infections aggravated the nation's unsettled mood. Governors in California, Illinois, and Virginia imposed fresh restrictions on activity in a bid to curb the outbreak.[32]

The stop-and-go economy was causing fundamental problems in supply chains, which were designed to handle a steady flow of goods from foreign factories to American consumers. Stuck at home, consumers slashed spending on in-person experiences such as restaurant meals, sporting events, and auto repairs. Instead they splurged on furniture, clothing, televisions, and fitness equipment. Many of these goods came from abroad in the belly of a ship or an aircraft.

At the same time that demand for goods was rising, manufacturers' ability to supply them was constrained. Factory shutdowns that started in China spread to Europe and the United States. Airlines dropped most passenger service to China in the pandemic's early weeks, eliminating air-freight capacity with each cancellation. Ocean carriers likewise reduced their calls at Chinese ports.

Across the globe, the rhythms of economic activity were out of whack. Some manufacturers were desperately waiting for parts from factories that were closed or operating at half-speed. In other cases, factories were shipping goods to American retailers that had closed to wait out the coronavirus, leading to stuffed warehouses on both sides of the Pacific.

Major ocean carriers, such as Maersk and Hapag-Lloyd, had reacted to the plunge in economic activity by canceling more than one thousand planned sailings in the first half of 2020.[33] The cutbacks kept cargo prices high and allowed the carriers to bank record profits. Maersk, which lost money in 2019, reported nearly $3 billion in net income for 2020. But when customer orders unexpectedly recovered in the summer of that year, the carriers were caught with too few vessels on the water.

By late January 2021, the combination of surging consumer orders and limited capacity sent ocean shipping costs up 80 percent.[34] Brand names such as Gap, WD-40, and Bang & Olufsen griped about unfamiliar transport headaches. The Port of Los Angeles, the country's top import gateway, quickly emerged as the center of the freight storm. Before the pandemic, container ships arriving from Asia typically sailed right into an unloading berth. But on one mid-January day, forty-two massive vessels were anchored offshore waiting for a spot at the docks, even as every warehouse within sixty miles was already full of merchandise.[35] Loading and unloading also were slowed by a shortage of dockworkers; many were sick.

No one had ever seen anything like it. For much of 2021, the supply chains that represented globalization's scaffolding seemed cursed. In March, the container ship *Ever Given* was blown off course by high winds and became lodged in the Suez Canal, blocking the trade artery for six days.

At the White House, Biden ordered a hundred-day review of the nation's supply chain for critical goods, such as computer chips, electric-vehicle batteries, and vital minerals.[36] "The American people should never face shortages for the goods they rely on," the president said.

Even as some advocated the "reshoring" of supply chains as an antidote to disruptions, domestic links in the nation's commercial pipeline also proved vulnerable. In February, up to nine days of "brutal and enduring cold" plunged Texas into its longest freeze in recorded history.[37] As power outages rolled across the state, chemical plants were deprived of the natural gas they needed for both heat and as a raw material. Many facilities suffered lasting damage because they did not receive the three to five days of warning needed to safely shut down.

With much of the state's chemical production sidelined, automakers ran short of substances like polycarbonate resin, a key ingredient in molded plastic parts, and polyvinyl chloride or PVC, which is used to make dashboards.[38]

Sogefi, an Italian auto parts maker, was forced to improvise after a shipment of resins that its US plant expected at the beginning of May failed to materialize. Months later, the February freeze was still reverberating through the petrochemical industry, causing a four-week delay in deliveries to the Prichard, West Virginia, facility.

From its site on the banks of the Big Sandy River, Sogefi produced engine manifolds and oil filters for most major automakers. Every six-cylinder engine in a Fiat or Chrysler car, for example, carried an oil filtration module from Sogefi. The multinational's sole US plant and its suppliers used almost four tons of the resin each week in their injection-molding operations. In April, when a supplier issue prevented Sogefi from delivering a key part, GM's assembly of diesel engines for Chevy Silverado pickup trucks stopped for an entire day.

A lack of resin wasn't Sogefi's only headache. Everything from cardboard boxes to computer chips had grown scarce. Prices for the wooden pallets it used to ship products had jumped to more than eighteen dollars apiece from ten dollars. Laborers were hard to find, as pandemic-era unemployment benefits left some choosy about job offers.

Raw material and component delivery delays hamstrung the company. When the plant ran short of twenty-six-cent cardboard boxes,

Sogefi was briefly unable to ship modules that sold for thirty-three dollars apiece. The lack of a twelve-cent part—one of twenty components in another product—idled an assembly line for two weeks. As supplies of the other nineteen components accumulated, Randy Simpkins, the plant's logistics manager, scrambled to find storage space. The plant was holding $2 million in excess inventory, about half of that tied to a GM assembly line that had been idled by a lack of semiconductors.[39]

As the United States clawed its way out of the pandemic, Sogefi's predicament was typical. One year earlier, the economy had been in a terrifying free fall. Now, businesses were overwhelmed by a flood of orders. "Companies and suppliers continue to struggle to meet increasing levels of demand. Record-long lead times, wide-scale shortages of critical basic materials, rising commodities prices and difficulties in transporting products are continuing to affect all segments of the manufacturing economy. Worker absenteeism, short-term shutdowns due to part shortages, and difficulties in filling open positions continue to be issues," said the Institute for Supply Management.[40]

The emergence of a new coronavirus variant designated "Delta" ignited a fresh round of supply snafus. In late May, the outbreak closed the southern Chinese port of Yantian for three days. Factories in Vietnam and Bangladesh were next to go offline. Elsewhere, two of the largest US railroads temporarily halted shipments from major West Coast seaports to their Midwestern hubs, which were overflowing with cargo.[41]

Across the economy, companies improvised workarounds. Programmers at Tesla rewrote software code to allow cars to use more readily available semiconductors.[42] Levi Strauss sent more of its jeans via aircraft and steered some ocean freight to East Coast ports instead of to Los Angeles.[43] General Electric and Honeywell redesigned products to reduce their dependence on unreliable suppliers.[44] Retailers appealed to the president to use the National Guard to help move freight.

At Stanley Black & Decker, executives blanched at freight costs that were seven times pre-pandemic levels. Computer chips needed for Stanley's power drills, saws, and sanders were stuck in trans-Pacific traffic jams. And the journey from Chinese factory to American retailer was taking almost ninety days, three times as long as before covid.[45]

Stanley responded to the supply chain snarls by accelerating plans to move production of its popular Craftsman-brand tools back to the United States at a new plant in Fort Worth, Texas, which the company had advertised as incorporating "some of the most advanced manufacturing technologies available."[46]

Producing products closer to where they were sold carried "a double benefit," Stanley said. Shorter supply chains were less vulnerable to interruption than those that stretched across oceans, and they enabled a faster response "to volatile changes in demand."[47]

Stanley moved away from the thin-inventory, just-in-time approach to manufacturing, bulking up on both finished goods and raw materials. Over a two-year period, the toolmaker added more than $3 billion to its inventories.[48]

But Stanley made less progress repatriating its supply chains than it had hoped. The company wanted to boost its share of American-made products to 70 percent from 40 percent.[49] But with demand surging amid Americans' pandemic shopping spree, Stanley's new Fort Worth factory and a second facility in Mexico could not keep up. The company remained dependent upon China.

"It's been difficult to ramp down the Asian production," confessed Don Allan, the company's chief financial officer.[50]

Total chaos

Persistent transport disruptions contributed to the highest inflation in forty years. Under pressure to act—and with few levers to pull—Biden in July issued an executive order to promote competition, taking particular aim at the movement of freight. Three ocean carrier alliances controlled more than 80 percent of the container shipping market, the White House said. Rail freight was carved up among four major railroads, with each one dominating a region where they privileged their cargoes over those of competitors.[51]

In August, as public discontent boiled, Brian Deese, the director of the National Economic Council, called veteran transportation specialist John Porcari about a new role as the president's port envoy. Porcari had extensive contacts and decades of experience. He had served as deputy secretary of transportation in the Obama administration and, earlier, as the State of Maryland's top transportation official. In that job, Porcari—unlike his counterparts in the other forty-nine states—oversaw every type of transport: highways, railroads, airports, and the Port of Baltimore.

If untangling the nation's supply chain amid a global pandemic and a historic demand surge was an all-but-impossible job, Biden at least had found the right man to try. For most of the next year, Porcari worked twelve-hour days as a volunteer, trying to corral industry figures who often were at odds.

On the day that the White House announced his appointment, forty ships were anchored off the coast of Southern California, waiting for room to tie up at the dock and unload. It was an unprecedented backlog and it was only getting worse. By the end of Porcari's first month, the traffic jam had grown to sixty-seven vessels. It topped one hundred on December 4.

The Port of Los Angeles symbolized the nation's supply chain crisis. An absolute avalanche of cargo had landed on the facility starting in the spring. Dockworkers handled more than 535,000 containers in May alone, 75 percent more than during the same month in 2020. Such comparisons were distorted by the pandemic. Yet even measured against 2019, Los Angeles had been swamped. The port's busiest month that year saw the arrival of more than 476,000 containers. In 2021, that monthly figure was exceeded four times.

The pandemic posed an acute challenge. But the supply chain had long been plagued by chronic ills. "Ideally, the intermodal transportation system should operate much like a pipeline, moving goods seamlessly from supplier to customer. However, in today's world, choke points and interruptions in the flow of commerce are common," the US Maritime Administration warned in 2005.[52]

A decade later, following a West Coast work slowdown by longshoremen, the Federal Maritime Commission, which regulates ocean carriers and terminal operators, found that little had changed. The nation's ports faced a "congestion crisis," the agency said.

It was different elsewhere. Foreign ports like Rotterdam in the Netherlands boasted sophisticated information systems that allowed everyone involved in the movement of freight to see the same information on a common software application. US ports entered the crisis with nothing similar.

One problem was money. Over the previous decade, East Coast and Gulf Coast ports had received $11 billion in federal funding, while West Coast facilities like Los Angeles and Long Beach, which handled more than one-third of US imports, got just $1 billion.[53] As vice president, Biden had said the ports were "the lifeblood of the US economy" and called for greater investment to modernize them.[54] But his plea went unheeded. In 2018, the World Bank ranked the United States just fourteenth in its logistics capabilities.[55]

The United States was also paying the price for railroad industry practices designed to maximize profits. Under a strategy called "precision scheduled railroading," the nation's major railroads had slashed payrolls and shuttered facilities. The push to maximize economies of scale resulted in trains that grew longer and longer; some stretched for three miles. Union Pacific, the nation's largest railroad, had eliminated one out of every three workers it employed in 2015, drawing the ire of federal regulators.[56] On the eve of the pandemic, UP's annual profits of almost $6 billion were roughly one-quarter larger than four years earlier despite flat sales.[57] It was another example of corporations pushing the doctrine of financial efficiency to an extreme.

The troubles were not confined to Los Angeles, and they would not be easy to resolve. Flush with cash from government rescue programs, consumers splurged on goods such as furniture, appliances, fitness gear, and electronics. One year after the pandemic, Americans' spending on merchandise was 30 percent higher than normal.[58]

The consequences could be seen at the gates of Chinese factories, on the waters of the Pacific Ocean, along the American rail and highway network, inside retailers' distribution centers, and on consumers' front stoops. Too much stuff was trying to move through too small a pipeline: $1 trillion worth of toys and furniture and clothing and electronics and chemicals and industrial parts competed for the same limited amount of cargo-moving capacity.

There was nothing fancy about the problem. But that didn't make it easy to fix. In the early stages of the crisis, finding enough truck chassis to carry containers to and from the docks was a major problem. Chassis were typical of the sort of prosaic issues snarling the supply chain. They were the most basic of equipment: just a wheeled metal frame that was pulled behind a truck cab and used to hold a shipping container.

But as the tsunami of cargo swept Los Angeles, chassis suddenly were in short supply. Or rather, they were both everywhere and yet not where they were needed. One of the great advantages of what was called the intermodal transport network was its modular design. A standard shipping container could be loaded aboard a ship in Shanghai, unloaded at a dock in Los Angeles, and immediately put aboard either a freight train or a truck chassis to be hauled to its destination.

That was the theory. In practice, warehouses and distribution centers that were stuffed with cargo simply could not find room for more. So rather than unloading a container and returning the chassis to the port, a truck would simply leave it and a fully loaded container in the parking lot. Once the warehouse lots were full, desperate drivers unhooked wherever they could find empty pavement.

"They weren't just at the distribution centers. I was talking to mayors and council members of Southern California municipalities. Some small, some large, where they're just parking them on their streets. They had had containers on chassis in front of people's houses for weeks on end. Crazy stuff," Porcari said.[59]

The July 2020 decisions by Union Pacific and BNSF Railway to halt all trains from West Coast ports helped the railroads dig out from under the mountain of containers clogging their Midwestern hubs. But that just pushed the problem back onto the ports, which received little warning of the plan.

"Once you stopped moving traffic east from the two ports, LA and Long Beach, everything cascaded from there," Porcari said.[60]

Railroad executives, in truth, had little choice. By the time Union Pacific put the brakes on new arrivals at its hub in Joliet, Illinois, the facility had been drowning in cargo for a year. At one point in July, trains were backed up for twenty-five miles trying to enter UP's "Global 4" yard.

Roughly eight thousand shipping containers—twice the figure from one year earlier—clogged the railroad's paved yard, making it hard for truckers to maneuver. Everything was taking longer. It took longer to find the right container to pick up, longer to find a chassis to put it on, longer to unload it at some local warehouse that had its own problems, and longer still to return with the empty chassis and start the cycle all over again. Routine freight movements had become complex industrial ballets.

Normally, it would take a driver three and a half days to load a container aboard a chassis, deliver it to a customer and then return for another pickup. Now, it took up to seventeen days. "Total chaos," Porcari recalled.

The system was overloaded with physical goods, but desperately short of information. People spoke of "the supply chain" as if it were an integrated whole. But it was actually a series of siloed operations. Surprisingly little real-time information flowed among the company shipping the goods, the ocean carrier, the terminal operator, the railroad, and the trucker. Instead, what transpired, Porcari said, was "a series of blind handoffs."

Some of the opacity reflected competitive sensitivities. Companies did not want their rivals knowing the details of their operations. Some of the secretiveness stemmed from security concerns. If everyone knew that a particular shipping container was full of fifty-inch flat-screen televisions, it might never make it to its scheduled destination. The most tight-lipped were railroad executives, who irritated Porcari by trying to fob him off on their industry association.

Porcari tried to encourage information sharing by staging regular Zoom calls with representatives of every link in the chain. Held at 8 a.m. every Monday, Wednesday, and Friday, some sessions drew hundreds of participants, all eager to unclog the system while parrying any unwelcome government requests.

The lack of information sharing was more than an annoyance. It also masked systemic vulnerabilities that had gone mostly unremarked until the crisis. Whenever corporations had faced a choice between efficiency and resilience in designing their supply chains, cost considerations had triumphed. For years, the lure of financial gain overrode any fear that concentration involved risk. Just three ports accounted for nearly half of the thirty-two million containers that arrived in the country.[61]

Shippers likewise had a habit of placing all their bets on the same horse. In 2021, for example, all hospitals in the United States obtained their blood transfusion kits through a handful of purchasing cooperatives. Those groups, in turn, bought the kits from the same factory in China. And that factory filled something like sixteen shipping containers with its products and placed them aboard the same container ship, which slowly made its way toward the United States as demand for transfusions soared amid the pandemic.

"The hospitals started screaming they were days away from running out of transfusion kits. That's not a traditional definition of a national security issue, but I would argue it very much is a national security issue," Porcari said.

The White House convinced the ocean carrier to divert the ship from the US West Coast, dock at a port in British Columbia, and ship the containers east by rail, averting a potential health care nightmare. But the episode exposed an underlying supply chain weakness: None of those involved—not the individual hospitals, the buying co-ops, or the Chinese supplier—were financially incentivized to establish a more resilient arrangement. Spreading the containers among five ships headed to multiple ports would have ensured that at least some transfusion kits would get through. But that would have cost someone more money.

With the supply chain almost entirely under private sector auspices, Porcari had to be creative. To motivate those who were reluctant to cooperate, he often threatened to invoke the Defense Production Act, the Korean War–era law that Trump used in the pandemic's first weeks to compel General Motors to produce ventilators.

But Porcari lacked the authority to invoke the law and was only vaguely aware of its particulars. He saw the DPA as a "great mallet... that was quite effective in focusing people on doing the right thing."

Some of his initiatives did not pay off. Looking for somewhere to store the containers that were blocking the docks and railroad ramps, he scoured federal government properties across Southern California without finding one that was suitable.

Other efforts—such as expanding the pool of available truck drivers—were more successful. Major shippers like Walmart had their own truck fleets. But since they generally moved goods between company facilities, their drivers lacked the credentials that would allow them access to the ports. Normally, obtaining the required Transportation Worker Identification Credential, or TWIC card, could take up to sixty days.

But Porcari arranged temporary trailers at the West Coast ports, which could offer drivers same- or next-day service. Quickly enrolling these new drivers in the federal system meant extra manpower that helped clear the docks.

By the autumn of 2021, persistent supply chain headaches were contributing to some of the highest inflation in decades and posing a significant political problem for the president. The White House needed to demonstrate progress that voters could understand. Biden was taking a personal interest in Porcari's work.

At Porcari's urging, the ports of Los Angeles and Long Beach in September announced extended night and weekend hours for trucks to pick up and return containers. The White House billed the announcement as moving the ports to "24/7 operation," signaling the sort of wartime urgency that consumers were demanding.

But the ports never really achieved round-the-clock status. Truckers were not even filling all of the existing appointment slots, let alone new ones in the middle of the night. From a driver's standpoint, it made little sense to collect a shipping container in the predawn darkness if the local distribution center it was bound for would not open for several more hours.

The president himself touted the idea of "24/7" operations, during an appearance at the Port of Baltimore, where he celebrated generations of Biden family "watermen."[62] But the claims of round-the-clock status were more public relations than reality.

Porcari had more success breaking down the barriers that prevented different supply chain players from sharing information. The Transportation Department built a software application called FLOW (Freight Logistics Optimization Works), which collected data from importers, carriers, ports, terminal operators, and trucking firms. FLOW went live in March 2022, drawing data from shippers such as Walmart, Home

Depot, and Nike; the largest ocean carriers, including Maersk; and maritime terminals in Newark, Long Beach, Savannah, and Houston.[63]

FLOW aggregated importers' purchase orders and compared anonymized demand details with the available freight-handling capacity. For the first time, participants in the nation's supply chain would get an advance look at the cargo moving through the system in time to do something about it.

By the spring of 2022, the nation's supply lines were improving. Carriers had begun redirecting some vessels to less crowded East Coast ports, like Savannah. The e-commerce shopping frenzy had eased, as the government stopped handing out coronavirus stimulus payments and the Federal Reserve began raising interest rates, which made borrowing more expensive and slowed the economy.

That meant fewer containers were arriving in Los Angeles. By June, the cost of shipping goods from China to the West Coast was half what it had been in the fall. Over the remainder of the year, there would be slow, steady improvement.[64]

Yet the prolonged disruptions had left a mark on global commerce. By reshaping trade patterns, the pandemic marked an end to the "era of country-agnostic globalization."[65] No longer would companies consider only cost in choosing how to organize their production. The risks involved in concentrating too much manufacturing in any one location—not just China and not just overseas—were now too obvious to ignore.

Roughly three of every four companies had made a significant change in their production networks, according to a Gartner survey of midsized companies.[66] There was no single strategy or location that would eliminate all supply chain risks. Life sciences companies added capacity in Eastern Europe. Retailers like Columbia Sportswear, which had sourced largely from China, added new suppliers in Central and South America while high-tech manufacturers bulked up in North America and Western Europe, often lured by government subsidies.

Flex, too, had been marked by the pandemic. For Advaithi, the legacy of the crisis was a massive stockpile of parts needed to produce the vacuum cleaners, cloud computing gear, and autonomous driving systems that Flex made for brand-name customers around the world. Flex had more than doubled the amount of raw material it kept on hand, raising its annual inventory expense by nearly $4 billion "to address continued component shortages and logistics constraints."[67]

The company's profits and its stock price were way up from the depths of the pandemic. But the costly inventory buildup left Advaithi frustrated—and hopeful that artificial intelligence might somehow prevent a repeat of the pandemic-era mismatch between what Americans wanted and what they could get.

It was "shocking," she said, that so much of the corporate response to the supply crisis had involved building up larger and more costly buffer stocks. "How do we still solve for these problems by putting too much inventory in place?" she asked. "That shouldn't be the world anymore."[68]

10

The Return of Big Government

J oe Biden, above all else, promised a return to normalcy. After a tumultuous Trump presidency capped by a global pandemic, economic collapse, and failed insurrection, Americans in January 2021 yearned for some peace and quiet.

But there would be no going back to the world of 2016. Too much had changed under Trump. Chinese imports now faced tariffs of up to 25 percent. Obama's signature trade deal, the Trans-Pacific Partnership, lay in ruins. And corporate America had lost its traditional influence over trade policy, with Biden proclaiming himself the most pro-union president in history.

The veteran pol had campaigned on a pledge to break with the approach to global economic integration that presidents of both parties had followed for decades before Trump's election. Biden said he would sign no new trade agreements before investing at home in education, infrastructure, and manufacturing. He vowed to appoint labor union leaders and environmentalists as US trade negotiators and to empower them to tackle currency manipulation by countries like China, despite Wall Street's opposition.

He opposed the special investor-state dispute panels that had allowed corporations to avoid foreign courts in countries like Mexico;

endorsed stronger "Buy America" rules; and committed himself to "revitalize communities impacted by globalization and automation."[1] Fulfilling these promises would amount to the most comprehensive overhaul in US engagement with the global economy in a generation.

But the extent of the promised break at first was not entirely clear. In some Washington circles, business representatives and mainstream economists held out hope that it would not be that dramatic. Biden, after all, was a centrist Democrat. He had voted for NAFTA and supported bringing China into the WTO. During the 2020 campaign, he had been critical of Trump's approach to China, promising an "immediate review" of his tariffs and outreach to allies to build a coalition to confront Beijing.

As the months passed and it became clear that Biden had no intention of reanimating any part of the old trade policy consensus, frustration grew in pro-globalization precincts. One of the earliest expressions of elite opposition to Biden's course came in an April 2021 piece in *Foreign Affairs* by the economist Adam Posen, who blasted the president for a "self-defeating economic retreat" from globalization founded on misplaced nostalgia for a golden age of manufacturing.[2] Many in Washington were baffled by the Biden team's support for economic nationalism. "They all know better," groused one former policymaker. The political climate was so unfriendly that Mark Kennedy, a former Republican congressman, wryly likened trade advocates to the Irish monks who labored during the Dark Ages to preserve the written word.

It was Biden's personal history that informed this epic shift. The president had been raised in a working-class Catholic family that was familiar with good times and bad times. His father, Joe Sr., did well during World War II after an uncle hired him to manage the Boston office of a company that produced a maritime sealant. The Bidens lived in a comfortable home in a Boston suburb, enjoying a life of "fur coats and fine China."[3] But after the war, the company's sales ebbed and Biden's father retreated to Scranton, Pennsylvania, his wife Jean's hometown, in search of work. By 1953, after a brief interlude cleaning industrial boilers, he had landed a job as a car salesman in a suburb of Wilmington, Delaware.[4]

His father's economic slide left a deep impression. Biden told a story about his dad and the meaning of work so often that the reporters who followed him on the campaign trail could recite it from memory.

"Joey, a job is about a lot more than a paycheck," the president would recall his father saying. "It's about your dignity. It's about respect. It's about being able to look your kid in the eye and say, 'Honey, it's going to be okay,' and mean it—and mean it."[5]

Biden the president bore the scars of Biden the son and father. He was ten years old when his family picked up and left the only home he had known. Two decades later, as a newly elected senator, his wife and infant daughter were killed in a car accident that left his two sons, Beau and Hunter, badly injured. He considered abandoning his Senate position even before he was sworn in, but was persuaded by older colleagues to take his seat. He could do so only because his sister Valerie moved in and agreed to serve as a de facto surrogate mother for the boys.

Those experiences left him with little sympathy for economists' bloodless insistence that residents of hard-hit factory towns should simply move to places that offered better prospects. Standing in the Oval Office, the president would tell aides that it was not always that simple. People say you have to move, Biden would say. Well, what if your kid has autism? What if you lost your husband and you're raising your kids by yourself? You can't just lose your community like that. Bill Clinton had promised "a global economy with a human face."[6] Biden was intent on bringing it about.

His view of most economic issues carried more than a whiff of class consciousness. Long after the president became wealthy, he called himself "Middle Class Joe," noting that he had often been the poorest member of the US Senate.[7] Biden, who was the first Democratic presidential nominee without an Ivy League degree since 1984, carried an evident chip on his shoulder.[8] "He would tell stories about the rich guys who would stab you in the back after they patted you on their way out the door. That was one of his favorite stories," said Jim Greene, his chief economic aide from 1992 until he became vice president in 2009.

Biden's votes for trade agreements in the 1990s had stemmed from his inclination to support whatever the Democratic Party mainstream backed at a given moment and his belief in the US-led international order. But his union ties meant these decisions were not always easy.

Delaware had three auto plants when Greene went to work for Biden, as the NAFTA debate was heating up. The senator's union allies who worked in them were opposed to the deal. Biden got an earful about the treaty from his wife, Jill, who was teaching English composition at Delaware Technical Community College. Many of her students were the sort of working-class people who worried the treaty would cost them their jobs.[9] Biden went through "the torture of the damned" before voting for NAFTA, Greene said.

Weighing in favor of the treaty were broad economic and foreign policy considerations. Even without NAFTA, auto jobs would be under pressure from lower-cost foreign competition. But by requiring Mexico to lower its tariffs—without the United States changing its own—the deal was likely to spur greater US exports, Biden said. He also was sensitive to the notion that the global trading system was essentially a US creation that made the world safe for American interests. Having international rules to referee trade conflicts was invaluable.

When Biden finally decided to support NAFTA, his Senate floor speech was a masterpiece of first trying to have it both ways. He shared "the fear and concerns" of the agreement's opponents, but nonetheless believed that it was the best deal the US could get. He scoffed at "the imaginary realm of econometric models" that promised all would be well while expressing faith that the US government would take steps to help the middle class.[10]

The treaty's effects had been exaggerated by both proponents and opponents, Biden said. Ross Perot's "giant sucking sound" was a chimera. NAFTA's impact would be dwarfed by the normal churn of the US economy. Biden's efforts to navigate the trade divide worked. The next day, Greene said, one of the Delaware papers gave him the headline he wanted: "Biden for NAFTA—and Labor."

The United States at the time was selling slightly more to Mexico than it was buying. Over the ensuing decades, American exports grew, but less quickly than imports from Mexico. The annual gap grew to more than $100 billion, a statistic that many economists said did not mean much, but which nonetheless carried political import.

A decade later as the China shock spread, Biden's enthusiasm for trade liberalization cooled. Big business was the big winner from China's rise. In the first several years after Beijing joined the WTO, corporate profits as a share of the economy doubled while labor's compensation slid.[11] "One thing I heard Biden rail about was labor not getting its cut out of the profits being made in China from his vote in favor of [permanent normal trade relations]," recalled Frank Jannuzi, who worked for him on the staff of the Senate Foreign Relations Committee.[12]

Biden voted in the 2000s against several small trade agreements with Chile, Singapore, Oman, and six Central American nations. And he supported Senate legislation that would have punished China for keeping the yuan's value artificially low, which made Chinese products less expensive than American ones. His voting record, the libertarian Cato Institute said, showed "great ambivalence about American participation in the global economy."[13]

During the Obama administration, the president's support of traditional trade liberalization left his vice president cold. Japanese diplomats who occasionally dealt with him in Obama's absence, for example, found Biden less enthusiastic about the administration's signature trade initiative, the Trans-Pacific Partnership. "His heart wasn't in it," one person recalled.

Set them free

In February 2022, Tim Draper, the venture capitalist who had soured on China, returned to Silicon Valley from a trip to Uruguay, where the center-right president, Luis Lacalle Pou, had charmed him by insisting on being addressed as "Luis." Draper arrived home just as Russian President Vladimir Putin ordered his military to invade neighboring Ukraine.

Draper had links to both belligerents. He had visited Ukraine in 2005 to look into a potential investment. Through an intermediary, he was invited to meet then-President Viktor Yushchenko for a discussion of ways to stimulate technological innovation.

Yushchenko, who had survived a poisoning one year earlier, was eager to develop financial ties with the West. Draper at first rejected the president's request to invest in Ukraine, complaining that it required six months and approvals from twenty-three bureaucrats just to incorporate a new business. Yushchenko rose from his chair and said with a flourish: "That will be one bureaucrat, one week!" [14]

Draper was impressed during a subsequent tour of the company he was eyeing. After visiting a room packed with busy engineers, and still enthused by his encounter with the pro-European president, he quickly agreed to invest $500,000 in the start-up. [15]

But it had all been a ruse. The "engineers" were playacting. The company was a money sink. The entrepreneur at its helm later could not explain what he had done with Draper's cash, leaving the venture capitalist believing he had been "cheated" for one of only three times in his career. Still, even though he never returned, Draper kept an eye on Ukraine. The vast pool of engineering talent there, a legacy of the Soviet era, meant great potential, he thought.

Draper also had a history with Russia. "When Gorbachev opened the place up, I started to get interested," he said. [16] Through Draper Fisher Jurvetson, he had tried on three separate occasions to set up a venture fund in Moscow, including via a 2007 partnership with VTB Bank. The Kremlin-backed bank was one of Russia's largest financial institutions. The DFJ-VTB Aurora fund drew half of its $150 million capital from the Russian government and one-fifth from the European Bank for Reconstruction and Development. [17] The partnership funded a handful of start-ups before VTB pulled out. [18] Years later, the contrast between Russian authoritarianism and Ukrainian aspirations for democracy was on Draper's mind as news of the invasion broke.

"Putin is jealous of the free world including #Ukraine. These countries are valuable, so he wants to steal them. But you can't steal #freedom and #trust. They are earned, and they are powerful economic engines. Trust your people, set them free, and they thrive," he wrote on the social media site X.

Draper also was exposed to geopolitics in Asia. After halting his investments in mainland China, he grew interested in several companies in Taiwan. He placed his first bets on TNL Media Group, a digital news and information company, and several other start-ups in 2021. [19] Taipei seemed an odd investment destination for someone who so distrusted Xi Jinping, the Chinese leader who had vowed to regain physical control over the island. But Draper took solace from the importance to the global economy of Taiwan's semiconductor industry, especially its flagship chipmaker, Taiwan Semiconductor Manufacturing Company (TSMC). "I think China would be really stupid to invade Taiwan," he said.[20]

Another prominent investor reached a different conclusion. Just a few months after Draper disclosed his Taiwan investments, Warren Buffett dumped Berkshire Hathaway's entire $4 billion stake in TSMC, citing geopolitical worries. It was an unusual move for Buffett, a famed buy-and-hold investor who had acquired a stake in the chipmaker only a few months before selling. "I don't like its location," he said.[21]

Recover together

Russia's invasion of Ukraine marked an emphatic end to an era of relative geopolitical calm that began in 1991. The post–Cold War world, of course, had not been entirely peaceful prior to the Russian attack. There were serial conflicts in the Balkans in the 1990s and US invasions of Iraq and Afghanistan following the terrorist attacks of September 11, 2001.

But Europe's largest state-on-state violence since 1945 shattered the European delusion that relying on Russian energy to fire its factories was risk-free. The conflict also disrupted global trade in food, fuel, and fertilizer, threatening parts of Africa and the Middle East with crop shortages and financial ruin while helping send inflation in the United States and Europe to forty-year highs.

A few weeks after Russian missiles hammered Kyiv, Larry Fink, CEO of BlackRock, the world's largest investment firm, said the war on Europe's periphery would prompt governments and companies around the world to rethink their operations. "The Russian invasion of Ukraine has put an end to the globalization we have experienced over the last three decades," said Fink, whose firm managed $10 trillion in assets.[22]

Within hours of the attack, US and European diplomats moved to sever Russia's links to the global economy. A Brussels summit late on the evening of the invasion, spurred by an emotional appeal from Ukrainian President Volodymyr Zelensky, ultimately agreed to impose punishing sanctions on Russia.[23] The United States, the European Union, Canada, and the United Kingdom barred major Russian banks from the SWIFT global financial messaging system, thus disrupting their ability to move funds across international borders, blacklisted Russian oligarchs, including Roman Abramovich, owner of the Chelsea Premier League football team, and froze €300 billion of Russian Central Bank assets held in Western banks.[24]

One of the first targets for US action was VTB Bank, the government-owned institution that Draper had partnered with almost fifteen years earlier. The Treasury Department imposed full blocking sanctions on the bank and twenty of its subsidiaries, terminating its ability to execute transactions through US financial channels. VTB was one of the largest banks the US had ever sanctioned. "This will sever a critical artery of Russia's financial system," the Treasury Department said.[25]

As Russia rained bombs and bullets on Ukraine, Putin's economy absorbed a financial beating. The ruble plunged, making Russians poorer. To halt free-falling share prices, the Moscow stock exchange closed temporarily. Russian banks, starved of dollars, struggled to move funds across borders. Russian businesses no longer had access to the world's most advanced technologies.

Day by day, the country's isolation deepened. Russian aircraft were barred from the skies over Europe and the United States. To prevent Putin's subjects from learning the truth of what was happening, regulators in Moscow blocked Facebook, one of the few sources of information that was not already under the government's thumb. In May, Italian authorities seized a yacht that reportedly belonged to Putin.[26] More than one thousand multinational corporations, including Ford, Siemens, IBM, Nike, and McDonald's, withdrew from the country.[27]

Fallout from the European conflict spread through the global economy. By the end of March, oil prices topped $110 per barrel, which fed into higher prices for a wide array of goods. Fertilizer prices rose 70 percent in the first six weeks of the war, beyond the ability of farmers in some African and Middle Eastern countries to pay. Grain shipments from the Black Sea were halted, leaving countries like Tunisia, which relied on Russia and Ukraine for more than half of its annual wheat imports, with dwindling supplies of bread.[28]

Europe's economy felt the war more directly than did the United States. The conflict dealt a lasting blow to Germany's policy of *Wandel durch Handel*, or "change through trade." Meant to justify unfettered commerce with authoritarian powers such as Russia and China, the German doctrine represented the purest distillation of the idea that globalization meant peace. American politicians for years had warned that Germany was sleepwalking into a dangerous dependence on an unreliable partner. In the invasion's aftermath, Germany began "coming to grips with something that many in this country have long ignored, namely that interdependence also involves risks and that trade is not necessarily followed by democratic change," said Foreign Minister Annalena Baerbock.[29]

At the invasion's outset, Germany was buying 38 percent of its natural gas from Russia. By September, after prices more than doubled, those purchases had stopped.[30] In the United States, too, consumers suffered. Retail gasoline prices, perhaps the most politically sensitive indicator for Americans, opened the year at $3.28 per gallon. By June, they topped $5.00, an all-time high.[31]

Before the war was a month old, it was evident that a reshaping of the global economic order was underway. Geopolitical calm, it turned out, had been a luxury, not an entitlement. Federal Reserve Chair Jerome H. Powell told Congress that Putin's invasion was "a game changer."[32] Any lingering hopes that countries like Russia would be part of a US-led international system had been exploded by the Russian leader's decision to invade his neighbor.

Coming after the pandemic exposed vulnerabilities in global supply chains, the war's disruption of merchandise and commodity trade only accelerated the corporate rethinking that was underway. US economic sanctions that segregated Russian oil shipments and capped their price effectively meant "the end of the global oil market," according to Daniel Yergin, vice chairman of S&P Global.[33]

Oil and gas, however, were not the only vital commodities affected by the conflict. Boeing and Airbus relied on a Russian state-owned firm, VSMPO-AVISMA, for titanium. Automakers bought palladium, which was used in catalytic converters, from Russian mines. US agribusiness giant Cargill owned two grain elevators, a terminal, and a sunflower seed processing and extraction plant in Ukraine. The sun-flower operation was located in the eastern Donetsk region, the scene of heavy fighting.

That fall, Biden traveled to Bali, Indonesia, for the annual sum-mit of the Group of 20, the global economy's steering committee, with much to discuss. The need for global cooperation was clear. And the G20 was supposed to be the place for it; world leaders had used the forum to mobilize trillions of dollars to fight the 2008 financial crisis.

But Biden found a muted gathering that showcased global divi-sion, not unity. Putin, anticipating ostracism over his brutal war, did not even show up. Xi, who did, proved uncooperative, casting the only negative vote on a proposal for poor-nation debt relief and publicly scolding the Canadian prime minister for leaking details of their private talks. Europe and South Korea, meanwhile, were at odds with the US over Biden's green energy subsidies, which discriminated against non-American companies. Even the G20 leaders' "family photo," a tradi-tional show of bonhomie, was canceled.

The highlight of Biden's stay on the resort island was a three-hour meeting with Xi. Flanked by aides, the two leaders spoke in a hotel ballroom with an enormous yellow, purple, and red floral arrangement between them. Biden had been warned that the meeting, aimed at ar-resting a deterioration in relations, would be all business; there would be no time for his customary icebreakers about Ireland or the beaches in his native Delaware. In the event, it was Xi who strayed from the agenda, speaking at length and with some passion about the vital role the Communist Party played in China's development. Afterward, the White House would say that the talks had been candid, a diplomatic euphemism for *blunt*, and the relationship stabilized. But after four de-cades of ever-tighter commercial links, the world's two largest econo-mies were drifting apart.

On his way to the airport for the flight home, Biden passed roadside billboards urging G20 participants to "Recover Together." In fact, they were doing anything but. The Bali summit showcased an erosion in the fabric of globalization that had begun with the 2008 financial crisis, accelerated with Donald Trump's trade wars, and blossomed with the supply chain disruptions caused by the coronavirus pandemic. When

Russia attacked Ukraine, it marked the end of a long era of relative geo-political calm that had enabled trade to flourish.

"Globalization is almost dead and free trade is almost dead. A lot of people still wish they would come back, but I don't think they will," Morris Chang, founder of Taiwan Semiconductor Manufacturing Company, the world's top chipmaker, said at the time.[34]

This could get some traction

In January 2023, midway through Biden's presidency, National Security Advisor Jake Sullivan decided it was time to publicly lay out the administration's new approach to international economic policy.

The seeds of what Sullivan planned to say had been germinating since 2016, when he served as Hillary Clinton's top policy adviser. Fending off populist attacks from Bernie Sanders on the left and Donald Trump on the right, Sullivan was forced to rethink economic nostrums that he had long taken for granted.

If Washington's governing elite could be distilled into a single human form, it would look like Jake Sullivan. He grew up in Minnesota. His father was a professor, his mother a high school guidance counselor. In high school, Sullivan was president of the student council and voted most likely to succeed. He graduated from Yale, was a Rhodes Scholar, and earned a master's degree in international relations from Oxford University before returning to New Haven for law school. After earning his law degree, he clerked for Supreme Court Justice Stephen Breyer, then worked on Capitol Hill, for Sen. Amy Klobuchar, and at the State Department, advising Clinton.[35]

Prior to 2016, he had never questioned the virtues of trade liberalization. But wrestling with the Sanders and Trump critiques began a reconsideration that blossomed following Hillary Clinton's defeat. While nursing his wounds at the Carnegie Endowment following the election, Sullivan had written a mea culpa, acknowledging that what he had taken for granted as received wisdom left millions of voters cold.

Sullivan was a moderate. But now he argued that a more assertive, freer-spending federal government was required to solve problems that the market neglected. Along with expensive public sector investments,

Washington needed new policies, such as wage insurance, to protect Americans "from unchecked market excess."[36] By the time Biden's 2020 campaign got underway, Sullivan had endorsed a wholesale overhaul of trade policy. Instead of prying open China's financial system for Goldman Sachs, trade negotiators should close the loopholes that allowed corporations to escape paying taxes needed to cushion workers against globalization, he said.[37]

When he looked back on 2016's heartbreak, TPP loomed large. Clinton, he thought, had approached the proposed trade pact "as more of a strategic issue" because of her experience as secretary of state.[38] But as he sought a path for his candidate, he dove into the pact's trade specifics, weighing arguments from the critics and supporters.

"A lot of the people who instinctively argued that TPP was just an inherent, innate good were not really grappling with the arguments being put forward by its critics. They glossed over the specifics. It was just sort of a general catechism that more trade is good. More trade agreements are good. This is important to do. Anyone who was arguing the other side of that is being either heretical or Neanderthal or knuckle-dragging," he said.

An example was the provision that would allow corporations to sue member governments in a private forum rather than gamble on the legal system in places like Vietnam or Mexico. It dawned on Sullivan that the goal of this investor-state dispute settlement procedure was to make other countries safe for US corporations; it would do nothing to promote investment or jobs at home.

Defenders of the system argued American corporations that moved their manufacturing to Mexico would add other jobs at their US headquarters. But Sullivan's point remained: Those headquarters jobs in marketing, product design, or human resources would be little help for laid-off factory workers.

During the general election, as Trump castigated China for the "rape" of the US economy, Sullivan grappled with fundamental questions about Chinese state capitalism.[39] China's market-oriented reforms had slowed, stalled, and then reversed within years of the country joining the WTO. In 2003, for example, Chinese leaders established the State-owned Assets Supervision and Administration Commission of the State Council (SASAC) to manage more than one hundred of China's top corporations. Mark Wu, an assistant professor at Harvard Law School who authored a seminal article on the system he called "China, Inc.," likened the organization's importance to having a single US government agency control "General Electric, General Motors, Ford, Boeing, US Steel, DuPont, AT&T, Verizon, Honeywell, and United Technologies."[40] Even after a Communist Party conclave a decade later granted the market a "decisive role" in allocating labor and capital resources, the backsliding continued.[41]

The theory behind allowing China to join the global trading system in 2001 was that it would continue its market-oriented reforms, ultimately converging with the world's advanced economies. "It became clearer and clearer to me, as we were having that back and forth on the campaign trail, you've got a whole international economic system designed around openness and market economies, and now you have the massive factor of a non-market economy sitting right in the middle. That has to be stared square in the face," Sullivan said. "And the whole globalization narrative doesn't just ignore that. It actually suggests that globalization will lead China to become the open market economy that the rest of the major players were. And that had manifestly not happened."

Sullivan found little support in establishment circles for reconsidering the conventional wisdom. His usually receptive audiences at the Aspen Strategy Group or the Council on Foreign Relations viewed his second thoughts as an overreaction to Hillary Clinton's loss in 2016. In truth, Sullivan had been struck by something that Jennifer Harris, one of his top aides, observed during the campaign. It seemed odd, she told Sullivan, that Democrats and Republicans had fundamental differences on domestic economic policies yet were in complete agreement on international economics.

Looking back, Sullivan saw the 2016 fight over trade as a long-overdue argument that the country had been denied by circumstances. In 2008, Obama rode to victory on voters' desire for change amid the wreckage of the housing bubble; his opponent, John McCain, was a national security specialist ill-equipped to challenge economic orthodoxy. Four years later, Mitt Romney had the financial expertise that McCain lacked. But as a wealthy private equity investor, he was not inclined to question the status quo.

In 2016, however, there finally was a candidate who validated workers' grievances and promised to set them right. Trump blended anti-immigration animus with an attack on the elite's failure to protect workers from "unfair" foreign competition. Academics would dispute whether identity or economics played the larger role in motivating Trump's coalition. Sullivan saw no reason to choose. "My own gut says it's a combination of both, probably a little heavier on the identity side than on the economic side. But the economic piece matters," he said.

Biden had long recognized the political dangers brewing in the American heartland. During the Obama administration, he supported hiring a White House manufacturing adviser and urged aides to promote factory jobs, recognizing in the wake of the financial crisis that economic distress in blue-collar towns would have political consequences, one aide recalled.

Two months after Trump's victory, Biden flew to Davos to address the World Economic Forum. Yes, globalization had lifted people from poverty in the developing world, he acknowledged. But for many people in advanced nations like the United States, it had meant a decline in living standards. "Globalization has not been an unalloyed good," Biden told the elite audience.

Urgent action was needed to "mitigate the economic trends that are stoking unrest in so many advanced economies and undermining people's basic sense of dignity," he said, calling for more education and job training, basic worker protections, easier access to capital, and tax reform.[42]

The address, by an outgoing vice president with forty-eight hours remaining in his tenure, drew little notice. Six years later, his views—polished by his national security advisor—were of greater moment. Appearing at the Brookings Institution in April 2023, Sullivan indicted the trade policies of the 1990s and called for "a new consensus" that integrated domestic and foreign policies. "Foreign policy for the middle class" had blossomed into government policy.

Biden had taken office with the nation's industrial base "hollowed out," the result of a generation of excessive deference to pure market outcomes, Sullivan said. Even before the pandemic depressed production, manufacturing output in late 2019 was lower than it had been in 2007.[43] The China shock "wasn't adequately anticipated and wasn't adequately addressed as it unfolded," Sullivan said, and that failure had eroded the social and economic cohesion that supported American democracy, leading—though Sullivan did not say this explicitly—to Trump.[44]

The 2008 financial crisis, subsequent weak recovery, and covid each had exposed vulnerabilities in the old approach. Placing economic efficiency above all other considerations had shortchanged workers and encouraged entire supply chains to migrate offshore. Biden's remedy was to use industrial policy to address this and other "market failures," such as insufficient investment in zero-carbon energy sources.

Sullivan skewered conventional trade policy, saying that through the 1990s the United States had pursued lower tariffs without paying sufficient attention to labor standards and supply chain resilience. The administration was committed to promoting trade, working through the WTO, and maintaining economic ties with China, he said. But the United States no longer could act as if it were dealing with the China of 2001. Recognizing Xi Jinping's challenge to the US-led international system, Biden would quarantine the most advanced technologies with a strategy he described as "a small yard with a high fence." This new emphasis on national security did not mean unilateralism or "America alone," Sullivan said.

It did not take long for traditionalists to object. Some questioned Sullivan's facts. The trade agreements of the 1990s were about more than tariff cuts, they said, citing intellectual property rules, investment protection, and regulatory harmonization.[45] Froman, his Obama administration colleague, wrote to say that it's not a new consensus when everyone disagrees with you. In some of the criticism, Sullivan detected grudging respect. Martin Wolf, the oracular *Financial Times* columnist, warned about all the ways that Biden's industrial policies might "backfire badly," but agreed that the fundamental objectives "make sense."[46]

Likewise, Larry Summers, the former treasury secretary whose support the administration coveted, visited Sullivan after the speech. Summers saw Sullivan's foreign policy for the middle class as "fairly misguided and dangerous" when it served as a justification for tariffs or the administration's "fetish" for promoting manufacturing jobs, which was doomed to fail given the march of automation.[47]

Sullivan thought that Summers's real fear was that the administration's logic would prove appealing. "Part of the reason I think people on the other side of this debate reacted to it, was that they looked at it and thought uh-oh. This could get some traction; this could get some legs," Sullivan said.

The longest of long shots

Wearing his trademark aviator sunglasses, the president was in a celebratory mood. On this August 2022 day, a large American flag hung from the arm of a Caterpillar backhoe on the lot behind him, the site of a $20 billion Intel semiconductor plant made possible by billions of dollars in federal subsidies. The government cash was needed to cover the 30 percent to 40 percent premium that building a plant in the United States cost compared to Asia, according to Pat Gelsinger, Intel's CEO.[48]

"Folks, the future of the chip industry is going to be made in America," the president told the crowd. "Made in America."[49]

The project in New Albany, Ohio, was evidence of one of Biden's signature accomplishments. The $53 billion CHIPS and Science Act, which he had signed less than two weeks earlier, was designed to regain the commanding position in computer chip production that the United States had surrendered during an era of offshoring.

Together with the Inflation Reduction Act, also signed that month, and the bipartisan infrastructure law passed the previous year, the CHIPS Act was part of an industrial policy push that promised the biggest shift in US government economic thinking in forty years.

"One thing that characterizes our administration is we see more market and more policy failures than previous administrations," said Jared Bernstein, chair of the Council of Economic Advisers.[50]

The change in direction was motivated by both domestic and foreign considerations. At home, the middle class had been squeezed, and public priorities such as developing renewable energy sources to address climate change had lagged. Abroad, China was challenging US leadership in a way that made it an untrustworthy supplier.

Biden aimed to revitalize domestic production, simultaneously strengthening thin supply chains, boosting working-class job prospects, and safeguarding national security.

Calls to "reindustrialize America" had been a feature of American politics for nearly half a century.[51] Trump, for all his bluster and bravado, failed to have a significant effect on manufacturing output or employment.[52] But this time, something was happening. Companies did not wait for the three bills to make their way through Congress. Spending on new factories tripled to a record high; more people were working construction than at the peak of the housing bubble.[53] The administration predicted total private and public spending in response to Biden's industrial policies of $3.5 trillion over the next decade.[54]

"Federal investments attract private investment. It creates jobs. It creates industries. It demonstrates we're all in this together," Biden said at the Intel groundbreaking ceremony.

The semiconductor plant represented a boost for Ohio's economy: seven thousand union construction jobs while the two-plant campus was being built, plus three thousand permanent positions paying an average annual salary of $135,000. Many would not require a college degree.

Almost one-third of the initial $736 billion in private sector investments made in response to the president's policies landed in China shock communities, according to research by Glencora Haskins, Mark Muro, and Maya Garg of the Brookings Institution. More than half of the money was for clean energy projects in hard-hit manufacturing regions, suggesting that Biden might succeed where his predecessors mostly failed to act.[55]

Yet there was no sign that voters gave the president much credit for it—and no sign that the long-term decline in manufacturing employment could be reversed. Once an electoral bellwether, Ohio was trending more Republican with every election. Biden had lost there to Trump by eight percentage points in 2020. In the RealClearPolitics average of polls, he trailed by a margin of 52 percent to 42 percent, before bowing out of the race in July.[56] In November, Trump would win the state by more than 11 percentage points.

Administration officials were more interested in touting the president's achievements than in acknowledging the limits of their manufacturing-centered strategy. It was true that factory employment had rallied from the pandemic low to reach a level unseen during the Trump years. Yet as Biden entered his final months in office, the gain over the pandemic-eve level was less than one hundred thousand jobs, a rounding error in the context of a labor force of nearly 160 million people.[57] As a share of total employment, the nearly thirteen million manufacturing jobs continued to tick down. Just 8 percent of all American jobs were found in the factories that drew so much attention from Washington policymakers.[58]

Manufacturing employment had been in decline since the early 1950s, when one out of every three American workers toiled on an assembly line. Long before NAFTA and the China shock, automation thinned factory payrolls, allowing individual workers to do more. From 1969 to 2000, the total number of factory jobs stayed roughly constant at around seventeen million. But manufacturing's share of all US jobs fell by half. Ten years later, factory employment stood at its lowest level since before the attack on Pearl Harbor.

"I think the question is: Can we have a manufacturing policy that gets the number of manufacturing jobs back to what it was for most of the pre-China-shock period?" said Bernstein. "We're certainly not ready to give up on that, by a long shot."

When Bernstein spoke, the United States was nearly four million factory jobs short of its pre-China-shock level. There is no precedent, in any advanced country, for regaining that many manufacturing jobs. The administration also never conducted any formal analysis of the likely jobs impact of Biden's industrial policies, according to one senior official.

Even friendly economists were skeptical. Jason Furman, the Harvard professor who served as Barack Obama's top White House economic adviser, said Biden's policies would deliver significant benefits in terms of domestic semiconductor production and climate-friendly energy projects. But as a jobs program, they would disappoint.

New government spending and tax incentives would boost investment in favored sectors, but with the economy already operating near full employment they would do so only by drawing money from elsewhere. As activity in computer chips and clean energy increased, interest rates would rise, making borrowed money for other businesses more expensive and hurting their ability to expand employment. "This will have basically zero impact on total employment and little to no impact on the number or share of those jobs that are in manufacturing," Furman said.[59]

Commerce Secretary Gina Raimondo led the high-stakes effort to rebuild America's domestic semiconductor capabilities. The former Rhode Island governor had transformed the sleepy backwater agency into the leading edge of government efforts to repatriate production of the computer brains used for everything from household appliances to the Pentagon's most advanced weaponry.

Raimondo was an unusual champion of government intervention in the market. Before entering politics, she had worked in the venture capital industry, eventually opening the first VC firm in Rhode Island. She described herself as a "pro-market person" and was viewed skeptically by some progressives who saw her as too close to the business community.[60]

But as a young girl, Raimondo had felt the market's sting. In 1983, her father, Joseph, lost his job as a chemist at the Bulova watch factory in Providence, after twenty-six years, when the company moved production to China.[61] His experience was replicated across the state. Between 1990 and the 2008 financial crisis, Rhode Island lost more than half of its factory jobs.[62]

"My family suffered significantly when Rhode Island's jewelry manufacturing industry collapsed. And all those jobs went to China. I lived it," she said in an interview. "And it wasn't just my family. We were relatively well-off compared to people who struggled. Entire communities in Rhode Island were destroyed because the factories went away. Many of them never really got over it."[63]

Biden prescribed industrial policy as the antidote to what he called "the trickle-down approach" that had hollowed out communities like Providence.[64] Almost three decades after Bill Clinton pronounced last rites for "the era of big government," Biden was bringing it back. One indication was the size of the federal budget deficit, which as a share of the economy, hit levels previously unseen outside of war or national crisis.

"You have a president who just feels that this whole development is a disaster for the country and for working-class Americans, and he really wants to reverse it," Treasury Secretary Janet Yellen said, referring to the China shock.[65]

New semiconductor plants, backed by federal subsidies, were under construction in Arizona, Texas, and New York, as well as in Ohio. By 2032, the US share of global production of advanced logic chips was expected to hit 28 percent, up from essentially nothing today, according to the Semiconductor Industry Association.

Raimondo said she expected the CHIPS program alone to create "one million-plus great jobs." But making computer chips is not labor-intensive. Even if the SIA's favorable forecasts are met, the industry is expected to add just 115,000 new jobs.

Manufacturing also faced structural headwinds. The value of the dollar by the spring of 2024 was 30 percent higher than a decade earlier, which made goods produced in the United States more expensive for overseas customers.[66]

The initial implementation of the Biden projects was a mixed bag. Intel, once the crown jewel of the US technology industry, reported nearly $2 billion in losses in the first half of 2024 while the Ohio plant's scheduled opening slipped. To boost the company, which was in line for perhaps $20 billion in government support, Raimondo began asking executives at Apple and Amazon to buy its chips.[67] Intel's financial plight, critics said, illuminated the danger that a more interventionist government could wind up yoked to a failing corporation.

Both of TSMC's semiconductor fabrication facilities in Arizona also suffered construction snags, related to a lack of skilled labor and licensing issues, which delayed their openings by at least a year.[68] Biden's "Buy America" requirement for federally funded projects, meanwhile, ran smack into the problem it meant to solve: a lack of American suppliers. In 2023, the nation's ports, for example, unsuccessfully sought a waiver of the domestic-content rules after discovering that no US manufacturer produced dock cranes and electric cargo-handling equipment.[69] And two years after Congress appropriated $7.5 billion for a nationwide network of electric-vehicle charging stations, a grand total of seven had been built.[70]

Raimondo had little patience for critics who regarded the administration's industrial policies as doomed to repeat earlier failures. Given the federal subsidies lavished on American farmers, airplane makers, and defense contractors, it was "rubbish" to paint the administration's initiatives as unprecedented, she said. Besides, the status quo was unsustainable. Deferring to the market had left the nation dependent upon Taiwan and South Korea for 100 percent of the advanced semiconductors needed for F-35 warplanes, drones, and other military hardware.

"The market, left to its own devices, optimizes on efficiency and profit," she said. "And if all you care about is efficiency and profit, it makes a ton of sense to manufacture in the places that have the lowest cost of capital and labor. And I think that's what you saw in the eighties and nineties. China was making eye-watering amounts of investment in their manufacturing infrastructure. They were giving away money. So capital was basically free. And labor was cheap. And so companies really fell in love with it, became addicted to the cheap labor, cheap capital, and increase in efficiency and profit. And to the extent that governments were enabling free trade, that only paved the way for more of that."[71]

The vulnerability was real. When car sales dropped by half between February and April 2020, US automakers idled assembly lines and slashed their chip orders. But sales unexpectedly recovered, and companies like GM were unable to obtain enough chips to keep up, disappointing would-be car buyers. The result was an unprecedented 50 percent spike in used car prices, as shoppers who could not obtain a new vehicle were pushed into the pre-owned market.[72] Some used cars sold for a higher price than they had when new.

The chip shortage rippled through the US economy. Many of the chips needed to make automobiles were so-called "legacy" semiconductors. These older devices were also used to make aircraft, consumer electronics, military equipment, and medical devices.[73] At Rockwell Automation in Milwaukee, a lack of chips meant that lead times for some of the company's factory robotic systems stretched to more than a year from a pre-pandemic average measured in days or weeks, CEO Blake Moret said.

That scarcity threatened to shut down assembly lines throughout American industry, since Rockwell equipment was used to produce automobiles, food packaging, energy, transportation, and individual doses of medicine.

Moret responded by stockpiling hard-to-get chips. By 2023, Rockwell's inventories of $1.4 billion were up 143 percent compared with pre-pandemic levels.[74] To reduce potential weak spots in Rockwell's supply lines, company engineers redesigned products to replace scarce chips with more readily available alternatives or to eliminate components produced by unreliable suppliers. Moret negotiated long-term supply contracts with chipmakers Texas Instruments, Intel, and Analog Devices and added redundancy to Rockwell's operations. If a problem occurred in Singapore, Rockwell's plant in Mequon, Wisconsin, could step in, and if Mequon suffered a hiccup, Monterrey, Mexico, could handle the load. Above all, both Rockwell and its customers wanted to avoid being dependent on one location in particular: China.

"If you think about the two ends of the spectrum, there's just-in-time and there's just-in-case. And, I think we're going to all end up somewhere in the middle," Moret said. "I don't think we're going to go back to just-in-time ever. Nor do I think that we're going to tolerate the inefficiencies of a complete just-in-case approach. But we are going to add additional resiliency because it's a big risk item. It's a risk item that we talk about in the boardroom."[75]

Shifting political winds

On a Saturday morning in the fall of 2022, Scott Lincicome of the Cato Institute was reading the *Financial Times* when he came across a column bemoaning the costs of globalization. Irritated by what he saw as flawed thinking, he fired off an email to Peter Goettler, Cato's president, suggesting a counteroffensive.

The result was Defending Globalization, a Cato project that included events and essays explaining the case for global economic integration. Lincicome was among those who believed that the China shock research had been misinterpreted to blame trade policy for conditions that actually were the result of the financial crisis and government policy failures. Rather than protect workers with tariffs, he said, policymakers should ease occupational licensing requirements, especially for skilled blue-collar jobs like plumbers. In any case, the solution to what ailed the US economy was more globalization, not less.

"We remain committed to the free movement of stuff and ideas and capital, and people, and we're going to champion that regardless of where the political winds are blowing," Lincicome said.[76]

Not long before, globalization had been viewed as inherently good. Amid a continuing backlash, it required a coordinated intellectual and political defense. The Cato project was part of the pushback against economic nationalism that emerged at prominent Washington think tanks during the Biden administration. The Council on Foreign Relations in 2024 launched an effort to underscore the trade-offs involved in overhauling international economic policy, such as the inflationary impact associated with more robust supply chains. The Peterson Institute for International Economics asked whether globalization was truly in retreat or had suffered just "a minor setback."[77]

As the backlash to the backlash built, the China shock research came under attack. Larry Summers called it "misleading," saying it ignored all the ways the US economy had benefited from trade with China. To Nicholas Lardy, one of the premier experts on the Chinese economy, its conclusions were "bogus."

The Biden administration, however, took it as received wisdom. Yellen, one of the country's most decorated economists, pronounced it "convincing" and added: "It's still how I think of what happened."[78]

MIT's David Autor, one of the China shock authors, scoffed at the critics. "It is the consensus of the literature, and there's hundreds of papers now written about it, by leading trade economists. They take it as a starting point and try to understand it. The period of 'This didn't happen; that can't be true' has passed by," he said.[79]

The Biden era's shifting political winds could be disorienting. In 2024, the US Chamber of Commerce attacked Lori Wallach after it obtained via the Freedom of Information Act internal emails from the office of the US Trade Representative that reflected her influence with trade negotiators. At issue was the US position on proposed global trade rules that would prohibit countries from interfering with the cross-border flow of digital data, which Wallach opposed as a giveaway to "big tech."

For years, the United States had supported such data flows, which were increasingly important for companies such as IBM, Citibank, FedEx, and Visa.[80] The old rules had been codified in previous US trade agreements, including Trump's NAFTA replacement. But the Biden administration in October 2023 suddenly withdrew its backing for them at the WTO, prompting outrage from the Chamber and other business groups.

The Chamber traced the negotiating switch to a January 19 "Hello Katherine" email from Wallach to Katherine Tai, the US Trade Representative. In a lengthy memo, Wallach took aim at five "problematic provisions" in the digital trade rules, which conflicted with other administration policies on privacy, artificial intelligence, and competition.

In its broadside, the Chamber derided Wallach's legal analysis as "faulty," "specious," and "delusive" and said the emails showed a "cozy" relationship between progressives like Wallach and Tai's top aides. The business group complained that USTR officials might have violated the law by communicating with Wallach via the encrypted Signal messaging service.[81]

A few weeks later, when Biden issued an executive order prohibiting the transfer of Americans' sensitive personal data—including financial, health, biometric, and genomic details—to countries such as China or Russia, Wallach said the change in strategy had made the new protections possible. The trade rules that the US previously supported would have prohibited Biden's action as an "illegal trade barrier," she said.[82]

The dustup showed the Chamber complaining about the sort of routine policy advocacy that experts all over Washington—including the business group's own lobbyists—engage in every working day. There was irony in Wallach's emergence as an insider, first under Trump and now with the Biden team. But there was also evidence of just how much had changed. Over a generation, the feisty activist had gone from inveighing against US trade policy to shaping it.

Saying things that needed to be said

Biden met Xi for the second time as president toward the end of 2023 in San Francisco. During previous summits, the most contentious exchanges were about the self-governing island of Taiwan, which Beijing claims as its territory. But this time, Xi grew most agitated when the talks turned to Biden's restrictions on sales to China of the most advanced US technology.

You're trying to suffocate us, the Chinese leader complained.[83]

Biden shot back: We know that some of this technology that you get from us you put in systems that are aimed at our aircraft carriers and designed to go after our young men and women serving in uniform, and I'm just not going to support that.

The blend of dialogue and confrontation was deliberate. If Sullivan represented the domestic political rethinking behind Biden's international economic policy, Kurt Campbell, the NSC's Asia director, personified the concomitant foreign policy shift. As the US and Chinese delegations faced off in San Francisco, Campbell—who had been assistant secretary of state for East Asian and Pacific affairs under Obama—was seated three chairs to Biden's left.

He was known for a controversial 2018 *Foreign Affairs* article, co-authored with Ely Ratner, now a Pentagon official. In "The China Reckoning," Campbell and Ratner argued that Washington, in engaging with China, had put excessive faith in its ability to influence Chinese political evolution. Contrary to the expectations of US policymakers from both parties, China—after an initial burst of market-oriented reforms—had reemphasized its state capitalist model. Intensified repression at home and provocative moves abroad, including in the contested South China Sea, disappointed US hopes for a cooperative relationship.

"Neither carrots nor sticks have swayed China as predicted. Diplomatic and commercial engagement have not brought political and economic openness. Neither US military power nor regional balancing has stopped Beijing from seeking to displace core components of the US-led system. And the liberal international order has failed to lure or bind China as powerfully as expected," Campbell and Ratner wrote.

The argument angered many of the China experts who had favored the engagement strategy. William Overholt of Harvard called it a "myth" that US policy had been predicated on eventual Chinese democratization and said the Biden team's initial hardline approach to China had been "one of the most dangerous, destructive moments in our modern history."[84] Princeton University's Thomas Christensen, writing with Patricia Kim of the Council on Foreign Relations, called the *Foreign Affairs* article "often inaccurate" and defended engagement as having produced prosperity and promoted peace. What was needed to address US complaints about Beijing's behavior were "more agreements" and continued efforts to persuade Chinese leaders to implement economic and political reforms.[85]

Whatever the errors on the US side, by the time Biden was inaugurated, China's own behavior had made a change of course unavoidable. Two decades of Beijing's foot-dragging on promised market openings, its rampant theft of Western intellectual property, and preferences for its domestic producers had exhausted American patience. Government-to-government dialogues designed to promote mutual understanding had become an engine of frustration. American officials once hoped that membership in the WTO would cause China to change; increasingly they worried that China instead was bending the global system to its will.

During his State Department years, Campbell had been inundated by US companies looking for help dealing with the Chinese government. They all told a version of the same story: After establishing a joint venture in China that enjoyed initial success, their Chinese partner had stolen their intellectual property and used it to establish a competitor. Formerly routine bureaucratic approvals suddenly became difficult to obtain and their business sagged. They came to the State Department hoping that a quiet US government intervention might put things right. "I probably met a hundred firms that had that experience, all of whom said the same thing: 'Don't go public.' For fear they'd be shamed or shunned by the Chinese," Campbell said.[86]

Privately, Campbell gave Trump credit for saying things about China that needed to be said. But Xi had helped stir the United States to action, presiding over a massive military buildup and unleashing China's "wolf warrior" diplomats in a high-decibel campaign that was meant to intimidate other nations but instead only awakened them to a potential threat. Xi's missteps, in this view, gave the Americans time to assemble a defensive coalition.

The various strands of Biden's domestic reinvestment strategy, his worker-centric trade policy, and the tougher approach to China eventually came together in a single initiative.

In May 2024, the president imposed 100 percent tariffs on Chinese electric vehicles and other clean energy products. After years of generous government subsidies, China's auto industry could produce ten million more cars annually than it could sell at home. If Washington failed to erect new trade barriers, that excess capacity could flood the US market with enough low-cost products to put many of the one million American autoworkers out of a job, administration officials feared.

Environmentalists complained that the new tariffs would slow the transition to a zero-carbon economy. But with a presidential election looming, the White House was taking no chances with the politics of trade. Biden in 2020 had criticized Trump's tariffs. Now he was cementing them in place and adding more of his own. The president was determined that there would be no second China shock.

11

What All the Wise Men Promised

Bob Ulrich was fifty-eight years old when the only job he'd ever had moved to Mexico. He had worked making steel doors at Amweld Building Products in Niles, Ohio, since returning from Vietnam in 1971. In October 2007, the private equity firm that owned the company closed its two plants in the Mahoning Valley and relocated to Monterrey, Mexico. By the time the equipment had been crated and shipped, the United States was in the throes of the worst financial crisis since the Great Depression.

Ulrich managed in the summer of 2008 to get hired at the General Motors plant in Lordstown, just a few miles away. But under the plant's two-tier wage system, he was brought in as a "temp," a twilight status that could last up to two years. "You're working on the line right next to the guy who actually got hired in to General Motors and he's making 28, 29 dollars an hour. And I was making $14.50," he said. "Standing right next to him on the line, doing the exact same thing." [1]

GM assigned him to the instrument panel line in Lordstown, installing countless screws and miles of wire in Chevy dashboards. Working an assembly line at his age took a toll. "It kicked my ass," Ulrich said. "You had to keep up. You don't shut that line down."

As the financial crisis deepened, auto sales plunged. Two days before Christmas, GM announced it was closing the Lordstown plant, putting Ulrich out of work for the second time in fourteen months. The following June, GM filed for bankruptcy. With the federal government's help, the automaker survived. But Ulrich had had enough.

Riddled with arthritis and suffering from a chronic inflammatory lung disease, he filed for Social Security disability insurance. The disability payments and a partial pension kept him afloat financially—as they did for so many other workers dislodged by imports. In areas hard hit by China's rise, the federal government spent more than thirty times as much per person on lifetime disability benefits as on the Trade Adjustment Assistance program designed to provide such workers income support and training.[2]

Like many older workers, Ulrich thought it was too late for him to start a new career. But his son, Brian, who was thirty-two at the time, and also worked at Amweld, enrolled in Kent State's nursing college and, after two years of study, became a registered nurse.

Brian once had expected to retire from Amweld, after a decades-long career like his dad's. Instead, Amweld's closure proved a blessing for the younger man. Unlike manufacturing, health care was booming. Nursing jobs would never be shipped to Mexico or China. It is impossible to administer medicine or comfort a worried patient from thousands of miles away.

His first job at Mercy Health, one of the largest health care systems in the country, paid about what he had made at Amweld. As he rose through the ranks to become a clinical nurse manager, overseeing other nurses at a local hospital, his earnings reached six figures.

Working three 12-hour shifts each week was draining, especially amid the horrors of covid. But the work had meaning. Brian learned that firsthand in 2014 when he was diagnosed with stage 4 lymphoma. Through several rounds of chemotherapy and dialysis, it was his fellow nurses who pulled him through a potentially fatal illness.

The Ulriches straddle the old and new American economies. The father, Bob, came of age in an era when the system repaid a willingness to work hard with a solid middle-class existence. His son was born in the mid-1970s, when the economy was shifting from manufacturing to services, and government spending on social programs was falling out of fashion. Bob struggled amid the trade shock that struck the United States in the first decade of the twenty-first century. Brian's success in navigating his transition provided a glimpse of the path more workers would need to tread in the future.

"Looking back on it, who do you blame? You blame Amweld for picking up and moving it down to Monterrey, Mexico, paying pennies on the dollar, basically, to what they were paying us up here to make that product. And shame on the government for letting that happen," he said. "These trade agreements have been going on for so many years. In our area, this Mahoning Valley here, back in the day, it was the steel mills that were here. And then all that went away. And then we had the smaller plants like an Amweld. We had GM was here. Well, now GM went away. It just seemed like everything's just going away. And what we get back are not the great-paying jobs that were gone."[3]

You can't get rid of China

Ohio's Trumbull County, where both Ulrich men live, gave Donald Trump 58 percent of the vote in his 2024 victory over Vice President Kamala Harris. Just a dozen years earlier, Barack Obama had thrashed Republican Mitt Romney in this part of eastern Ohio by a margin of 60 percent to 38 percent. But Trump since then had cemented his hold on these Ohioans. One reason: Nearly two-thirds of the county's manufacturing jobs had disappeared in the past two decades.[4]

Earlier in the year, when a second Joe Biden term seemed possible, corporate executives debated whether he might adjust his stance if reelected and launch new trade negotiations. In the months after his sudden exit from the race, the views of his replacement as the Democratic candidate had been sufficiently opaque that such a turnabout still seemed possible.

Trump's decisive win put an end to such hopes. He had campaigned on a message of full-throated economic nationalism, promising to impose tariffs on all of the $3 trillion in annual US imports: 60 percent levies on goods from China—potentially closing the US market to many

Chinese products—and 10 percent or 20 percent on everything that the United States bought from other countries. And he began implementing his vision within days of taking office, launching a trade war against Mexico and Canada while threatening to make the European Union his next target.

China loomed large in Trump's crosshairs. The campaign platform that he had personally dictated vowed to revoke China's trade status, reversing the US decision to grant "permanent normal trade relations" in 2000. Imports from China of essential goods—"everything from electronics to steel to pharmaceuticals"—would be reduced to zero in four years, Trump said. "The most urgent priority should be strategic decoupling from China," wrote Robert E. Lighthizer, his first-term trade chief, who remained an informal adviser.[5]

Trump also launched what he promised would be the largest deportation operation in history.[6] He would use the military, if needed, to round up and expel ten million or perhaps twenty million illegal migrants. Along with his "America First" plans for trade and immigration, Trump began centralizing governing power in the presidency. He acted to circumvent the Senate's constitutional authority to advise on and consent to cabinet nominations by pressuring Republicans to allow him to appoint department heads while Congress was in recess. And he refused to spend funds authorized by Congress, something Richard Nixon had tried in the 1970s before lawmakers passed legislation prohibiting the practice.[7]

As always with Trump, it was difficult to tell how much was real and how much was bluster. But if he followed through on everything he had suggested, it seemed that the once and future president might well inaugurate an era of hyper-nationalism to replace the discredited hyper-globalization that had first brought him to power in 2016. Enacting Trump's second-term agenda, one supportive commentator wrote, "would mean the decisive abandonment of the dream of a globally integrated economy."[8]

The days of "hyper-globalization," to be sure, are over.[9] But despite Trump's rhetoric, globalization itself is not ending, only changing. Merchandise trade growth has plateaued and faces new restrictions in dozens of countries.[10] But cross-border flows of services such as portfolio management and investment advice, travel and tourism, and outsourced call centers have increased since 2008 three or four times as fast as the trade in goods and are expected to mushroom in the years ahead.[11] One new product in particular, software services offering simultaneous speech translation, "will transform the global economy," according to Richard Baldwin, a professor of international economics at the International Institute for Management Development in Lausanne, Switzerland.[12]

The product shortages of the pandemic and alarm over Chinese intentions are driving the US government and many corporations to recalibrate key supply chains. Instead of focusing exclusively on cost and efficiency, logisticians now aim for resilience in supplies of semiconductors, electric vehicles and their batteries, and some types of medical and pharmaceutical products.

Many corporations are planning for a less China-focused future. HP and Lego produce some goods now in Mexico that once were made in Chinese factories. Rubbermaid and Logitech, a maker of computer peripherals, also are shifting their manufacturing from China. In perhaps the most dramatic change, new investment by foreigners in Chinese businesses has collapsed. As recently as 2022, foreign investors poured more than $100 billion into Chinese companies in a single three-month period. But by mid-2023, those investors were selling their stakes and withdrawing more than $11 billion in ninety days. It was the first time in a quarter century of Chinese government record-keeping that those figures had turned negative.[13] Merchandise flows also changed. Through the spring of 2024, total US-China trade was down more than 20 percent compared to just two years earlier. China accounted for less than 17 percent of all US imports, down from nearly 22 percent in 2017, reflecting what some economists called "a great reallocation" of supply chains.[14]

But those figures were misleading. Some Chinese suppliers, like those making rulers, paper trimmers, and pencil sharpeners for Westcott of Shelton, Connecticut, set up new factories in countries such as Thailand and the Philippines to get around US tariffs.[15] Other Chinese companies routed products such as integrated circuits, telephone sets, and textiles to the United States through Mexico. Having a modest amount of finishing work performed there qualified goods as "Mexican" rather than "Chinese" when they arrived at a US port.[16]

If the next iteration of globalization looks less China-centric, there is no sign of significant reshoring of manufacturing work to the United States. The jobs that left during the China shock are gone for good. Moreover, the United States cannot execute a wholesale rupture of its commercial relationship with China and is unlikely to even try. Even after more than five years of trade war and acrimony, the two nations exchange nearly $600 billion worth of merchandise each year.

Chinese suppliers have a near chokehold on important US markets, including the rare earth materials needed for smartphones, wind turbines, and military aircraft; vital medicines; and some industrial components. Sixty percent of the US commercial drone market is controlled by DJI, a Chinese manufacturer.[17]

China's role as a US supplier is even greater than those overall numbers indicate. As the world's top manufacturing power, accounting for nearly one-third of global value added, China makes an array of parts and materials that are marbled through just about every conceivable industry in ways that are not immediately evident.[18]

Along with the products that American companies import directly from China, the US has a "hidden exposure" to Chinese parts that are contained in finished goods from Thailand or Mexico or India or Vietnam. In the vehicles industry, for example, the United States indirectly imports four times as much Chinese hardware as it buys directly from China, according to research published by the Brookings Institution.[19]

Shifting supply lines out of China also costs money. Buying goods from Vietnam is roughly 10 percent more expensive. Mexican goods, on average, cost more than 3 percent more than Chinese models.[20] "The costs of following through with current US industrial policies may be broader and more extensive than publicly realized," concluded one study.[21]

In his second White House term, Trump is likely to intensify efforts that have been underway for several years to reduce the United States' dependence on China. But it is important not to exaggerate the extent of the ongoing shift. In early 2024, the percentage of businesses planning to reduce their sourcing from China was more than twice the share of those intending to buy more from Chinese factories, according to a survey by QIMA, a global factory inspection and audit firm. But 45 percent of respondents, by far the largest proportion, planned no changes.[22]

As wages in China have risen, its signature advantage has changed from low-cost labor, which can be found elsewhere, to manufacturing scale and infrastructure that no other country can match. It would take years for a company to replicate its Chinese supply chain somewhere else, said Sébastien Breteau, QIMA's chief executive.

"China is not dead," Breteau said in early 2024. "You can't get rid of China."[23]

We're entering a new era

There is, however, a tension between these supply chain realities and geopolitics. American companies are likely to remain far more entangled with China than the makers of US foreign policy would prefer.

The ultimate shape of the global economy will depend on whether the United States and China find a durable rationale for stable relations. The impetus for warm ties between the United States and China has changed over time. In the 1970s and 1980s, shared opposition to Soviet power brought together the American superpower and Mao's isolated and impoverished Communist state. After the Soviet Union collapsed, the relationship was remade on the basis of mutual economic interest. China would develop its economy with Western help, and American businesses would enjoy fabulous profits in return.

That economic rationale is fraying as Xi Jinping's China turns inward and the multinational business community loses patience with Chinese government favoritism for domestic companies. The shift can be seen in the fortunes of General Motors, which once thrived in China and now is flailing. Each year between 2010 and 2022, the company sold more vehicles in China than in the United States, making this American industrial icon ever more dependent upon decisions in Beijing. But after lagging domestic producers in bringing new models to market, GM in 2023 managed to sell only half as many vehicles to Chinese customers as it had in 2017. Income from its Chinese operations has plunged by nearly 80 percent since 2014 and analysts now openly speculate that GM may soon be forced to exit the Chinese market altogether.[24]

The strategic landscape is even gloomier. Over the next decade, it is easier to see the US-China relationship getting worse rather than better. The US military is actively preparing for a possible war with the Chinese People's Liberation Army over the island of Taiwan, which Beijing regards as its own.[25] US officials have said publicly that Xi has directed the Chinese military to be prepared to fight for Taiwan as soon as 2027.

Many in Washington speak as if open conflict between the United States and China is inevitable. In the spring of 2024, Matt Pottinger and Mike Gallagher, the former chairman of the House Select Committee on the Chinese Communist Party, published a striking essay in the journal *Foreign Affairs*, which eschewed "forcible regime change" but said "the only workable destination" is "a China free from communist dictatorship."[26]

Other prominent figures on the political right are openly bellicose. "We're going to go to a kinetic war one day. There's no doubt because they've made a decision. They're going to have their system and we're going to have our system," said Stephen Bannon, Trump's former White House strategist. "And that's the way it's going to be. But there will not be any integration. The super hawks don't believe in the legitimacy of the Chinese Communist Party as the government entity that rules the Chinese people. We think that they absolutely have to be taken down."[27]

In 2024, the public's view of China hit an all-time low in Chicago Council on Global Affairs polling that began in 1978. A majority of Americans agreed that trade with China hurts the United States and that US leaders should "actively work to limit the growth of China's power." Even so, full-scale military conflict between the United States and China would be disastrous for winner and loser alike; 69 percent of those surveyed said the United States' top objective should be to avoid a war with China.[28]

The immediate dilemma for the United States is not so much how to spur greater decoupling as it is how to manage the deep linkages between the two nations that are destined to remain. Preserving a cold economic peace will be challenging, when the political chorus in favor of confrontation is so loud.

The loss of strategic trust between Washington and Beijing has economic consequences. The Biden administration left in place Trump-era tariffs, added its own, and imposed regulations that block China's access to the most advanced semiconductors and the machines and personnel needed to produce them. These new limits are predicated on a view of China as an adversary, a sentiment that researchers at the IMF say is already reshaping global commerce. Trump has been inconsistent on the strategic threat posed by China, alternately targeting Chinese companies such as ZTE and TikTok with economic sanctions and agreeing to revive them.

Kristalina Georgieva, the Bulgarian economist who runs the International Monetary Fund, has sounded a deeply personal alarm about "a deepening fragmentation in the world economy." Georgieva, sixty-nine, grew up under communism; as a young mother, she rose each day at 4 a.m. to join the queue for milk. Now she fears that the major powers are splitting into a new pair of rival blocs. "I lived through the first Cold War on the other side of the Iron Curtain. And, yeah, it is quite cold out there.... We may be sleepwalking into a world that is poorer and less secure," she said.[29]

Since Russia's invasion of Ukraine, trade flows have held up better among politically like-minded nations while shrinking between rival groupings, according to the IMF.[30] Many nations, such as those in Southeast Asia that trade heavily with both the US and China, will resist taking sides. The fund's warnings about a split in the global economy have been discussed by central bankers and finance ministers from around the world. But not everyone is sold on the argument. "I do think the IMF overdoes it on the costs of fragmentation. And I think that they're doing scenarios that go beyond anything that's really happening," said Treasury Secretary Janet Yellen.[31]

In seeking to contain China's military development, Biden administration officials insisted their "small yard, high fence" strategy will cordon off just a sliver of potential trade while allowing most commerce to continue. But these measures—which the White House says are intended to ensure the US maintains "as large of a lead as possible" in the most vital technologies—already are having a corrosive effect on links between the two countries. In 2022, BlackRock, the world's largest asset manager, abandoned plans to market a new Chinese bond fund, fearing that US policymakers would object to even this plain-vanilla financing of the Chinese government.[32] And it is likely that the American "yard" deemed off-limits to Chinese customers will only grow over time. Jamieson Greer, whom Trump nominated to be US trade representative in his second term, has called for tougher restrictions on exports to China of "a broader range of critical industries."[33]

Other investors, meanwhile, are reconsidering their stakes in China and preparing for the worst. If the US were to impose Ukraine-style sanctions in response to a Chinese invasion of Taiwan, the global bond market could be upended. Of the 170 corporate bonds issued over a three-year period by Chinese banks, investment firms, and insurance companies, none allowed repayment in any currency other than the dollar, S&P Global Ratings told investors in Hong Kong.[34] If Chinese institutions were cut off from US-dollar transactions and unable to make interest payments on their bonds during a Taiwan crisis, the resulting financial losses in China, and elsewhere, could be mammoth.

Political developments within China also will work against deeper economic ties. The US restrictions are matched by Beijing's efforts to reduce its reliance upon other nations and to develop its own homegrown technologies. Companies alarmed by Xi's authoritarianism are placing their bets elsewhere. In a 2023 survey by the American Chamber of Commerce in Shanghai, 40 percent of companies said they were redirecting investment from China to other markets, twice the share that did so in 2018, at the height of Trump's trade war.[35] Among the companies seeking to spread their manufacturing across multiple countries is Apple, which is moving some iPhone production to India and Vietnam.

As Russian missiles batter Ukraine, and China descends into one-man rule, it seems incredible that US policymakers ever believed these authoritarian states would join a US-led international system. What President George H. W. Bush once called "an era of possibility and hope" has instead devolved into a confused and dangerous age.[36]

The political climate in Washington is now uniformly anti-China. The support that once existed for integrating this emerging rival into a US-led global economy has evaporated as has the intellectual justification for it: that expanded trade would encourage Beijing to liberalize both its economic and political systems. Perhaps the best that now can be hoped—at least so long as Xi rules—is to avoid the worst.

Sen. Marco Rubio of Florida, before becoming secretary of state in the second Trump administration, took stock of a quarter century of US-led globalization at a Senate Foreign Relations Committee hearing. Exaggerating only slightly, Rubio said that US foreign policy for a generation had been premised on "a gamble" that trade would bind nations in prosperity, democracy, freedom, and peace.

Wealth had grown, Rubio acknowledged. Yet neither China nor Russia had become more democratic or more peaceful. In fact, both had doubled down on autocratic rule. Russia had invaded Ukraine twice, in 2014 and 2022, while China had militarized the South China Sea and vowed to regain control of Taiwan, by force, if necessary.

"I think it's fair to say that gamble failed," Rubio said. "And we are now entering a new era."[37]

Where the elite gets the blame

The economist Paul Krugman often cites an old joke to illustrate the impossibility of undoing the China shock: A truck driver runs over a pedestrian. Noticing the damage, he apologizes and says, let me make things right. So he backs up the truck, flattening the victim for a second time.[38]

Unwinding the current commercial relationship between the United States and China will do nothing to help workers who suffered from the rise of Chinese imports in the early 2000s. In fact, full decoupling from China would unleash a reverse China shock that could prove as painful as the original.

The original China shock largely ended by 2010, though many of the affected communities still bear the scars.[39] US officials in both parties today are worried about history repeating itself. Beijing continues to provide generous subsidies for advanced manufacturing, including low-cost financing by state banks. The result is massive excess production capacity—especially in the renewable energy sectors that the United States sees as critical to future growth and is supporting with its own subsidies.

Both the United States and the European Union have responded to the threat of surging Chinese electric vehicle shipments, for example, by raising trade barriers. Those may delay China's dominance of the global auto market. But at least for the United States, the tariffs enacted to date are unlikely to represent a long-term solution. BYD, one of China's leading car makers, is building a plant in Szeged, Hungary, and may move forward with a second European facility in 2025.[40] Those factories are billed as serving European customers. But there is nothing yet to prevent them from one day shipping inexpensive Chinese EVs to the United States.

Focusing exclusively on the competitive threat from China, however, risks missing the point. Even if the United States does hold off a fresh surge of Chinese manufactured goods, there will be other labor market shocks in the future, such as the rise of artificial intelligence and the transition to a low-carbon economy, which will test the resilience of individual Americans and their government. Hardest-hit in these future convulsions are likely to be women without a college degree, who dominate the occupations that the government expects to shrink the most over the next decade, according to an analysis by Third Way, a center-left think tank.[41] The US safety net that proved so inadequate amid the tumult of globalization is not ready for what lies ahead.

Roughly 60 percent of all jobs in advanced economies like the United States will be "impacted by AI," with about one-half of that number negatively affected, according to an IMF study. That suggests more than forty-five million American workers—far more than the number directly affected by the China shock—could see demand for their services shrink, resulting in lower wages and fewer job opportunities.[42]

The sheer amount of technological upheaval over the next decade "will dwarf" what's happened over the past thirty years, billionaire Mark Cuban told Bloomberg Television in 2024. This time, the fallout will not be confined to the voiceless, the least-educated and least-skilled members of the workforce. By automating the process of automation, machine learning and AI will eliminate the need for many well-paid professionals. "It's bad news for employment and bad news for people who are disrupted," Cuban said.[43]

In fact, blue-collar workers who suffered the most from China's rise may escape generative AI's impact. Rather than automate physical activity, as already has happened on assembly lines, AI will take over cognitive tasks, leading to "broad transformations across nearly all categories of white-collar occupations." Lawyers, Hollywood writers and actors, financial analysts, auditors, accountants, software coders, and journalists will be affected. Companies like Morgan Stanley, McKinsey & Co., and Google will feel the sting.[44]

"AI is going to make globalization look like peanuts. And our existing system isn't going to be able to cope with it," said Howard Rosen, the former congressional aide who specializes in workforce development issues.

Each wave of technological progress since the cotton gin has prompted fears of mass worker obsolescence. In the end, technology always creates more jobs than it destroys. But the risk today is that AI will develop so quickly that its disruptive force—even if positive in the long run—upends groups of workers faster than they can retool for new opportunities. Labor market shifts that once took twenty years may now happen in five, according to Cuban.

In one respect, AI's effects may be reminiscent of what happened as Chinese goods became more widely available in the United States. The economy as a whole will almost certainly benefit. The productivity gains as workers learn to use AI as a helpmate could be enormous, allowing "most workers" to enjoy higher incomes.[45] The spread of AI will equip a broader population of workers with access to expertise, "restoring the middle-skill, middle-class heart of the US labor market that has been hollowed out by automation and globalization," said MIT's David Autor, one of the principal China shock researchers.[46]

But just as the growth of Chinese imports benefited some Americans and hurt others, AI will have distributional consequences.[47] And the United States is little better prepared today to cope with a major labor market shock than it was at the beginning of China's global rise. The Affordable Care Act, a.k.a. "Obamacare," addressed one significant hole in the safety net: the tie between an individual's job and their health insurance. But for dislocated workers, it was no panacea. And there have been no other major safety net enhancements.

Generous government aid during the pandemic, which kept millions of Americans afloat and dramatically reduced poverty rates, gave a hint of what more ambitious social policies could accomplish. The combination of economic impact payments, plus extended and enhanced unemployment benefits, allowed the typical family to maintain its pre-crisis consumption roughly 50 percent longer than it otherwise would have, according to a Federal Reserve study.[48] But pushback from many employers who saw the extra jobless aid as discouraging Americans from returning to work brought an end to such programs when the pandemic ebbed.

If there is a major employment upheaval in the next several years, American workers will navigate it much as they have in the past: on their own. As the US economy experienced transformative change in the decades after the Cold War, both parties failed to provide for globalization's losers. The near certainty of new labor market shocks argues for the United States to belatedly construct a better safety net for *all* workers who lose their jobs—not just those affected by trade. Otherwise, the United States is likely to suffer continuing populist ferment and political polarization.

"How do you take care of those people that are left behind? That is a challenge. That's where we fail. That's where the elite gets the blame," said former Treasury Secretary Henry Paulson. "Unless we develop policy responses, technology and automation will continue to hollow out the middle class."[49]

There is historical precedent for government action. Over a century ago, as Americans moved off the farm and into factory work, the nation exerted itself to better educate its workers. From less than 10 percent in 1910, the share of the population with a high school diploma rose to nearly 40 percent in 1935.

Today, there is no shortage of worthwhile ideas. In 2019, Paulson developed with the Aspen Institute Economic Strategy Group a proposed $22 billion federal grant program for the nation's community colleges. The aim was to credential twenty-eight million additional workers with a college degree or its equivalent by 2030.[50]

More recently, economist Daron Acemoglu, who received the 2024 Nobel Prize in Economics, warned that the rise of AI, profound changes in the global economy, and societal aging threatened to deliver the greatest labor market shock in nearly fifty years. In response, he called for devoting greater attention to training American workers to make better use of automation. The United States risks "more pain for manufacturing" if it does not get creative with tax credits or subsidies to equip people to work alongside futuristic technology, Acemoglu said.[51]

Policies tailored to the needs of individual communities, like the ones that Catherine Novelli credited with helping Greenville, South Carolina, recover, also deserve more attention. Of course, regional economic development is notoriously difficult, and not every town threatened by economic change can be saved. But the plight of so many hollowed-out American hometowns warrants greater government effort and policy experimentation to remediate.

Nearly one in five Americans live in "left behind" places that suffer from lagging population and income growth, according to the Economic Innovation Group, a Washington think tank. Since the 2008 financial crisis, the market has steered almost three-quarters of all new jobs to superstar cities like San Francisco, Boston, and New York, research by the Brookings Institution shows.[52] That lopsided pattern is not entirely the fault of globalization. But it has left an awful lot of Americans feeling neglected and alienated from the system.

Paying for a more robust social safety net would seem to be an insurmountable hurdle when forecasts of federal budget deficits are daunting and interest rates are expected to remain higher than in recent decades. The federal government in fiscal 2025 will spend more than $1 trillion paying interest on the national debt, more than twice what it spent just three years earlier.[53]

The answer lies in reforming the tax system that has allowed corporations to shirk their societal responsibilities. If corporations today paid as much in federal taxes relative to the size of the economy as they did before Ronald Reagan was elected president, the government would have nearly $300 billion in additional annual revenue.[54] That sum could be devoted to shrinking the federal budget deficit, funding new social programs, or both.

Such reforms, of course, will not be easy. The last three American presidents have tried to reduce the tax code's incentives for companies to book profits offshore rather than in the United States.[55] None have succeeded.

Trump's 2017 tax-cut legislation was advertised as reducing the incentive to shift profits to offshore havens such as Ireland and the

Cayman Islands. But a new tax on intangible income booked abroad, such as intellectual property payments, was set at just half of the new 21 percent corporate tax rate. So the gamesmanship continued.[56] Biden sought to crack down on profit shifting by joining an international effort to establish a new global minimum tax, but Congress balked.

Tax avoidance is especially acute in the pharmaceutical industry, which increasingly chooses to produce its most profitable products outside the United States in order to escape paying taxes on their US sales, according to economist Brad Setser of the Council on Foreign Relations.[57] Leading pharmaceutical manufacturers generate the majority of their revenue in the United States. But they sell the right to profit from innovative new drugs to their overseas subsidiaries. By assigning most of their profits to low-tax foreign jurisdictions, major drugmakers such as AbbVie, Johnson & Johnson, Amgen, and Merck legally escape paying tens of billions of dollars in taxes that should go to the US government.[58] Closing these loopholes could bring in around $50 billion annually, Setser said.[59]

The need for action is undeniable. Failing to address the original China shock contributed to a growing gap between rich and poor, which helped poison American politics. From 1979 to 2007, the richest 1 percent of American households saw their share of after-tax income more than double while the portion earned by the poorest fifth of society fell.[60] One long-term study found that US trade liberalization and income inequality rose in near lockstep over that period.[61] And the reason was that the US tax system became less progressive—even as the need for redistribution grew.

"The political rhetoric that has fuelled the backlash against globalization will remain a challenge unless tax systems do a better job of providing a safety net or offering active labor-market policies to those individuals experiencing negative trade-related income shocks, such as job dislocations caused by import competition," wrote Pol Antràs, an economics professor at Harvard University, one of the study's authors.[62]

Flat no more

In 1829, when Britain's Catholic Emancipation Act failed to fully placate the king's restive Catholic subjects, as its leading advocates had promised, the Prime Minister Lord Melbourne famously exclaimed: "What all the wise men promised has not happened and what all the damned fools said would happen has come to pass."

It was not the last time that elite certainty would prove misplaced. From nineteenth-century Britain to Vietnam War–era America, wise men confidently insisted that theirs was the right approach when they might instead have taken counsel from their critics.

The experience of the hyper-globalization era is just the latest example. Post–Cold War trade liberalization was to have produced shared prosperity and a harmonious US-led international system that included a cooperative China and Russia. Today, after generating significant but uneven benefits at home and unexpected reversals abroad, that formula has lost its appeal. Both major political parties have turned their back on the global economic policy of openness and liberalization that held sway for decades. In doing so, they are responding to public sentiment. By a margin of 59 percent to 37 percent, Americans say the United States "has lost more than it has gained" from trade, according to a 2024 Pew Research Center survey.[63]

On a strictly economic accounting, that belief is almost certainly wrong, at least at the aggregate level. It also overlooks the meaningful gains that expanded trade produced in the developing world. But the potency of such public sentiment, whether entirely justified or not, requires a political and policy response.

The United States needs to confront the unresolved domestic questions from the era of hyper-globalization. To date, both political parties have offered inadequate solutions, primarily involving industrial policies or tariffs. Yet discontent simmers. Those who favor further trade liberalization should support greater protection for workers against economic calamities, whether the result of trade, technology, or any other cause— as the proposal advanced thirty years ago by the economist Lawrence Katz during the NAFTA debate would have done.

Otherwise, if the lessons of post–Cold War globalization are not learned, the extraordinary global gains of this period are at risk. Recent decades have been governed by simplistic binaries: Globalization or protectionism? Laissez-faire labor markets or sclerosis? US policymakers should acknowledge the need for nuance and be honest about the trade-offs involved. To support globalization and additional trade liberalization requires recognizing the imperative to fulfill US leaders' promise to assist those who would otherwise be left behind. But meeting unaddressed needs will not be costless.

As the US tries to course correct from its bad bet on unfettered globalization, it risks overcompensating. Few once dissented from the belief that greater trade would generate shared prosperity at home and encourage political change abroad. Today, a less monolithic, still-contested argument favors the use of government subsidies or tariffs to promote domestic manufacturing. Expanded production of certain strategic items in the United States would benefit national security. But many policymakers exaggerate the potential employment gains from such industrial policies while others minimize the likely costs of disengaging from China.

Industrial policy will not deliver a meaningful renaissance in factory employment. Most of the jobs in the new semiconductor plants supported by government funding, for example, will require skills that most blue-collar workers lack. The bulk of the work done in any new manufacturing facility, as has long been true, will be carried out by machines. Likewise, the evidence from Trump's first-term trade war suggests that tariffs' most noteworthy effects were political, not economic. The net effect on employment of US tariffs and foreign nations' retaliatory measures "was at best a wash," though the experience did make people in trade-exposed areas more likely to vote for Trump, one study found.[64]

The manufacturing jobs that preoccupy both political parties once allowed millions of less-skilled Americans to enjoy middle-class lifestyles. But today, they no longer reliably provide higher wages than other blue-collar occupations. The wage premium for production jobs "disappeared" by 2006, according to a Federal Reserve Board study.[65] Preserving a critical mass of domestic manufacturing—especially in strategic sectors—is essential given the links between the location of production and related innovations. But rather than devote disproportionate attention to manufacturing *employment* as opposed to manufacturing *activity*, the government should encourage the development of good-paying jobs in the services industries that account for more than 70 percent of US employment.

Politicians' perpetual promises to regain lost factory jobs are guaranteed to disappoint the voters they are meant to impress, ensuring continued domestic discontent and antiestablishment politics. Likewise, redrawing supply chains to emphasize redundancy rather than efficiency will, by definition, increase costs. Corporate shareholders will resist paying; taxpayers may not be given a choice.

The global outlook is also fraught. Russia has been all but expelled from the global economy. Both the US and China are taking steps to reduce their reliance on each other and on the outside world. Industrial policy subsidies enacted in Washington and Beijing are prompting responses in London, Berlin, Paris, and Seoul. Wars rage in Europe and the Middle East; a potential third conflict beckons in the Taiwan Strait.

The emerging global economic division will not replicate the Cold War's tidy East-West split. Instead, some industries, notably including advanced technologies, will be segregated, while most consumer products will easily cross borders. And technology itself will enable some elements of globalization to move ahead—albeit not as uniformly as once expected.

One thing is clear: The world is no longer flat.

Donald Trump's 2024 election victory cements the US turn away from bipartisan 1990s-style globalization. Looking ahead, neither the unconstrained globalism of the 1989–2008 period nor a retreat into autarky is in the cards. Instead, countries and companies will be navigating a far more complex world, choosing industry by industry, one product at a time, whether collaboration or self-reliance is best. Amid the return of geopolitical risk, including that emanating from a less predictable United States, national security considerations will take precedence over economic efficiency.

Much as globalization created winners and losers, this new era of economic nationalism will do likewise. Some industries will be favored with government largesse or protection; others will not. Some occupations will be disrupted in the next labor market shock; others will be spared. Moving supply chains away from their lowest-cost venue will act like Trump's tariffs, raising costs and hurting those who can least afford higher prices.

For a generation, globalization delivered consistently low inflation for American consumers, robust profits for multinational corporations, and a better life for more than one billion people in the developing world. Many American workers enjoyed new or more rewarding jobs. But too many others, with fewer skills and opportunities, languished. As their needs were ignored, they understandably grew resentful. If globalization is to fulfill its potential and truly become "what all the wise men promised," a new approach is needed.

Epilogue

A New Pitch for Globalization?

No American did more to lay the groundwork for twenty-first-century globalization than Bill Clinton. As the forty-second president of the United States—the leader of the world's largest economy and sole superpower—he shepherded a historic North American trade deal through Congress and celebrated China's entry into the World Trade Organization. Clinton embraced globalization, championed it, and sought to shape it as a force for good.

When he left the White House in 2001, Clinton's public approval rating was a remarkable 66 percent.[1] The US economy had boomed on his watch; almost twenty-three million more Americans were working at the end of Clinton's presidency than at the beginning. Abroad, he had presided over an era of US supremacy. Former adversaries in Moscow and Beijing cooperated with Washington, hoping to imbibe the secrets of American prosperity.

More than two decades later, the glow of those years has dimmed. Clinton's captaincy of global integration no longer looks like an unalloyed success. The most recent book-length study of his presidency was entitled *A Fabulous Failure*.[2] Clinton's management of globalization, and its consequences at home and abroad, now draws criticism from across the political spectrum.

On the left, the Democratic Party's progressive wing disdains his market-oriented economics. The most recent Democrat to occupy the White House, Joe Biden, scorned Clinton-style trade deals, choosing instead to promote domestic manufacturing. It was an article of faith in the Biden White House that voters injured by foreign competition helped deliver the presidency to Donald Trump in 2016.

Conservatives, meanwhile, assail Clinton's handling of China. He was naive, they say, to believe that Chinese Communists would ever surrender their monopoly on power, even if in Western eyes full economic liberalization required political reform. Like many others, Clinton wrongly expected technology to erode Chinese authoritarianism.

On a midwinter day in early 2024, Clinton was ready to talk about globalization—the greatest engine of global prosperity the world has ever seen—and how it went off track. Thinner than in his White House years, thanks to the vegan diet he had adopted after a brush with heart disease, he still had a thick head of hair. His eyes were clear. On his wrist, he wore an Apple Watch with a band of safety-vest orange.

"It's gotten to be that there's not a lot of clear thinking about the upsides of globalization," he said at the start of a seventy-five-minute interview in his midtown Manhattan office.

Leaning back in his chair, with his legs stretched out before him, Clinton acknowledged that events have not turned out as he had expected. He agreed that US leaders failed to provide the help they had promised for those Americans left behind in a globalized world and had underestimated the resentments percolating among the working class.

Part of the problem, he said, was that the private sector had outfoxed the public sector. As capital grew more mobile, governments struggled to raise enough money by taxing corporations and the wealthy to pay for the social programs that would have softened the blow for workers.

"Look, I was amazed that we held off as long as we did in this kind of nationalist reaction, because you could see all over America and all over the world that the thing that was killing globalization was that the policies had to be ratified by nations. But their ability to nationalize the benefits was limited, either by their tax base or their wealth or their understanding or whatever—it was just limited," he said. "So there was going to be a reaction sooner or later."

When the reaction came in the United States, it revolved around trade and immigration. As Clinton spoke, in fact, Washington was convulsed by the latest political crisis over the nation's porous southern border. Chronic chaos there was "deeply unsettling" to voters and was sapping the Democratic Party's appeal, he said. The biggest drop in Democratic Party support anywhere in the nation in recent decades had occurred between San Antonio and the US-Mexican border.

"I carried that area," Clinton said, referring to his election triumphs in 1992 and 1996. But by 2020, Democratic backing there had withered. In rural Jim Wells County, just west of Corpus Christi, where Clinton had beaten George H. W. Bush by a margin of better than two to one, Trump romped.

A few months shy of his seventy-eighth birthday, Clinton was by turns formidable and nostalgic. His comments were punctuated by a nagging cough, but his political memory was undimmed: He accurately quoted the vote shares that Ronald Reagan and Walter Mondale received in their 1984 showdown and retold with relish detailed stories of his career in Arkansas. Reminded at one point of election night in Little Rock in November 1992, he said with a wistful smile, "That was a good night."

His Clinton Foundation office was not particularly imposing. A pair of photos hung on the wall behind his desk. One showed his wife Hillary, the former secretary of state, standing with her hands clasped in front of her, head thrown back in laughter. On the opposite wall was a black-and-white image taken in the Oval Office: Clinton and George W. Bush in conversation, with Barack Obama looking on.

Clinton boasted of completing nearly three hundred trade deals during his eight years in Washington. Today, neither political party shows any interest in matching that record. In a bitter twist, aggrieved Rust Belt voters, feeling themselves victims of Clinton's trade policies, wrecked his wife's 2016 presidential bid.

Long before Trump came on the scene, public discontent was evident, Clinton said. Relentless automation and a rising tide of Chinese imports destroyed five million manufacturing jobs while the response to the 2008 financial crisis compounded the pain. Each aspect of globalization—trade, finance, technology, ideas, and people—raised difficult questions that Washington struggled to answer. Sometimes, it barely seemed to try.

Those who failed to flourish in what Clinton once called "the new economy" turned against the conventional wisdom on trade,

immigration, and change itself. "You could just see it. They were just…
seething," he said. The old politician understood the anger among those
who were ill-equipped for this new, borderless world. He just thought
his wife could outrun it. "We didn't appreciate how much built-up frustration there was," he said.

The irony in Hillary Clinton's 2016 defeat lay in her husband's earlier clairvoyance. As president, Clinton had warned that support for
trade deals would evaporate if the government did not help those who
lacked the skills or education to capitalize on the globalized economy.
Yet Washington failed to act. In his first years in the White House,
Clinton prioritized deficit reduction. Then, Democrats lost control of
Congress, making new social spending politically impossible.

Clinton had an ambitious safety-net agenda of health care reform,
universal training, and place-based investments, according to Gene
Sperling, who directed Clinton's National Economic Council. But
the Republicans, who controlled Congress for six of his eight years in
office, neutered it. "Looking back, he feels we should have insisted that
the major domestic investments and protections happen before or at
least at the same time as any market opening. And it clearly pains him
that it didn't," Sperling said.[3]

From his first days as a politician in the mid-1970s, Clinton drew
support from rural voters and blue-collar whites. His political base
overlapped with Trump's. Both men understood the importance of the
working-class vote, but their political strategies could not have been
more dissimilar. Barnstorming for his wife in 2016, Clinton approached
blue-collar audiences the way he had addressed his neighbors back in
Arkansas. He took their concerns seriously and sought to win them over
by connecting arcane policy choices to their lives.

"You can't tell people they're stupid, and you've got to give them
a chance to like you. So you have to show you like them. And then
you don't really change their mind. *They* change *their* mind based on
what their lived experience is," Clinton said. A few minutes later, he
added: "You can't go around and deny that nobody ever lost a job because of these trade deals, or you can't go around and claim that there
was never any currency manipulation or any other changes that broke
the rules."

Trump, to put it mildly, took a different approach. The brighter future he peddled was a retreat to an imagined past. He did not explain the intricacies of automation, rising productivity, and global interdependence. Instead, he railed about "American carnage," economic "rape," and treasonous elites, including Clinton's wife.

If Clinton was disappointed in the way events had unfolded at home, the outcome abroad was little better. He had been confident in the 1990s that the internet would undermine dictators' ability to control their people and to keep democracy at bay. But the strongmen had proven more resilient than expected. China's "Great Firewall" shielded most Chinese citizens from Western ideas while steering them instead to government-approved information. Meanwhile, in the United States, popular social media sites were replete with racism, libel, and nonsense.

Just that morning, Clinton said, he had read a Pew Research Center study of attitudes toward social media. Out of nineteen countries surveyed, the most negative views of sites like X and Facebook were found in the United States. Sixty-four percent of Americans—including Clinton—believed such products were bad for democracy.[4] They contaminated "the information ecosystem," he said, fueling popular frustration with government.

Clinton understood the backlash to globalization as a blend of economic, cultural, and emotional influences. He noted that most of those arrested during the insurrection on January 6, 2021, were not hurting financially. Many were college-educated small business owners or farmers.

"I think that it was a revolt of the stymied, of the people who felt stuck, not necessarily poor. You can go to New York here and walk into all kinds of neighborhoods where people's incomes are below the average, but they seem lively and everything, because everybody's got a job and people believe they can make tomorrow better. What kills people is when they look in the mirror every morning [and] they think every tomorrow is going to be just like yesterday," he said.

Voters also did not approach trade policy like participants in a Washington think tank debate, coolly weighing the aggregate effects of powerful economic forces. Many Americans felt doubly battered by what they saw as cultural insults layered atop economic losses.

"The reaction against globalization was amplified by the very rapid social changes that were going on in America and other places where urban areas saw the rising acceptance of gay rights and gay marriage and all kinds of other things. And then the transgender issue came up and all that. So on social media, the people who were against all this [globalization] said, 'Oh here's a way we can maybe get ahold of this and marry people who are against the social change to people who are feeling left out of the economic change,'" Clinton said.

Globalization's defenders were part of the problem. Purists, chiefly on the coasts, dismissed any dissent, any defense of factory labor, any small-town attachment to community as ignorant protectionism. Treating the livelihoods of individuals and communities as just another variable in an equation might be the right way to run a regression, but it was the wrong way to win and hold political power.

To prove the point, Clinton recalled an episode from 1998 when he was trying to secure passage of legislation that would discourage youth smoking. Visiting tobacco farmers in North Carolina who saw the initiative as an existential threat to their way of life, he offered them government aid to switch crops, absolved them of responsibility for what was, after all, a societal challenge, and promised to help. He did not tell them to pack their bags and move, economists' standard advice for factory workers on the losing end of globalization.

"One of the problems we have is when people who have experience of all this talk about it, they have to be damn careful not to sound like they're know-it-alls or arrogant or clueless," he said.

A hint of defensiveness crept into the former president's tone only once, when he was asked about his expectations for China in the late 1990s, as it prepared to join the global trading system. "I thought what I said. I thought they would gradually become more open and more inclusive. . . . And I thought they would eventually replace us as the biggest economy in the world. And my goal was to make sure that when that happens, it wouldn't be bad for us or dangerous for them," he said. "I was much more hopeful."

By now, the midwinter sunshine streaming in the windows had warmed the room, and the former president was late for his next appointment. Before leaving, he pulled from a shelf *The Social Conquest of*

Earth, a book by the biologist Edward O. Wilson. Leaning closer, Clinton said that Wilson had found that the most successful species since the last mass extinction were ants, spiders, termites, and humans—creatures that found ways to work together on common challenges.

"My globalization position is just that I think that our capacity to solve every problem we face, including climate change, is dramatically amplified by cooperation. I think the cultural and other identity issues are basically challenges to our ability to sit here and [do] what we're doing like this," he said. "But they just have to be met with and dealt with."

It was time, Clinton said, to make "a new pitch for globalization," one that could overcome a rising tide of nationalism. "You got two choices. You can pretend there's going to be no change. If you do, we'll lose more jobs than we gain. Or you can make change your friend," he said. "But if you want to have a free enterprise system, there's going to be some losers when investment patterns change. The obligation of the government is to minimize loss and find people something else to do so we can keep growing."

That's sensible enough, as far as it goes. But that "new pitch" is precisely the argument that Clinton made, and other politicians echoed, thirty years ago. And it didn't work. Globalization made the United States as a whole wealthier. But the "obligation" to ensure that globalization's gains were widely shared was only identified, never fulfilled. The people Clinton had worried would be left behind were, in fact, left behind, and the political consequences—for his legacy, his wife's ambitions, and the country's future—were precisely what he had foretold.

Acknowledgments

It may be a cliché that every journalist is only as good as his or her sources. But that doesn't make it any less true. I know that I have been fortunate over the years to benefit from frequent conversations with experts on the global economy, financial markets, trade, and China.

I have many people to thank for helping me as I wrote this book.

Bill Reinsch has been my first call on countless trade stories since I moved home from China in 2005. Never too busy to answer a question or ten, he has been a reliable guide to the ins and outs of US trade policy.

Others who have been especially helpful over the years, even when they disagreed with my conclusions, include: Tim Adams, Ted Alden, Dean Baker, Myron Brilliant, Marc Chandler, Wendy Cutler, Greg Daco, Jason Furman, Scott Kennedy, Nick Lardy, Phil Levy, Scott Paul, Dan Price, Doug Rediker, Dan Rosen, Brad Setser, Nathan Sheets, Michael Strain, John Veroneau, Mike Wessel, Dennis Wilder, and Rufus Yerxa.

As I put the finishing touches on this manuscript, I was saddened to learn of Bill Overholt's passing. He always offered a distinctive and well-informed take on what was happening between the United States and China. Bill will be missed.

I worked with Michael Duffy for about five minutes 40 years ago and have been dunning him for favors ever since. It was his suggestion during a casual brainstorming session that led to my using *The World's Worst Bet* as my title. He remains one of the sharpest journalists I know.

Duffy, my old grad school pal Andy Collier, and my former Bloomberg colleague Larry Roberts each read a portion of the draft and provided valuable advice. I appreciate their assistance.

I covered many of the events described in this book as a correspondent in Washington, London, and Beijing. Along with drawing on those firsthand observations, I conducted more than 125 interviews with current and former policymakers, economists, business executives, and workers in preparing this manuscript. Of the interviews I sought, only Gary Cohn and Tim Geithner declined my request.

The idea for this history of post–Cold War globalization came to me as I was preparing to cover the G20 leaders' summit in Bali, Indonesia, in November 2022. It took me two years to complete the thinking, reading, writing, and research that went into the final product.

Along the way, I was fortunate enough to be offered a fellowship at the Woodrow Wilson International Center for Scholars, one of Washington's underappreciated gems. The Wilson Center afforded me a quiet place to work and access to a community of specialists in subjects too numerous to list. In particular, Mark Kennedy, director of the center's Wahba Institute for Strategic Competition, was a welcoming program host. When we weren't discussing trade politics, we shared an interest in genealogy and Guinness.

I am also indebted to Amb. Mark Green, the center's president and CEO, and his associates Robert Litwak, Lindsay Collins, and Nicole Gaouette. Wilson's professional librarians—Janet Spikes, Michelle Kamalich, and Andrea Britten—were indispensable.

Gail Ross has been my agent since she took a chance on a first-time author in 2010. She was enthusiastic about the idea for this book from the start and did a masterful job of selling it.

Editor John Mahaney and the entire crew at PublicAffairs did yeoman's work turning my draft into what you now hold in your hands. I am in their debt. Throughout the process, John was a congenial, supportive, and smart partner. He very much lived up to his stellar reputation.

At *The Washington Post*, which remains one of the best news organizations on the planet and a place at which I am proud to work, my editors were generous in granting me book leave. Special thanks go to Sally Buzbee, Matt Murray, Lori Montgomery, and Jen Liberto.

With my wife Kathy, I spent several delightful mid-August days polishing my draft at the Nantucket home of our friends Monica and

Terry Toth. They were wonderful hosts, who kept me supplied with chocolate chip cookies and beer as I raced to meet my deadline.

My wife, of course, deserves the greatest thanks, both for putting up with me for more than thirty years of marriage and for providing her customary outstanding editing.

Vienna, Virginia
January 2025

Notes

Introduction: We Might Have Done Things Differently, If We Had Known What Was Coming

1. Senator Biden speaking on measure to authorize extension of nondiscriminatory treatment to the People's Republic of China, Congressional Record, Senate, bound edition, vol. 146, part 13, 18331–18389, https://www.govinfo.gov/content/pkg/CRECB-2000-pt13/html/CRECB-2000-pt13-Pg18331-7.htm. Further senatorial quotes in this section are from the same source.

2. Jannuzi interview with the author, October 18, 2023.

3. "To Paris, US Looks Like a 'Hyperpower,'" *International Herald Tribune*, February 5, 1999, https://www.nytimes.com/1999/02/05/news/to-paris-us-looks-like-a-hyperpower.html. The term was coined by French Foreign Minister Hubert Védrine.

4. Transcript of the Senate debate can be found here: https://www.govinfo.gov/content/pkg/CRECB-2000-pt13/html/CRECB-2000-pt13-Pg18331-7.htm.

5. Henry Rowen, "The Short March: China's Road to Democracy," *National Interest*, Fall 1996, https://nationalinterest.org/article/the-short-march-chinas-road-to-democracy-416. In the event, China reached the $7,000 mark in 2013, two years earlier than expected, just as Xi Jinping was settling into power.

6. George W. Bush, "A Distinctly American Internationalism," remarks at Ronald Reagan Presidential Library, Simi Valley, California, November 19, 1999, https://www.washingtonpost.com/archive/business/technology/1999/11/19/text-of-remarks-prepared-for-delivery-by-texas-gov-george-w-bush-at-ronald-reagan-presidential-library-simi-valley-calif-on-november-19-1999/1e893802-88ce-40de-bcf7-a4e1b6393ad2/.

7. "World GDP (Constant Dollars 2015)," World Bank, https://data.worldbank.org/indicator/NY.GDP.MKTP.KD.

8. According to the Bureau of Labor Statistics' import price index, Chinese imports in aggregate cost Americans no more in 2023 than they had in 2003: https://data.bls.gov/PDQWeb/ei.

9. Xavier Jaravel and Erick Sager, "What Are the Price Effects of Trade? Evidence from the US and Implications for Quantitative Trade Models," Working Paper No. 2019-68, Finance and Economics Discussion Series (FEDS), Board of Governors of the Federal Reserve System, August 2019, 5, footnote 7, http://dx.doi.org/10.17016/FEDS.2019.068.

10. Ben S. Bernanke et al., "International Capital Flows and the Returns to Safe Assets in the United States, 2003–2007," International Finance Discussion Paper No. 1014, Board of Governors of the Federal Reserve System, February 2011, https://www .federalreserve.gov/pubs/ifdp/2011/1014/ifdp1014.pdf; Carol Bertaut et al., "ABS Inflows to the United States and the Global Financial Crisis," International Finance Discussion Paper No. 1028, Board of Governors of the Federal Reserve System, August 2011, https://www.federalreserve.gov/pubs/ifdp/2011/1028/ifdp1028.pdf.

11. Anne Case and Angus Deaton, *Deaths of Despair and the Future of Capitalism* (Princeton University Press, 2020), 2–7.

12. Case and Deaton, *Deaths of Despair*, 220.

13. "Monetary Policy Report," Bank of England, November 2019, 34, https://www .bankofengland.co.uk/-/media/boe/files/monetary-policy-report/2019/november /monetary-policy-report-november-2019.pdf.

14. "Exit Polls," CNN, updated November 23, 2016, https://www.cnn.com/election /2016/results/exit-polls.

15. Dani Rodrik, "Why Does Globalization Fuel Populism? Economics, Culture, and the Rise of Right-Wing Populism," *Annual Review of Economics* 13, no. 1 (2021): 139, https://drodrik.scholar.harvard.edu/files/dani-rodrik/files/why_does_globalization _fuel_populism.pdf.

16. "Trade, Percentage of Gross Domestic Product," World Bank, https://data.world bank.org/indicator/NE.TRD.GNFS.ZS?locations=1W.

17. "Banks from All Reporting Countries; Consolidated Total Claims in All Currencies with Residents of All Countries, Etc.," Consolidated Banking Statistics, Bank of International Settlements, https://data.bis.org/topics/CBS/BIS,WS_CBS_PUB,1.0 /Q.S.5A.4R.F.C.A.A.TO1.A.5J.

18. Yasmeen Abutaleb, Rick Noack, and Toluse Olorunnipa, "Biden Says He Might Meet with Putin—but Not Now," *Washington Post*, December 1, 2022, https://www .washingtonpost.com/politics/2022/12/01/macron-biden-warning-western-alliance/.

19. Dimon spoke at a meeting on June 13, 2024, with the *Washington Post* editorial board, with author in attendance.

20. Glenn Hubbard, *The Wall and the Bridge: Fear and Opportunity in Disruption's Wake* (Yale University Press, 2022), 12.

21. Paul Krugman, "Globalization: What Did We Miss?," in *Meeting Globalization's Challenges: Policies to Make Trade Work for All*, ed. Luis A. V. Catao and Maurice Obstfeld (International Monetary Fund and Princeton University Press, 2019), 118.

22. Paul Krugman, "How Economists Like Me Got Globalization Wrong," *Bloomberg Opinion*, October 10, 2019, https://www.bloomberg.com/view/articles/2019-10-10 /inequality-globalization-and-the-missteps-of-1990s-economics.

23. From 1996 to 2002, the federal budget recorded a surplus four times and posted a negligible deficit twice. Congressional Budget Office's budget and economic outlook historical data is available at https://www.cbo.gov/data/budget-economic-data#2.

24. Mario Draghi, "Economic Policy in a Changing World," Volcker Award acceptance speech, National Association of Business Economics Economic Policy Conference, February 15, 2024, https://files.constantcontact.com/668faa28001/a33105a7-25c1 -4102-9a8e-f7becb95e8c3.pdf.

25. Hubbard interview with the author, November 18, 2023.
26. Froman interview with the author, December 8, 2023.
27. Thomas L. Friedman, "Read All About It," *New York Times*, January 12, 1997, 17.
28. Rush Doshi, *The Long Game: China's Grand Strategy to Displace American Order* (Oxford University Press, 2021), 54–55.
29. Paul Ryan, "Paul Ryan Says Even MAGA Diehards Believe Trump Can't Win in 2024," interview by David Marchese, *New York Times Magazine*, March 3, 2023, https://www.nytimes.com/interactive/2023/03/06/magazine/paul-ryan-interview.html.
30. Susan Shirk, *Overreach: How China Derailed Its Peaceful Rise* (Oxford University Press, 2023), 14.
31. Joshua Cooper Ramo, "The Committee to Save the World," *Time*, February 15, 1999.
32. Rubin interview with the author, September 26, 2023.

Chapter 1: The Strongest in the World

1. Associated Press TV footage of summit arrivals, available at https://www.youtube.com/watch?v=CCXBGBMvMnY.
2. William J. Clinton, "Remarks in Littleton, Colorado," June 19, 1997, in *Public Papers of the Presidents of the United States*, book I for 1997 (US Government Printing Office, 1998), 762–767, https://www.govinfo.gov/content/pkg/PPP-1997-book1/html/PPP-1997-book1-doc-pg762.htm.
3. E. J. Dionne Jr., "Great Countries Don't Boast," *Washington Post*, June 27, 1997, A25; Steven Pearlstein and Paul Blustein, "In the Best of Both Worlds, Consider a Third Option," *Washington Post*, June 23, 1997, A12; Steven R. Weisman, "The Big Boys in Denver," *New York Times*, June 24, 1997, 18.
4. Samuel R. Berger and Daniel K. Tarullo, "Memorandum for the President," June 16, 1997, declassified, Clinton Presidential Records, https://clinton.presidentiallibraries.us/items/show/100496.
5. Bill Clinton, *My Life* (Alfred A. Knopf, 2004), 758.
6. Lawrence Summers, "Promoting Global Financial Stability," speech, Institute for International Economics, June 12, 1997, https://home.treasury.gov/news/press-releases/sp061297.
7. John Kifner, "Mao's Heir Finds Path: Wall Street," *New York Times*, November 1, 1997, https://archive.nytimes.com/www.nytimes.com/library/world/110197us-china.html.
8. White House, "Meeting with Russian President Yeltsin," memorandum of conversation, June 20, 1997, https://nsarchive.gwu.edu/document/16837-document-10-memorandum-conversation-meeting.
9. Stephanie Baker, "Russia: Deal on Paris Club Entry Seen as Political Victory," Radio Free Europe/Radio Liberty, June 9, 1997, https://www.rferl.org/a/1085238.html.
10. George H. W. Bush, "Remarks at the Yale University Commencement Ceremony in New Haven, Connecticut," May 27, 1991, in *Public Papers of the Presidents of the United States*, book I for 1991 (US Government Printing Office, 1992), 565, https://www.govinfo.gov/content/pkg/PPP-1991-book1/html/PPP-1991-book1-doc-pg565.htm.

11. Gwen Ifill, "The 1992 Campaign: The Democrats; With Reservations, Clinton Endorses Free-Trade Pact," *New York Times*, October 5, 1992, A1; Peter Behr, "Clinton's Conversion on NAFTA," *Washington Post*, September 19, 1993, https://www.washingtonpost.com/archive/business/1993/09/19/clintons-conversion-on-nafta/3a5b9cb5-dfc8-4b5c-9ae6-30781f0a99fc/.

12. William J. Clinton Presidential History Project, "Interview with David Kusnet," Miller Center, University of Virginia, 35–36, https://s3.amazonaws.com/web.poh.transcripts/ohp_2010_0319_kusnet.pdf.

13. Waldman interview with the author, September 11, 2023.

14. Katz interview with the author, January 13, 2025.

15. White House, "Remarks by President Clinton, President Bush, President Carter, President Ford, and Vice President Gore in Signing of NAFTA Side Agreements," September 14, 1993, https://clintonwhitehouse6.archives.gov/1993/09/1993-09-14-remarks-by-clinton-and-former-presidents-on-nafta.html.

16. Waldman interview with the author, September 11, 2023.

17. NAFTA Debate, CNN, transcript, November 9, 1993, https://ggallarotti.web.wesleyan.edu/govt155/goreperot.htm.

18. Kenneth J. Cooper, "House Approves US-Canada-Mexico Trade Pact 234–200, Giving Clinton Big Victory," *Washington Post*, November 18, 1993, A1.

19. US Bureau of Labor Statistics, "All Employees Manufacturing," Federal Reserve Bank of St. Louis, updated January 10, 2025, https://fred.stlouisfed.org/series/MANEMP#0.

20. Jiwon Choi et al., "Local Economic and Political Effects of Trade Deals: Evidence from NAFTA," *American Economic Review* 114, no. 6 (2024): 1540–1575, https://pubs.aeaweb.org/doi/pdfplus/10.1257/aer.20220425.

21. "Meeting with Former Secretary of State Henry Kissinger and Three Others re China," declassified memorandum of conversation, Oval Office, July 13, 1995, Clinton Presidential Records, https://clinton.presidentiallibraries.us/items/show/101840.

22. Reuters, "Beijing Blasts US, Gingrich," *Washington Post*, July 11, 1995, https://www.washingtonpost.com/archive/politics/1995/07/12/beijing-blasts-us-gingrich/9ed2b014-fc0c-48b2-886e-981ad4d048b5/.

23. John F. Harris, "Clinton, Jiang Confer," *Washington Post*, October 24, 1995, https://www.washingtonpost.com/archive/politics/1995/10/25/clinton-jiang-confer/8609ca72-a44d-4977-8757-f0576709a0aa/.

24. William J. Clinton Presidential History Project, "Interview with Mickey Kantor," Miller Center, University of Virginia, 46, https://s3.amazonaws.com/web.poh.transcripts/ohp_2002_0628_kantor.pdf.

25. William J. Clinton Presidential History Project, "Interview with Sandy Berger," Miller Center, University of Virginia, 111, https://s3.amazonaws.com/web.poh.transcripts/ohp_2005_0324_berger.pdf.

26. William J. Clinton, "The President's News Conference in Hong Kong Special Administrative Region," July 3, 1998, in *Public Papers of the Presidents of the United States*, book II for 1998 (US Government Printing Office, 1999): 1177–1178, https://www.govinfo.gov/content/pkg/PPP-1998-book2/html/PPP-1998-book2-doc-pg1174.htm.

27. "Vice President's Meeting with Chinese President Jiang Zemin," declassified memorandum of conversation, November 16, 1998, Clinton Presidential Records, https://clinton.presidentiallibraries.us/items/show/101542.

28. Douglas Irwin, *Clashing over Commerce: A History of US Trade Policy* (University of Chicago Press, 2017), 667.

29. Justin R. Pierce and Peter K. Schott, "The Surprisingly Swift Decline of US Manufacturing Employment," *American Economic Review* 106, no. 7 (2016): 4–6, in online appendix, https://www.aeaweb.org/articles?id=10.1257/aer.20131578.

30. Karen Lee Scrivo, "Foreign Affairs—Door-to-Door Diplomacy," *National Journal*, May 20, 2000.

31. Barshefsky interview with the author, April 19, 2023.

32. *Assessment of the Economic Effects on the United States of China's Accession to the WTO* (US International Trade Commission, 1999), xx, https://www.usitc.gov/publications/docs/pubs/332/PUB3229.PDF.

33. Charlene Barshefsky, in Hearing Before the Committee on Agriculture of the House of Representatives, 106th Congress, Second Session, "The Administration's Proposal for Permanent Normal Trade Relations with China," May 17, 2002, 45, https://commdocs.house.gov/committees/ag/hag10652.000/hag10652_0f.htm.

34. William J. Clinton, "Address Before a Joint Session of Congress on Administration Goals," February 17, 1993, in *Public Papers of the Presidents of the United States*, book I for 1993 (US Government Printing Office, 1994): 115, https://www.govinfo.gov/content/pkg/PPP-1993-book1/html/PPP-1993-book1-doc-pg113-2.htm.

35. William J. Clinton Presidential History Project, "Interview with Anthony Lake," Miller Center, University of Virginia, 11, https://s3.amazonaws.com/web.poh.transcripts/ohp_2002_0521_lake.pdf.

36. William J. Clinton Presidential History Project, "Interview with Warren Christopher and Strobe Talbott," Miller Center, University of Virginia, 31, https://s3.amazonaws.com/web.poh.transcripts/ohp_2002_0415_christophertalbott.pdf.

37. Donnie Radcliffe, "Governors' Night Out; Tea, Toasts; Tea and Toasts at a Japanese Embassy Fete," *Washington Post*, February 27, 1979, https://www.washingtonpost.com/archive/lifestyle/1979/02/27/governors-night-out/f94cfc8e-ad7e-45b0-8112-61775420a08d/; Elisabeth Bumiller, "Trade Routes to the Great Wall," *Washington Post*, February 26, 1980, https://www.washingtonpost.com/archive/lifestyle/1980/02/26/trade-routes-to-the-great-wall/ed19458b-e5c9-47cb-9c34-0e702bf2e348/.

38. Allan Janesch, "US Governors' Travel Abroad 'Opens the Door' to Increased Exports and Jobs for Their States," *Business America*, May 7, 1990.

39. Kantor interview with the author, September 12, 2023.

40. Elizabeth Kolbert, "The 1992 Campaign: Democrats; Both Kerreys Searching for Campaign Strategy," *New York Times*, January 16, 1992, A16; David E. Rosenbaum with Keith Bradsher, "Candidates Playing to Mood of Protectionism," *New York Times*, January 26, 1992, 1.

41. William J. Clinton Presidential History Project, "Interview with Sandy Berger," Miller Center, University of Virginia, 27, https://s3.amazonaws.com/web.poh.transcripts/ohp_2005_0324_berger.pdf.

42. Waldman interview with the author, September 11, 2023.

43. William J. Clinton, "A New Covenant for Economic Change: Remarks to Students at Georgetown University," November 20, 1991, https://thetechnocratictyranny .com/PDFS/1991_Clinton_New_Covenant_economy.pdf.

44. White House, "Remarks by Clinton, Bush, Carter, Ford, Gore."

45. Mohamed Younis, "Sharply Fewer in US View Foreign Trade as Opportunity," Gallup, March 31, 2021, https://news.gallup.com/poll/342419/sharply-fewer-view -foreign-trade-opportunity.aspx.

46. Kantor interview with the author, September 12, 2023.

47. Memo from Christopher Dorval to Don Baer, "Trade," Clinton Presidential Records, https://clinton.presidentiallibraries.us/items/show/34683. Confirmed in Baer interview with the author, October 13, 2023, that Dorval's memo was written in January 1996.

48. Memo from Dorval to Baer, "Trade."

49. Clinton, "Remarks in Littleton, Colorado," 762–767.

50. William J. Clinton Presidential History Project, "Interview with Sandy Berger," Miller Center, University of Virginia, 28, https://s3.amazonaws.com/web.poh .transcripts/ohp_2005_0324_berger.pdf.

51. Robert Reich, *Locked in the Cabinet* (Vintage Books, 1997), 104–105, 119.

52. Reich, *Locked in the Cabinet*, 194–195.

53. Reich, *Locked in the Cabinet*, 256–257.

54. Jack Lew and Laura D'Andrea Tyson, "Status of the Workforce Development Legislation—Your GI Bill," memorandum for the president, Office of Management and Budget, June 25, 1996, 18, Clinton Presidential Records, https://clinton.presidential libraries.us/item/show/32923.

55. Rubin interview with the author, September 26, 2023.

56. Joseph E. Stiglitz, Council of Economic Advisers, "Memorandum for the President: Second-Term Initiatives," November 8, 1996, Clinton Presidential Records, https:// clinton.presidentiallibraries.us/items/show/60798.

57. Dani Rodrik, *Has Globalization Gone Too Far?* (Institute of International Economics, 1997), 11.

58. Rodrik, *Has Globalization Gone Too Far?*, 6.

59. Office of the Executive Secretary, "The President's Trip to Denver, Colorado, for the Summit of the Eight," June 19–22, 1997, declassified, Clinton Presidential Records, https://clinton.presidentiallibraries.us/items/show/100496.

60. Daniel K. Tarullo, assistant to the president, speech to National Press Club, June 16, 1997, https://clintonwhitehouse3.archives.gov/WH/New/Eight/npc.html.

61. US Department of the Treasury, "Promoting Global Financial Stability: The G7 Agenda—Deputy Secretary Lawrence H. Summers—Institute for International Economics, Washington, DC," press release, June 12, 1997, https://home.treasury .gov/news/press-releases/sp061297.

62. Clinton, "Remarks in Littleton, Colorado," 762–767.

63. R. Barry Johnston et al., "Sequencing Capital Account Liberalization: Lessons from the Experiences in Chile, Indonesia, Korea and Thailand," Working Paper No. 97/157, International Monetary Fund, November 1997, 29–32, https://www.imf .org/external/pubs/ft/wp/wp97157.pdf.

64. Robert Wade, "The Coming Fight over Capital Flows," *Foreign Policy*, Winter 1998–1999, https://ciaotest.cc.columbia.edu/olj/fp/fp_99war01.html.

65. Alejandro Lopez-Mejia, "Large Capital Flows: Causes, Consequences and Policy Responses," *Finance and Development*, International Monetary Fund, September 1999, 1, https://www.imf.org/external/pubs/ft/fandd/1999/09/lopez.htm.

66. "67th Annual Report," Bank for International Settlements, June 9, 1997, 108, https://www.bis.org/publ/ar67f01.pdf.

67. Robert Rubin and Jacob Weisberg, *In an Uncertain World: Tough Choices from Wall Street to Washington* (Random House, 2003), 217.

68. Lopez-Mejia, "Large Capital Flows," 4.

69. Lopez-Mejia, "Large Capital Flows," 18.

70. Clinton, *My Life*, 806–807.

71. Rubin and Weisberg, *In an Uncertain World*, 221.

72. "Trading Analysis of October 27 and 28, 1997," Division of Market Regulation, US Securities and Exchange Commission, September 1998, https://www.sec.gov/news/studies/tradrep.htm#:~:text=On%20Monday%2C%20October%2027%2C%20the,in%20the%20index%20since%201915.

73. Rubin and Weisberg, *In an Uncertain World*, 230–234.

74. White House, "Conversation with South Korean President Kim Young Sam," memorandum of conversation, November 27, 1997, Clinton Presidential Records, https://clinton.presidentiallibraries.us/items/show/118552.

75. Rubin and Weisberg, *In an Uncertain World*, 235.

76. White House, "Telcon with Korean President-Elect Kim Dae-jung," memorandum of telephone conversation, December 18, 1997, Clinton Presidential Records, https://clinton.presidentiallibraries.us/items/show/118555.

77. Timothy Geithner, *Stress Test: Reflections on Financial Crises* (Crown, 2014), 61.

78. Rubin and Weisberg, *In an Uncertain World*, 240.

79. William J. Clinton, "Remarks to the Council on Foreign Relations in New York City," September 14, 1998, in *Public Papers of the Presidents of the United States*, book II for 1998 (US Government Printing Office, 1999), 1575, https://www.govinfo.gov/content/pkg/PPP-1998-book2/html/PPP-1998-book2-doc-pg1572.htm.

80. Geithner, *Stress Test*, 66.

81. James Harrigan, "The Impact of the Asia Crisis on US Industry: An Almost-Free Lunch?," *Economic Policy Review—Federal Reserve Bank of New York* 6, no. 3 (2000): 79, https://www.newyorkfed.org/medialibrary/media/research/epr/00v06n3/0009harr.pdf.

82. US Department of Commerce, International Trade Administration, "Report to the President: Global Steel Trade: Structural Problems and Future Solutions," July 2000, 1, 22, https://permanent.fdlp.gov/lps12229/lps12229/steelreport726.htm.

83. Homi Kharas et al., "An Analysis of Russia's 1998 Meltdown: Fundamentals and Market Signals," *Brookings Papers on Economic Activity*, no. 1 (2001): 2, https://www.brookings.edu/wp-content/uploads/2001/01/2001a_bpea_kharas.pdf.

84. White House, "President Boris Yeltsin of Russia," declassified memorandum of telephone conversation, August 14, 1998, Clinton Presidential Records, https://clinton.presidentiallibraries.us/items/show/101533.

85. Taylor Branch, *The Clinton Tapes* (Simon & Schuster, 2009), 512.

86. White House, "President Boris Yeltsin of Russia," declassified memorandum of telephone conversation, September 12, 1998, Clinton Presidential Records, https://clinton.presidentiallibraries.us/items/show/101535.

87. James Boughton, "Russia: From Rebirth to Crisis to Recovery," in *Tearing Down Walls: The International Monetary Fund, 1990–1999* (International Monetary Fund, 2012), 343.

88. Michael Waldman, *POTUS Speaks* (Simon & Schuster, 2000), 232.

89. William J. Clinton, "Remarks to the Council," 1572.

90. Branch, *The Clinton Tapes*, 513.

91. Michael Siconolfi, Anita Raghavan, and Mitchell Pacelle, "All Bets Are Off: How the Salesmanship and Brainpower Failed at Long-Term Capital," *Wall Street Journal*, November 16, 1998, A1.

92. This figure includes off-balance-sheet derivatives. Meeting of the Federal Open Market Committee, transcript, Federal Reserve, September 29, 1998, 111, https://www.federalreserve.gov/monetarypolicy/files/FOMC19980929meeting.pdf.

93. Meeting on September 29, 1998, of the Federal Open Market Committee, 108.

94. Gary Schinasi, "Systemic Aspects of Recent Turbulence in Mature Markets," *Finance and Development*, International Monetary Fund, March 1999, 3, https://www.imf.org/external/pubs/ft/fandd/1999/03/schinasi.htm.

95. Meeting on September 29, 1998, of the Federal Open Market Committee, 100.

96. Meeting on September 29, 1998, of the Federal Open Market Committee, 100.

Chapter 2: Whose Streets?

1. Wallach interview with the author, September 6, 2023.

2. Moises Naim, "Lori's War," *Foreign Policy*, Spring 2000, 30.

3. Wallach interview with the author, September 6, 2023.

4. "Statement by H. E. William J. Clinton, President," World Trade Organization, May 1998, https://www.wto.org/english/thewto_e/minist_e/min98_e/anniv_e/clinton_e.htm.

5. "Statement by William J. Clinton."

6. Richard Baldwin, *The Great Convergence: Information Technology and the New Globalization* (Belknap, 2016), 1–7.

7. Charlene Barshefsky, "Toward Seattle: The Next Round and America's Stake in the Trading System," Council on Foreign Relations, October 19, 1999, 6, accessed on USTR website.

8. PBS *Commanding Heights* transcript of interview with Lori Wallach, https://www.pbs.org/wgbh/commandingheights/shared/minitext/int_loriwallach.html.

9. William J. Clinton, "Address Before a Joint Session of the Congress on the State of the Union," January 19, 1999, American Presidency Project, UC Santa Barbara, https://www.presidency.ucsb.edu/documents/address-before-joint-session-the-congress-the-state-the-union-6.

10. So named for the 1996 WTO ministerial that was held in Singapore. Craig VanGrasstek, *The History and Future of the World Trade Organization* (WTO, 2013), 373.

11. Barshefsky, "Toward Seattle."

12. Naim, "Lori's War," 50.

13. Lori Wallach personal papers, Folder "WTO-Seattle-Road to Seattle."
14. Helene Cooper, "Activists' Boot Camp Teaches How to Confront Trade Leaders," *Wall Street Journal*, September 20, 1999, https://www.wsj.com/articles/SB9377792 54498198737.
15. Lori Wallach personal papers, "Ruckus Camp Notice," July 12, 1999.
16. "Seattle General Strike Project," University of Washington, https://depts.washington .edu/labhist/strike/.
17. Foster interview with the author, September 8, 2023.
18. Foster interview with the author, September 8, 2023.
19. Edward J. Wasilewski Jr., "A Look Back at the Kaiser Aluminum and United Steelworkers Dispute," Bureau of Labor Statistics, January 30, 2003, https://www.bls.gov/opub /mlr/cwc/a-look-back-at-the-kaiser-aluminum-and-united-steelworkers-dispute.pdf.
20. Foster interview with the author, September 8, 2023.
21. Ron Judd, interview by Jeremy Simer, WTO History Project, University of Washington, https://depts.washington.edu/wtohist/interviews/Judd.pdf.
22. Mike Dolan, interview by Jeremy Simer, WTO History Project, University of Washington, http://depts.washington.edu/wtohist/interviews/Dolan%20-%20Simer.htm.
23. Lori Wallach personal papers, email to Michael Dolan, October 19, 1999.
24. Lori Wallach personal papers, group email chain, July 13–23, 1999.
25. Lori Wallach personal papers, email from Wallach to Dolan, October 14, 1999; Peter Bjarkman, "Fidel Castro and Baseball," Society for American Baseball Research, March 25, 2016, https://sabr.org/bioproj/topic/fidel-castro-and-baseball/; Castro did not opt out of the conference until November 28, per Seattle Police Department, "After Action Report: World Trade Organization Ministerial Conference Seattle, Washington, November 29–December 3, 1999," April 4, 2000, 31, https://media .cleveland.com/pdextra/other/Seattle%20PD%20after%20action%20report.pdf.
26. Seattle Police Department, "After Action Report," 10.
27. Barshefsky interview with the author, September 12, 2023.
28. Seattle Police Department, "After Action Report," 18.
29. Ronald G. Shafer, "Nervous in Seattle: Concerns Grow About Expected Anti-Trade Protests," *Wall Street Journal*, August 13, 1999, A1.
30. VanGrasstek, *History of World Trade Organization*, 385.
31. VanGrasstek, *History of World Trade Organization*, 386.
32. William J. Clinton Presidential History Project, "Interview with Charlene Barshefsky," Miller Center, University of Virginia, 46, https://s3.amazonaws.com/web.poh .transcripts/ohp_2005_0302_barshefsky.pdf.
33. Wallach interview with the author, August 9, 2023.
34. Protesters complained that the WTO had elevated global trade rules above legitimate US efforts to protect endangered species. But the WTO ruled against the US for the manner in which it implemented the import ban, not the ban itself. The US provided Caribbean countries with financial and technical assistance and gave them longer to prepare for the new rules, benefits it did not extend to Asian countries. "The US lost the case, not because it sought to protect the environment but because it discriminated between WTO members," the trade judges ruled: https://www.wto.org /english/tratop_e/envir_e/edis08_e.htm.

Notes to Chapter 2

35. Alex Tizon, "Monday, Nov. 29," *Seattle Times*, December 5, 1999, A14.
36. Seattle Police Department, "After Action Report," 18–19.
37. Wallach interview with the author, September 6, 2023.
38. Rally footage, https://www.c-span.org/video/?153918-1/rally-march-global-justice.
39. Seattle Police Department, "After Action Report," 37.
40. Seattle Police Department, "After Action Report," 38–40.
41. Seattle Police Department, "After Action Report," 37–38.
42. Seattle Police Department, "After Action Report," 20.
43. Alex Tizon, "Monday, Nov. 29," *Seattle Times*, December 5, 1999, A14.
44. "Countdown to Chaos in Seattle," *Seattle Times*, December 5, 1999, B1.
45. Wallach interview with the author, September 6, 2023.
46. Shesol interview with the author, September 4, 2023.
47. William J. Clinton, "Remarks by the President on Parental Leave," White House, November 30, 1999, https://clintonwhitehouse4.archives.gov/textonly/WH/New/html/19991130.html. Video available at https://www.c-span.org/video/?153915-1/family-leave.
48. "WTO—Seattle Ministerial 12/1/99 WTO Ministers' Lunch Drafts," Speechwriting Office, Jeff Shesol, Clinton Presidential Records, https://clinton.presidentiallibraries.us/items/show/12237.
49. Shesol interview with author, September 4, 2023.
50. "Schedule of the President for Tuesday, Nov. 30, 1999, Final Schedule," Clinton Presidential Records, https://clinton.presidentiallibraries.us/items/show/12719; White House, "Press Briefing by United States Trade Representative Charlene Barshefsky and National Economic Advisor Gene Sperling," December 1, 1999, https://clintonwhitehouse3.archives.gov/WH/New/WTO-Conf-1999/briefings/19991201-1607.html.
51. VanGrasstek, *History of World Trade Organization*, 390.
52. Michael Paulson, "Clinton Says He Will Support Trade Sanctions for Worker Abuse," *Seattle Post-Intelligencer*, December 1, 1999, 1.
53. William J. Clinton Presidential History Project, "Interview with Charlene Barshefsky," Miller Center, University of Virginia, 47, https://s3.amazonaws.com/web.poh.transcripts/ohp_2005_0302_barshefsky.pdf.
54. Barshefsky interview with the author, September 12, 2023.
55. William J. Clinton, "Remarks by the President to the Luncheon in Honor of the Ministers Attending the Meetings of the World Trade Organization," White House, December 1, 1999, https://clintonwhitehouse3.archives.gov/WH/New/WTO-Conf-1999/remarks/19991201-1505.html.
56. "Press Briefing by Barshefsky and Sperling," 1.
57. Wallach interview with the author, August 9, 2023.
58. "Presidential Approval Ratings: Bill Clinton," Gallup, https://news.gallup.com/poll/116584/presidential-approval-ratings-bill-clinton.aspx.
59. Frank Newport, "Americans Favor China Trade Agreement, but Agree That Workers Could Be Hurt," Gallup, November 30, 1999, https://news.gallup.com/poll/3439/americans-favor-china-trade-agreement-agree-workers-could-hurt.aspx.
60. Barshefsky interview with the author, September 12, 2023.
61. Naim, "Lori's War," 40.

332

62. VanGrasstek, *History of World Trade Organization*, 394.
63. William J. Clinton Presidential History Project, "Interview with Charlene Barshefsky," Miller Center, University of Virginia, 46, https://s3.amazonaws.com/web.poh .transcripts/ohp_2005_0302_barshefsky.pdf.
64. William J. Clinton Presidential History Project, "Interview with James Steinberg," Miller Center, University of Virginia, 37, https://s3.amazonaws.com/web.poh .transcripts/steinberg_2008_taggedtranscript.pdf.
65. Cassidy interview with the author, September 21, 2023.
66. Seattle Police Department, "After Action Report," 3–4.
67. Seattle Police Department, "After Action Report," 71.
68. Seattle Police Department, "After Action Report," 48–49.
69. Thomas Friedman, "Senseless in Seattle," *New York Times*, December 1, 1999, A23.
70. Wallach interview with the author, September 12, 2023.
71. Dolan interview with the author, September 21, 2023.
72. Nash interview with the author, September 22, 2023.
73. Nash interview with the author, September 22, 2023.
74. William C. Rempel, Henry Weinstein, and Alan C. Miller, "Testimony Links Top China Official, Funds for Clinton," *Los Angeles Times*, April 4, 1999, https://www .latimes.com/archives/la-xpm-1999-apr-04-mn-24189-story.html.
75. Taylor Branch, *The Clinton Tapes: Wrestling History with the President* (New York: Simon & Schuster, 2009), 544.
76. Branch, *The Clinton Tapes*, 545.
77. White House, "Joint Press Conference with President Clinton and Premier Zhu Rongji of the People's Republic of China," April 8, 1999, https://clintonwhitehouse4 .archives.gov/WH/New/html/19990408-1109.html.
78. Bob Davis and Lingling Wei, *Superpower Showdown* (Harper Business, 2020), 69.
79. Thomas Pickering, under secretary of state, "Oral Presentation to the Chinese Government Regarding the Accidental Bombing of the PRC Embassy in Belgrade," June 17, 1999, released July 6, 1999, US State Department, https://1997-2001.state.gov /policy_remarks/1999/990617_pickering_emb.html.
80. Some of the details in this account are based on an interview with a former US government official with direct knowledge of the situation.
81. Sperling interview with the author, October 12, 2023.
82. Rush Doshi, *The Long Game: China's Grand Strategy to Displace American Order* (Oxford University Press, 2021), 146.
83. Lieberthal interview with the author, April 5, 2023.
84. Doshi, *The Long Game*, 152–156.

Chapter 3: Sense of Menace

1. Matt Marshall, "VC Geography: Financier's Global Vision Leads Way; Silicon Valley Lives Changed by Globalization," *San Jose Mercury News*, December 28, 2005, M1.
2. William Booth, "School Voucher Initiative Roils Race," *Washington Post*, July 19, 2000, https://www.washingtonpost.com/archive/politics/2000/07/19/school-voucher -initiative-roils-race/e036d38c-8983-41b0-b8ac-33bcefc2b4d6/.

3. Oral history interview with General William H. Draper Jr., Harry S. Truman Library, National Archives January 11, 1972, https://www.trumanlibrary.gov/library/oral-histories/draperw#transcript.

4. William H. Draper III, *The Startup Game: Inside the Partnership Between Venture Capitalists and Entrepreneurs* (Palgrave Macmillan, 2011), 13.

5. "Our 40-Year Journey in China: 1979–2019," United Nations Development Program, https://www.undp.org/china/publications/our-40-year-journey-china-1979-2019.

6. Draper interview with the author, April 10, 2023.

7. Draper III, *The Startup Game*, 139–140.

8. Draper III, *The Startup Game*, 229.

9. Draper III, *The Startup Game*, 229–230.

10. Draper interview with the author, April 10, 2023.

11. Draper email to author, December 23, 2022.

12. Draper email to author, December 23, 2022.

13. Baidu, Prospectus for Initial Public Offering of American Depositary Shares, August 4, 2005, 115, https://ir.baidu.com/static-files/15c8e098-e46f-4e22-85c7-d348e14df301.

14. Draper interview with the author, April 10, 2023.

15. Draper email to author, December 23, 2022.

16. Draper interview with the author, April 10, 2023.

17. David J. Lynch, "Emerging Middle Class Reshapes China," *USA Today*, November 12, 2002, A13.

18. Draper interview with the author, April 10, 2023.

19. Michelle Tsai, "DFJ Affiliate ePlanet Winning Over Doubters," *Dow Jones Venture Capital Analyst*, October 2005, https://webreprints.djreprints.com/sampleVCcr.pdf.

20. Rieschel interview with the author, October 20, 2023. "Pat never gets the credit for really being the first. He was really the first person to set up an institutional Silicon Valley style partnership in China. And so Pat deserves the credit for being the first," Rieschel said.

21. Sebastian Mallaby, *The Power Law: Venture Capital and the Making of the New Future* (Penguin, 2022), 226.

22. Mallaby, *The Power Law*, 228–231.

23. Mallaby, *The Power Law*, 231–232.

24. Rieschel interview with the author, October 20, 2023.

25. "US capital, legal structures, and talent were central to the development of China's digital economy," concluded Mallaby, *The Power Law*, 233.

26. "Full Text of Clinton's Speech on China Trade Bill," *New York Times*, March 9, 2000, https://archive.nytimes.com/www.nytimes.com/library/world/asia/030900clinton-china-text.html.

27. Memo from Ken Lieberthal to Paul Orzulak, April 29, 2000, Clinton Presidential Records, https://clinton.presidentiallibraries.us/files/original/7d1a983fb4a7eb717d9a7d62d65239a1.pdf.

28. The US trade deficit with China was more than $202 billion in 2005, compared with almost $84 billion in 2000, according to the Census Bureau: https://www.census.gov/foreign-trade/balance/c5700.html#2005.

29. Douglas Irwin, *Clashing over Commerce: A History of US Trade Policy* (University of Chicago Press, 2017), 664.

30. Brilliant interview with the author, October 24, 2023.

31. Karen Lee Scrivo, "Foreign Affairs—Door-to-Door Diplomacy," *National Journal*, May 20, 2000.

32. "US Economists Sign Letter Supporting China's WTO Entry," Office of International Information Programs, US Department of State, April 26, 2000, https://usinfo.org/wf-archive/2000/000426/epf303.htm.

33. "Xin Qiao Electronics," China Labor Watch, January 2, 2000, https://chinalaborwatch.org/xin-qiao-electronics/.

34. Juliet Eilperin and David Broder, "Despite UAW Threat, Low Risk Seen in China Vote," *Washington Post*, May 24, 2000, A14.

35. Matthew Vita and Juliet Eilperin, "China Trade Bill Gains Supporters; 10 Democrats, 4 Republicans Declare on Eve of House Vote," *Washington Post*, May 24, 2000, A1.

36. Bob Davis and Lingling Wei, *Superpower Showdown: How the Battle Between Trump and Xi Threatens a New Cold War* (Harper Business, 2020), 94.

37. William J. Clinton, "Remarks by the President on Passage of Permanent Normal Trade Relations with China," White House, May 24, 2000, https://www.presidency.ucsb.edu/documents/remarks-permanent-normal-trade-relations-with-china.

38. Robert Samuelson, "Overselling the China Deal," *Washington Post*, May 24, 2000, A37.

39. William J. Clinton, "Remarks to the World Economic Forum and a Question-and-Answer Session in Davos, Switzerland," January 29, 2000, in *Public Papers of the Presidents of the United States*, book I for 2000 (US Government Printing Office, 2001), 150–161, https://www.govinfo.gov/content/pkg/PPP-2000-book1/html/PPP-2000-book1-doc-pg150.htm.

40. Anne Swardson, "Clinton Appeals for Compassion in Global Trade; World Economic Forum Told Don't Leave 'Little Guys' Out," *Washington Post*, January 30, 2000, A18.

41. Bill Clinton, *My Life* (Alfred A. Knopf, 2004), 928.

42. Taylor Branch, *The Clinton Tapes: Wrestling History with the President* (Simon & Schuster, 2009), 639.

43. Stephen J. Hadley, ed., *Hand-Off: The Foreign Policy George W. Bush Passed to Barack Obama* (Brookings Institution Press, 2023), 418.

44. "Excerpts from Bush's Remarks on National Security and Arms Policy," *New York Times*, May 24, 2000, A21; Condoleezza Rice, his secretary of state, was even more direct during the primary season, writing: "Trade in general can open up the Chinese economy and, ultimately, its politics, too. This view requires faith in the power of markets and economic freedom to drive political change, but it is a faith confirmed by experiences around the globe." Condoleezza Rice, "Campaign 2000: Promoting the National Interest," *Foreign Affairs* 79, no. 1 (2000): 45–62.

45. George W. Bush, "Remarks to the Los Angeles World Affairs Council in Los Angeles, California," May 29, 2001, in *Public Papers of the Presidents of the United States*, book I for 2001 (US Government Printing Office, 2002), 593–598, https://www.govinfo.gov/content/pkg/PPP-2001-book1/html/PPP-2001-book1-doc-pg593.htm.

46. Jannuzi interview with the author, October 18, 2023.
47. Jeremy Page, "Senators Bring US-Style Politics to China Village," Reuters, August 10, 2001.
48. Hadley, *Hand-Off*, 420.
49. Paul Blustein, "142 Nations Reach Pact on Trade Negotiations," *Washington Post*, November 15, 2001, A1.
50. Irwin, *Clashing over Commerce*, 482.
51. White House, "USTR Briefing on Steel: Press Briefing by US Trade Representative Robert Zoellick," March 5, 2002, https://georgewbush-whitehouse.archives.gov/news/releases/2002/03/text/20020305-10.html.
52. George W. Bush Oral History Project, "Interview 2 with Karl Rove," Miller Center, University of Virginia, 104, https://s3.amazonaws.com/web.poh.transcripts/Rove_Karl2.final3.pdf.
53. "Trade Under Trump," Gallup, 2019, 2, https://news.gallup.com/reports/267386/trade-under-trump-gallup-briefing.aspx.
54. White House, "USTR Briefing on Steel."
55. Elizabeth Becker, "US Tariffs on Steel Are Illegal, World Trade Organization Says," *New York Times*, November 11, 2003, https://www.nytimes.com/2003/11/11/business/us-tariffs-on-steel-are-illegal-world-trade-organization-says.html.
56. Bergsten interview with the author, October 31, 2023.
57. David J. Lynch, "Maryland Factory Feels Heat from China; Trade Prowess Raises Suspicions at US Firm," *USA Today*, March 6, 2007.
58. United States Trade Representative, "2003 Report to Congress on China's WTO Compliance," December 11, 2003, 3, https://ustr.gov/archive/assets/Document_Library/Reports_Publications/2003/asset_upload_file425_4313.pdf.
59. USTR, "2003 Report to Congress," 33.
60. United States Trade Representative, "2022 Report to Congress on China's WTO Compliance," February 2023, 27, https://ustr.gov/sites/default/files/2023-02/2022%20USTR%20Report%20to%20Congress%20on%20China's%20WTO%20Compliance%20-%20Final.pdf.
61. Cass Johnson, in Hearing Before the Committee on Small Business of the House of Representatives, 108th Congress, First Session, "The Effect of Foreign Currency Manipulation on Small Manufacturers and Exporters," June 25, 2003, https://www.govinfo.gov/content/pkg/CHRG-108hhrg92726/html/CHRG-108hhrg92726.htm.
62. George W. Bush Oral History Project, "Interview with John Snow and Chris Smith," Miller Center, University of Virginia, 97, https://s3.amazonaws.com/web.poh.transcripts/Snow_John.final2.pdf.
63. "Snow Business: The Bush Administration's Desire for Stronger Asian Currencies May Backfire," *The Economist*, September 4, 2003; "Fuzzy Economic Thinking; Blaming Beijing," Opinion, *New York Times*, September 3, 2003, https://www.nytimes.com/2003/09/03/opinion/fuzzy-economic-thinking-blaming-beijing.html.
64. David Barboza and Joseph Kahn, "China No Longer to Peg Currency Only to Dollar," *New York Times*, July 22, 2005, https://www.nytimes.com/2005/07/22/business/worldbusiness/china-no-longer-to-peg-currency-only-to-dollar.html.

65. George W. Bush Oral History Project, "Interview with John Snow and Chris Smith," Miller Center, University of Virginia, 99, https://s3.amazonaws.com/web.poh .transcripts/Snow_John.final2.pdf. The reference is to Senator Reed Smoot and Rep. Willis Hawley, principal authors of the disastrous legislation that raised US industrial and agricultural tariffs and ignited a global rush to protectionism.

66. Matt Pottinger, Russell Gold, Michael M. Phillips, and Kate Linebaugh, "Oil Politics: Cnooc Drops Offer for Unocal, Exposing US-Chinese Tensions—Delay Imposed by Fierce Foes in Congress, Plus Missteps by Bidder, Doomed Move—Sale to Chevron All but Certain," *Wall Street Journal*, August 3, 2005, A1.

67. Paula Span, "The Many Lives of Stanley Pottinger," *Washington Post*, May 13, 1995, https://www.washingtonpost.com/archive/lifestyle/1995/05/13/the-many-lives-of -stanley-pottinger/57bd1250-9066-4406-9665-69b168a59248/.

68. Bob Woodward, *The Secret Man* (Simon & Schuster, 2005), 131–135.

69. Pottinger interview with the author, July 11, 2023.

70. Kaufman interview with the author, October 24, 2023.

71. "WHO Issues a Global Alert About Cases of Atypical Pneumonia," World Health Organization, March 12, 2003, https://www.who.int/emergencies/disease -outbreak-news/item/2003_03_12-en.

72. Matt Pottinger and Rebecca Buckman, "Holding Their Breath: A Mystery Illness Spreads in Asia, and So Does Fear—in Hong Kong, Empty Offices and Canceled Travel Plans; a Market for Bambi Masks—Official: It's 'Not Rampaging,'" *Wall Street Journal*, March 28, 2003, A1.

73. Antonio Regalado, Matt Pottinger, and Betsy McKay, "Germ Warfare: Across the Globe, a Race to Prepare for SARS Round 2—amid Fears of New Outbreak, New Research, Assessment of Last Year's Lessons—Culprits: Palm Civets and Labs," *Wall Street Journal*, December 9, 2003, A1.

74. Matt Pottinger, "Outraged Surgeon Forces China to Take a Dose of the Truth—Dr. Jiang Went Public to Put an End to SARS Coverup; Watching a Lie on TV," *Wall Street Journal*, April 22, 2003, A1.

75. Matt Pottinger, "Return of SARS Sparks Concerns About Lab Safety—Eight Cases Are Linked to Researchers in Beijing; WHO May Alter Guidelines," *Wall Street Journal*, April 26, 2004, A13.

76. Pottinger interview with the author, July 11, 2023.

77. Matt Pottinger, "Mightier Than the Pen," *Wall Street Journal*, December 15, 2005, https://www.wsj.com/articles/SB113461636659623128.

78. "A Virtual Conversation with Deputy National Security Advisor Matt Pottinger," Ronald Reagan Foundation and Institute, September 30, 2020, https://www .youtube.com/watch?v=3mSdp-fZEjo.

Chapter 4: China Shock

1. R. C. Forrester, "Obion County," Tennessee Encyclopedia, https://tennesseeencyclo pedia.net/entries/obion-county/.

2. Kate Bronfenbrenner et al., "Impact of US-China Trade Relations on Workers, Wages and Employment," US-China Security Review Commission/US Trade Deficit Review

Commission, June 30, 2001, ii, 18–19, https://govinfo.library.unt.edu/tdrc/research /china1.pdf.

3. Figure for 2008 was nearly $54 billion. Data is from the Bureau of Economic Analysis database: https://apps.bea.gov/iTable/?reqid=2&step=1&isuri=1#eyJhcHBpZCI6Mi wic3RlcHMiOlsxLDIsMyw0LDUsNywxMF0sImRhdGEiOltbIlN0ZXAxUHJvb XB0MSIsIjEiXSxbIlN0ZXAxUHJvb XB0MiIsIjEiXSxbIlN0ZXAyUHJvb XB0My IsIjEiXSxbIlN0ZXAzUHJvb XB0NCIsIjMwIl0sWyJTdGVwNFByb21wdDUiL CI0Il0sWyJTdGVwNVByb21wdDYiLCIxLDIiXSxbIlN0ZXA3UHJvb XB0O CIsWyIxMywxNCwxNSwxNiwxNywxOCwxOSwyMCwyMSwyMiwyMywy NCwyNSwyNiwyNywyOCwyOSwzMCwzMSwzMiwzMywzNCwzNSwzNiwzN ywzOCwzOSw0MCw0MSw0Miw0Myw0OCw0OSw1Miw1NSw1Niw1OCw2MC w2MSw2NSw2NiJdXSxbIlN0ZXA4UHJvb XB0OUEiLFsiMiJdXSxbIlN0ZXA4 UHJvb XB0MTBBIixbIjg1Il1dXX0=.

4. David Autor of the Massachusetts Institute of Technology; Gordon Hanson of Harvard Kennedy School; and David Dorn of the University of Zurich collaborated on a series of research papers under the "China Shock" heading, available here: https:// chinashock.info/.

5. Daron Acemoglu et al., "Import Competition and the Great US Employment Sag of the 2000s," *Journal of Labor Economics* 34, no. S1, part 2 (2016): S147, https:// economics.mit.edu/sites/default/files/publications/Import%20Competition%20 and%20the%20Great%20US%20Employment%20Sag.pdf.

6. Autor interview with the author, August 17, 2023.

7. The Labor Department certified petitions seeking Trade Adjustment Assistance benefits for workers at each of these companies. Details available at https://www.citizen .org/article/trade-adjustment-assistance-database/.

8. Data from the Bureau of Labor Statistics' Quarterly Census of Employment and Wages.

9. US International Trade Commission, "Certain Passenger Vehicle and Light Truck Tires from China," Investigation No. TA-421-7, July 2009, C-3, https://www.usitc .gov/publications/safeguards/pub4085.pdf.

10. US International Trade Commission, "Certain Tires from China," 62.

11. McGuire interview with the author, November 15, 2023.

12. Leath interview with the author, November 14, 2023.

13. Leath interview with the author, November 14, 2023.

14. Goodyear Corporate Responsibility Report, July 22, 2008.

15. Waggoner interview with the author, September 25, 2023.

16. Spending is described in Goodyear's 1998 annual report and its 10-K reports to the Securities and Exchange Commission for 1999 and 2000.

17. US International Trade Commission, "Certain Passenger Vehicle and Light Truck Tires from China," Investigation Nos. 701-TA-522 and 731-TA-1258 (Final), August 2015, 51.

18. Goodyear Tire & Rubber Co., Q3 2002 Earnings call, October 30, 2002.

19. Goodyear Tire & Rubber Co., Q4 2002 Earnings call, April 3, 2003.

20. Goodyear Tire & Rubber Co., *2003 Annual Report*, 2–6, https://corporate.goodyear .com/content/dam/goodyear-corp/documents/annualreports/2003annual.pdf.

21. Goodyear Tire & Rubber Co., *2009 Annual Report*, 1, https://corporate.goodyear
    .com/content/dam/goodyear-corp/documents/annualreports/2009ar.pdf.
22. Goodyear, *2009 Annual Report*, 5.
23. US International Trade Commission, "Certain Tires from China," 51; Zaneta Lowe,
    "Opelika Tire Plant to Shut Down," WTVM, April 13, 2009, https://www.wtvm
    .com/story/10174900/opelika-tire-plant-to-shut-down/.
24. US General Accountability Office, "US-China Trade: The United States Has Not
    Restricted Imports Under the China Safeguard," GAO-05-1056, September 2005,
    https://www.gao.gov/assets/gao-05-1056.pdf.
25. Barshefsky interview with the author, April 19, 2023.
26. Zoellick interview with the author, November 1, 2023.
27. Yeling Tan, *Disaggregating China, Inc.: State Strategies in the Liberal Economic Order*
    (Cornell University Press, 2021), 5–15.
28. Tan, *Disaggregating China, Inc.*, 10.
29. Zoellick interview with the author, November 1, 2023.
30. United States Trade Representative, "Report to Congress on China's WTO Compli-
    ance," December 11, 2007, 5, https://china.usc.edu/sites/default/files/article/attachments
    /2007%20China%20Report%20to%20Congress.pdf.
31. Paul interview with the author, November 17, 2023.
32. Goodyear Tire & Rubber Co., Form 8-K, June 15, 2009. The company reported a
    $60 million after-tax restructuring charge associated with the buyouts.
33. Goodyear earnings call, July 30, 2009.
34. John Bussey, "Get-Tough Policy on Chinese Tires Falls Flat," *Wall Street Journal*,
    January 20, 2012, https://www.wsj.com/articles/SB10001424052970204301404577
    171130489514146.
35. Barack Obama, "Remarks by the President in the State of the Union Address," White
    House, January 24, 2012, https://obamawhitehouse.archives.gov/the-press-office
    /2012/01/24/remarks-president-state-union-address.
36. Gary Clyde Hufbauer and Sean Lowry, "US Tire Tariffs: Saving Few Jobs at High
    Cost," Policy Brief No. 12-9, Peterson Institute for International Economics, April
    2012, https://www.piie.com/publications/policy-briefs/us-tire-tariffs-saving-few-jobs
    -high-cost.
37. Barack Obama, "Remarks by the President in the State of the Union Address," White
    House, January 24, 2012, https://obamawhitehouse.archives.gov/the-press-office
    /2012/01/24/remarks-president-state-union-address.
38. Greer interview with the author, November 14, 2023.
39. Greer interview with the author, November 14, 2023.
40. Goodyear Tire & Rubber Co., Securities and Exchange Commission, Form DEF
    14A, March 14, 2014, 52, http://pdf.secdatabase.com/1482/0001193125-14-099083
    .pdf; Goodyear Tire & Rubber Co., Securities and Exchange Commission, Form
    DEF 14A, March 8, 2011, 36, https://www.sec.gov/Archives/edgar/data/42582
    /000095012311023118/l41553def14a.htm.
41. Waggoner interview with the author, September 25, 2023.
42. Calculations from Bureau of Labor Statistics' Quarterly Census of Employment and
    Wages.

43. Jackie Starks, "Illegally Subsidized Imports Take Jobs from 1,900 Tire Builders; United Steelworkers," available at https://m.usw.org/act/campaigns/fair-trade/profiles /illegally-subsidized-imports-take-jobs.

44. John F. Kennedy, "Special Message to the Congress on Foreign Trade Policy," January 25, 1962, American Presidency Project, UC Santa Barbara, https://www.presidency .ucsb.edu/documents/special-message-the-congress-foreign-trade-policy.

45. Kennedy, "Special Message on Trade Policy."

46. Douglas Irwin, *Clashing over Commerce: A History of US Trade Policy* (University of Chicago Press, 2017), 523.

47. John F. Kennedy, "Remarks upon Signing the Trade Expansion Act," October 11, 1962, American Presidency Project, UC Santa Barbara, https://www.presidency .ucsb.edu/documents/remarks-upon-signing-the-trade-expansion-act.

48. Congressional Research Service, "Trade Adjustment Assistance (TAA) and Its Role in US Trade Policy," August 5, 2013, 7, https://www.everycrsreport.com/reports /R41922.html.

49. Lori G. Kletzer and Howard Rosen, "Easing the Adjustment Burden on US Workers," in *The United States and the World Economy: Foreign Economic Policy for the Next Decade*, ed. C. Fred Bergsten (The Peterson Institute for International Economics, 2005), 317.

50. CRS, "Trade Adjustment Assistance," 8.

51. William Overholt, "The Great Betrayal: How America's Elites Are Failing to Confront the Challenge of Trade Politics," *International Economy* 31, no. 1 (2017): 34, http://www.international-economy.com/TIE_W17_Overholt.pdf.

52. Kletzer and Rosen, "Easing the Adjustment Burden," 317.

53. Alan Blinder, "The Free Trade Paradox: The Bad Politics of a Good Idea," *Foreign Affairs* 98, no. 1 (2019): 119–128.

54. Kletzer and Rosen, "Easing the Adjustment Burden," 323, footnote 14.

55. Social Policy Research Associates and Mathematica Policy Research, "Estimated Impacts for Participants in the Trade Adjustment Assistance (TAA) Program Under the 2002 Amendments," prepared for US Department of Labor Employment and Training Administration, August 2012, 12, https://www.mathematica.org/publications /estimated-impacts-for-participants-in-the-trade-adjustment-assistance-taa-program -under-the-2002-amendments. The study concluded that the program's net benefit to society was a negative $53,802.

56. George W. Bush, "President Bush Discusses Job Training Initiative in North Carolina," White House, November 7, 2003, https://georgewbush-whitehouse.archives .gov/news/releases/2003/11/text/20031107-6.html.

57. Leath interview with the author, August 6, 2023.

58. Jooyoun Park, "Does Occupational Training by the Trade Adjustment Assistance Program Really Help Reemployment?," September 23, 2011, https://papers.ssrn .com/sol3/papers.cfm?abstract_id=1962169.

59. "Estimated Impacts for Trade Adjustment Assistance," X-1.

60. Kara M. Reynolds and John S. Palatucci, "Does Trade Adjustment Assistance Make a Difference?," Working Paper No. 2008-12, American University Department of Economics, August 2008, 2, https://w.american.edu/cas/economics/repec/amu/working papers/2008-12.pdf.

61. Barnow interview with the author, November 9, 2023.
62. Burt S. Barnow and Jeffrey Smith, "Employment and Training Programs," in *Economics of Means-Tested Transfer Programs in the United States*, ed. Robert A. Moffitt, vol. 3 (University of Chicago Press, 2016), 152–153. In 2007, total education and training spending consumed 0.04 percent of US gross domestic product compared with 0.07 percent in 1989.
63. George W. Bush, "Fact Sheet: President Bush Acts on Helping Unemployed Americans," American Presidency Project, UC Santa Barbara, https://www.presidency.ucsb.edu/documents/fact-sheet-president-bush-acts-helping-unemployed-americans.
64. Congressional Research Service, "Supplemental Appropriations FY2003: Iraq Conflict, Afghanistan, Global War on Terrorism, and Homeland Security," May 5, 2003, 3, https://www.everycrsreport.com/files/20030505_RL31829_db039ba8aea300f5819d16e57f303fcfc852e001.pdf.
65. David J. Lynch, "On the Harley Free Trade Brigade: Like Others Before Him, Bush Uses Bikemaker to Tout Globalization," *USA Today*, August 17, 2006, B1.
66. US Department of Defense, "75 Years of the GI Bill: How Transformative It's Been," January 9, 2019, https://www.defense.gov/News/Feature-Stories/story/Article/1727086/75-years-of-the-gi-bill-how-transformative-its-been/. Among the millions of Americans who received a college education only because the GI Bill made it possible was the author's father.
67. Kletzer and Rosen, "Easing the Adjustment Burden," 315–316.
68. Claus Thustrup Kreiner and Michael Svarer, "Danish Flexicurity: Rights and Duties," *Journal of Economic Perspectives* 36, no. 4 (2022): 82, 85, https://pubs.aeaweb.org/doi/pdfplus/10.1257/jep.36.4.81.
69. Kreiner and Svarer, "Danish Flexicurity," 93.
70. Kerwin Kofi Charles, Erik Hurst, and Matthew J. Notowidigdo, "Housing Booms, Manufacturing Decline, and Labor Market Outcomes," Working Paper No. 18949, National Bureau of Economic Research, April 2013, https://www.nber.org/system/files/working_papers/w18949/w18949.pdf.
71. "Restoring America's Promise of Opportunity, Prosperity and Growth," Hamilton Project, Brookings Institution, April 5, 2006, https://www.hamiltonproject.org/wp-content/uploads/2022/11/Restoring_Americas_Promise_of_Opportunity_Prosperity_and_Growth_Transcript.pdf.
72. "Restoring America's Promise."
73. Lynch, "On the Harley Brigade."
74. Aldonas interview with author, November 17, 2023.
75. Grant Aldonas, Robert Lawrence, and Matthew Slaughter, "An Adjustment Assistance Program for American Workers," Financial Services Forum, July 2008, 4.
76. Aldonas, Lawrence, and Slaughter, "An Adjustment Assistance Program," 7.
77. Hubbard interview with the author, November 18, 2023.
78. Susan Houseman, "Understanding the Decline of US Manufacturing Employment," Working Paper No. 18-287, Upjohn Institute, 2018, 28, https://research.upjohn.org/up_workingpapers/287/.
79. Economists' estimates vary for the relative contribution of trade and technology to manufacturing job losses. Michael Hicks and Srikant Devaraj of Ball State

University conclude that technology is responsible for 88 percent of factory jobs lost between 2000 and 2010: Michael Hicks and Srikant Devaraj, "The Myth and the Reality of Manufacturing in America," Center for Business and Economic Research, Ball State University, April 2017, 6; Melissa Kearney and Katharine Abraham of the University of Maryland find that competition from Chinese imports is to blame for roughly twice as much of the manufacturing employment decline between 1999 and 2018 as was automation: Melissa Kearney and Katharine Abraham, "Explaining the Decline in the US Employment-to-Population Ratio," Working Paper No. 24333, National Bureau of Economic Research, February 2018, 51, https://www.nber.org/system/files/working_papers/w24333/w24333.pdf.

80. David H. Autor et al., "The China Syndrome: Local Labor Market Effects of Import Competition in the United States," *American Economic Review* 103, no. 6 (2013): 2140, https://economics.mit.edu/sites/default/files/publications/the%20china%20syndrome%202013.pdf.

81. Johnson interview with the author, March 12, 2024.

82. Irwin, *Clashing over Commerce*, 666–667.

83. Robert C. Feenstra and Akira Sasahara, "The 'China Shock,' Exports and US Employment: A Global Input-Output Analysis," Working Paper No. 24022, National Bureau of Economic Research, November 2017, 3, https://www.nber.org/papers/w24022.

84. Zhi Wang et al., "Re-Examining the Effects of Trading with China on Local Labor Markets: A Supply Chain Perspective," Working Paper No. 24866, National Bureau of Economic Research, October 2018, 2, https://www.nber.org/papers/w24886.

85. Data from the Tennessee Department of Health: https://www.tn.gov/content/dam/tn/health/documents/TN_Marriages_Divorces_-_2009.pdf.

86. August Benzow, "Economic Renaissance or Fleeting Recovery? Left-Behind Counties See Boom in Jobs and Businesses amid Widening Divides," Economic Innovation Group, July 8, 2024, https://eig.org/left-behind-places/.

87. Nicholas Bloom et al., "The China Shock Revisited: Job Reallocation and Industry Switching in US Labor Markets," Working Paper No. 33098, National Bureau of Economic Research, November 2024, http://www.nber.org/papers/w33098.

88. Zhi Wang et al., "Re-Examining the Effects," 56.

89. Yellen interview with the author, June 28, 2024.

90. Justin R. Pierce, Peter K. Schott, and Cristina Tello-Trillo, "To Find Relative Earnings Gains After the China Shock, Look Outside Manufacturing and Upstream," Working Paper No. 32438, National Bureau of Economic Research, May 2024, https://www.nber.org/papers/w32438.

91. Bloom et al., "The China Shock Revisited."

92. Patrick J. Purcell, "Geographic Mobility and Annual Earnings in the United States," *Social Security Bulletin* 80, no. 2 (2002): chart 1, https://www.ssa.gov/policy/docs/ssb/v80n2/v80n2p1.html.

93. Waggoner interview with the author, November 14, 2023.

94. Lisa B. Kahn et al., "Racial and Ethnic Inequality and the China Shock," Working Paper No. 30646, National Bureau of Economic Research, July 2024, 35, https://www.nber.org/system/files/working_papers/w30646/w30646.pdf.

95. Kahn et al., "Racial and Ethnic Inequality," 29.
96. Kahn et al., "Racial and Ethnic Inequality," 38.
97. Zillow Home Value Index, for Single-family Home Time Series by county, accessed here: https://www.zillow.com/research/data/.
98. Martin Neil Baily and Robert Z. Lawrence, "What Happened to the Great US Job Machine? The Role of Trade and Electronic Offshoring," *Brookings Papers on Economic Activity*, no. 2 (2004): 213, https://www.brookings.edu/wp-content/uploads/2004/06/2004b_bpea_baily.pdf.

Chapter 5: Sleepwalking Toward Disaster

1. Hearing Before the Committee on Foreign Relations, United States Senate, 110th Congress, Second Session, "United States–China Relations in the Era of Globalization," May 15, 2008, https://www.govinfo.gov/content/pkg/CHRG-110shrg48013/pdf/CHRG-110shrg48013.pdf.
2. Fox Butterfield, "Senators Cautioned on Taiwan by Deng," *New York Times*, April 20, 1979, A9.
3. US Department of State, "Deng Xiaoping Meeting with Codel Church/Javits," April 19, 1979, confidential, https://aad.archives.gov/aad/createpdf?rid=13829&dt=2776&dl=2169.
4. Philip Taubman, "US and Peking Join in Tracking Missiles in Soviet," *New York Times*, June 18, 1981, A1; Rush Doshi, *The Long Game: China's Grand Strategy to Displace American Order* (Oxford University Press, 2021), 47.
5. Joe Biden, in "US-China Relations" hearing, 12, 19, and 48.
6. Joe Biden, in "US-China Relations" hearing, 2.
7. Robert B. Zoellick, deputy secretary of state, "Whither China: From Membership to Responsibility?," remarks to the National Committee on US-China Relations, September 21, 2005, https://2001-2009.state.gov/s/d/former/zoellick/rem/53682.htm.
8. David J. Lynch, "Suspect Imports Raise Questions About the Real Value of Getting Lowest Price; 'Sometimes, It's a Shock to Discover How Poor the Quality Processes Are,'" Money section, *USA Today*, July 3, 2007 cover story.
9. David J. Lynch, "FBI Goes on Offensive vs. Tech Spies; China Linked to About One-Third of All Economic Espionage Cases," Money section, *USA Today*, July 24, 2007, cover story.
10. US Department of Justice, "Former Metaldyne Employees Sentenced to Prison in Conspiracy to Steal Confidential Business Information to Benefit Chinese Competitor," February 13, 2009, https://www.justice.gov/sites/default/files/criminal-ccips/legacy/2012/03/15/lockwoodSent2.pdf.
11. Laura Silver et al., "How Global Public Opinion of China Has Shifted in the Xi Era," Pew Research Center, September 28, 2022, https://www.pewresearch.org/global/2022/09/28/how-global-public-opinion-of-china-has-shifted-in-the-xi-era/.
12. James Mann, *The China Fantasy* (Viking Penguin, 2007), 25–26.
13. David M. Lampton, "*The China Fantasy*, Fantasy," review of *The China Fantasy: How Our Leaders Explain Away Chinese Repression*, by James Mann, *China Quarterly* (September 2007): 745–749.

14. Mann interview with the author, December 7, 2023.
15. Pottinger interview with the author, October 27, 2023.
16. Henry M. Paulson, *On the Brink: Inside the Race to Stop the Collapse of the Global Financial System* (Business Plus, 2010), 82–83.
17. Steven J. Hadley, ed., *Hand-Off: The Foreign Policy George W. Bush Passed to Barack Obama* (Washington: Brookings Institution Press, 2023), 423.
18. Hadley, *Hand-Off*, 424.
19. Interview with the author, December 7, 2023.
20. Jie Li, "International System in Transition: From the Perspective of Financial Crisis," *China International Studies* 16 (2009): 12.
21. Henry M. Paulson Jr., *Dealing with China: An Insider Unmasks the New Economic Superpower* (Twelve, 2015), 240.
22. US Department of the Treasury, "Transcript of US Delegation Press Conference at the Fourth Meeting of the US China Strategic Economic Dialogue," June 18, 2008, https://home.treasury.gov/news/press-releases/hp1048.
23. US Department of the Treasury, "Transcript of US Delegation Press Conference."
24. Paulson Jr., *Dealing with China*, 259.
25. Yeling Tan, "How the WTO Changed China: The Mixed Legacy of Economic Engagement," *Foreign Affairs* 100, no. 2 (2021): 90–102.
26. Timothy Geithner, *Stress Test: Reflections on Financial Crises* (Crown, 2014), 357.
27. Andrew Ross Sorkin, *Too Big to Fail: The Inside Story of How Wall Street and Washington Fought to Save the Financial System—and Themselves* (Viking Penguin, 2009), 445.
28. Paulson Jr., *Dealing with China*, 256.
29. Interview with the author, December 7, 2023.
30. Paulson Jr., *Dealing with China*, 251.
31. Paulson interview with the author, December 12, 2023.
32. Paulson Jr., *Dealing with China*, 249.
33. The relationship between bilateral merchandise and financial flows is not this direct. Flows of goods and cash must balance at the global level, though not for each country-to-country account.
34. Paulson Jr., *On the Brink*, 64, 439–440.
35. Ben S. Bernanke et al., "International Capital Flows and the Returns to Safe Assets in the United States, 2003–2007," International Finance Discussion Paper No. 1014, Board of Governors of the Federal Reserve System, February 2011, 20, https://www.federalreserve.gov/pubs/ifdp/2011/1014/ifdp1014.pdf.
36. Foreign purchases of US government bonds shaved eighty basis points off the yield on the ten-year Treasury in the year ending May 2005, say Francis E. Warnock and Veronica Cacdac Warnock, "International Capital Flows and US Interest Rates," *Journal of International Money and Finance* 28, no. 6 (2009), 904, https://www.sciencedirect.com/science/article/abs/pii/S0261560609000461.
37. "The Great Pandemic Mortgage Refinance Boom," *Liberty Street Economics* (blog), Federal Reserve Bank of New York, May 15, 2023, https://libertystreeteconomics.newyorkfed.org/2023/05/the-great-pandemic-mortgage-refinance-boom/.

38. Carol Bertaut et al., "ABS Inflows to the United States and the Global Financial Crisis," International Finance Discussion Paper No. 1028, Board of Governors of the Federal Reserve System, August 2011, 33–34, https://www.federalreserve.gov/pubs /ifdp/2011/1028/ifdp1028.pdf.

39. Bernanke et al., "International Capital Flows," 3.

40. Setser interview with the author, December 1, 2023.

41. Anthony di Iorio, "Deutsche Bank 2006 Results: Roadshow Edinburgh/Dublin," March 15–16, 2007, https://investor-relations.db.com/files/documents/other-presentations -and-events/Roadshow_EDI_DUB_15-16_Mar_Tony_di_Iorio.pdf?language_id=1.

42. Tamim Bayoumi, *Unfinished Business: The Unexplored Causes of the Financial Crisis and the Lessons Yet to Be Learned* (International Monetary Fund, 2018), 10, 30.

43. Jill Treanor, "Farewell to the FSA—and the Bleak Legacy of the Light-Touch Regu- lator," *The Guardian*, March 23, 2013, https://www.theguardian.com/business/2013 /mar/24/farewell-fsa-bleak-legacy-light-touch-regulator.

44. Alan Greenspan, "World Finance and Risk Management," remarks, Federal Re- serve, September 25, 2002, https://www.federalreserve.gov/boarddocs/speeches/2002 /200209253/default.htm.

45. "United States Article IV Consultation," International Monetary Fund, August 2007, 26, https://www.imf.org/external/pubs/ft/scr/2007/cr07264.pdf.

46. Bertaut et al., "ABS Inflows," 2.

47. Robert McCauley, "The 2008 Crisis: Transpacific or Transatlantic?," *BIS Quarterly Review*, December 2018, 49, https://www.bis.org/publ/qtrpdf/r_qt1812f.pdf; Viral Acharya and Philipp Schnabl, "Do Global Banks Spread Global Imbalances? The Case of Asset-Backed Commercial Paper During the Financial Crisis of 2007–09," paper presented at the 10th Jacques Polak Annual Research Conference, hosted by the International Monetary Fund, Washington, DC, November 5–6, 2009, 2, https://www.imf.org/external/np/res/seminars/2009/arc/pdf/acharya.pdf.

48. Details of Sachsen's holdings, including its Ormond Quay holdings and funding are taken from Acharya and Schnabl.

49. Acharya and Schnabl, "Do Global Banks?," 23.

50. Martin Hellwig, "Germany and the Financial Crisis 2007–2017," draft version, June 2018, 18, https://www.riksbank.se/globalassets/media/konferenser/2018/germany-and -financial-crises-2007-2017.pdf.

51. Aaron Kirchfield and Jacqueline Simmons, "Lehman Toxic Debt Advice Led Leipzig Bank to Ruin Via Dublin," Bloomberg News, October 28, 2008, https://www.anderson .ucla.edu/documents/areas/adm/loeb/09g10.pdf.

52. National Commission on the Causes of the Financial and Economic Crisis in the United States, *Financial Crisis Inquiry Report* (US Government Printing Office, 2011), 140, https://fcic-static.law.stanford.edu/cdn_media/fcic-reports/fcic_final_report _full.pdf.

53. Deborah Lucas, "Measuring the Cost of Bailouts," *Annual Review of Financial Economics* 11 (December 2019): 85–108, https://www.annualreviews.org/content /journals/10.1146/annurev-financial-110217-022532.

54. National Commission on Crisis, *Financial Crisis Inquiry Report*, 352.

55. Distributional Financial Accounts, Board of Governors of the Federal Reserve System, available at https://www.federalreserve.gov/releases/z1/dataviz/dfa/compare/chart/#quarter:73;series:Assets;demographic:networth;population:all;units:levels.

56. US Treasury, "Report on Foreign Holdings of US Securities at End-June 2008," June 30, 2009, https://home.treasury.gov/news/press-releases/tg116#:~:text=The%20survey%20measured%20foreign%20holdings,of%20non%2DABS%20securities)%2C; US Treasury, "Report on Foreign Holdings of US Long-Term Securities as of March 31, 2000," April 2002, https://ticdata.treasury.gov/Publish/shl2000r.pdf.

57. Anton Brender and Florence Pisani, *Global Imbalances and the Collapse of Globalized Finance* (Center for European Policy Studies, 2010), 1.

58. Sharada Dharmasankar and Bhash Mazumder, "Have Borrowers Recovered from Foreclosures During the Great Recession?," *Chicago Fed Letter*, no. 370 (June 2016): 1–5, https://www.chicagofed.org/publications/chicago-fed-letter/2016/370.

59. Bernanke et al., "International Capital Flows," 16.

60. Bayoumi interview with the author, September 15, 2023.

61. Ben Bernanke, *21st Century Monetary Policy: The Federal Reserve from the Great Inflation to COVID-19* (W. W. Norton, 2022), 163.

62. CNBC's Rick Santelli Chicago Tea Party, February 12, 2009, https://www.youtube.com/watch?v=zp-Jw-5Kx8k.

63. Elizabeth Price Foley, *The Tea Party Movement: Three Principles* (Cambridge University Press, 2012), 76.

64. Walter Russell Mead, "The Tea Party and American Foreign Policy: What Populism Means For Globalism," *Foreign Affairs* 90, no. 2 (2011): 34.

65. Ginia Bellafante, "Gunning for Wall Street with Faulty Aim," *New York Times*, September 25, 2011, https://www.nytimes.com/2011/09/25/nyregion/protesters-are-gunning-for-wall-street-with-faulty-aim.html.

66. John Judis, *The Populist Explosion* (Columbia Global Reports, 2016), 60.

67. Wallach interview with the author, December 18, 2023.

68. "Public Divided over Occupy Wall Street Movement; Tea Party Draws More Opposition Than Support," Pew Research Center, October 24, 2011, https://www.pewresearch.org/politics/2011/10/24/public-divided-over-occupy-wall-street-movement/.

69. Barack Obama, "Remarks by the President on the Economy in Osawatomie, Kansas," White House, December 6, 2011, https://obamawhitehouse.archives.gov/the-press-office/2011/12/06/remarks-president-economy-osawatomie-kansas#:~:text=I'm%20here%20in%20Kansas,Democratic%20values%20or%20Republican%20values.

70. Wallach interview with the author, December 18, 2023.

71. "Gregory with VP Biden at Washington Ideas Forum," *NBC News*, October 5, 2011, https://www.nbcnews.com/video/gregory-with-vp-biden-at-washington-ideas-forum-44580419829.

72. "Fukushima Daiichi Accident," World Nuclear Association, updated August 2023, https://world-nuclear.org/information-library/safety-and-security/safety-of-plants/fukushima-daiichi-accident.aspx.

73. Marc Levinson, *The Box: How the Shipping Container Made the World Smaller and the World Economy Bigger* (Princeton University Press, 2006), 1.

74. Measured in twenty-foot equivalent (TEU) units. Annual data from the United Nations Conference on Trade and Trade Development, "Handbook of Statistics 2023," https://hbs.unctad.org/maritime-transport-indicators/, and 1990 figure from Linton Nightingale, "One Hundred Ports: The Numbers Tell the Story," Lloyd's List, August 18, 2022, https://lloydslist.com/LL1141949/One-Hundred-Ports-The-numbers-tell-the-story#:~:text=Container%20port%20volumes%20went%20through,a%20figure%20approaching%20250m%20teu.

75. Bill Hurles, retired GM supply chain executive, interview with the author, December 15, 2023.

76. Levinson, *The Box*, 266.

77. Congressional Research Service, "The Motor Vehicle Supply Chain: Effects of the Japanese Earthquake and Tsunami," May 23, 2011, 7, https://www.everycrsreport.com/reports/R41831.html.

78. Dennis Fisher, "Japan Disaster Shakes Up Supply-Chain Strategies," *Harvard Business School Working Knowledge*, May 31, 2011, https://hbswk.hbs.edu/item/japan-disaster-shakes-up-supply-chain-strategies.

79. Christoph E. Boehm et al., "The Role of Global Supply Chains in the Transmission of Shocks: Firm-Level Evidence from the Tōhoku Earthquake," Finance and Economics Discussion Series (FEDS) Note, Board of Governors of the Federal Reserve System, May 2, 2016, https://www.federalreserve.gov/econresdata/notes/feds-notes/2016/role-of-global-supply-chains-in-the-transmission-of-shocks-20160502.html.

80. Yossi Sheffi, *The Power of Resilience: How the Best Companies Manage the Unexpected* (MIT Press, 2017), 7, 54–63.

81. "Motor Vehicle Supply Chain," 13.

82. Flextronics International Ltd., Q4 2011 Earnings Calls, April 27, 2011.

83. Flextronics International Ltd., Form 10-Q, for the period ending July 1, 2011, filed August 9, 2011, 19, https://d1lge852tjjqow.cloudfront.net/CIK-0000866374/34e68be7-72dd-4f6d-b1ad-603aab55eba6.pdf.

84. Sheffi, *The Power of Resilience*, 67.

85. Flextronics International Ltd., Form 10-Q, for the period ending December 31, 2011, filed February 2, 2012, 5, https://d1lge852tjjqow.cloudfront.net/CIK-0000866374/47a48382-dffc-4444-92b2-5ba049da26e7.pdf.

86. Sheffi, *The Power of Resilience*, 23–25.

87. "World Economic Outlook: War Sets Back the Global Recovery," International Monetary Fund, April 2022, 99, https://www.imf.org/en/Publications/WEO/Issues/2022/04/19/world-economic-outlook-april-2022#:~:text=War%20slows%20recovery&text=Global%20growth%20is%20projected%20to,percent%20over%20the%20medium%20term.

88. Hurles interview with author, December 15, 2023.

89. "Corporate Profits After Tax (Without IVA and CCAdj)/Gross Domestic Product," FRED Economic Data, Federal Reserve Bank of St. Louis, https://fred.stlouisfed.org/graph/?g=1Pik.

90. James B. Rice Jr., "The Japan Disaster: What Lessons Learned for the Supply Chain?," talk at Imperial College London, August 12, 2011, 7, https://www.imperial.ac.uk

/media/imperial-college/research-centres-and-groups/centre-for-transport-studies
/seminars/2011/The-Japan-Disaster-What-Lessons-Learned-for-the-Supply-Chain.pdf.

91. Barry Lynn, "The Fragility That Threatens the World's Industrial Systems," *Financial Times*, 19.

92. Michael T. Osterholm, "Preparing for the Next Pandemic," *Foreign Affairs* 84, no. 4 (2005): 24–37.

93. Lynn interview with the author, November 28, 2023.

94. Barack Obama, *A Promised Land* (Crown, 2020), 176–177, 346.

95. Evan Osnos, *Joe Biden: The Life, the Run, and What Matters Now* (Scribner, 2020), 104.

96. Full text: "Biden's Announcement That He Won't Run for President," *Washington Post*, October 21, 2015, https://www.washingtonpost.com/news/post-politics/wp /2015/10/21/full-text-bidens-announcement-that-he-wont-run-for-president/.

Chapter 6: No More Money into China

1. Richard Byrne Reilly, "VC Steve Jurvetson: Elon Musk Is More Capable Than Steve Jobs Was," *VentureBeat*, April 24, 2014, https://venturebeat.com/entrepreneur/vc -steve-jurvetson-elon-musk-is-more-capable-than-steve-jobs-was/.

2. Sharon Lim, "DFJ Leads $5 Million Financing Round of China's Yeepay," *Infrastructure Investor*, October 6, 2006, https://www.infrastructureinvestor.com/dfj -leads-5m-financing-round-of-chinas-yeepay/.

3. Wang Xu, "Pay Package," *China Business Weekly*, June 25, 2007, https://www.china daily.com.cn/bw/2007-06/25/content_901146.htm.

4. YeePay did not respond to multiple emailed requests for an interview with company executives. Chen Yu, the company's president and co-founder, also did not respond to an interview request.

5. This account of the YeePay situation comes from an interview with Draper on April 10, 2023.

6. US Ambassador Jon Huntsman, "Portrait of Vice President Xi Jinping: 'Ambitious Survivor' of the Cultural Revolution," confidential cable, November 16, 2009, available at WikiLeaks: https://www.wikileaks.org/plusd/cables/09BEIJING3128_a .html.

7. US Ambassador Clark Randt, "Zhejiang Party Secretary Touts Economic Successes and Work Towards Rule of Law at Ambassador's Dinner," confidential cable, March 19, 2007, available at WikiLeaks: https://www.wikileaks.org/plusd/cables/07BEI JING1840_a.html.

8. Chun Han Wong, *Party of One: The Rise of Xi Jinping and China's Superpower Future* (Avid Reader, 2023), 42.

9. Sebastian Mallaby, *The Power Law: Venture Capital and the Making of the New Future* (Penguin, 2022), 248.

10. Joseph Kahn, "China Detains Dissident, Citing Subversion," *New York Times*, December 30, 2007, https://www.nytimes.com/2007/12/30/world/asia/web30china .html.

11. May Hui, "TA Associates Invests in Venture Capital-Backed YeePay," *Greater China Private Equity Review*, March 18, 2015.

12. "China Headlines: New Regulation on Third-Party Payments Stirs Controversy," Xinhua's China Economic Information Service, August 3, 2015, https://www.ecns .cn/business/2015/08-03/175594.shtml.

13. "Chinese Police Warn Third Party Payment Firms Against Pornography," Xinhua News Agency, July 20, 2009.

14. Zhou Xiaochuan, "Order No. 2 [2010] of the People's Bank of China-Administrative Measures for the Payment Services Provided by Non-Financial Institutions," People's Bank of China, June 14, 2010, http://www.pbc.gov.cn/en/3688253/3689009/37884 74/3926128/index.html.

15. "PBOC Punishes Some Third-Party Payment Firms on Acquirer Business," Xinhua News Agency, March 31, 2014.

16. "China's Unionpay Fines Payment Companies for Unlawful Operations," Electronic Payments International, July 29, 2014, https://www.electronicpaymentsinternational .com/news/china-unionpay-fines-payment-companies-for-unlawful-operations -290714-4328959/. The standard service fees, which are divided among the bank that issued the card, the payment firm, and UnionPay, vary by type of business. Restaurants, for example, paid 1.25 percent of the transaction value while supermarkets paid 0.38 percent.

17. "PBOC Punishes Payment Companies for Mishandling Bank Card Transactions," Caixin Online, September 16, 2014, https://www.caixinglobal.com/2014-09-16/pboc -punishes-payment-companies-for-mishandling-bank-card-transactions-101013044 .html.

18. "China Headlines: New Regulation on Third-Party Payments Stirs Controversy," Xinhua's China Economic Information Service, August 3, 2015, https://www.ecns .cn/business/2015/08-03/175594.shtml.

19. Chiu-Wan Liu, "The Chinese Fintech Boom and the Consolidation of Recentralized Authoritarian Capitalism," *Asian Survey* 61, no. 6 (2021): 981, https://doi .org/10.1525/as.2021.1428111.

20. Duncan Clark interview with the author, November 3, 2023.

21. "China Protests by Fanya Metal Exchange Investors," *BBC News*, September 21, 2015, https://www.bbc.com/news/world-asia-china-34318344; Sun Yu and Thomas Hale, "China Fights a Financial Fraud Explosion," *Financial Times*, December 2, 2021, https://www.ft.com/content/77f61cf0-5b9d-4ea8-854a-4f220039dcb7.

22. "Fool's Gold: An Investigative Report," Radio Free Asia, December 20, 2016, https:// www.rfa.org/english/multimedia/fanya-12202016115113.html.

23. Richard McGregor, *The Party: The Secret World of China's Communist Rulers* (Harper-Collins, 2010), 52.

24. Rieschel interview with the author, October 20, 2023.

25. Source interview with the author, July 10, 2023, and subsequent emails.

26. "Local Government Debt: Interest Payment: Heilongjiang: Qitaihe," CEIC, https://www.ceicdata.com/en/china/local-government-debt-prefecture-level -city-interest-payment/cn-local-government-debt-interest-payment-heilongjiang -qitaihe; Meredith Chen, "How China's Smaller Private Firms May Be Paying the Price for Huge Local Government Debts," *South China Morning Post*, November 3, 2024, https://www.scmp.com/news/china/politics/article/3285016

/how-chinas-smaller-private-firms-may-be-paying-price-huge-local-government
-debts.

27. Nicholas Lardy, *Integrating China into the Global Economy* (Brookings Institution Press, 2002), 34.

28. Lardy, *Integrating China*, 23.

29. Yeling Tan, "How the WTO Changed China: The Mixed Legacy of Economic Engagement," *Foreign Affairs* 100, no. 2 (2021): 6.

30. Lee Branstetter and Nicholas Lardy, "China's Embrace of Globalization," Working Paper No. 12373, National Bureau of Economic Research, July 2006, 30, https://www.nber.org/system/files/working_papers/w12373/w12373.pdf.

31. Tan, "How the WTO Changed China," 9.

32. Jeffrey Bader, *Obama and China's Rise: An Insider's Account of America's Asia Strategy* (Brookings Institution Press, 2012), 69.

33. Bader, *Obama and China's Rise*, 113–114.

34. Office of the US Trade Representative, "Chinese Export Subsidies Under the 'Demonstration Bases–Common Service Platform' Program Terminated Thanks to US-China Agreement," April 14, 2016, https://ustr.gov/about-us/policy-offices/press-office/press-releases/2016/april/chinese-export-subsidies-under.

35. Froman interview with the author, December 8, 2023.

36. US Department of Commerce, International Trade Administration, "Aluminum Extrusions from the People's Republic of China: Preliminary Affirmative Countervailing Duty Determination, and Alignment of Final Determination with Final Antidumping Duty Determination," March 11, 2024, https://www.federalregister.gov/documents/2024/03/11/2024-05070/aluminum-extrusions-from-the-peoples-republic-of-china-preliminary-affirmative-countervailing-duy.

37. Data drawn from annual Pew Research Center reports: https://www.pewresearch.org/global/2014/07/14/chapter-2-chinas-image/ and https://www.pewresearch.org/global/2011/07/13/chapter-4-views-of-china/.

38. Froman interview with the author, December 8, 2023.

39. "Report of the Commission on the Theft of American Intellectual Property," National Bureau of Asian Research, May 2013, 3, https://www.nbr.org/wp-content/uploads/pdfs/publications/IP_Commission_Report.pdf.

40. Hickton interview with the author, December 28, 2023.

41. Dennis Wilder, former deputy associate director of the Central Intelligence Agency's East Asia Mission Center, interview with the author, January 2, 2024.

42. Tom Donilon, "Remarks by Tom Donilon, National Security Advisor to the President, the United States and the Asia-Pacific in 2013," White House, March 11, 2013, https://obamawhitehouse.archives.gov/the-press-office/2013/03/11/remarks-tom-donilon-national-security-advisor-president-united-states-an.

43. "US Charges Five Chinese Military Hackers for Cyber Espionage Against US Corporations and a Labor Organization for Commercial Advantage," Office of Public Affairs, US Department of Justice, May 19, 2014, https://www.justice.gov/opa/pr/us-charges-five-chinese-military-hackers-cyber-espionage-against-us-corporations-and-labor.

44. "America, China and the Hacking Threat," Editorial Board, *New York Times*, May 25, 2014, https://www.nytimes.com/2014/05/25/opinion/sunday/america-china-and -the-hacking-threat.html.

45. Tom Fontaine, "Chinese Hacker Indictment a Publicity Stunt, Says Former Governor Ridge," *Trib Total Media*, June 10, 2014, https://archive.triblive.com/local/pittsburgh -allegheny/chinese-hacker-indictment-a-publicity-stunt-says-former-governor-ridge/.

46. Karoun Demirjian, "Chinese Hackers Stole 60,000 State Dept. Emails in Breach Reported in July," *New York Times*, September 27, 2023, https://www.nytimes .com/2023/09/27/us/politics/chinese-hackers-state-department.html.

47. National Security Agency, "Huawei Surveillance Program Notes," Snowden Archive, accessed December 31, 2023, https://snowden.glendon.yorku.ca/items/show/789.

48. Ellen Nakashima, "Indictment of Chinese Hackers Part of Broad Strategy," *Washington Post*, May 23, 2014, A8.

49. Ellen Nakashima, "US Developing Sanctions Against China over Cyberthefts," *Washington Post*, August 30, 2015, https://www.washingtonpost.com/world/national -security/administration-developing-sanctions-against-china-over-cyberespionage /2015/08/30/9b2910aa-480b-11e5-8ab4-c73967a143d3_story.html.

50. White House, "Remarks by President Obama and President Xi of the People's Republic of China in Joint Press Conference," September 25, 2015, https:// obamawhitehouse.archives.gov/the-press-office/2015/09/25/remarks-president -obama-and-president-xi-peoples-republic-china-joint.

51. Hearing Before the Committee on Armed Services, United States Senate, "Hearing to Receive Testimony on United States Cyber Command in Review of the Defense Authorization Request for Fiscal Year 2017 and the Future Years Defense Plan," April 5, 2016, 70, https://www.armed-services.senate.gov/imo/media/doc/16-35_4-05-16.pdf.

52. David J. Lynch and Geoff Dyer, "Chinese Hacking of US Companies Declines," *Financial Times*, April 13, 2016, https://www.ft.com/content/d81e30de-00e4-11e6 -99cb-83242733f755.

53. "US Charges Three Chinese Hackers Who Work at Internet Security Firm for Hacking Three Corporations for Commercial Advantage," Office of Public Affairs, US Department of Justice, November 27, 2017, https://www.justice.gov/opa/pr/us-charges-three -chinese-hackers-who-work-internet-security-firm-hacking-three-corporations.

54. Josh Chin, "Chinese Firm Behind Alleged Hacking Was Disbanded This Month," *Wall Street Journal*, November 29, 2017, https://www.wsj.com/articles/chinese-firm -behind-alleged-hacking-was-disbanded-this-month-1511881494.

55. Chin, "Chinese Firm Disbanded"; Council on Foreign Relations, "Indictment of APT 3 Threat Actors," November 2017, https://www.cfr.org/cyber-operations/indictment -apt-3-threat-actors.

56. Michael S. Chase, "Xi in Command: Downsizing and Reorganizing the People's Liberation Army," Commentary, RAND Corporation, September 14, 2015, https://www .rand.org/pubs/commentary/2015/09/xi-in-command-downsizing-and-reorganizing -the-peoples.html.

57. "US Charges Three Chinese Hackers Who Work at Internet Security Firm for Hacking Three Corporations for Commercial Advantage," Office of Public Affairs,

US Department of Justice, November 27, 2017, 8, https://www.justice.gov/opa/pr
/us-charges-three-chinese-hackers-who-work-internet-security-firm-hacking-three
-corporations.

58. Dan Levin, "China Names 14 Generals Suspected of Corruption," *New York Times*,
March 2, 2015, A10, https://www.nytimes.com/2015/03/03/world/china-names-14
-generals-suspected-of-corruption.html.

59. Evanina interview with the author, December 29, 2023.

60. International Trade Commission, "US-Korea Free Trade Agreement: Potential
Economy-Wide and Selected Sectoral Effects," Investigation No. TA-2104-24,
USITC Publication 3949, September 2007, https://www.usitc.gov/publications/pub
3949.pdf.

61. John Parkinson, "House Passes Three Free Trade Agreements," *ABC News*,
October 13, 2011, https://abcnews.go.com/blogs/politics/2011/10/house-passes-three
-free-trade-agreeements; Jim Abrams, "Obama Signs Three Trade Deals, Biggest
Since NAFTA," *NBC News*, October 21, 2011, https://www.nbcnews.com/id/wbna
44989775.

62. China's trade status was made permanent seven years after the NAFTA vote with
73 Democratic votes. When the House approved a Central American trade deal in
2005, only 15 Democrats joined the majority.

63. Hillary Clinton, "America's Pacific Century: The future of politics will be decided
in Asia, not Afghanistan or Iraq, and the United States will be right at the center
of the action," *Foreign Policy*, October 11, 2011, https://foreignpolicy.com/2011/10/11
/americas-pacific-century/#:~:text=In%20Asia%2C%20they%20ask%20whether,We
%20can%2C%20and%20we%20will.

64. Wallach interview with the author, December 18, 2023.

65. David J. Lynch, "Obama's Goals Clash as Allies Say Trade Push Widens Income
Gap," Bloomberg News, January 30, 2014.

66. Rep. Mark Pocan, "Democrats Call on Administration to Release Confidential Labor Advisory Committee Report," press release, June 11, 2015, https://pocan.house
.gov/sites/evo-subsites/pocan-evo.house.gov/files/wysiwyg_uploaded/Modified%20
TPP%20Interim%20Report%20redacted%20052915.pdf.

67. Lauren French, Jake Sherman, and John Bresnahan, "Democrats Deal Obama Huge
Defeat on Trade," *Politico*, June 12, 2015, https://www.politico.com/story/2015/06
/barack-obama-capitol-hill-trade-deal-118927.

68. Public Law 114-26, "Trade Promotion Authority," 129 STAT 320, June 29, 2015,
https://www.congress.gov/114/plaws/publ26/PLAW-114publ26.pdf.

69. Cutler interview with the author, December 18, 2023.

70. Jonathan Weisman, "Trade Authority Bill Wins Final Approval in Senate," *New York
Times*, June 24, 2015, https://www.nytimes.com/2015/06/25/business/trade-pact
-senate-vote-obama.html.

71. Glenn Kessler, "Fact Check: Clinton Did Call TPP 'The Gold Standard,'" *Washington Post*, September 26, 2016, https://www.washingtonpost.com/politics/2016
/live-updates/general-election/real-time-fact-checking-and-analysis-of-the-first
-presidential-debate/fact-check-clinton-dod-call-tpp-the-gold-standard/.

72. Mark Murray, Chuck Todd, and Andrew Rafferty, "First Read: Jeb Bush Leads the GOP Pack," *NBC News*, June 22, 2015, https://www.nbcnews.com/meet-the-press /first-read-jeb-bush-leads-gop-pack-n379601.

73. Simas interview with the author, January 5, 2024.

74. *Time* staff, "Here's Donald Trump's Presidential Announcement Speech," *Time*, June 16, 2015, https://time.com/3923128/donald-trump-announcement-speech/.

75. Froman interview with the author, December 8, 2023.

76. "Real Median Household Income in the United States," FRED, Federal Reserve Bank of St. Louis, updated September 11, 2024, https://fred.stlouisfed.org/series /MEHOINUSA672N.

77. Mayhill Fowler, "Obama: No Surprise that Hard-Pressed Pennsylvanians Turn Bitter," *HuffPost*, November 17, 2008, https://www.huffpost.com/entry/obama-no -surprise-that-ha_b_96188.

78. Maureen Burke, "People in Economics: The $787 Billion Question," *Finance and Development*, International Monetary Fund, March 2013, https://www.imf.org/external /pubs/ft/fandd/2013/03/people.htm; Noam Scheiber, "Exclusive: The Memo That Larry Summers Didn't Want Obama to See," *New Republic*, February 22, 2012, https:// newrepublic.com/article/100961/memo-larry-summers-obama.

79. Jackie Calmes, "Obama Unveils New Budget Cuts," *New York Times*, May 7, 2009, https://www.nytimes.com/2009/05/08/us/politics/08budget.html.

80. Robert E. Scott, "Worst Recovery in Postwar Era Largely Explained by Cuts in Government Spending," Economic Policy Institute, August 2, 2016, https://www.epi.org/blog /worst-recovery-in-post-war-era-largely-explained-by-cuts-in-government-spending/.

81. "Employment-Population Ratio, 25–54 Years," FRED Economic Data, Federal Reserve Bank of St. Louis, https://fred.stlouisfed.org/series/LNS12300060.

82. Data drawn from the Bureau of Economic Analysis interactive website showing a 34.5 percent real increase in GDP between 2001 and 2016 compared with a 61.1 percent gain between 1986 and 2001 measured in chained 2017 dollars: https://apps.bea.gov/iTable/?reqid=19&step=2&isuri=1&categories=survey&_gl =1*sb5q7f*_ga*OTkwNDU3MTMyLjE3MDM0NDg2NTA.*_ga_J4698JNN FT*MTcwMzQ0ODY0OS4xLjEuMTcwMzQ0ODcxOC41OS4wLjA.#eyJh cHBpZCI6MTksInN0ZXBzIjpbMSwyLDMsM10sImRhdGEiOltbImNhd GVnb3JpZXMiLCJTdXJ2ZXkiXSxbIk5JUEFfVGFibGVfTGlzdCIsIjYiXSxb IkZpcnN0X1llYXIiLCIxOTg2Il0sWyJMYXN0X1llYXIiLCIyMDAxIl0sWy JTY2FsZSIsIi05Il0sWyJTZXJpZXMiLCJBIl1dfQ==.

83. US nonfarm employment grew by 4.8 percent between January 2008 and October 2016, according to the Bureau of Labor Statistics. Comparable figures for the three states were 1.4 percent for Pennsylvania, 2.4 percent for Michigan, and 1.8 percent for Wisconsin.

84. Lawrence Summers, "A Deal Worth Getting Right," *Washington Post*, March 9, 2015, https://www.washingtonpost.com/opinions/its-worth-getting-the-tpp-trade-deal -right/2015/03/08/a1017428-c42f-11e4-ad5c-3b8ce89f1b89_story.html.

85. David J. Lynch, "Obama's Goals Clash as Allies Say Trade Push Widens Income Gap," Bloomberg News, January 30, 2014.

86. "Satisfaction with the United States," Gallup, https://news.gallup.com/poll/1669/general-mood-country.aspx.
87. Reich interview with the author, November 30, 2023.

Chapter 7: Everything Wrong with Globalization and Trade

1. Jonathan Allen and Amie Parnes, *Shattered: Inside Hillary Clinton's Doomed Campaign* (Crown, 2017), 184–185.
2. Allen and Parnes, *Shattered*, 176.
3. John Judis, *The Populist Explosion* (Columbia Global Reports, 2016), 83–84.
4. Chelsea Schneider and Brian Eason, "Clinton Touts Manufacturing in Northern Indiana," *Star Press*, April 27, 2016, A2.
5. Ahiza Garcia, "Carrier Workers' Rage over Move to Mexico Caught on Video," CNN, February 19, 2016, https://money.cnn.com/2016/02/12/news/companies/carrier-moving-jobs-mexico-youtube/.
6. Nick Carey, "Sanders, Trump Give Union Hope in Fight for Carrier Jobs," Reuters, February 18, 2016, https://www.reuters.com/article/world/sanders-trump-give-union-hope-in-fight-for-carrier-jobs-idUSKCN0VS02E/.
7. This account comes from a person familiar with the company's internal deliberations who spoke on the condition of anonymity.
8. Team Fix, "The CBS News Republican Debate Transcript, Annotated," *Washington Post*, February 13, 2016, https://www.washingtonpost.com/news/the-fix/wp/2016/02/13/the-cbs-republican-debate-transcript-annotated/.
9. Carey, "Sanders, Trump Give Union Hope."
10. Michael Anthony Adams, "Hundreds Protest Carrier's Move to Mexico," *IndyStar*, March 23, 2016, https://www.indystar.com/videos/news/2016/03/23/82192072/.
11. Schneider and Eason, "Clinton Touts Manufacturing."
12. "Bill Clinton Discusses Carrier at Indy Rally," WRTV, April 26, 2016, https://news.yahoo.com/news/bill-clinton-discusses-carrier-indy-172838582.html.
13. Kane Farabaugh, "Jobs, Trade Agreements Among Top Concerns for Indiana Workers," *Voice of America*, April 29, 2016.
14. "Former Pres. Bill Clinton Talks NAFTA, Carrier Corp. During Fort Wayne Visit," WBOI News, April 30, 2016, https://www.wboi.org/news/2016-04-30/former-pres-bill-clinton-talks-nafta-carrier-corp-during-fort-wayne-visit.
15. David J. Lynch, "Trump's Carrier Deal Fades as Economic Reality Intervenes," *Washington Post*, October 26, 2020, https://www.washingtonpost.com/business/2020/10/26/trump-carrier-manufacturing-jobs/.
16. Data from the US Bureau of Labor Statistics.
17. Political transcripts by CQ, "Donald Trump, Republican Presidential Candidate Delivers Remarks at a Campaign Rally in Indianapolis," May 2, 2016.
18. "Full Transcript: Donald Trump's Jobs Plan Speech," *Politico*, June 28, 2016, https://www.politico.com/story/2016/06/full-transcript-trump-job-plan-speech-224891.
19. "Trump's Jobs Plan Speech."
20. "2016 General Election: Trump vs. Clinton," RealClear Polling, https://www.realclearpolling.com/polls/president/general/2016/trump-vs-clinton.

21. David J. Lynch, "Immigrations Fears Boost Trump Far from Mexican Border," *Financial Times*, July 4, 2016, https://www.ft.com/content/bfd425f8-3f0d-11e6-8716 -a4a71e8140b0.

22. "Full Transcript: First 2016 Presidential Debate," *Politico*, September 27, 2016, https://www.politico.com/story/2016/09/full-transcript-first-2016-presidential -debate-228761.

23. Allen and Parnes, *Shattered*, 307–308.

24. US Bureau of Labor Statistics, "Educational Attainment for Workers 25 Years and Older by Detailed Occupation"; Congressional Research Service, "Real Wage Trends, 1979 to 2019," updated December 28, 2020, 12, https://sgp.fas.org/crs/misc/R45090.pdf.

25. Annie Linskey, "A Wistful, Resolute Bill Clinton Works Small-Town Trail Anew," *Boston Globe*, October 6, 2016, A1.

26. John Wagner, "Clinton Plans New Effort to Win Over White Working-Class Men," *Washington Post*, October 8, 2016, https://www.washingtonpost.com/politics/clinton -plans-new-effort-to-win-over-white-working-class-men/2016/10/07/6ffb7e1a-8ca0 -11e6-875e-2c1bfe943b66_story.html.

27. Allen and Parnes, *Shattered*, 366.

28. Allen and Parnes, *Shattered*, 375.

29. Allen and Parnes, *Shattered*, 379.

30. Trip Gabriel, "How Erie Went Red: A Democratic Bastion Undone by Job Losses," *New York Times*, November 13, 2016, A27.

31. David Maraniss, "A Dynasty Undone by Its Building Blocks," *Washington Post*, November 10, 2016, A1.

32. "How Trump's Taj Mahal Casino Went from '8th Wonder of the World' to Closure After Years of Losses," *ABC News*, October 17, 2016, https://abcnews.go.com/US /trumps-taj-mahal-casino-8th-world-closure-years/story?id=42762369.

33. Morrison interview with the author, February 21, 2018, previously unpublished.

34. Clinton interview with the author, February 6, 2024.

35. Robert Griffin and Ruy Teixeira, "The Story of Trump's Appeal: A Portrait of Trump's Voters," Democracy Fund Voter Study Group, June 2017, https://www .voterstudygroup.org/publication/story-of-trumps-appeal.

36. "Voter Study Group Releases New Longitudinal Poll and Reports on the American Electorate," Democracy Fund Voter Study Group, June 13, 2017, https://www.voter studygroup.org/newsroom/press-release-june-13-2017.

37. Griffin and Teixeira, "The Story of Trump's Appeal."

38. John Sides et al., *Identity Crisis: The 2016 Presidential Campaign and the Battle for the Meaning of America* (Princeton University Press, 2018), 2.

39. Diana C. Mutz, *Winners and Losers: The Psychology of Foreign Trade* (Princeton University Press, 2021), 243.

40. Diana C. Mutz, "Status Threat, Not Economic Hardship, Explains the 2016 Presidential Vote," *Proceedings of the National Academy of Sciences* 115, no. 19 (2018): E4330–E4339, https://www.pnas.org/doi/10.1073/pnas.1718155115.

41. Diana C. Mutz, "Response to Morgan: On the Role of Status Threat and Material Interests in the 2016 Election," *Socius* 4 (2018): 3, https://journals.sagepub.com/doi /epub/10.1177/2378023118808619.

42. Sullivan interview with the author, April 5, 2024.

43. Morgan interview with the author, January 10, 2024.

44. Stephen L. Morgan, "Status Threat, Material Interests, and the 2016 Presidential Vote," *Socius* 4 (2018), https://journals.sagepub.com/doi/epub/10.1177/2378023118788217.

45. Justin Grimmer and William Marble, "Who Put Trump in the White House? Explaining the Contribution of Voting Blocs to Trump's Victory," draft version, December 12, 2019, 33, https://williammarble.co/docs/vb.pdf.

46. Dani Rodrik, "Why Does Globalization Fuel Populism? Economics, Culture, and the Rise of Right-Wing Populism," *Annual Review of Economics* 13, no. 1 (2021): 133–170, https://drodrik.scholar.harvard.edu/files/dani-rodrik/files/why_does_globalization _fuel_populism.pdf.

47. Rodrik, "Why Does Globalization Fuel Populism?," 139.

48. Rodrik, "Why Does Globalization Fuel Populism?," 139.

49. J. Lawrence Broz et al., "Populism in Place: The Economic Geography of the Globalization Backlash," *International Organization* 75, no. 2 (2021): 465, https://www .cambridge.org/core/journals/international-organization/article/populism-in-place -the-economic-geography-of-the-globalization-backlash/98ED873D925E0590C B9A78AEC68BB439.

50. Broz et al., "Populism in Place," 470.

51. Broz et al., "Populism in Place," 477.

52. Edward Wolff, "Household Wealth Trends in the United States, 1962 to 2016: Has Middle Class Wealth Recovered?," Working Paper No. 24085, National Bureau of Economic Research, November 2017, 2, https://www.nber.org/system/files/working _papers/w24085/w24085.pdf.

53. Bob Davis and Jon Hilsenrath, "How the China Shock, Deep and Swift, Spurred the Rise of Trump," *Wall Street Journal*, August 11, 2016, https://www.wsj.com/articles /how-the-china-shock-deep-and-swift-spurred-the-rise-of-trump-1470929543.

54. David Autor et al., "Importing Political Polarization? The Electoral Consequences of Rising Trade Exposure," *American Economic Review* 110, no. 10 (2020): 3139, 3177, https://pubs.aeaweb.org/doi/pdfplus/10.1257/aer.20170011.

55. Autor et al., "Importing Political Polarization?," 3175.

56. Hubbard interview with the author, November 18, 2023.

57. Election data from the office of the Tennessee secretary of state, available at https:// sos.tn.gov/elections/results.

58. Bannon interview with the author, January 10, 2024.

59. David J. Lynch, "Trump Moves to Crack Down on China Trade with $60 Billion in Tariffs on Imported Products," *Washington Post*, March 22, 2018, https://www .washingtonpost.com/business/economy/trump-moves-to-crack-down-on-china -trade-with-50-billion-in-tariffs-on-imported-products/2018/03/22/c09309e8-2de3 -11e8-8ad6-fbc50284fce8_story.html.

60. Hillary Rodham Clinton, *What Happened* (Simon & Schuster, 2017), 410.

61. "Watch President-elect Donald Trump Speak from Carrier Plant," *PBS Newshour*, December 1, 2016, https://www.youtube.com/watch?v=QlT_j98Qdy8.

62. Peggy Noonan, "Declarations: Trump's Carrier Coup and a Lesson From JFK," *Wall Street Journal*, December 3, 2016, A11.

63. Ylan Mui, "Trump Demonstrates the Art of Celebrating the Deal," *Washington Post*, December 3, 2016, A1.

64. "United Technologies CEO Greg Hayes: Trump's 'No Quid Pro Quo' Request," CNBC, December 6, 2016, https://www.youtube.com/watch?v=7q6v0yd9eRE.

65. Carrier filed the required Worker Adjustment and Retraining Notice on May 19, 2017, https://www.in.gov/dwd/warn-notices/current-warn-notices/.

66. There were 12.2 million manufacturing workers in January 2021 and 12.4 million in January 2017. "All Employees—Manufacturing," FRED Economic Data, Federal Reserve Bank of St. Louis, https://fred.stlouisfed.org/series/MANEMP#0.

67. Jill Aitoro, "Raytheon CEO on Trump Meeting: President Appears to Understand Value of UTC-Raytheon Tie-up," *DefenseNews*, June 19, 2019, https://www.defensenews.com/digital-show-dailies/paris-air-show/2019/06/19/raytheon-ceo-trump-clearly-understands-the-value-of-the-raytheon-utc-tie-up/.

68. David J. Lynch and Shawn Donnan, "Police Arrest More Than 200 in Inauguration Protests," *Financial Times*, January 20, 2017, https://www.ft.com/content/5e5e3f08-df57-11e6-9d7c-be108f1c1dce.

69. Peter Baker, "Trump Abandons Trans-Pacific Partnership, Obama's Signature Trade Deal," *New York Times*, January 24, 2017, A1.

70. Lighthizer interview with the author, February 21, 2024.

71. "President Trump Meeting with Union Leaders and Workers," C-SPAN, January 23, 2017, https://www.c-span.org/video/?422483-1/president-trump-meeting-union-leaders-workers.

72. Cutler interview with the author, December 18, 2023.

Chapter 8: One of the Most Significant People in the Entire US Government

1. Matthew Forbes Pottinger, interviewed by Select Committee to Investigate the January 6th Attack on the US Capitol, US House of Representatives, April 7, 2022, 7, https://www.govinfo.gov/content/pkg/GPO-J6-TRANSCRIPT-CTRL0000062447/pdf/GPO-J6-TRANSCRIPT-CTRL0000062447.pdf.

2. Major General Michael T. Flynn, USA Captain Matt Pottinger, USMC Paul D. Batchelor, DIA, "Fixing Intel: A Blueprint for Making Intelligence Relevant in Afghanistan," Center for a New American Security, January 2010, 4, https://s3.us-east-1.amazonaws.com/files.cnas.org/hero/documents/AfghanIntel_Flynn_Jan2010_code507_voices.pdf.

3. Pottinger interview with the author, July 11, 2023.

4. Pottinger interview with the author, July 11, 2023.

5. "US Strategic Framework for the Indo-Pacific," White House, 2017, January 5, 2021, declassified, 1, https://trumpwhitehouse.archives.gov/wp-content/uploads/2021/01/IPS-Final-Declass.pdf.

6. "US Strategic Framework for the Indo-Pacific," White House, 2017, January 5, 2021, declassified, 2, https://trumpwhitehouse.archives.gov/wp-content/uploads/2021/01/IPS-Final-Declass.pdf.

7. "US Strategic Framework for the Indo-Pacific," White House, 2017, January 5, 2021, declassified, 6, https://trumpwhitehouse.archives.gov/wp-content/uploads/2021/01/IPS-Final-Declass.pdf.

8. James Lighthizer interview with the author, February 14, 2018.

9. Damian Paletta, "Top Trump Trade Officials Still at Odds After Profane Shouting Match in Beijing," *Washington Post*, May 16, 2018, https://www.washington post.com/news/business/wp/2018/05/16/top-trump-trade-officials-still-at-odds -after-profane-shouting-match-in-beijing/.

10. Bannon interview with the author, January 10, 2024.

11. "A Trump Sampler: His Changing Views," *New York Times*, May 7, 2016, https:// www.nytimes.com/interactive/2016/05/08/sunday-review/a-trump-sampler-his -changing-views.html.

12. Jennifer M. Miller, "Let's Not Be Laughed at Anymore: Donald Trump and Japan from the 1980s to the Present," *Journal of American-East Asian Relations* 25, no. 2 (2018): 139, https://jennifermmiller.com/wp-content/uploads/2019/06/final-trump-article.pdf.

13. "Lou Dobbs Tonight," transcript, aired April 20, 2004, National Foundation for American Policy, https://nfap.com/newarticle/lou-dobbs-tonight/.

14. Donald Trump, "'Trump Revealed': The Reporting Archive," interview by Bob Woodward and Robert Costa, *Washington Post*, March 31, 2016, https://www .washingtonpost.com/wp-stat/graphics/politics/trump-archive/docs/donald-trump -interview-with-bob-woodward-and-robert-costa.pdf.

15. Miller, "Let's Not Be Laughed at Anymore," 149.

16. Yumiko Ono, "Trump's Condos Lose Their Luster for Tokyo Buyers," *Wall Street Journal*, June 22, 1990, A5.

17. Guajardo interview with the author, August 16, 2023.

18. "Executive Order: Border Security and Immigration Enforcement Improvements," White House, January 25, 2017, https://trumpwhitehouse.archives.gov/presidential -actions/executive-order-border-security-immigration-enforcement-improvements/.

19. Full text of Xi Jinping keynote at the World Economic Forum, available at https://america .cgtn.com/2017/01/17/full-text-of-xi-jinping-keynote-at-the-world-economic-forum.

20. Stephen Schwarzman, *What It Takes: Lessons in the Pursuit of Excellence* (Simon & Schuster, 2019), 317.

21. White House footage of expanded bilateral meeting with Xi Jinping, available at https://www.youtube.com/watch?v=ICD6Prj-qEA.

22. Bob Davis and Lingling Wei, *Superpower Showdown: How the Battle Between Trump and Xi Threatens a New Cold War* (Harper Business, 2020), 181.

23. Bannon interview with the author, January 10, 2024.

24. Robert E. Lighthizer, "What Did Asian Donors Want?," *New York Times*, February 25, 1997, https://www.nytimes.com/1997/02/25/opinion/what-did-asian-donors-want.html.

25. David J. Lynch and Gerry Shih, "Crossed Wires: Why the US and China Are Struggling to Reach a Trade Deal," *Washington Post*, October 24, 2018, https:// www.washingtonpost.com/business/economy/crossed-wires-why-the-us-and-china -are-struggling-to-reach-a-trade-deal/2018/10/24/69f859e6-d2dc-11e8-8c22 -fa2ef74bd6d6_story.html.

26. Binyamin Applebaum, "US Begins Nafta Negotiations with Harsh Words," *New York Times*, August 16, 2017, https://www.nytimes.com/2017/08/16/business/economy /nafta-negotiations-canada-mexico.html.

27. Peter Baker and Susan Glasser, *The Divider: Trump in the White House, 2017–2021* (Doubleday, 2022), 74.

28. Author interview with a diplomat, who asked not to be identified.

29. Damian Paletta, "Trump Considers Order That Would Start Process of Withdrawing from NAFTA," *Washington Post*, April 26, 2017, https://www.washingtonpost.com/news/wonk/wp/2017/04/26/trump-close-to-notifying-canada-mexico-of-intent-to-withdraw-from-nafta/.

30. Jan-Albert Hootsen, "The 'Colossal Failure' of Trump's Mexico Visit," *Politico*, September 2, 2016, https://www.politico.com/magazine/story/2016/09/trump-mexico-visit-pena-nieto-failure-214211/.

31. Author interview with a presidential adviser who asked not to be identified, February 8, 2024.

32. "The full incidence of the tariff falls on domestic consumers," concluded Mary Amiti et al., "The Impact of the 2018 Trade War on US Prices and Welfare," Working Paper No. 25672, National Bureau of Economic Research, March 2019, https://www.nber.org/system/files/working_papers/w25672/w25672.pdf.

33. David J. Lynch, "Companies Can Escape Trump's Steel Tariffs. But It Won't Be Easy," *Washington Post*, June 19, 2018, https://www.washingtonpost.com/business/economy/companies-can-escape-trumps-steel-tariffs-but-it-wont-be-easy/2018/06/19/9c03da20-701a-11e8-bd50-b80389a4e569_story.html.

34. Veljko Fotak et al., "The Political Economy of Tariff Exemption Grants," *Journal of Financial and Quantitative Analysis*, ahead of print, July 29, 2024, https://jfqa.org/wp-content/uploads/2024/08/23440-Tariff-Exemptions.pdf.

35. Carrier Corp., "Section 301 Investigation: China's Acts, Policies and Practices Related to Technology Transfer, Intellectual Property and Innovation—Form to Request Exclusion of Product," USTR-2018-032-2579, December 18, 2018.

36. Carrier Corp., "Section 301 Investigation."

37. "Placing Carrier's components on the final list of proposed tariffs, therefore, will only raise costs on US businesses and consumers, and threaten American jobs without producing the policy changes sought by USTR," Reilly Kimmerling, Carrier's senior director of international trade compliance, testified before a USTR panel. "Section 301 Tariffs Public Hearing," 301 Committee, US Trade Representative, June 25, 2019, 260, https://ustr.gov/sites/default/files/enforcement/301Investigations/Section_301_Hearing_Transcript_on_Proposed_Tariffs_Day_7.pdf.

38. Joseph Barloon, general counsel, "Exclusion Denied," Office of the United States Trade Representative, May 7, 2019, https://www.regulations.gov/document/USTR-2018-0032-2579.

39. Strain interview with the author, February 27, 2020.

40. Kimberly Clausing, "Fixing Our 'America Last' Tax Policy," *The Hill*, April 11, 2019, https://thehill.com/opinion/finance/438274-fixing-our-america-last-tax-policy/.

41. Data drawn from table 1A, column F on this Internal Revenue Service page: https://www.irs.gov/statistics/soi-tax-stats-country-by-country-report. By 2020, the most recent data available, the gap had widened: Corporations claimed to have made $46 billion in profits in Ireland and $33 billion in China.

42. Applied Materials, Form 10-K for the Fiscal Year Ended October 28, 2018, 91, https://ir.appliedmaterials.com/static-files/e32d0616-758c-4703-b49b-84c3a3c21db5. The company's rate temporarily jumped the following year, reflecting the transition

to the new corporate tax regime, which provided a one-time incentive to repatriate and pay deferred taxes on some of the $2 trillion in deferred profits that companies had accumulated in offshore accounts. Economist Brad Setser of the Council on Foreign Relations was the first to comment on Applied Materials' tax situation: https://x .com/Brad_Setser/status/1762217221110067682.

43. For pace of growth, see "Real Private Nonresidential Fixed Investment," FRED Economic Data, Federal Reserve Bank of St. Louis, https://fred.stlouisfed.org/series /OB000336Q; for level relative to size of the economy, see "Share of Gross Domestic Product: Gross Private Domestic Investment," FRED Economic Data, Federal Reserve Bank of St. Louis, https://fred.stlouisfed.org/series/A006RE1Q156NBEA.

44. International Trade Commission, "US-Mexico-Canada Trade Agreement: Likely Impact on the US Economy and on Specific Industry Sectors," April 2019, 14, https://www.usitc.gov/publications/332/pub4889.pdf. The ITC projected a total gain of 176,000 jobs compared with the 2018 average monthly increase of 223,000, according to the Bureau of Labor Statistics, https://www.bls.gov/opub/mlr/2019 /article/employment-growth-accelerates-in-2018.htm#:~:text=According%20to%20 data%20from%20the,monthly%20gain%20of%20223%2C000%20jobs.

45. Lena Sun, "Top White House Official in Charge of Pandemic Response Exits Abruptly," *Washington Post*, May 10, 2018, https://www.washingtonpost.com/news /to-your-health/wp/2018/05/10/top-white-house-official-in-charge-of-pandemic -response-exits-abruptly/.

46. Wallach interview with the author, March 18, 2024.

47. Wallach interview with the author, March 18, 2024.

48. "Commanding Heights: Lori Wallach," PBS, https://www.pbs.org/wgbh/commanding heights/shared/minitext/int_loriwallach.html#1.

49. Peter Baker, "Trump Abandons Trans-Pacific Partnership, Obama's Signature Trade Deal," *New York Times*, January 23, 2017, https://www.nytimes.com/2017/01/23/us /politics/tpp-trump-trade-nafta.html.

50. Chris Hayes, "Fighting over Trade Wars with Lori Wallach: Podcast and Transcript," *NBC News*, January 15, 2019; available at https://www.nbcnews.com/think/opinion /fighting-over-trade-wars-lori-wallach-podcast-transcript-ncna958876.

51. Sullivan interview with the author, April 5, 2024.

52. "US Foreign Policy for the Middle Class: Perspectives from Ohio," Carnegie Endowment for International Peace, 2018, 21, https://carnegieendowment.org/files/USForeign Policy_Ohio_final.pdf.

53. "Roundtable: The Future of Globalization," International Monetary Fund, October 11, 2017, https://www.imf.org/en/Videos/view?vid=5607414429001.

54. Industry employment plunged to about 20,000 in 2008 from roughly 55,000 in 2001, according to Joseph C. Von Nesen, "Economic Impact of GADC," Division of Research, Moore School of Business, University of South Carolina, April 2021, 4, https://upstatebusinessjournal.com/wp-content/uploads/sites/2/2021/04/Growing -Greenville-Gvl-County-Economic-Impact-Study-2021.pdf.

55. Novelli interview with author, August 16, 2023.

56. Damien Paletta, David J. Lynch, and Josh Dawsey, "Trump's Claims on China Trade Deal Already Fracturing," *Washington Post*, December 5, 2018, A1.

57. David J. Lynch, "President Delays Tariff Hikes to Help China Talks," *Washington Post*, February 25, 2019, A1.

58. Robert E. Lighthizer, *No Trade Is Free: Changing Course, Taking on China, and Helping America's Workers* (Broadside Books, 2023), 175.

59. David J. Lynch, "US Says China Reneged on Trade Commitments," *Washington Post*, May 7, 2019, A1.

60. United States Attorney's Office Eastern District of New York, "Chinese Telecommunications Conglomerate Huawei and Huawei CFO Wanzhou Meng Charged with Financial Fraud," press release, January 28, 2019, https://www.justice.gov/usao-edny/pr/chinese -telecommunications-conglomerate-huawei-and-huawei-cfo-wanzhou-meng-charged.

61. David J. Lynch, "US Companies Banned from Selling to China's ZTE Telecom Maker," *Washington Post*, April 16, 2018, https://www.washingtonpost.com/news/business /wp/2018/04/16/u-s-companies-banned-from-selling-to-chinas-zte-telecom-maker/.

62. Damian Paletta, Ellen Nakashima, and Steven Mufson, "China Telecom Sparks Talks," *Washington Post*, May 14, 2018, A6.

63. Michael Crowley, "The White House Official Trump Says Doesn't Exist," *Politico*, May 30, 2018, https://www.politico.com/magazine/story/2018/05/30/donald -trump-matthew-pottinger-asia-218551/.

64. Michael Barbaro and Steve Eder, "Under Oath, Donald Trump Shows His Raw Side," *New York Times*, July 28, 2015, https://www.nytimes.com/2015/07/29/us /politics/depositions-show-donald-trump-as-quick-to-exaggerate-and-insult.html.

65. Pottinger interview with the author, April 1, 2024.

66. David J. Lynch, "Trump's Next Round of Trade Limits Could Hurt the US Tech Industry He Wants to Help," *Washington Post*, May 21, 2018, https://www .washingtonpost.com/business/economy/trumps-next-round-of-trade-limits-could -hurt-the-us-tech-industry-he-wants-to-help/2018/05/21/7b2507ee-587c-11e8-b656 -a5f8c2a9295d_story.html.

67. Susan Shirk, *Overreach: How China Derailed Its Peaceful Rise* (Oxford University Press, 2023), 258–261.

68. Audrey Fritz, "China's Evolving Conception of Civil-Military Collaboration," Center for Strategic and International Studies, August 2, 2019, https://www.csis.org/blogs /trustee-china-hand/chinas-evolving-conception-civil-military-collaboration; "The Chinese Communist Party's Military-Civil Fusion Policy," US Department of State fact sheet, https://2017-2021.state.gov/military-civil-fusion/#:~:text=What%20is%20Military %2DCivil%20Fusion,world%20class%20military%E2%80%9D%20by%202049.

69. Rush Doshi, *The Long Game: China's Grand Strategy to Displace American Order* (Oxford University Press, 2021), 287.

70. Doshi, *The Long Game*, 286–290.

71. Lee Branstetter and Guangwei Li, "Does 'Made in China 2025' Work for China? Evidence from Chinese Listed Firms," October 20, 2022, 1, 16, http://dx.doi.org /10.2139/ssrn.4254356.

72. David J. Lynch, "How the US-China Trade War Became a Conflict over the Future of Tech," *Washington Post*, May 22, 2019, https://www.washingtonpost.com /business/economy/how-the-us-china-trade-war-became-a-conflict-over-the-future -of-tech/2019/05/22/18148d1c-7ccc-11e9-8ede-f4abf521ef17_story.html.

73. House Permanent Select Committee on Intelligence, "Investigative Report on the US National Security Issues Posed by Chinese Telecommunications Companies Huawei and ZTE," October 8, 2012, https://intelligence.house.gov/sites/intelligence.house .gov/files/documents/huawei-zte%20investigative%20report%20(final).pdf.

74. Pottinger interview with the author, March 20, 2024.

75. David Nakamura, Carol D. Leonnig, and Ellen Nakashima, "Matthew Pottinger faced Communist China's intimidation as a reporter. He's now at the White House shaping Trump's hard line policy toward Beijing," *Washington Post*, April 29, 2020, https:// www.washingtonpost.com/politics/matthew-pottinger-faced-communist-chinas -intimidation-as-a-reporter-hes-now-at-the-white-house-shaping-trumps-hard-line -policy-toward-beijing/2020/04/28/5fb3f6d4-856e-11ea-ae26-989cfce1c7c7_story.html.

76. Ryan Hass, *Stronger: Adapting America's China Strategy in an Age of Competitive Interdependence* (Yale University Press, 2021), 99.

77. David J. Lynch, "Trump Signs Partial Economic Deal with China, Calls Trade Pact a 'Momentous Step,'" *Washington Post*, January 15, 2020, https://www.washingtonpost .com/business/economy/trumps-new-china-deal-cements-emergence-of-managed -trade/2020/01/15/7892c446-372b-11ea-bf30-ad313e4ec754_story.html.

78. "Disease Outbreak News—Japan," World Health Organization, January 17, 2020, https://www.who.int/emergencies/disease-outbreak-news/item/2020-DON237.

Chapter 9: These Stupid Supply Chains

1. Gerry Shih and Lena H. Sun, "China Identifies New Strain of Coronavirus as Source of Pneumonia Outbreak," *Washington Post*, January 10, 2020, A12.

2. "World Development Report 2020: Trading for Development in the Age of Global Value Chains," World Bank, xiii, https://www.worldbank.org/en/publication/wdr2020.

3. Joyce Gannon, "Charging Ahead: Eaton Electrical Unit Chief 'Giving Space,'" *The Pittsburgh Post-Gazette*, May 31, 2012, D1.

4. Much of the Flex case study is drawn from David J. Lynch, "Business Unusual: How a Little-Known Company Navigated the Shortages and Shutdowns of the Pandemic While Pointing the Way to a Less China-Centric Future," *Washington Post*, July 30, 2020, A1, https://www.washingtonpost.com/graphics/2020/world/corona virus-globalization-manufacturing/.

5. White House, "Economic Report of the President," March 2024, 196, https://www .whitehouse.gov/wp-content/uploads/2024/03/ERP-2024.pdf.

6. White House, "Economic Report of the President," March 2024, 195, https://www .whitehouse.gov/wp-content/uploads/2024/03/ERP-2024.pdf.

7. Willy C. Shih, "What Really Makes Toyota's Production System Resilient," *Harvard Business Review*, November 15, 2022, https://hbr.org/2022/11/what-really-makes -toyotas-production-system-resilient.

8. "Judge Orders Ports Opened," CNN, October 9, 2002, https://money.cnn.com/2002 /10/08/news/ports_longshoremen/.

9. US Census Bureau, "Manufacturers: Inventories to Sales Ratio [MNFCTRIRSA]," FRED Economic Data, Federal Reserve Bank of St. Louis, accessed April 26, 2024, https://fred.stlouisfed.org/series/MNFCTRIRSA.

10. "Basic Concept of the Toyota Production System," Toyota, https://www.toyota-global
.com/company/history_of_toyota/75years/data/automotive_business/production
/system/change.html.

11. Jeffrey H. Dyer, "Dedicated Assets: Japan's Manufacturing Edge," *Harvard Business Review*, November–December 1994, https://hbr.org/1994/11/dedicated-assets
-japans-manufacturing-edge.

12. David J. Lynch, "Tactics of Fiery White House Trade Adviser Draw New Scrutiny as Some of His Pandemic Moves Unravel," *Washington Post*, September 2, 2020, https://
www.washingtonpost.com/us-policy/2020/09/02/navarro-pandemic-coronavirus/.

13. White House, "Remarks by President Trump, Vice President Pence, and Members of the Coronavirus Task Force in Press Briefing," March 15, 2020, https://trumpwhite
house.archives.gov/briefings-statements/remarks-president-trump-vice-president
-pence-members-coronavirus-task-force-press-briefing-2/.

14. Flex Ltd., Form 10-K for the fiscal year ended March 31, 2019, 32, https://s202
.q4cdn.com/732614612/files/doc_financials/2020/q4/Q4-20-10K.pdf.

15. Flex Ltd., Form 10-K for the fiscal year ended March 31, 2015, 39, https://www.sec
.gov/Archives/edgar/data/866374/000104746915004931/a2224823z10-k.htm.

16. Flex Ltd., Form 10-K for the fiscal year ended March 31, 2020, 36, https://s202
.q4cdn.com/732614612/files/doc_financials/2020/q4/Q4-20-10K.pdf.

17. Advaithi interview with the author, June 22, 2020.

18. Advaithi interview with the author, June 22, 2020.

19. Flex Ltd., "Q3 2020 Earnings Call," January 30, 2020, https://s202.q4cdn.com
/732614612/files/doc_financials/2020/q3/flex_fy20q3_transcript.pdf.

20. Advaithi interview with the author, June 22, 2020.

21. David J. Lynch, "Coronavirus Fallout Is Choking Economic Pipelines," *Washington Post*, February 14, 2020, A1.

22. Wang interview with the author, June 30, 2020.

23. Inventories data can be found in the condensed consolidated balance sheets contained in Flex quarterly filings. Pre-pandemic inventories figure is here: Flex Ltd., Form 10-Q for the quarterly period ended December 31, 2019, 4, https://s202
.q4cdn.com/732614612/files/doc_financials/2020/q3/flex_10-q_fy20q3.pdf.

24. Advaithi interview with the author, June 22, 2020.

25. Lynch, "Coronavirus Fallout."

26. Torrel interview with the author, June 24, 2020.

27. Flex, Form 10-Q for the quarterly period ended June 26, 2020, 28, https://
d18rn0p25nwr6d.cloudfront.net/CIK-0000866374/6760c976-a0f6-4c5a-985f
-d5419e0c009d.pdf.

28. Torrel interview with the author, June 24, 2020.

29. Lynch, "Business Unusual."

30. Ana Swanson and Alan Rappeport, "Wilbur Ross Says Coronavirus Could Bring Jobs Back to the US," *New York Times*, January 31, 2020, https://www.nytimes
.com/2020/01/30/business/economy/wilbur-ross-coronavirus-jobs.html.

31. Donald J. Trump, "Remarks at a White House Coronavirus Task Force Press Briefing," April 2, 2020, American Presidency Project, UC Santa Barbara, https://www.presidency
.ucsb.edu/documents/remarks-white-house-coronavirus-task-force-press-briefing-18.

32. David J. Lynch, "Raging Virus Triggers New Shutdown Orders and Economy Braces for Fresh Wave of Pain," *Washington Post*, November 15, 2020, A1.

33. International Trade Commission, "The Impact of the Covid-19 Pandemic on Freight Transportation Services and US Merchandise Imports," https://www.usitc.gov /research_and_analysis/tradeshifts/2020/special_topic.html#_ftn16.

34. David J. Lynch, "Shipping Woes Spell Trouble for Consumers," *Washington Post*, January 25, 2021, A1.

35. Lynch, "Shipping Woes."

36. White House, "Executive Order on America's Supply Chains," February 24, 2021, https://www.whitehouse.gov/briefing-room/presidential-actions/2021/02/24 /executive-order-on-americas-supply-chains/.

37. "The Great Texas Freeze: February 11–20, 2021," National Centers for Environmental Information, National Oceanic and Atmospheric Administration, February 24, 2023, https://www.ncei.noaa.gov/news/great-texas-freeze-february-2021.

38. Jesse Thompson, "Texas Winter Deep Freeze Broke Refining, Petrochemical Supply Chains," Southwest Economy, Second Quarter 2021, Federal Reserve Bank of Dallas, Southwest Economy, https://www.dallasfed.org/research/swe/2021/swe2102 /swe2102c#n2.

39. David J. Lynch, "West Virginia Factory Is Center Stage in Supply Chain Crisis, Showing Economy's Strains," *Washington Post*, May 8, 2021, https://www.washingtonpost .com/business/2021/05/08/manufacturing-supply-chain-crisis/.

40. Institute for Supply Management, "Manufacturing PMI at 61.2%; May 2021 Manufacturing ISM Report on Business," press release, June 1, 2021, https://www .prnewswire.com/news-releases/manufacturing-pmi-at-61-2-may-2021-manufacturing -ism-report-on-business-301301816.html.

41. David J. Lynch, "Global Supply-Line Woes May Soon Clear Shelves," *Washington Post*, July 28, 2021, A1.

42. International Monetary Fund, "Chapter 4: Global Trade and Value Chains During the Pandemic," World Economic Outlook, April 2022, 95, https://www.imf.org/en /Publications/WEO/Issues/2022/04/19/world-economic-outlook-april-2022.

43. David J. Lynch, "Biden Targets High Shipping Costs," *Washington Post*, July 15, 2021, A19.

44. David J. Lynch, "As Supply Lines Strain, Some Corporations Rewrite Production Playbook," *Washington Post*, November 15, 2021, https://www.washingtonpost.com /business/2021/11/15/supply-chains-companies-strategy/.

45. Lynch, "As Supply Lines Strain."

46. "Stanley Black & Decker Announces Opening of New Craftsman Plant in Fort Worth, Texas," Stanley Black & Decker, May 15, 2019, https://www.stanleyblackanddecker.com /stanley-black-decker-announces-opening-new-craftsman-plant-fort-worth-texas.

47. Stanley Black & Decker, Q1 2022 Earnings Call Transcript, April 28, 2022, 13, https://s29.q4cdn.com/245094436/files/doc_financials/2022/q1/SWK-USQ _Transcript_2022-04-28.pdf.

48. Comparing the end of 2022 to the end of 2020. Figures drawn from Stanley Black & Decker Inc., Form 10-K for the fiscal year ended December 31, 2022, 76, https:// d18rn0p25nwr6d.cloudfront.net/CIK-0000093556/c6f30c27-3877-4e39-9dc8

-5ee04111da68.pdf; and Stanley Black & Decker Inc., Form 10-K for the fiscal year ended January 2, 2021, 80 https://d18rn0p25nwr6d.cloudfront.net/CIK -0000093556/7d346892-892a-41c7-adbf-ef6caf981b58.pdf.

49. Lynch, "As Supply Lines Strain."

50. Stanley Black & Decker, Q1 2022 Earnings Call Transcript, April 28, 2022, 13, https:// s29.q4cdn.com/245094436/files/doc_financials/2022/q1/SWK-USQ_Transcript _2022-04-28.pdf.

51. White House, "Fact Sheet: Executive Order on Promoting Competition in the American Economy," July 9, 2021, https://www.whitehouse.gov/briefing-room/statements -releases/2021/07/09/fact-sheet-executive-order-on-promoting-competition-in-the -american-economy/.

52. US Department of Transportation, Maritime Administration, "Report to Congress on the Performance of Ports and the Intermodal System," June 2005, iv, https:// rosap.ntl.bts.gov/view/dot/18108.

53. David J. Lynch, "Inside America's Broken Supply Chain," *Washington Post*, September 30, 2021, https://www.washingtonpost.com/business/interactive/2021/supply -chain-issues/?itid=ap_davidj.%20lynch.

54. Michael Graczyk, "Biden Pitches Infrastructure Improvements," Associated Press, November. 12, 2014.

55. World Bank, "Connecting to Compete: Trade Logistics in the Global Economy," 2018, 45, https://documents1.worldbank.org/curated/en/576061531492034646/pdf /Connecting-to-compete-2018-trade-logistics-in-the-global-economy-the-logistics -performance-index-and-its-indicators.pdf.

56. Lynch, "Inside America's Broken Supply Chain."

57. Union Pacific Corporation, Form 10-K for the fiscal year ended December 31, 2019, 24, https://www.up.com/cs/groups/public/@uprr/@investor/documents/investordocuments /pdf_up_10k_02072020.pdf.

58. "How Changes in Consumption Caused by COVID-19 Affected Inflation," *FRED Blog*, Federal Reserve Bank of St. Louis, January 5, 2023, https://fredblog.stlouisfed .org/2023/01/how-changes-in-consumption-caused-by-covid-19-affected-inflation/.

59. Porcari interview with the author, April 25, 2024.

60. Porcari interview with the author, April 25, 2024.

61. Federal Maritime Commission, Bureau of Trade Analysis, "US Container Port Congestion and Related International Supply Chain Issues: Causes, Consequences and Challenges," July 2015, 1, https://www.fmc.gov/wp-content/uploads/2019/04/Port ForumReport_FINALwebAll.pdf.

62. White House, "Remarks by President Biden on the Bipartisan Infrastructure Deal," November 10, 2021, https://www.whitehouse.gov/briefing-room/speeches -remarks/2021/11/10/remarks-by-president-biden-on-the-bipartisan-infrastructure -deal-2/.

63. Bureau of Transportation Statistics, US Department of Transportation, "Freight Logistics Optimization Works," https://www.bts.gov/flow.

64. Improvement can be seen in the Global Supply Chain Pressure Index maintained by the Federal Reserve Bank of New York, https://www.newyorkfed.org/research /policy/gscpi#/interactive.

65. Vicky Forman and Ronak Gohel, "Reglobalization Is Driving Supply Chain Performance," Gartner, July 15, 2024.
66. Forman and Gohel, "Reglobalization."
67. Quote is from Flex Ltd., Form 10-K for the fiscal year ended March 31, 2023, p. 46; nearly $4 billion calculation represents the difference in total inventories disclosed on pg. 63 of the 2023 and 2019 10-Ks. The 2023 and 2019 forms are available at https://d18rn0p25nwr6d.cloudfront.net/CIK-0000866374/8a9b202b-597e-43b3-ac3d-a1e1f7bbfd42.pdf and https://d18rn0p25nwr6d.cloudfront.net/CIK-0000866374/e1a8df5c-924f-41c8-912e-d67df1be1fd2.pdf.
68. Advaithi was interviewed at *The Wall Street Journal*'s CEO Council Summit on December 12, 2023, https://www.wsj.com/video/events/leading-in-uncertain-times/4D7F4756-1942-4BB1-A159-E4CEC3F6EC45.html.

Chapter 10: The Return of Big Government

1. Joe Biden, United Steelworkers union candidate questionnaire, May 17, 2020.
2. Adam Posen, "The Price of Nostalgia: America's Self-Defeating Economic Retreat," *Foreign Affairs* 100, no. 3 (2021): 28–43.
3. Adam Entous, "The Untold History of the Biden Family," *New Yorker*, August 15, 2022, https://www.newyorker.com/magazine/2022/08/22/the-untold-history-of-the-biden-family.
4. Steven Levingston, "Joe Biden: Life Before the Presidency," Miller Center, University of Virginia, https://millercenter.org/president/biden/life-before-the-presidency; Entous, "Untold History of Biden Family."
5. White House, "Remarks by President Biden at a Campaign Event, Scranton, PA," April 16, 2024, https://www.whitehouse.gov/briefing-room/speeches-remarks/2024/04/16/remarks-by-president-biden-at-a-campaign-event-scranton-pa-2/.
6. William J. Clinton, "Address at Convocation, University of Chicago," June 12, 1999, https://1997-2001.state.gov/policy_remarks/1999/990612_clinton_chicago.html.
7. Matt Viser, "Once the Poorest Senator, 'Middle Class Joe' Biden Has Reaped Millions in Income Since Leaving the Vice Presidency," *Washington Post*, June 25, 2019, https://www.washingtonpost.com/politics/once-the-poorest-senator-middle-class-joe-biden-has-reaped-millions-in-income-since-leaving-the-vice-presidency/2019/06/25/931458a8-938d-11e9-b570-6416efdc0803_story.html.
8. Evan Osnos, *Joe Biden: The Life, the Run, and What Matters Now* (Scribner, 2020), 24.
9. Greene interview with the author, December 1, 2023.
10. Congressional Record, Senate, bound edition, vol. 139, part 21, November 19, 1993, 30676–30678, https://www.congress.gov/bound-congressional-record/1993/11/19/senate-section.
11. "Corporate Profits After Tax (without IVA and CCAdj)/Gross Domestic Product," FRED Economic Data, Federal Reserve Bank of St. Louis, https://fred.stlouisfed.org/graph/?g=1Pik; "Share of Gross Domestic Income: Employee Compensation Paid," FRED Economic Data, Federal Reserve Bank of St. Louis, https://fred.stlouisfed.org/series/A4002E1A156NBEA.
12. Jannuzi interview with the author, October 18, 2023.

13. Daniel Griswold, "Joe Biden's So-So Record on Trade," Cato Institute, August 25, 2008, https://www.cato.org/blog/joe-bidens-so-so-record-trade.
14. Tim Draper, "I Will Promote Freedom at All Costs," *Medium*, October 27, 2017, https://medium.com/@TimDraper/i-will-promote-freedom-at-all-costs-c1a8316e415e.
15. Illia Kabachynskyi, "Ukraine's Ministry of Defense Launches Accelerator of Innovative Development. Its Coordinator Is Loboyko, Mentioned in Tim Draper's Book," *AIN.Capital*, July 4, 2023, https://ain.capital/2023/07/04/ministry-of-defense-launches-accelerator-of-innovative-development/.
16. Draper interview with the author, March 11, 2024.
17. Eric Eldon, "Venture Firm Draper Fisher Jurvetson Goes to Russia," *VentureBeat*, September 27, 2007, https://venturebeat.com/business/venture-firm-draper-fisher-jurvetson-goes-to-russia/.
18. Rebecca Fannin, "The Silicon Valley Fallout from Waging Economic War Against Russia," *CNBC.com*, March 17, 2022, https://www.cnbc.com/2022/03/17/the-silicon-valley-fallout-from-waging-economic-war-against-russia.html.
19. Joyu Wang, "Tim Draper Touts Decision to Pull Out of China," *Wall Street Journal*, November 18, 2022, https://www.wsj.com/articles/tim-draper-touts-decision-to-pull-out-of-china-11668768693.
20. Draper interview with author, March 11, 2024.
21. "2023 Annual Meeting," Warren Buffett Archive, May 6, 2023, https://buffett.cnbc.com/2023-berkshire-hathaway-annual-meeting/.
22. Larry Fink's Chairman's Letter, "To Our Shareholders," BlackRock, March 24, 2022, https://www.blackrock.com/corporate/investor-relations/2022-larry-fink-chairmans-letter.
23. David J. Lynch, Michael Birnbaum, Ellen Nakashima, and Paul Sonne, "Historic Sanctions on Russia Had Roots in Emotional Appeal from Zelensky," *Washington Post*, February 27, 2022, https://www.washingtonpost.com/business/2022/02/27/russia-ukraine-sanctions-swift-central-bank/.
24. "EU Sanctions Against Russia Explained," European Council, last reviewed December 16, 2024, https://www.consilium.europa.eu/en/policies/sanctions-against-russia/sanctions-against-russia-explained/.
25. US Department of the Treasury, "US Treasury Announces Unprecedented & Expansive Sanctions Against Russia, Imposing Swift and Severe Economic Costs," press release, February 24, 2022, https://home.treasury.gov/news/press-releases/jy0608.
26. Henry Farrell and Abraham Newman, *Underground Empire: How America Weaponized the World Economy* (Henry Holt, 2023), 139.
27. "Yale CELI List of Companies Leaving and Staying in Russia," Chief Executive Leadership Institute, Yale School of Management, updated May 19, 2024, https://www.yalerussianbusinessretreat.com/.
28. David J. Lynch, "Tunisia Among Countries Seeing Major Economic Consequences from War in Ukraine," *Washington Post*, April 14, 2022, https://www.washingtonpost.com/business/2022/04/14/ukraine-war-economic-impact-tunisia/.
29. Federal Foreign Office, "Speech by Foreign Minister Annalena Baerbock at the Business Forum of the 20th Conference of the Heads of German Missions," September 6, 2022, https://www.auswaertiges-amt.de/en/newsroom/news/business-forum-amb-conference/2551336.

30. Julian Wettengel, "Germany, EU Remain Heavily Dependent on Imported Fossil Fuels," *Clean Energy Wire*, April 3, 2024, https://www.cleanenergywire.org/factsheets/germanys-dependence-imported-fossil-fuels.

31. "US Regular All Formulations Gas Price," FRED Economic Data, Federal Reserve Bank of St. Louis, https://fred.stlouisfed.org/series/GASREGW.

32. David J. Lynch, "War Could Be a Global Economic 'Game Changer,' Not Just for Now," *Washington Post*, March 7, 2022, A1, https://www.washingtonpost.com/business/2022/03/05/global-economy-russia-ukraine/.

33. Daniel Yergin, "Putin Can't Count on the Global Oil Market," *Wall Street Journal*, December 26, 2022, https://www.wsj.com/articles/putin-cant-count-on-the-global-oil-market-price-cap-revenue-production-cut-friedman-biden-eu-russia-energy-11672065849.

34. Cheng Ting-Fang, "TSMC Founder Morris Chang Says Globalization 'Almost Dead,'" *Nikkei Asia*, December 7, 2022, https://asia.nikkei.com/Spotlight/Most-read-in-2022/TSMC-founder-Morris-Chang-says-globalization-almost-dead.

35. Devin Henry, "Jake Sullivan: Minneapolis Native Among Those to Hatch Iranian Nuclear Deal," *MinnPost*, November 27, 2013, https://www.minnpost.com/dc-dispatches/2013/11/jake-sullivan-minneapolis-native-among-those-hatch-iranian-nuclear-deal/.

36. Jake Sullivan, "The New Old Democrats," *Democracy*, June 20, 2018, https://democracyjournal.org/arguments/the-new-old-democrats/.

37. Jennifer Harris and Jake Sullivan, "America Needs a New Economic Philosophy. Foreign Policy Experts Can Help," *Foreign Policy*, February 7, 2020.

38. Sullivan interview with the author, April 5, 2024.

39. Nick Gass, "Trump: 'We can't continue to allow China to rape our country,'" *Politico*, May 2, 2016, https://www.politico.com/blogs/2016-gop-primary-live-updates-and-results/2016/05/trump-china-rape-america-222689.

40. Mark Wu, "The 'China, Inc.' Challenge to Global Trade Governance," *Harvard International Law Journal* 57, no. 2 (2016): 270–272, https://www.law.berkeley.edu/wp-content/uploads/2020/05/WuMark.pdf.

41. David J. Lynch, "China Government Control Endures Through Xi's Embrace of Market," Bloomberg, December 3, 2014, https://www.bloomberg.com/news/articles/2014-12-04/china-government-control-endures-through-xi-s-embrace-of-market?embedded-checkout=true.

42. White House, "Remarks by Vice President Joe Biden at the World Economic Forum," January 18, 2017, https://obamawhitehouse.archives.gov/the-press-office/2017/01/18/remarks-vice-president-joe-biden-world-economic-forum.

43. "Industrial Production: Manufacturing (NAICS)," FRED Economic Data, Federal Reserve Bank of St. Louis, https://fred.stlouisfed.org/series/IPMAN.

44. White House, "Remarks by National Security Advisor Jake Sullivan on Renewing American Economic Leadership at the Brookings Institution," April 27, 2023, https://www.whitehouse.gov/briefing-room/speeches-remarks/2023/04/27/remarks-by-national-security-advisor-jake-sullivan-on-renewing-american-economic-leadership-at-the-brookings-institution/.

45. In Sullivan's defense, the US weighted average tariff rate dropped from 3.9 percent in 1990 to 2.1 percent in 2000 while the world average fell from a peak of 8.6 percent

to 5 percent, according to the World Bank: https://data.worldbank.org/indicator/TM.TAX.MRCH.WM.AR.ZS?locations=US-1W.

46. Martin Wolf, "America Is Feeling Buyer's Remorse at the World It Built," *Financial Times*, June 27, 2023, https://www.ft.com/content/77faa249-0f88-4700-95d2-ecd7e9e745f9.

47. Summers interview with the author, June 12, 2024.

48. "Biden: The Future of the Chip Industry Is 'Made in America,'" CNBC, September 9, 2022, https://www.youtube.com/watch?v=QckvbzJJoi4.

49. White House, "Remarks by President Biden on Rebuilding American Manufacturing Through the CHIPS and Science Act," September 9, 2022, https://www.whitehouse.gov/briefing-room/speeches-remarks/2022/09/09/remarks-by-president-biden-on-rebuilding-american-manufacturing-through-the-chips-and-science-act/.

50. Bernstein interview with the author, May 10, 2024.

51. Nelson Lichtenstein and Judith Stein, *A Fabulous Failure: The Clinton Presidency and the Transformation of American Capitalism* (Princeton University Press, 2023), 54.

52. Even discounting the pandemic, real manufacturing output at the end of 2019 was marginally lower than when Trump took office in 2017. Factory employment rose by 419,000 over the same period, a marginal improvement over the 383,000 gained during Obama's second term. See "Industrial Production: Manufacturing (NAICS)," FRED Economic Data, Federal Reserve Bank of St. Louis, https://fred.stlouisfed.org/series/IPMAN; and "All Employees, Manufacturing," FRED Economic Data, Federal Reserve Bank of St. Louis, https://fred.stlouisfed.org/series/MANEMP#0.

53. "Total Construction Spending: Manufacturing in the United States," FRED Economic Data, Federal Reserve Bank of St. Louis, https://fred.stlouisfed.org/series/TLMFGCONS; "All Employees, Construction," FRED Economic Data, Federal Reserve Bank of St. Louis, https://fred.stlouisfed.org/series/USCONS.

54. White House, "Remarks by National Security Advisor Jake Sullivan on Renewing American Economic Leadership at the Brookings Institution," April 27, 2023, https://www.whitehouse.gov/briefing-room/speeches-remarks/2023/04/27/remarks-by-national-security-advisor-jake-sullivan-on-renewing-american-economic-leadership-at-the-brookings-institution/.

55. Glencora Haskins, Mark Muro, and Maya Garg, "'Place-based Industrial Strategy' Responds to Past and Future Industrial and Labor Market Shocks," Brookings Institution, August 29, 2024, https://www.brookings.edu/articles/place-based-industrial-strategy-responds-to-past-and-future-industrial-and-labor-market-shocks/?share=interactive-1784920.

56. "2024 Ohio Election: Trump vs. Biden Polls," RealClear Polling, May 2024, https://www.realclearpolling.com/polls/president/general/2024/ohio/trump-vs-biden.

57. As of October 2024.

58. "All Employees: All Employees Manufacturing/All Employees Nonfarm," FRED Economic Data, Federal Reserve Bank of St. Louis, https://fred.stlouisfed.org/graph/?g=1Gor.

59. Furman interview with the author, May 9, 2024.

60. Raimondo interview with the author, May 31, 2024.

61. Josh Boak, "Commerce Head Out to Save US Jobs, 1 Computer Chip at a Time," Associated Press, October 18, 2021, https://apnews.com/article/joe-biden-technology-business-united-states-rhode-island-7dc6ee7312bf4653c16d873643b9ac90.

62. "All Employees: Manufacturing in Rhode Island," FRED Economic Data, Federal Reserve Bank of St. Louis, https://fred.stlouisfed.org/series/RIMFG.

63. Raimondo interview with the author, May 31, 2024.

64. White House, "Remarks by President Biden on Bidenomics," June 28, 2023, https://www.whitehouse.gov/briefing-room/speeches-remarks/2023/06/28/remarks-by-president-biden-on-bidenomics-chicago-il/.

65. Yellen interview with the author, June 28, 2024.

66. "Real Broad Dollar Index," FRED Economic Data, Federal Reserve Bank of St. Louis, https://fred.stlouisfed.org/series/RTWEXBGS.

67. Ana Swanson and Tripp Mickle, "The White House Bet Big on Intel. Will It Backfire?," *New York Times*, October 24, 2024, https://www.nytimes.com/2024/10/24/us/politics/intel-chips-biden.html.

68. Joelle Anselmo, "TSMC Delays Second Arizona Chip Plant to 2027 or 2028," *Manufacturing Dive*, January 19, 2024, https://www.manufacturingdive.com/news/tsmc-delays-second-arizona-chip-factory-to-2027/704937/.

69. David J. Lynch, "Biden's 'Buy America' Bid Runs into Manufacturing Woes It Aims to Fix," *Washington Post*, February 18, 2023, https://www.washingtonpost.com/us-policy/2023/02/18/biden-buy-america-roads-bridges/.

70. Shannon Osaka, "Biden's $7.5 Billion Investment in EV Charging Has Only Produced 7 Stations in Two Years," *Washington Post*, March 29, 2024, https://www.washingtonpost.com/climate-solutions/2024/03/28/ev-charging-stations-slow-rollout/.

71. Raimondo interview with the author, May 31, 2024.

72. "Consumer Price Index for All Urban Consumers: Used Cars and Trucks in US City Average," FRED Economic Data, Federal Reserve Bank of St. Louis, https://fred.stlouisfed.org/series/CUSR0000SETA02.

73. Sujai Shivakumar, Charles Wessner, and Thomas Howell, "The Strategic Importance of Legacy Chips," Center for Strategic and International Studies, March 3, 2023, https://www.csis.org/analysis/strategic-importance-legacy-chips.

74. Rockwell Automation, "2023 Annual Report on Form 10-K," November 8, 2023, 45, https://www.rockwellautomation.com/content/dam/rockwell-automation/documents/pdf/company/about-us/ir/2023/Web-Ready_Rockwell-Automation_2023-Annual-Report_Web.pdf.

75. Moret interview with the author, January 31, 2024.

76. Lincicome interview with the author, May 24, 2024.

77. "Is Globalization Really in Retreat?," Peterson Institute for International Economics, October 30, 2023, https://www.piie.com/events/globalization-really-retreat.

78. Yellen interview with the author, June 28, 2024.

79. Autor interview with the author, August 17, 2023.

80. David J. Lynch, "The US Dominates the World of Big Data. But Trump's NAFTA Demands Could Put That at Risk," *Washington Post*, November 29, 2017, https://www.washingtonpost.com/business/economy/trumps-trade-deficit-obsession-could-hurt-leading-american-industries/2017/11/27/b2b8122c-cbb5-11e7-8321-481fd63f174d_story.html.

81. "US Chamber FOIA Requests on US Digital Trade Policy," US Chamber of Commerce, January 31, 2024, https://www.uschamber.com/international/trade-agreements/u-s-chamber-foia-requests-on-u-s-digital-trade-policy.

82. Rethink Trade, "Biden Digital Trade Update Paved Way for Smart Data Security Executive Order," press release, February 28, 2024, https://rethinktrade.org/wp-content/uploads/2024/02/PressRelease_2.28.2024.pdf.

83. This account of the San Francisco meeting comes from a source with direct knowledge of the events.

84. William H. Overholt, "Another Outing for Myth-Based Diplomacy," *Global Asia* 18, no. 4 (2023), https://www.globalasia.org/v18no4/focus/another-outing-for-myth-based-diplomacy_william-h-overholt; Overholt interview with the author, August 16, 2024.

85. Wang Jisi et al., "Did America Get China Wrong? The Engagement Debate," *Foreign Affairs* 97, no. 4 (2018): 183–195.

86. Campbell interview with the author, December 12, 2023.

Chapter 11: What All the Wise Men Promised

1. Bob Ulrich interview with the author, June 13, 2024.

2. David H. Autor et al., "The China Syndrome: Local Labor Market Effects of Import Competition in the United States," *American Economic Review* 103, no. 6 (2013): 2140, https://economics.mit.edu/sites/default/files/publications/the%20china%20syndrome%202013.pdf.

3. Brian Ulrich interview with the author, June 10, 2024.

4. In 2023, Trumbull County manufacturing employment of 9,429 was down 65 percent from 26,867 in 2001 according to US Bureau of Labor Statistics, "All Employees in Private Manufacturing for All Establishment Sizes in Trumbull County, Ohio, NSA," Quarterly Census of Employment and Wages, accessed via database at https://www.bls.gov/data/home.htm.

5. Robert E. Lighthizer, *No Trade Is Free: Changing Course, Taking on China, and Helping America's Workers* (Broadside Books, 2023), 318.

6. "2024 Republican Party Platform," July 8, 2024, American Presidency Project, UC Santa Barbara, https://www.presidency.ucsb.edu/documents/2024-republican-party-platform.

7. Jeff Stein, "Trump Aides Explore Plans to Boost Musk Effort by Wresting Control from Congress," *Washington Post*, November 13, 2024, https://www.washingtonpost.com/business/2024/11/13/elon-musk-government-efficiency-congress-budget-law/.

8. Matthew Schmitz, "There's One Person Trump Absolutely Needs in His Administration," *New York Times*, November 20, 2024, https://www.nytimes.com/2024/11/20/opinion/trump-treasury-robert-lighthizer.html.

9. Arvind Subramanian, Martin Kessler, and Emanuele Properzi, "Trade Hyperglobalization Is Dead. Long Live . . . ?," Peterson Institute for International Economics, November 2023, https://www.piie.com/publications/working-papers/trade-hyperglobalization-dead-long-live.

10. M. Ayhan Kose and Alen Mulabdic, "Global Trade Has Nearly Flatlined. Populism Is Taking a Toll on Growth," World Bank, February 22, 2024, https://blogs.worldbank.org/en/voices/global-trade-has-nearly-flatlined-populism-taking-toll-growth.

11. For services trade growth relative to goods trade, see Richard Baldwin, "The Third Big Shift in Globalization: The Future of Trade Is Intermediate Services," virtual presentation at Bendheim Center for Finance, Princeton University, June 27, 2024, https://www.linkedin.com/pulse/my-charts-from-27-june-2024-presentation-markus-academy-baldwin-fln9e/. For forecast of future growth see Richard Baldwin, "The Peak Globalisation Myth: Part 4—Services Trade Did Not Peak," VoxEU, September 3, 2022, https://cepr.org/voxeu/columns/peak-globalisation-myth-part-4-services-trade-did-not-peak.

12. Richard Baldwin, "Spotlight Intervention," 60th Anniversary of UN Trade and Development Global Leaders Forum, June 13, 2024, https://unctad.org/system/files/non-official-document/unctad-at-60-ppt-richard-baldwin_en.pdf.

13. Francois de Soyres and Dylan Moore, "Assessing China's Efforts to Increase Self-Reliance," Finance and Economics Discussion Series (FEDS) Note, Board of Governors of the Federal Reserve System, February 2, 2024, https://doi.org/10.17016/2380-7172.3436.

14. Laura Alfaro and Davin Chor, "Global Supply Chains: The Looming 'Great Reallocation,'" paper prepared for the Jackson Hole Symposium, organized by the Federal Reserve Bank of Kansas City, August 24–26, 2023, 3, https://www.kansascityfed.org/documents/9747/JH_Paper_Alfaro.pdf.

15. Acme United, Q3 2024 Earnings Call, October 18, 2024.

16. Alfaro and Chor, "Global Supply Chains," 27–28.

17. Grace Fan, "US-China Decoupling," TS Lombard, June 21, 2024, 4.

18. David J. Lynch, "Flood of Chinese Imports Could Renew Trade Tensions, Threaten US Jobs," *Washington Post*, March 18, 2024, https://www.washingtonpost.com/business/2024/03/18/china-imports-trade-cars-electronics/.

19. Richard Baldwin et al., "Hidden Exposure: Measuring US Supply Chain Resilience," paper drafted for the Brookings Papers on Academic Activity conference, September 28–29, 2023, 19, https://www.brookings.edu/wp-content/uploads/2023/09/2_Baldwin-et-al_unembargoed.pdf.

20. Alfaro and Chor, "Global Supply Chains," 22.

21. Alfaro and Chor, "Global Supply Chains," 33.

22. "Q1 Procurement Uptick: A Beacon of Hope for Western Retail?," Q2 Barometer, QIMA, April 7, 2024, https://www.qima.com/qima-news/q2-2024-barometer.

23. Breteau interview with the author, February 14, 2024.

24. David J. Lynch and Jeanne Whalen, "US and Chinese Automakers Are Headed in Completely Different Directions," *Washington Post*, May 18, 2024, https://www.washingtonpost.com/business/2024/05/18/china-us-ev-cars/.

25. Helene Cooper, "New Vehicles, Face Paint and a 1,200-Foot Fall: The US Army Prepares for War with China," *New York Times*, October 29, 2024, https://www.nytimes.com/2024/10/29/us/politics/us-military-army-china.html.

26. Matt Pottinger and Mike Gallagher, "No Substitute for Victory: America's Competition with China Must Be Won, Not Managed," *Foreign Affairs* 103, no. 3 (2024): 25–39.

27. Bannon interview with the author, January 10, 2024.

28. Craig Kafura, "American Views of China Hit All-Time Low," 2024 Chicago Council Survey, Chicago Council on Global Affairs, October 24, 2024, https://globalaffairs .org/research/public-opinion-survey/american-views-china-hit-all-time-low.

29. David J. Lynch, "US-China Rivalry Risks Splintering Global Economy, IMF Chief Warns," *Washington Post*, November 12, 2022, https://www.washington post.com/business/2022/11/12/us-china-rivalry-risks-splintering-global-economy -imf-chief-warns/.

30. "Steady but Slow: Resilience amid Divergence," World Economic Outlook, International Monetary Fund, April 2024, 24, https://www.imf.org/en/Publications/WEO /Issues/2024/04/16/world-economic-outlook-april-2024.

31. Yellen interview with the author, June 28, 2024.

32. Sun Yu, "BlackRock Shelves China Bond ETF," *Financial Times*, November 12, 2022, https://www.ft.com/content/5bc4c8c6-ebac-4b2b-84a5-c918dc4de614.

33. Jamieson L. Greer, "Testimony Before the US-China Economic and Security Review Commission," May 23, 2024, Hearing on Key Economic Strategies for Leveling the US-China Playing Field: Trade, Investment, and Technology, 30, https://www.uscc .gov/sites/default/files/2024-05/Jamieson_Greer_Testimony.pdf.

34. David J. Lynch, "US-China Economic Ties Continue to Fray, Despite Biden–Xi Meeting," *Washington Post*, November 18, 2022, https://www.washingtonpost.com /business/2022/11/17/china-trade-investors-markets/.

35. American Chamber of Commerce in Shanghai, *China Business Report 2023*, not publicly available, 15.

36. George H. W. Bush and Brent Scowcroft, *A World Transformed* (Alfred A. Knopf, 1998), xiii.

37. Committee on Foreign Relations, United States Senate, 118th Congress, First Session, "Evaluating US-China Policy in the Era of Strategic Competition," February 9, 2023, https://www.foreign.senate.gov/imo/media/doc/95df7f8b-9b07-07c6-ac3f -6cdeeb25e3f4/02%2009%2023%20—%20Evaluating%20US-China%20Policy %20in%20the%20Era%20of%20Strategic%20Competition.pdf.

38. Paul Krugman, "Hair of the Dog," *New York Times*, March 3, 2008, https://archive .nytimes.com/krugman.blogs.nytimes.com/2008/03/03/hair-of-the-dog/.

39. David Autor et al., "On the Persistence of the China Shock," Working Paper No. 29401, National Bureau of Economic Research, October 2021, https://www.nber .org/system/files/working_papers/w29401/w29401.pdf.

40. Nick Carey, "China's BYD Will Consider Second Europe Plant in 2025, Executive Says," Reuters, May 9, 2024, https://www.reuters.com/business/autos-transportation /byd-will-consider-second-european-plant-2025executive-says-2024-05-09/.

41. Curran McSwiggan, "The Future for Non-College Women Is Bleak," *Third Way*, October 24, 2023, https://www.thirdway.org/memo/the-future-for-non-college-women -is-bleak?utm_source=newsletter&utm_medium=email&utm_campaign=newsletter _axiosam&stream=top.

42. Kristalina Georgieva, "AI Will Transform the Global Economy. Let's Make Sure It Benefits Humanity," International Monetary Fund, January 14, 2024, https://www.imf.org/en/Blogs/Articles/2024/01/14/ai-will-transform-the-global -economy-lets-make-sure-it-benefits-humanity.

43. "Mark Cuban Reveals AI's Job Impact," Bloomberg Television, March 15, 2024, https://www.youtube.com/watch?v=XAxmbswoO2s.

44. Burning Glass Institute and the Society for Human Resource Management, "Generative Artificial Intelligence and the Workforce," February 1, 2024, 4–5, https://shrm-res.cloudinary.com/image/upload/v1706729099/AI/CPR-230956_Research_Gen-AI-Workplace_FINAL_1.pdf.

45. Mauro Cazzaniga et al., "Gen-AI: Artificial Intelligence and the Future of Work," *IMF Staff Discussion Notes*, January 2024, 2, https://www.imf.org/en/Publications/Staff-Discussion-Notes/Issues/2024/01/14/Gen-AI-Artificial-Intelligence-and-the-Future-of-Work-542379.

46. David Autor, "AI Could Actually Help Rebuild the Middle Class," *Noema*, February 12, 2024, https://www.noemamag.com/how-ai-could-help-rebuild-the-middle-class/.

47. Cazzaniga et al., "Gen-AI," 15.

48. James Aylward, Elizabeth Laderman, Luiz E. Oliveira, and Gladys Teng, "How Much Did the CARES Act Help Households Stay Afloat?," *FRBSF Economic Letter*, July 6, 2021, https://www.frbsf.org/wp-content/uploads/el2021-18.pdf.

49. Paulson interview with the author, December 12, 2023.

50. "Expanding Economic Opportunity for More Americans: Bipartisan Policies to Increase Work, Wages, and Skills," Aspen Institute Economic Strategy Group, February 2019, 20, https://www.aspeninstitute.org/wp-content/uploads/2019/01/ESG_Report_Expanding-Economic-Opportunity-for-More-Americans.pdf.

51. Daron Acemoglu, "America Is Sleepwalking into an Economic Storm," *New York Times*, October 17, 2024, https://www.nytimes.com/2024/10/17/opinion/economy-us-aging-work-force-ai.html.

52. David J. Lynch, "For Pa. Presidential Bellwether, Inflation Is Just the Latest Challenge," *Washington Post*, August 17, 2024, https://www.washingtonpost.com/business/2024/08/17/erie-politics-inflation-left-behind/.

53. "An Update to the Budget and Economic Outlook: 2024 to 2034," Congressional Budget Office, June 18, 2024, https://www.cbo.gov/publication/60039.

54. In 2023, corporate income taxes were equal to 1.6 percent of gross domestic product, down from 2.6 percent of GDP in 1979, the year before Reagan's election. One percent of the $29 trillion GDP would be $290 billion. Statistics from "historical budget data" section of this report: "Update to the Budget: 2024 to 2034," Congressional Budget Office, https://www.cbo.gov/publication/60039.

55. David J. Lynch, "Biden Wants to Crack Down on Corporate Tax Loopholes, Resuming a Battle His Predecessors Lost," *Washington Post*, April 20, 2021, https://www.washingtonpost.com/us-policy/2021/04/20/corporate-tax-loopholes-biden/.

56. David J. Lynch, "Biden Wants to Crack Down."

57. Brad Setser, "Cross-Border Rx: Pharmaceutical Manufacturers and US International Tax Policy," in Testimony before the Finance Committee, Senate, 118th Congress, First Session, May 11, 2023, https://www.cfr.org/report/cross-border-rx-pharmaceutical-manufacturers-and-us-international-tax-policy.

58. Setser, "Cross-Border Rx"; Brad Setser, "The Dangerous Myth of Deglobalization: Misperceptions of the Global Economy Are Driving Bad Policies," *Foreign Affairs*, June 4, 2024, https://www.foreignaffairs.com/china/globalization-dangerous-myth-economy-brad-setser.

59. Setser interview with the author, June 6, 2024.

60. "Trends in the Distribution of Income," Congressional Budget Office, October 25, 2011, https://www.cbo.gov/publication/42537.

61. Pol Antràs et al., "Globalization, Inequality and Welfare," *Journal of International Economics* 108 (2017): 388, https://scholar.harvard.edu/files/antras/files/agi_published.pdf.

62. Pol Antràs, "De-Globalization? Global Value Chains in the Post-Covid Age," Working Paper No. 28115, National Bureau of Economic Research, November 2020, 5, https://www.nber.org/system/files/working_papers/w28115/w28115.pdf.

63. Shanay Gracia, "Majority of Americans Take a Dim View of Increased Trade with Other Countries," Pew Research Center, July 29, 2024, https://www.pewresearch.org/short-reads/2024/07/29/majority-of-americans-take-a-dim-view-of-increased-trade-with-other-countries/.

64. David Autor et al., "Help for the Heartland? The Employment and Electoral Effects of the Trump Tariffs in the United States," Working Paper No. 32082, National Bureau of Economic Research, January 2024, https://www.nber.org/system/files/working_papers/w32082/w32082.pdf.

65. Kimberly Bayard, Tomaz Cajner, Vivi Gregorich, and Maria D. Tito, "Are Manufacturing Jobs Still Good Jobs? An Exploration of the Manufacturing Wage Premium," Finance and Economics Discussion Series (FEDS), Board of Governors of the Federal Reserve System, 1, https://doi.org/10.17016/FEDS.2022.011.

Epilogue: A New Pitch for Globalization?

1. "Presidential Approval Ratings: Bill Clinton," Gallup, https://news.gallup.com/poll/116584/presidential-approval-ratings-bill-clinton.aspx.

2. Nelson Lichtenstein and Judith Stein, *A Fabulous Failure: The Clinton Presidency and the Transformation of American Capitalism* (Princeton University Press, 2023).

3. Sperling interview with the author, October 12, 2023.

4. Richard Wike et al., "Social Media Seen as Mostly Good for Democracy Across Many Nations, but US Is a Major Outlier," Pew Research Center, December 6, 2022, https://www.pewresearch.org/global/2022/12/06/social-media-seen-as-mostly-good-for-democracy-across-many-nations-but-u-s-is-a-major-outlier.

Selected Bibliography

Books

Acemoglu, Daron, and Simon Johnson. *Power and Progress: Our 1000-Year Struggle over Technology & Prosperity*. PublicAffairs, 2023.

Allen, Jonathan, and Amie Parnes. *Shattered: Inside Hillary Clinton's Doomed Campaign*. Crown, 2017.

Applebaum, Anne. *Autocracy, Inc.: The Dictators Who Want to Run the World*. Doubleday, 2024.

Bader, Jeffrey. *Obama and China's Rise: An Insider's Account of America's Asia Strategy*. Brookings Institution Press, 2012.

Baker, Peter, and Susan Glasser. *The Divider: Trump in the White House, 2017–2021*. Doubleday, 2022.

Baldwin, Richard. *The Great Convergence: Information Technology and the New Globalization*. Belknap, 2016.

Barnow, Burt S., and Jeffrey Smith. "Employment and Training Programs." In vol. 2 of *Economics of Means-Tested Transfer Programs in the United States*, edited by Robert A. Moffitt. University of Chicago Press, 2016.

Bayoumi, Tamim. *Unfinished Business: The Unexplored Causes of the Financial Crisis and the Lessons Yet to Be Learned*. Yale University Press, 2018.

Bergsten, Fred, and Joseph E. Gagnon. *Currency Conflict and Trade Policy: A New Strategy for the United States*. Peterson Institute for International Economics, 2017.

Bernanke, Ben S. *21st Century Monetary Policy: The Federal Reserve from the Great Inflation to COVID-19*. W. W. Norton, 2022.

Blustein, Paul. *Schism: China, America and the Fracturing of the Global Trading System*. Centre for International Governance Innovation, 2019.

Boughton, James. "Russia: From Rebirth to Crisis to Recovery." In *Tearing Down Walls: The International Monetary Fund, 1990–1999*. International Monetary Fund, 2012.

Branch, Taylor. *The Clinton Tapes: Wrestling History with the President*. Simon & Schuster, 2009.

Brender, Anton, and Florence Pisani. *Global Imbalances and the Collapse of Globalized Finance*. Center for European Policy Studies, 2010.

Bush, George H. W., and Brent Scowcroft. *A World Transformed*. Alfred A. Knopf, 1998.

Selected Bibliography

Case, Anne, and Angus Deaton. *Deaths of Despair and the Future of Capitalism*. Princeton University Press, 2020.

Catao, Luis A. V., and Maurice Obstfeld, eds. *Meeting Globalization's Challenges: Policies to Make Trade Work for All*. International Monetary Fund and Princeton University Press, 2019.

Clinton, Bill. *My Life*. Alfred A. Knopf, 2004.

Clinton, Hillary Rodham. *What Happened*. Simon & Schuster, 2017.

Davis, Bob, and Lingling Wei. *Superpower Showdown: How the Battle Between Trump and Xi Threatens a New Cold War*. Harper Business, 2020.

Doshi, Rush. *The Long Game: China's Grand Strategy to Displace American Order*. Oxford University Press, 2021.

Draper III, William H. *The Startup Game: Inside the Partnership Between Venture Capitalists and Entrepreneurs*. Palgrave Macmillan, 2011.

Farrell, Henry, and Abraham Newman. *Underground Empire: How America Weaponized the World Economy*. Henry Holt, 2023.

Foer, Franklin. *The Last Politician: Inside Joe Biden's White House and the Struggle for America's Future*. Penguin, 2023.

Foley, Elizabeth Price. *The Tea Party Movement: Three Principles*. Cambridge University Press, 2012.

Friedberg, Aaron L. *Getting China Wrong*. Polity, 2022.

Frieden, Jeffry A. *Global Capitalism: Its Fall and Rise in the Twentieth Century*. W. W. Norton, 2006.

Friedman, Thomas L. *The Lexus and the Olive Tree*. Farrar, Straus and Giroux, 1999.

Geithner, Timothy F. *Stress Test: Reflections on Financial Crises*. Crown, 2014.

Gerstle, Gary. *The Rise and Fall of the Neoliberal Order: America and the World in the Free Market Era*. Oxford University Press, 2022.

Goldberg, Pinelopi Koujianou. *The Unequal Effects of Globalization*. With Greg Larson. MIT Press, 2023.

Goodman, Peter. *How the World Ran Out of Everything: Inside the Global Supply Chain*. Mariner Books, 2024.

Hadley, Stephen J., ed. *Hand-Off: The Foreign Policy George W. Bush Passed to Barack Obama*. Brookings Institution Press, 2023.

Hass, Ryan. *Stronger: Adapting America's China Strategy in an Age of Competitive Interdependence*. Yale University Press, 2021.

Hubbard, Glenn. *The Wall and the Bridge: Fear and Opportunity in Disruption's Wake*. Yale University Press, 2022.

Irwin, Douglas A. *Clashing over Commerce: A History of US Trade Policy*. University of Chicago Press, 2017.

Judis, John. *The Populist Explosion*. Columbia Global Reports, 2016.

Judis, John B., and Ruy Teixeira. *Where Have All the Democrats Gone? The Soul of the Party in the Age of Extremes*. Henry Holt, 2023.

Klein, Matthew, and Michael Pettis. *Trade Wars Are Class Wars*. Yale University Press, 2020.

Kletzer, Lori G., and Howard Rosen. "Easing the Adjustment Burden on US Workers." In *The United States and the World Economy: Foreign Economic Policy for the Next*

Decade, edited by C. Fred Bergsten. Peterson Institute for International Economics, 2005.

Lardy, Nicholas. *Integrating China into the Global Economy.* Brookings Institution Press, 2002.

Levinson, Marc. *The Box: How the Shipping Container Made the World Smaller and the World Economy Bigger.* Princeton University Press, 2006.

Lichtenstein, Nelson, and Judith Stein. *A Fabulous Failure: The Clinton Presidency and the Transformation of American Capitalism.* Princeton University Press, 2023.

Lighthizer, Robert E. *No Trade Is Free: Changing Course, Taking on China, and Helping America's Workers.* Broadside Books, 2023.

Mallaby, Sebastian. *The Power Law: Venture Capital and the Making of the New Future.* Penguin, 2022.

Mann, James. *The China Fantasy.* Viking Penguin, 2007.

Maraniss, David. *First in His Class: The Biography of Bill Clinton.* Simon & Schuster, 1995.

McGregor, Richard. *The Party: The Secret World of China's Communist Rulers.* HarperCollins, 2010.

Miller, Chris. *Chip War: The Fight for the World's Most Critical Technology.* Scribner, 2022.

Mohsin, Saleha. *Paper Soldiers: How the Weaponization of the Dollar Changed the World Order.* Portfolio Penguin, 2024.

Mutz, Diana C. *Winners and Losers: The Psychology of Foreign Trade.* Princeton University Press, 2021.

Obama, Barack. *A Promised Land.* Crown, 2020.

Osnos, Evan. *Joe Biden: The Life, the Run, and What Matters Now.* Scribner, 2020.

Paulson Jr., Henry M. *Dealing with China: An Insider Unmasks the New Economic Superpower.* Twelve, 2015.

Paulson Jr., Henry M. *On The Brink: Inside the Race to Stop the Collapse of the Global Financial System.* Business Plus, 2010.

Reddaway, Peter, and Dmitri Glinski. *The Tragedy of Russia's Reforms: Market Bolshevism Against Democracy.* United States Institute of Peace Press, 2001.

Reich, Robert. *Locked in the Cabinet.* Vintage Books, 1997.

Rodrik, Dani. *Has Globalization Gone Too Far?* Institute of International Economics, 1997.

Rubin, Robert E., and Jacob Weisberg. *In an Uncertain World: Tough Choices from Wall Street to Washington.* Random House, 2003.

Rudd, Kevin. *The Avoidable War: The Dangers of a Catastrophic Conflict Between the US and Xi Jinping's China.* PublicAffairs, 2022.

Schwarzman, Stephen. *What It Takes: Lessons in the Pursuit of Excellence.* Simon & Schuster, 2019.

Sheffi, Yossi. *The Power of Resilience: How the Best Companies Manage the Unexpected.* MIT Press, 2017.

Shirk, Susan. *Overreach: How China Derailed Its Peaceful Rise.* Oxford University Press, 2023.

Sides, John, Michael Tesler, and Lynn Vavreck. *Identity Crisis: The 2016 Presidential Campaign and the Battle for the Meaning of America.* Princeton University Press, 2018.

Sorkin, Andrew Ross. *Too Big to Fail: The Inside Story of How Wall Street and Washington Fought to Save the Financial System—and Themselves*. Viking Penguin, 2009.

Sperling, Gene. *Economic Dignity*. Penguin Books, 2021.

Stiglitz, Joseph. *Globalization and Its Discontents Revisited: Anti-Globalization in the Era of Trump*. W. W. Norton, 2018.

Tan, Yeling. *Disaggregating China, Inc.: State Strategies in the Liberal Economic Order*. Cornell University Press, 2021.

Tooze, Adam. *Crashed: How a Decade of Financial Crises Changed the World*. Viking, 2018.

VanGrasstek, Craig. *The History and Future of the World Trade Organization*. WTO, 2013.

Waldman, Michael. *POTUS Speaks*. Simon & Schuster, 2000.

Wilson, Edward O. *The Social Conquest of Earth*. W. W. Norton, 2012.

Wong, Chun Han. *Party of One: The Rise of Xi Jinping and China's Superpower Future*. Avid Reader, 2023.

Woodward, Bob. *The Secret Man*. Simon & Schuster, 2005.

Zelizer, Julian, ed. *The Presidency of Donald J. Trump*. Princeton University Press, 2022.

Articles

Acemoglu, Daron, David H. Autor, David Dorn, Gordon H. Hanson, and Brendan Price. "Import Competition and the Great US Employment Sag of the 2000s." *Journal of Labor Economics* 34, no. S1, part 2 (2016): S141–S198. https://economics.mit.edu/sites/default/files/publications/Import%20Competition%20and%20the%20Great%20US%20Employment%20Sag.pdf.

Acharya, Viral, and Philipp Schnabl. "Do Global Banks Spread Global Imbalances? The Case of Asset-Backed Commercial Paper During the Financial Crisis of 2007–09." Paper presented at the 10th Jacques Polak Annual Research Conference, hosted by the International Monetary Fund, Washington, DC, November 5–6, 2009. https://www.imf.org/external/np/res/seminars/2009/arc/pdf/acharya.pdf.

Alfaro, Laura, and Davin Chor. "Global Supply Chains: The Looming 'Great Reallocation.'" Paper prepared for the Jackson Hole Symposium, organized by the Federal Reserve Bank of Kansas City, August 24–26, 2023. https://www.kansascityfed.org/documents/9747/JH_Paper_Alfaro.pdf.

Amiti, Mary, Stephen J. Redding, and David Weinstein. "The Impact of the 2018 Trade War on US Prices and Welfare." Working Paper No. 25672. National Bureau of Economic Research, March 2019. https://www.nber.org/system/files/working_papers/w25672/w25672.pdf.

Antràs, Pol. "De-Globalization? Global Value Chains in the Post-Covid Age." Working Paper No. 28115. National Bureau of Economic Research, November 2020. https://www.nber.org/system/files/working_papers/w28115/w28115.pdf.

Antràs, Pol, Alonso de Gortaria, and Oleg Itskhokib. "Globalization, Inequality and Welfare." *Journal of International Economics* 108 (2017): 387–412. https://scholar.harvard.edu/files/antras/files/agi_published.pdf.

Autor, David H., Anne Beck, David Dorn, and Gordon H. Hanson. "Help for the Heartland? The Employment and Electoral Effects of the Trump Tariffs in the United States." Working Paper No. 32082. National Bureau of Economic Research, January 2024. https://www.nber.org/system/files/working_papers/w32082/w32082.pdf.

Selected Bibliography

Autor, David H., David Dorn, and Gordon H. Hanson. "The China Syndrome: Local Labor Market Effects of Import Competition in the United States." *American Economic Review* 103, no. 6 (2013): 2121–2168. https://economics.mit.edu/sites/default/files/publications/the%20china%20syndrome%202013.pdf.

Autor, David H., David Dorn, and Gordon H. Hanson. "On the Persistence of the China Shock." Working Paper No. 29401. National Bureau of Economic Research, October 2021. https://www.nber.org/system/files/working_papers/w29401/w29401.pdf.

Autor, David H., David Dorn, Gordon H. Hanson, and Kaveh Majlesi. "Importing Political Polarization? The Electoral Consequences of Rising Trade Exposure." *American Economic Review* 110, no. 10 (2020): 3139–3183. https://pubs.aeaweb.org/doi/pdfplus/10.1257/aer.20170011.

Baily, Martin Neil, and Robert Z. Lawrence. "What Happened to the Great US Job Machine? The Role of Trade and Electronic Offshoring." *Brookings Papers on Economic Activity*, no. 2 (2004): 211–281. https://www.brookings.edu/wp-content/uploads/2004/06/2004b_bpea_baily.pdf.

Baldwin, Richard, Rebecca Freeman, and Angelos Theodorakopoulos. "Hidden Exposure: Measuring US Supply Chain Resilience." Paper drafted for the Brookings Papers on Academic Activity conference, September 28–29, 2023. https://www.brookings.edu/wp-content/uploads/2023/09/2_Baldwin-et-al_unembargoed.pdf.

Benzow, August. "Economic Renaissance or Fleeting Recovery? Left-Behind Counties See Boom in Jobs and Businesses amid Widening Divides." Economic Innovation Group, July 8, 2024. https://eig.org/left-behind-places/.

Bernanke, Ben, Carol Bertaut, Laurie Pounder DeMarco, and Steven Kamin. "International Capital Flows and the Returns to Safe Assets in the United States, 2003–2007." International Finance Discussion Paper No. 1014. Board of Governors of the Federal Reserve System, February 2011. https://www.federalreserve.gov/pubs/ifdp/2011/1014/ifdp1014.pdf.

Bertaut, Carol, Laurie Pounder DeMarco, Steven Kamin, and Ralph Tryon. "ABS Inflows to the United States and the Global Financial Crisis." International Finance Discussion Paper No. 1028. Board of Governors of the Federal Reserve System, August 2011. https://www.federalreserve.gov/pubs/ifdp/2011/1028/ifdp1028.pdf.

Blinder, Alan. "The Free Trade Paradox: The Bad Politics of a Good Idea." *Foreign Affairs* 98, no. 1 (2019): 119–128.

Bloom, Nicholas, Kyle Handley, André Kurmann, and Philip Luck. "The China Shock Revisited: Job Reallocation and Industry Switching in US Labor Markets." Working Paper No. 33098. National Bureau of Economic Research, November 2024. http://www.nber.org/papers/w33098.

Boehm, Christoph E., Aaron Flaaen, and Nitya Pandalai-Nayar. "The Role of Global Supply Chains in the Transmission of Shocks: Firm-Level Evidence from the Tōhoku Earthquake." Finance and Economics Discussion Series (FEDS) Note, Board of Governors of the Federal Reserve System, May 2, 2016. https://www.federalreserve.gov/econresdata/notes/feds-notes/2016/role-of-global-supply-chains-in-the-transmission-of-shocks-20160502.html.

Branstetter, Lee, and Nicholas Lardy. "China's Embrace of Globalization." Working Paper No. 12373. National Bureau of Economic Research, July 2006. https://www.nber.org/system/files/working_papers/w12373/w12373.pdf.

Branstetter, Lee, and Guangwei Li. "Does 'Made in China 2025' Work for China? Evidence from Chinese Listed Firms." October 20, 2022. http://dx.doi.org/10.2139/ssrn.4254356.

Broz, J. Lawrence, Jeffry Frieden, and Stephen Weymouth. "Populism in Place: The Economic Geography of the Globalization Backlash." *International Organization* 75, no. 2 (2021): 464–494. https://www.cambridge.org/core/journals/international-organization/article/populism-in-place-the-economic-geography-of-the-globalization-backlash/98ED873D925E0590CB9A78AEC68BB439.

Charles, Kerwin Kofi, Erik Hurst, and Matthew J. Notowidigdo. "Housing Booms, Manufacturing Decline, and Labor Market Outcomes." Working Paper No. 18949. National Bureau of Economic Research, April 2013. https://www.nber.org/system/files/working_papers/w18949/w18949.pdf.

Chase, Michael S. "Xi in Command: Downsizing and Reorganizing the People's Liberation Army." Commentary, RAND Corporation, September 14, 2015. https://www.rand.org/pubs/commentary/2015/09/xi-in-command-downsizing-and-reorganizing-the-peoples.html.

Choi, Jiwon, Ilyana Kuziemko, Ebonya L. Washington, and Gavin Wright. "Local Economic and Political Effects of Trade Deals: Evidence From NAFTA." *American Economic Review* 114, no. 6 (2024): 1540–1575. https://pubs.aeaweb.org/doi/pdfplus/10.1257/aer.20220425.

Dharmasankar, Sharada, and Bhash Mazumder. "Have Borrowers Recovered from Foreclosures During the Great Recession?" *Chicago Fed Letter*, no. 370 (June 2016): 1–5. https://www.chicagofed.org/publications/chicago-fed-letter/2016/370.

Dyer, Jeffrey H. "Dedicated Assets: Japan's Manufacturing Edge." *Harvard Business Review*, November–December 1994. https://hbr.org/1994/11/dedicated-assets-japans-manufacturing-edge.

Feenstra, Robert C., and Akira Sasahara. "The 'China Shock,' Exports and US Employment: A Global Input-Output Analysis." Working Paper No. 24022. National Bureau of Economic Research, November 2017. https://www.nber.org/papers/w24022.

Fisher, Dennis. "Japan Disaster Shakes Up Supply-Chain Strategies." *Harvard Business School Working Knowledge*, May 31, 2011. https://hbswk.hbs.edu/item/japan-disaster-shakes-up-supply-chain-strategies.

Fotak, Veljko, Hye Seung (Grace) Lee, William L. Megginson, and Jesus M. Salas. "The Political Economy of Tariff Exemption Grants." *Journal of Financial and Quantitative Analysis*, ahead of print, July 29, 2024. https://jfqa.org/wp-content/uploads/2024/08/23440-Tariff-Exemptions.pdf.

Grimmer, Justin, and William Marble. "Who Put Trump in the White House? Explaining the Contribution of Voting Blocs to Trump's Victory." Draft version, December 12, 2019. https://williammarble.co/docs/vb.pdf.

Harrigan, James. "The Impact of the Asia Crisis on US Industry: An Almost-Free Lunch?" *Economic Policy Review—Federal Reserve Bank of New York* 6, no. 3 (2000): 71–81. https://www.newyorkfed.org/medialibrary/media/research/epr/00v06n3/0009harr.pdf.

Hellwig, Martin. "Germany and the Financial Crises 2007–2017." Draft version, June 2018. https://www.riksbank.se/globalassets/media/konferenser/2018/germany-and-financial-crises-2007-2017.pdf.

Hicks, Michael, and Srikant Devaraj. "The Myth and the Reality of Manufacturing in America." Center for Business and Economic Research, Ball State University, April 2017. https://conexus.cberdata.org/files/MfgReality.pdf.

Houseman, Susan. "Understanding the Decline of US Manufacturing Employment." Working Paper No. 18-287. Upjohn Institute, 2018. https://research.upjohn.org/cgi/viewcontent.cgi?article=1305&context=up_workingpapers.

Hufbauer, Gary Clyde, and Sean Lowry. "US Tire Tariffs: Saving Few Jobs at High Cost." Policy Brief No. 12-9. Peterson Institute for International Economics, April 2012. https://www.piie.com/publications/policy-briefs/us-tire-tariffs-saving-few-jobs-high-cost.

Jaravel, Xavier, and Erick Sager. "What Are the Price Effects of Trade? Evidence from the US and Implications for Quantitative Trade Models." Working Paper No. 2019-68. Finance and Economics Discussion Series (FEDS), Board of Governors of the Federal Reserve System, September 2019. http://dx.doi.org/10.17016/FEDS.2019.068.

Johnston, R. Barry, Salim M. Darbar, and Claudia Echeverria. "Sequencing Capital Account Liberalization: Lessons from the Experiences in Chile, Indonesia, Korea and Thailand." Working Paper No. 97/157. International Monetary Fund, November 1997. https://www.imf.org/external/pubs/ft/wp/wp97157.pdf.

Kahn, Lisa B., Lindsay Oldenski, and Geunyong Park. "Racial and Ethnic Inequality and the China Shock." Working Paper No. 30646. National Bureau of Economic Research, July 2024. https://www.nber.org/system/files/working_papers/w30646/w30646.pdf.

Kearney, Melissa, and Katharine Abraham. "Explaining the Decline in the US Employment-to-Population Ratio." Working Paper No. 24333. National Bureau of Economic Research, February 2018. https://www.nber.org/system/files/working_papers/w24333/w24333.pdf.

Kharas, Homi, Brian Pinto, and Sergei Ulatov. "An Analysis of Russia's 1998 Meltdown: Fundamentals and Market Signals." *Brookings Papers on Economic Activity*, no. 1 (2001): 1–68. https://www.brookings.edu/wp-content/uploads/2001/01/2001a_bpea_kharas.pdf.

Kreiner, Claus Thustrup, and Michael Svarer. "Danish Flexicurity: Rights and Duties." *Journal of Economic Perspectives* 36, no. 4 (2022): 81–102. https://pubs.aeaweb.org/doi/pdfplus/10.1257/jep.36.4.81.

Lampton, David M. "*The China Fantasy*, Fantasy." Review of *The China Fantasy: How Our Leaders Explain Away Chinese Repression*, by James Mann. *China Quarterly* (September 2007): 745–749. https://doi.org/10.1017/S0305741007001786.

Li, Jie. "International System in Transition: From the Perspective of Financial Crisis." *China International Studies* 16 (2009): 4–23.

Liu, Chiu-Wan. "The Chinese Fintech Boom and the Consolidation of Recentralized Authoritarian Capitalism." *Asian Survey* 61, no. 6 (2021): 971–978. https://doi.org/10.1525/as.2021.1428111.

Lucas, Deborah. "Measuring the Cost of Bailouts." *Annual Review of Financial Economics* 11 (2019): 85–108. https://www.annualreviews.org/content/journals/10.1146/annurev-financial-110217-022532.

McCauley, Robert. "The 2008 Crisis: Transpacific or Transatlantic?" *BIS Quarterly Review*, December 2018. https://www.bis.org/publ/qtrpdf/r_qt1812f.pdf.

Mead, Walter Russell. "The Tea Party and American Foreign Policy: What Populism Means for Globalism." *Foreign Affairs* 90, no. 2 (2011): 28–44.

Miller, Jennifer. "Let's Not Be Laughed at Anymore: Donald Trump and Japan from the 1980s to the Present." *Journal of American–East Asian Relations* 25, no. 2 (2018): 138–168. https://jennifermmiller.com/wp-content/uploads/2019/06/final-trump-article.pdf.

Morgan, Stephen L. "Status Threat, Material Interests, and the 2016 Presidential Vote." *Socius* 4 (2018). https://journals.sagepub.com/doi/epub/10.1177/2378023118788217.

Mutz, Diana C. "Response to Morgan: On the Role of Status Threat and Material Interests in the 2016 Election." *Socius* 4 (2018). https://journals.sagepub.com/doi/epub/10.1177/2378023118808619.

Mutz, Diana C. "Status Threat, Not Economic Hardship, Explains the 2016 Presidential Vote." *Proceedings of the National Academy of Sciences* 115, no. 19 (2018): E4330–E4339. https://www.pnas.org/doi/10.1073/pnas.1718155115.

Osterholm, Michael T. "Preparing for the Next Pandemic." *Foreign Affairs* 84, no. 4 (2005): 24–37.

Overholt, William H. "Another Outing for Myth-Based Diplomacy." *Global Asia* 18, no. 4 (2023): 96–100. https://www.globalasia.org/v18no4/focus/another-outing-for-myth-based-diplomacy_william-h-overholt.

Overholt, William H. "The Great Betrayal: How America's Elites Are Failing to Confront the Challenge of Trade Politics." *International Economy* 31, no. 1 (2017): 33–35, 69. http://www.international-economy.com/TIE_W17_Overholt.pdf.

Park, Jooyoun. "Does Occupational Training by the Trade Adjustment Assistance Program Really Help Reemployment?" September 23, 2011. https://dx.doi.org/10.2139/ssrn.1962169.

Pierce, Justin R., and Peter K. Schott. "The Surprisingly Swift Decline of US Manufacturing Employment." *American Economic Review* 106, no. 7 (2016): 1632–1662, online appendix. https://www.aeaweb.org/articles?id=10.1257/aer.20131578.

Pierce, Justin R., Peter K. Schott, and Cristina Tello-Trillo. "To Find Relative Earnings Gains After the China Shock, Look Outside Manufacturing and Upstream." Working Paper No. 32438. National Bureau of Economic Research, May 2024. https://www.nber.org/papers/w32438.

Posen, Adam. "The Price of Nostalgia: America's Self-Defeating Economic Retreat." *Foreign Affairs* 100, no. 3 (2021): 28–43.

Pottinger, Matt, and Mike Gallagher. "No Substitute for Victory: America's Competition with China Must Be Won, Not Managed." *Foreign Affairs* 103, no. 3 (2024): 25–39.

Purcell, Patrick J. "Geographic Mobility and Annual Earnings in the United States." *Social Security Bulletin* 80, no. 2 (2020). https://www.ssa.gov/policy/docs/ssb/v80n2/v80n2p1.html.

Reynolds, Kara M., and John S. Palatucci. "Does Trade Adjustment Assistance Make a Difference?" Working Paper No. 2008-12. American University Department of Economics, August 2008. https://w.american.edu/cas/economics/repec/amu/workingpapers/2008-12.pdf.

Rodrik, Dani. "Why Does Globalization Fuel Populism? Economics, Culture, and the Rise of Right-Wing Populism." *Annual Review of Economics* 13, no. 1 (2021): 133–170.

https://drodrik.scholar.harvard.edu/files/dani-rodrik/files/why_does_globalization
_fuel_populism.pdf.

Setser, Brad. "The Dangerous Myth of Deglobalization: Misperceptions of the Global Economy Are Driving Bad Policies." *Foreign Affairs*, June 4, 2024. https://www.foreign affairs.com/china/globalization-dangerous-myth-economy-brad-setser.

Shih, Willy C. "What Really Makes Toyota's Production System Resilient." *Harvard Business Review*, November 15, 2022. https://hbr.org/2022/11/what-really-makes-toyotas -production-system-resilient.

Silver, Laura, Christine Huang, and Laura Clancy. "How Global Public Opinion of China Has Shifted in the Xi Era." Pew Research Center, September 28, 2022. https:// www.pewresearch.org/global/2022/09/28/how-global-public-opinion-of-china -has-shifted-in-the-xi-era/.

Sullivan, Jake. "The New Old Democrats." *Democracy*, June 20, 2018. https://democracy journal.org/arguments/the-new-old-democrats/.

Tan, Yeling. "How the WTO Changed China: The Mixed Legacy of Economic Engagement." *Foreign Affairs* 100, no. 2 (2021): 90–102.

Wang Jisi et al. "Did America Get China Wrong? The Engagement Debate." *Foreign Affairs* 97, no. 4 (2018): 183–195.

Wang, Zhi, Shang-Jin Wei, Xinding Yu, and Kunfu Zhu. "Re-Examining the Effects of Trading with China on Local Labor Markets: A Supply Chain Perspective." Working Paper No. 24866. National Bureau of Economic Research, October 2018. https:// www.nber.org/papers/w24886.

Warnock, Francis E., and Veronica Cacdac Warnock. "International Capital Flows and US Interest Rates." *Journal of International Money and Finance* 28, no. 6 (2009). https://www.sciencedirect.com/science/article/abs/pii/S0261560609000461.

Wolff, Edward. "Household Wealth Trends in the United States, 1962 to 2016: Has Middle Class Wealth Recovered?" Working Paper No. 24085. National Bureau of Economic Research, November 2017. https://www.nber.org/system/files/working_papers /w24085/w24085.pdf.

Wu, Mark. "The 'China, Inc.' Challenge to Global Trade Governance." *Harvard International Law Journal* 57, no. 2 (2016): 261–324. https://www.law.berkeley.edu/wp -content/uploads/2020/05/WuMark.pdf.

Index

Index

Index

Index

Credit: Photo courtesy of the author.

David J. Lynch is the global economics correspondent of *The Washington Post*. The recipient of the National Press Foundation's Hinrich Award for Distinguished Reporting on Trade in 2020, Lynch has reported from more than sixty countries for the *Post* and earlier in his career for the *Financial Times* of London, Bloomberg News, and *USA Today*. He lives in Vienna, Virginia, with his wife, Kathy.

RAISING READERS
Books Build Bright Futures

Thank you for reading this book and for being a reader of books in general. As an author, I am so grateful to share being part of a community of readers with you, and I hope you will join me in passing our love of books on to the next generation of readers.

Did you know that reading for enjoyment is the single biggest predictor of a child's future happiness and success?

More than family circumstances, parents' educational background, or income, reading impacts a child's future academic performance, emotional well-being, communication skills, economic security, ambition, and happiness.

Studies show that kids reading for enjoyment in the US is in rapid decline:

- In 2012, 53% of 9-year-olds read almost every day. Just 10 years later, in 2022, the number had fallen to 39%.
- In 2012, 27% of 13-year-olds read for fun daily. By 2023, that number was just 14%.

Together, we can commit to Raising Readers and change this trend. How?

- Read to children in your life daily.
- Model reading as a fun activity.
- Reduce screen time.
- Start a family, school, or community book club.
- Visit bookstores and libraries regularly.
- Listen to audiobooks.
- Read the book before you see the movie.
- Encourage your child to read aloud to a pet or stuffed animal.
- Give books as gifts.
- Donate books to families and communities in need.

BOB1217

Books build bright futures, and **Raising Readers** is our shared responsibility.

For more information, visit **JoinRaisingReaders.com**

Sources: National Endowment for the Arts, National Assessment of Educational Progress, WorldBookDay.org, Nielsen BookData's 2023 "Understanding the Children's Book Consumer"